Heroines of the Crusades

Heroines of the Crusades

Outstanding Women
During the Eight Crusades

C. A. Bloss

LEONAUR

Heroines of the Crusades
Outstanding Women During the Eight Crusades
by C. A. Bloss

First published under the title
Heroines of the Crusades

Leonaur is an imprint of Oakpast Ltd

Copyright in this form © 2012 Oakpast Ltd

ISBN: 978-0-85706-936-8 (hardcover)
ISBN: 978-0-85706-937-5 (softcover)

http://www.leonaur.com

Publisher's Notes

Contents

To my pupils,
The "Heroines of the Crusades"
Is affectionately dedicated
By the author

Preface

To those whom it has been my privilege and pleasure to lead through the devious and darkened paths of the past, to all who cordially receive the doctrine that *actions* and not faint desires for excellence form the character, I address a few words by way of explanation and preface.

Jerusalem, the capital of Palestine, whether glorious in the beauty of her first temple, and the excellent wisdom of her philosopher king, or veiled in the darkness of that fatal eclipse in which the solemn scenes of Calvary consummated her glory and shame, has occupied a position in the great drama of human events, more interesting and important than any other city on the globe.

But Jerusalem, in the gloom of that moral night which gathered over the nations after the fall of the Western Empire of the Romans, exerted a greater influence upon the minds of men than at any former period. The insulting Moslem felt a degree of veneration for the splendid ruins over which he walked with all a Conqueror's pride—the African anchorite left his solitary hermitage to weep upon Mount Olivet—the European adventurer wreathed his staff with the branching palm from her holy hills—the despairing Jew sat in sackcloth at her fallen gates, and even the mingled barbarians of the East united with the Christian to revere the spot where art achieved its proudest monument, and poetry found the theme of its sublimest song.

This natural reverence, exalted into piety by the decrees of the church, resulted necessarily in the practice of pilgrimage. Anxious, restless guilt, fled from the scene of its enormities to the sweet valleys where the Saviour whispered peace to his disciples; poetry sought inspiring visions on the Mount of Transfiguration; penitence lingered in the garden of Passion, and remorse expiated its crimes in weary vigils at the Holy Sepulchre.

At the dawn of the eleventh century, one sublime idea pervaded Christendom. The thousand years of the Apocalypse were supposed to be accomplished, and a general belief prevailed that on the Mount of Olives, whence the Son of God ascended in his chariot of cloud to heaven, he would reappear in all the pomp of his Second Advent. From every quarter of the Latin world the affrighted Christians, deserting their homes and kindred, crowded to the Holy Land—terror quickened devotion, curiosity stimulated enthusiasm. But insult and outrage awaited the pilgrims in Palestine, and in Jerusalem itself they encountered the scoffing taunts of idolatry and infidelity.

To free those holy courts from the polluting tread of the sandalled Paynim, to prepare a pure resting-place for the Son of Man. Superstition roused the martial spirit of the age, and enlisted chivalry under the banners of the cross.

Thus began the *Crusades*, those romantic expeditions which, combining religious fervour with military ardour, united the various nations of Europe from the shores of the Baltic to the Straits of Gibraltar, and from the banks of the Danube to the Bay of Biscay, in one common cause, and poured the mingled tide of fanatics, warriors and adventurers, upon the plains of Asia. For nearly two centuries the mightiest efforts and best blood of Christendom were wasted in the useless struggle, and it is computed that not less than six millions of people devoted their lives and fortunes to this desperate undertaking.

But though the Crusades are so important to the historian as involving the politics of all nations; to the philosopher as fraught with consequences affecting the happiness of succeeding generations; and to the scholar as commencing the era when Genius, brooding over the ruins of the past, rose Phœnix-like from the ashes of Arabian splendour, and soaring in the clearer light of Christianity, scattered from her wing the dew of refinement upon the barbarians of the North; yet the general reader feels that his knowledge of them is so vague as to detract materially from his pleasure in allusions to them, and continually to force upon his mind a painful sense of ignorance upon points where he ought to be informed.

In some measure to supply a deficiency which common history cannot obviate, to make the period of the Crusades interesting, by giving to it the tangible thread of authentic narrative, these biographies of the "Heroines" who inspired the troubadour, animated the warrior, or in person "took the cross," have, with much care and labour, been selected and compiled.

The era opens about the time of the Conquest, when William I., unquestionably the greatest ruler of his time, returns in triumph to Normandy. No two writers agreeing as to the age of his children, I have arranged them as best suited my purpose, making Cicely the eldest, the betrothed of Harold; and the second daughter, Agatha, the bride of Earl Edwin; and Adela, whose ambitious character is well authenticated, the heroine of the First Crusade.

The character and superstitions of the Saxons, with their love of "legendary lore," I have endeavoured to embody in the early life of Maude, while I have endeavoured to make her riper years illustrate the principles and piety of a teacher to whom you are all much attached.

The half-*infidel* Hardrager, who was necessary to show both the plan of Battle Abbey and the causes and character of pilgrimage, might really have been the leader of the assassins, since they established themselves in Mount Lebanon, and incorporated in their belief some of the doctrines of the New Testament about that period.

Eleanor of Aquitaine was one of the few women whose mature years in some measure atoned for a youth of folly. Agnes Strickland cites authorities to show that Fair Rosamond passed nineteen years in a convent, and died with the reputation of a saint. You will excuse me that I permitted death to cut her off in "her young beauty's bloom" to present a more affecting picture of the sad effects of guilt. The ballads are not mine; some I found in obsolete works, and one was versified from a legend of the early romancers.

For the tournament, and contest with the lion in Berengaria, I am indebted to the same veracious authority, though I cannot account for Richard's finding the lion's heart so conveniently situated at the bottom of the throat, except from the fact that "Physiology and Hygiene" had not then assigned the true position to the internal organs.

I was very sorry not to make Joanna as interesting as Edith in the Talisman, but this was clearly impossible—first, from the fact that I had not the genius of Scott; and second, because I made it my study to adhere strictly to truth. It was Saphadin and not Saladin who sought to ally himself with the princely house of Plantagenet, and I found it convenient to console his disappointment by bestowing upon him the fictitious lady I had brought to seek her fortune in the East. Michelet confirms this decision by his statement that this was emphatically the era of women, and that for some years a female exercised the sovereign power over the territories of Islamism.

Blondell, upon whose very existence so many doubts have been cast, is, I think, a well-authenticated character, who *"plays his part"* with great fidelity and truth.

Had I not been limited as to space, the *ring* in the hand of Violante's grandson would have projected the catastrophe of the Sicilian Vespers. For the same reason, I could only allude to the strife between the Guelphs and Ghibellines, to the civil wars of France and England, to the Crusade against the Albigenes, and the founding of the Inquisition by St. Dominic, when, in quest of heresy, he traversed the hills and vales of Languedoe, and doomed to death those brave spirits who dared to exercise the right of private judgment.

Eva is the only purely fictitious character of any importance in the work, and she was drawn from life, a portrait which some of you may recognize. Fuller, in his *Holy War*, contradicts the legend of Eleanora's drawing the poison from Edward's wound, but adds, "he who shall disprove this pretty fiction shall get to himself little credit," and I confess I had not the courage thus warned to attempt it.

I would here gratefully acknowledge my obligations to the gentlemen of the Rochester University, through whose politeness I have been permitted to consult several works of early English authors not republished in this country, from which I have made liberal extracts both of facts and language.

In conclusion, I can only say I have endeavoured to set before you a true history in a series of entertaining stories. In the former, I am confident I have succeeded both as regards events and chronology; of the latter I am somewhat doubtful; but if my "Heroines" have the effect to awaken curiosity and induce research, I shall feel that "they have their reward."

Clover Street Sem., Nov. 30th, *1852.*

Leaders of Crusades

Godfrey of Boulogne,	First Crusade	
Stephen, Count of Blois,	,,	,,
Louis VII. of France,	Second	,,
Frederic I. Barbarossa,	Third	,,
Philip II. Augustus,	,,	,,
Richard I. Coeur de Lion,	,,	,,
Henry, Count of Champagne,	Fourth	,,
Conrad of Germany,	,,	,,
Thibaut, Count of Champagne,	Fifth	,,
Dandolo, Doge of Venice,	,,	,,
Jean de Brienne, King of Jerusalem,	,,	,,
Hugh X. de Lusignan, Count la Marche,	,,	,,
Andrew II. of Hungary,	Sixth	,,
Frederic II. of Germany,	,,	,,
Louis IX. of France	Seventh	,,
Charles d'Anjou, King of Sicily,	,,	,,
Edward I. of England,	Eighth	,,

ADELA. COUNTESS OF BLOIS.

Adela

CHAPTER 1: THE NIGHT OF THE 20TH OF MARCH, 1067

Wave high your torches on each crag and cliff
Let many lights blaze on our battlements,
Shout to them in the pauses of the storm
And tell them there is no hope.

Maturin's Bertram

All night long the Lady Matilda, with her becoming children, knelt before the holy shrine in the old Abbey of Feschamp.

Anxiously had they watched through the lingering twilight, for the whitening sails of the Conqueror's fleet. No sails appeared, and the night fell dark and stormy upon the English channel. Meet was it that prayer should ascend to Him who rules the destiny of nations, for the hopes of all future times were rocked upon that midnight sea. The field of Hastings was won, Harold was slain, England was subdued, and the ships of William the Conqueror, filled with the flower of Norman chivalry, and followed by the sad remnant of Saxon nobles, were speeding to the Norman coast.

Was it Woden the storm-throned, that thus with relentless fury pursued the Viking's progeny,—despoilers of the Saxon race? Was it Thor the thunder-voiced, warning the proud Conqueror that the great heart of England still throbbed with the pulse of freedom, though the vale of Sanguelac was red with the blood of her bravest sons? Was it the spirit of a milder Faith that prevailed over that night of darkness, spread a calm morning on those troubled waters, and through that all-pervading sunlight scattered blessings countless as the liquid jewels that paved the track of the rescued ships?

The *Mora* with its splendid convoy was in sight, the bells rang out merrily their *matin* chimes, and while Matilda lingered to unite in the

15

anthem of thanksgiving and praise, the little Adela, escaping from the care of the attendants, found her way through the dim aisles, to the door of the church, where she stood the radiant picture of delight, gazing with childish interest upon the scene before her.

The solemn service over, Matilda with her stately train emerged from the abbey and encircled by a princely retinue of knights and ladies, watched the swelling canvass, which under the pressure of a steady breeze, bore the gallant vessels into port. Impatient of delay, the royal children ran eagerly down the green slope to the water's edge. "Now brothers mine," said the fiery William, "the fair and goodly land of England, to him who in three stones' cast shall twice strike yon fisherman's buoy." Seizing a pebble as he spoke, he was about to hurl it towards the destined mark, when Adela thoughtlessly grasped his arm. The stone dropped idly into the wave, sprinkling the short cloaks, and embroidered tunics of the little group. A derisive laugh followed this exploit, and Adela, familiar with the effects of William's anger, fled from his uplifted hand to the protecting care of Richard, who, sheltering her with his arm, exclaimed, "Robert, imagine yon buoy a Saxon Earl, and try your prowess upon him. I resign all claim to the conquered realm."

"Book and bell, Latin prayers, and a pilgrimage for my brother Richard," replied Robert, selecting a smooth pebble and preparing to throw, but, ere the stone left his hand, a well directed missile from William struck the buoy, and sank it for a moment beneath the waves. With a look of proud disdain Robert hurled the stone. It fell dimpling the waters far beyond the mark.

"England is mine," shouted William, as again with unerring aim he dashed the buoy beneath the surface. "England is mine," he repeated, pointing exultingly to the Saxon banner grasped in the hand of his own effigy upon the prow of the *Mora*. Robert smiled contemptuously, and rejoined his mother.

All eyes were now directed towards the gallant bark which rode proudly into port, amid the joyous flutter of banners, gonfanons, pennons, and streamers which from every mast, spar, and standard, waved and flapped in the morning breeze.

A glad shout burst from the assembled multitude, and cries of "Long live the Conqueror William! Long live our good Duke of Normandy!" echoed by the clangour of trumpet, and chiming of bells, welcomed the victor on shore. Fondly embracing his lovely wife and children, and graciously receiving the greeting of his rejoicing subjects, he turned to present the noble Saxons, that swelled the pomp of his train.

"My Matilda will welcome Edgar Atheling, in whose veins flows the blood of her sire Alfred the Great. The brave Earls Morcar and Edwin, the noble Waltheof, and his beautiful daughter Maude, are also guests at our court, and must lack no courtesy at our hands."

While Matilda with high-born grace and dignity received her reluctant guests, the little Adela accustomed to the sight of mail-clad barons, and princely array, felt herself irresistibly attracted by the timid girl, who clung tremblingly to the arm of Earl Waltheof. Other eyes than hers were fascinated by the appearance of the lovely stranger. A yellow kirtle of the finest wool fell in graceful folds to her feet; over this was thrown a purple robe, which confined at the bodice by a girdle exquisitely wrought, draped without concealing the delicate proportions of a figure cast in nature's finest mould. A crimson coverchief half hid the jewelled network, from which her fair brown hair, brightening to gold in the sunshine, escaped in rich abundance over a neck of snow. The steady light of her meek violet eyes fell lovingly on Adela, and the faint tinge upon her cheek deepened into a brilliant blush, as the sprightly child kindly taking her hand, led her forward to receive the kiss of welcome from the Queen Duchess Matilda.

CHAPTER 2

But doth the exile's heart serenely dwell in sunshine there?

A succession of brilliant pageants, and knightly entertainments awaited the Conqueror, his nobles and hostages, in their pompous progress through all the towns and cities of Normandy, from Feschamp to Bayeux.

Robert already wearing the spurs of knighthood, girt with silver baldric, and bearing high the lance with its pointed banderol, led the van; gallantly conducting the young Earls Morcar and Edwin, and the royal Atheling: while the aspiring Prince William, attaching himself to a band of his father's best trained bowmen, practised on bright winged birds, those feats of archery in which he subsequently became so cruelly skilful.

Adela obtained a place near the gentle Maude, and strove by every childish art to charm back the smiles that transiently enlivened the sad countenance of the Saxon maiden. Not less assiduously, and not more successfully did the Duke King, and his haughty consort, employ the fascinations of easy grace, and polished wit, to beguile the gloomy musings of the captive Waltheof. So passed they on, the sad hearts with the gay. So sat they in the halls of mirth, the one keeping strict Lenten fast, the other revelling in triumphal feasts; one sole thought embittering the fast, and sweetening the feast—and that thought *England*.

In a chamber in the palace of Bayeux were assembled the household of the Conqueror, busy in their daily occupations. Groups of girls, with nimble fingers, wrought silently under the eye of Matilda, the sad epic of England's fall.

"Leave thy tangled skeins to these fair maids, and the skilful Turold, and come thou apart with me," said William, abruptly entering and drawing his queen aside, within the deep embrasure of the window, "'tis of thy glory and mine that I would speak."

The conference lasted long. The young princes summoned the maidens to the mimic tourney in the tiltyard, and waiting clouds prepared the gorgeous couch of sun, beyond the hills of Bretagne, ere the wily statesman had completed the unfoldings of all his schemes, for fixing the Norman line securely upon the throne of Edward the Confessor. He revealed his apprehensions from the stern character of Waltheof, and his hopes from the fascinations of his niece Judith d'Aumale.

From Edgar Atheling he feared little. The boy reared in a foreign court, a stranger to Saxon language and manners, had neither desire nor capacity to contend for a dignity unsuited to his years. He was already hand and glove with Robert, and subject to the imperious will of the young knight.

But Morcar and Edwin were more dangerous foes. Kinsmen of the late king, at the least disaffection they might rouse the friends of the famous Earl Siward, vanquisher of Macbeth; the thegns of Norfolk, Ely, Huntingdon, and Northumbria, stretching far to the Scottish border; and the valiant man of Mercia allied to the terrible Welsh.

"The victory at Hastings, my Queen," said William, with his blandest smile, "does not establish peaceful rule o'er all the hills and vales of merrie England. Let policy complete what valour has commenced. Methinks our pretty Cicely might bind the restive Edwin in the silken toils of love, more securely than unwilling homage or extorted oath."

"Cicely, the betrothed of Harold!" exclaimed Matilda. "Could'st thou have seen her agony when tidings of Harold's death came with news of thy victory, thou would'st scarcely speak to her of love."

"A childish fancy," impatiently cried William, "the breath of praise soon dries the tears on a maiden's cheeks. She must be the Saxon's bride."

"It is impossible," replied the queen. "In Notre-Dame de Bonnes Nouvelles, while my soul was filled with joy for thy safety, did I dedicate thy broken-hearted child to be the bride of Heaven. The holy Lanfranc has already sanctioned the vow."

William strode hastily up and down the chamber, tying and untying the rich cordon of his cloak in uncontrollable anger and disappointment.

Matilda laid her hand soothingly upon his arm. "Agatha is fairer than Cicely—Adela hath wit beyond her years, and child as she is, will readily comprehend all thy schemes."

"Talk not of Adela, she hath a head for intrigue equal to my brother Odo. Wed her to one who might foster her ambition, and neither crown nor throne would be beyond her aspirations."

"Agatha hath a loving heart," pleaded Matilda.

"Thou sayest truth *bien aimie*, 'tis by the heart woman rules. Agatha shall be the affianced of Edwin before he leaves these shores."

Thus it was settled. The new queen received the title of the manor of Gloucester, and condemned the owner, her former lover, to perpetual imprisonment. The fair Maude was to dwell in exile a hostage for the fidelity of her father, till a fitting opportunity might occur to make her hand the bond of amity between the Conqueror and some disaffected peer.

Other hostages with their various possessions were disposed of in a similar manner, and thus the shades of evening stole into that darkened chamber, and brooded like palpable forms over the sacrifices which the new sovereigns covertly laid upon the altar of avarice and ambition.

The ceremony of betrothal took place on the following evening. There were guests in embroidered garments and costly jewels, there were lights and music, and more than wonted festivity: yet Maude saw only Edwin, and when taking the hand of the little princess, he pronounced with unhesitating voice, "Thine, and thine only," the colour faded from her lip and cheek, as if a mortal woe had fastened on her heart.

There were gifts and congratulations, and as Edwin presented his bride a miniature shield of silver, saying gallantly, "This shall thy heart from other love defend," a gleam of triumph on the countenance of William assured Matilda that Edwin was won.

CHAPTER 3

Oh! the joy
Of young ideas painted on the mind,
In the warm glowing colours fancy spreads
On objects not yet known, when all is new
And all is lovely.

Hannah More,

When the spring deepened into summer, Edwin, exulting in the pride of his youthful elegance and princely alliance, returned loaded with honours to his restored domains.

Agatha wept sore at his departure, but no tear trembled on the cheek of Maude. All external emotions were buried in the grave of hopeless love, and thenceforth in her pale, changeless beauty, she looked the ivory shrine, where the ashes of some holy thing were preserved, to work daily miracles upon the restless spirits by which she was surrounded.

In her society the turbulent, and self-willed children of the Conqueror became calm and docile. Often in the long still twilight would she hold them a charmed circle, listening with breathless awe to wild tales and ghostly legends of the terrible Vikings; who drove their daring keels into unknown seas, and immured their wailing captives in sunless dungeons of northern ice, or left them naked and shivering upon a barren coast, a prey to the wolfish winds, that lifted and tossed them ever on the red and bristling spears of Aurora's giant demons.

The story of the Babe of Bethlehem—cradled among the beasts of the stall—heralded by angels, and worshiped by the eastern sages, passing, a holy presence that diffused joy and comfort to every heart, through the green vales of Judea—walking unsandalled upon the glassy waves of Galilee, and standing in robes white as the light upon the top of Tabor, agonizing in Gethsemane, and suffering upon Calvary for the redemption of a ruined race, recited in the mellow tones of Maude, imparted an interest to the scenes of the Saviour's life and passion, which all the sacred relics and saintly effigies of the church had failed to awaken.

But especially did Robert and Adela delight in tales of the turbaned Paynim. The long caravan winding its spicy track through emerald oases, or glistening sands—the dark-browed Saracens with spear and scimitar careering in battle on Arab steeds, fleet as the desert wind—terrible Turks from the wilds of Khosser, swifter than leopards, and more fierce than the evening wolves—swarthy Nubians clustering like locusts in the holy places—toil-worn pilgrims scourged and massacred, and Christian children slaughtered to furnish diabolical repasts for Moslem fiends, were themes that never failed to excite the most intense curiosity, and to rouse the direct imprecations of vengeance.

From one of these narrations, Robert rose with a determined air, and exclaimed—"My grandsire, Robert le Diable, say the monks, was carried to heaven on the backs of fiends; but if by the favour of St. Stephen, I ever visit the Holy Land, it shall be not with pilgrim's staff, but with sword and lance, to drive those cursed fiends back to their place of torture."

"It were a holy work," said Richard, "and one the saints would bless."

"Were I a knight, or might a woman set lance in rest," cried Adela, "those heathen dogs should no longer feed upon the flesh of Christian babes. Shame to the peers of Normandy, that sit quietly in Rouen while the Holy Sepulchre is in the hands of *infidels*."

"The peers of Normandy will sit quietly in Rouen only till my father returns from his conference with Lanfranc," said William. "Last night a small vessel anchored off the coast, and a messenger came in breathless haste to the palace. I could not gain speech with him, but I know he brings tidings from Fitz Osborne, and our Uncle Odo. Hugh de Glaville conjectures there is treason in England."

"My mother dismissed her maidens at an earlier hour than is her wont, and sent away Turold with a frown, when he brought her his pattern of the wooden fort," said Cicely, with a sigh, "my heart misgave me then that some peril was impending."

"Pray God it may not reach Edwin," said Agatha, with white lips.

"Pray God the troubles may continue till my father moves his court to London," said William, as rising from the mossy bank upon which they had been sitting, the anxious party returned through the pleasance, to the great hall where the evening meal was prepared.

When the silent repast was finished, Maude led the weeping Agatha to her own chamber, and lifting the curtain of the oratory, stood with her before an altar covered with a richly embroidered velvet pall. Upon the altar was placed a golden crucifix, before which burned a silver lamp, and in a niche above, an alabaster image of the Madonna.

"Daughter of the Norman William," said she, taking Agatha's hands and kneeling before the altar, "with the holy cross before thee, and the eyes of our blessed lady looking down upon thee, tell me truly, lovest thou the Saxon Edwin?" and Agatha whispered low but firmly, "I love the Saxon Edwin."

"Turn thy eyes to the stars, emblems of unchanging faith, and tell me truly, wilt thou be to Edwin a guardian Fylga in weal or woe?" and Agatha answered, "I will guard Edwin in weal or woe."

"Lay thy hand upon this holy shrine," again said Maude, lifting the purple pall, and revealing a jewelled casket, "and tell me truly, though father, mother, brother, friend, or priest, compel, wilt thou with Edwin keep thy plighted troth?" and Agatha answered, "I will with Edwin keep my plighted troth."

"The pure Mary, the sleepless stars, and this holy relic of St. John the divine aid thee to keep thy vow, Amen."

And Agatha responded solemnly—"Amen."

All that night the patient Maude wrought with a magic bodkin upon the trothgift of Edwin, inscribing thereon a Saxon charm, that worn upon the breast of his mistress should shield him from danger, defeat, and death! the trusting Agatha keeping silent vigils by her side, while from the courtyard below echoed the tramp of steeds, and the heavy tread of mail-clad warriors hastening preparations for departure.

CHAPTER 4

That cruel word her tender heart so thrilled
That sudden cold did run through every vein,
And stony horror all her senses filled,
With dying fit, that down she fell for pain.
Spenser's *Fairy Queen.*

When sorrows come, they come not single spies,
But in battalions.
Shakespeare's *Hamlet.*

The conjectures of Prince William were well founded. The peers of Normandy were again summoned from their castles to attend the Conqueror, and the following spring the royal family removed to Winchester.

The coronation of Matilda was the most imposing pageant that had ever been seen in England. Foreign princes and peers graced the brilliant ceremonial—a numerous and lordly company of Normans attended her to the church, and a bodyguard of Anglo-Saxons, among whom Agatha distinguished Edwin, conspicuous alike for the beauty of his person, and the almost oriental magnificence of his apparel, reconducted the new queen and her beautiful children to the palace, where a splendid banquet closed the festivities. This season of rejoicing was followed by events of a sad and gloomy character. The peculiar miseries which fell upon England during the disastrous years of 1069-70 compelled the queen with the ladies of her court, again to seek safety in Normandy. The revolt of Earl Waltheof—the invasion of the Danes—the flight of Edgar Atheling—the hostility of Malcolm, King of Scotland—the destruction of the city of York—the death of Aldred, its beneficent, and much loved bishop—the desolation of Northumberland—the laying waste the county of Hampshire—the confiscation of private property—and the cry of houseless wanderers, perishing of want, furnished a scene of unexampled calamities, while the odious revival of the Danegelt, and the still more odious imposition of the *couvre feu*, goaded the exasperated inhabitants to desperation, and excited constant rebellions and insurrections.

The heart of the king, grieved and irritated, became entirely alienated from his Saxon subjects; and when Earl Edwin demanded the hand of Agatha, his claim was rejected with reproach and scorn.

Meanwhile the ladies of the Norman court, no less than Matilda, deplored the absence of their lords, and murmurings and complaints succeeded to sadness and discontent, as month after month, and year after year rolled on, and still the troubles in England required the constant exercise of the Norman arms.

The unheralded arrival of the Conqueror, with a military escort at Caen, excited a brief sensation of pleasure, but small cause had his family to rejoice in his coming.

The princesses were listening with rapt attention while Maude related the romance of a northern Jarl, who each night when the moon hung her silver lamp on high, moored his ocean palace beneath the shadow of a castle, beetling the sea, to woo fair Ulnah the pearl of the Orkneys. The maiden, leaning spell-bound from the lattice, had yielded to the enchanter's song, and dropped a pale pearl upon the deck of the war-ship; the wizard-bird that nestled in its shroudings had spread its broad wings and hovered broodingly above the casement, when flaming torches—splashing oars—and wild shouts, announced the coming of her father's fleet.

At this point of the story a messenger hastily entered and summoned Agatha to the presence of her dread father.

With sad presentiments the princess rose and silently obeyed the mandate. None were present with the Conqueror in the audience chamber save Matilda, Lanfranc, and the Saxon secretary, Ingulfus.

"Seat thyself beside me, daughter, and listen to my words," said the haughty monarch, with unwonted tenderness. "That I bade thee pledge thy hand to Earl Edwin to secure the peace of England, instead of trusting that event to my good sword, hath long grieved me sore; and often have I prayed the holy saints to absolve me of the sin. Heaven has heard my prayer and averted thy doom."

An involuntary shudder shook the slight frame of Agatha, but no sound escaped her lips.

"The brave Alphonso, King of Gallicia," continued the king, "has sent to woo thee for his bride; ambassadors wait in the antechamber, and the good Lanfranc has consented to release thee from thy extorted vow. With this costly ring the prince of Spain plights thee his faith."

Agatha instinctively drew back her hand.

"Nay, shrink not, my daughter. The Saxon was unworthy of thy love. Knowest thou not he is leagued with thy father's foes? Resign thou his troth-gift, I will restore it to the proud Rebel. Bid thy maidens robe thee in apparel befitting thy rank, (certes, the Spanish diadem will well become thy jetty locks.) Even now a splendid convoy of vessels ride at anchor in the harbour to convey thee to thy future lord, and the pious Ingulfus, who hath long desired to visit the Holy Sepulchre, shall attend thee to the coast of Spain."

Agatha neither spoke nor moved.

"Give me thy troth-gift, silly girl," cried her father angrily, bending his brow upon her, with the terrible frown, at which bold hearts were wont to quail.

Mechanically the trembling victim, drew from her bosom the talismanic shield. Lanfranc took it from her hand, placed the ring upon her finger, repeated the words of absolution, and the ceremony of betrothal, and when he ceased, Agatha lay at her father's feet, pale and cold in a death-like swoon. But bitterly as Matilda wept over her suffering daughter, her heart was torn with still keener anguish, at the maledictions pronounced upon her first-born and favourite son. Robert had been betrothed in infancy to the heiress of Maine; and had cherished the most romantic attachment for his affianced bride. On the death of the princess the people demanded him for their lord, and the young regent, generous and rash, had proceeded to take possession of the duchy, and administer justice in his own name.

William now required him to resign the fief, not only, but to give his hand to Maude, the beautiful captive, who had so long been the companion of his sisters. With the true spirit of chivalry, Robert indignantly replied;

"The lovely Maude hath already bestowed her affections on Earl Edwin, and Robert's bride shall never bear to the altar a reluctant heart. Thou hast sacrificed the meek Agatha to the lust of dominion, but the gentle Maude shall never suffer from thy tyranny, while the sword of a belted knight can defend her. If ever I am king of England, the lands of Huntingdon shall be hers, with free right to choose her own lord."

"Boast not thyself of tomorrow, England shalt thou never have. I have won it by mine own good sword, the vicars of Christ have set its crown upon my head, and placed its sceptre in my hand, and all the world combined shall not take it from me," cried the monarch in a paroxysm of rage.

"I only demand the suzerainship of Normandy and Maine, which all men say is my just inheritance," replied Robert.

"Thou would'st do well to remember the fate of Absalom, and the misfortunes of Rehoboam, and beware of evil counsellors," retorted William.

Robert insolently rejoined, "I did not come hither to listen to sermons, but to claim the investiture which has been promised me. Answer me positively, are not these things my right?"

"It is not my custom to strip before I go to bed," replied the Conqueror; "and as long as I live, I will not divide my native realm, Normandy, with another, for it is written in the holy evangelists, 'Every kingdom divided against itself shall become desolate.'"

"If it is inconvenient for thee to keep thy word, I will depart from Normandy, and seek justice from strangers, here I will not remain a subject," retorted Robert, with equal pride and scorn.

"*Par le splendeur de Dé,*" shouted William, half unsheathing his sword. "It is not to be borne, that he who owes his existence to me, should aspire to be my rival in mine own dominions. May the curse of Cain light upon thy undutiful head."

Thus they parted, Robert to take refuge with his mother's brother, in Flanders, and William to return to his distracted kingdom, where the fires of civil war still smouldered in the ashes of freedom.

In such scenes was Adela nurtured, and thus in an atmosphere of intrigue and superstition, was a character naturally penetrating and im-

25

petuous, prepared to devise and carry forward the wildest schemes.

Public calamities, and domestic vexations, impaired the peace and irritated the temper of the English monarch. Bodesmen from the north, brought news of leagues and plots against his power, while messengers from Normandy, conveyed tidings of the disaffections of his peers, and the hostilities of the French king.

Richard, his most dutiful and affectionate son, had accompanied him to England. The young prince was exceedingly fond of the chase, and often spent whole days hunting in the New Forest of Hampshire.

The malaria of the depopulated district, and the painful emotions awakened in his sensitive nature, by the sight of famishing wretches, vainly seeking food and shelter, brought on a delirious fever, which soon terminated his life. He was interred in Winchester Cathedral.

The last tone of the curfew bell was reverberating through the silent halls of the palace, when the distracted father, haunted by the piteous lamentations, and reproachful ravings of his departed son, threw himself despairingly upon his couch.

"News from beyond seas," said the chamberlain, entering, and presenting him a letter. William cut the silk and read.

"In the name of the blessed Mary, ever virgin, St. Michael, and St. Valery, doth thy poor scribe Ingulfus pray, that strength may be given thee, duke William, by grace of God, king of England, to bear the dreadful tidings, which much it grieves me to convey. When this comes to thee thou wilt know that thy sweet daughter, Agatha, liveth no more. From the day of our departure she shed no tears, but a tender wailing sound, like the moan of a wounded dove, issued ever from her lips. Her heart, she said, was devoted to her first spouse, and she prayed that the Most High would rather take her to himself, than allow her ever to be wedded to another. Her prayer was granted.

"The faintness which we witnessed at her betrothal, returned upon her by night and by day, but she never murmured; and on the eve of the blessed St. Agnes, having received the rites of our holy Church, she died, with the crucifix in her hand, and the name of Edwin on her lips."

The scroll dropped from the hand of the stricken father and a remorseful pang wrung his heart.

Again the chamberlain entered ushering in a dark figure wrapped in a long serge cloak, like those usually worn by monks. Kneeling at the monarch's feet, the stranger spoke. "Knowing, oh king! thy munificence to thy faithful servants, and moved by the love I bear thy throne and realm, I have discovered to Fitz Osborne the secret haunts of thine enemies, and to obtain thy royal favour, have brought from the Isle of Ely, that which I hope will please thee well. Behold the head of the Saxon chief."

The Conqueror shrank back in horror, as the well-known features of Edwin, pale and distorted with the death agony, and the long, fair locks all dabbled with gore, met his bewildered gaze.

"Cursed traitor!" shouted he, starting from his seat, "dost thou think to win my favour by bringing me the head of thy murdered lord? Ho! *seneschal*, convey this Judas to the lowest cell of the donjon. There shall he learn how William rewards the betrayer of innocent blood." The prisoner was borne from his presence.

The monarch buried his face in his hands, and burst into tears of uncontrollable anguish.

"Woe is me, my daughter,—Done to death by thy father's un-holy ambition—Thy Edwin hunted and slain on his own hearth-stone. What has this sceptre brought me? Toilsome days, and sleepless nights,—a divided household,—and children cut off in the flower of their youth. Truly, saith the Scripture; '*Woe unto him that coveteth an evil covetousness unto his house.*'"

As he bowed his head his eyes fell upon the fatal, silver shield. Lifting it reverently from the floor, and wiping the clotted blood from its polished surface, with some difficulty, he deciphered the Saxon inscription, which has been thus elegantly translated.

Edwin his pledge has left in me,
Now to the battle prest:
His guardian angel may she be,
Who wears me on her breast.

To him true hearted may she prove,
Oh! God, to thee I pray;
Edwin shall well requite her love,
Returning from the fray.

But if, forgetful of her vows,
May Heaven avert the thought,
She sell this love-charm of her spouse,
Which never could be bought;

If of her own free will she cast
This talisman away;

May Edwin's life no longer last,
To rue that fatal day.

CHAPTER 5

Still to the truth direct thy strong desire,
And flee the very air where dwells a liar.
Fail not the mass, there still with reverent feet,
Each morn be found, nor scant thy offering meet,
Haste thee, sir knight, where dames complain of wrong ;
Maintain their right, and in their cause be strong.

The last act in the bloody tragedy of England's subjection, was consummated in the year 1074, when Earl Waltheof, having been drawn into a plot against the crown, and betrayed by his Norman wife, Judith, to her uncle, the Conqueror, was beheaded on a rising ground, just without the gates of Winchester, the first Anglo-Saxon that perished by the hand of the executioner.

The perfidious Judith had fixed her affections on a French Count, but William had already secured a willing agent of his own purposes, in the person of Simon, a Norman noble, lame and deformed, on whom he designed to bestow her hand, with the rich earldoms of Northampton and Huntingdon.

The haughty Judith scorned the alliance, and stripped of rank and power, retired to the wilds of Yorkshire in obscurity and contempt.

The bitter tears occasioned by the melancholy fate of Agatha and Edwin, were fresh upon the cheek of Maude, when the heavy tidings of her father's cruel death, overwhelmed her in a tide of deeper anguish. A lingering illness followed, yet sweet dreams stole ever upon her rest, and the watchful Adela comprehended, that transported to the home of her childhood, in the gaiety of life's early morn, she trod again the breezy upland, and fragrant glade, wandered through wood and wold, with Edwin by her side, or sitting by the star-lit fountain, challenged the nightingale from out the leafy holt, with snatches of Runic rhyme, and Saxon melody. But young life combating disease, slowly led her back from the gates of the grave. One by one the bright visions faded, and sadly her eyes unclosed to a consciousness of the dark realities before her.

William had determined that the hand of the beautiful heiress of Huntingdon, should compensate the pliant Simon for the mortifying refusal of her stepmother. The betrothal was to take place directly on the Conqueror's arrival in Normandy, but the happy oblivion of

Maude, no less than the entreaties of Adela, and the menacing of Robert served to delay the doom they could not finally avert.

William had subdued the rebel province of Maine, and moved by the declining health, and incessant pleading of his beloved queen, had accorded to his refractory son a full pardon for his late rebellion, "promising at the same time, to grant him everything that he could expect from the affection of a father consistently with the duty of a king."

Thus peace was restored throughout the Conqueror's dominions, and the royal family happy in their reunion, kept merry Christmas in the capital city of Rouen.

"Sweet sister mine," said Robert to Adela, as she sat engaged upon the famous Bayeux tapestry, "pray leave the royal nose of our valiant sire, which thou hast punctured and cross-stitched, till verily it seems to bleed beneath thy fingers, and lend an ear to thy brother's words."

"Now, gramercy! Curthose," said Adela, laughing, "thou must have a distinct impression of thy noble father's visage, since thou canst not distinguish his nose from the 'fiery train' of the terrific comet."

"Nay," said Robert, taking up the simile, "the Conqueror's fiery train in England, has wrought more terror than all the comets since the days of Julius Cæsar, as the inhabitants of York will testify; but come, lay aside that odious tapestry, I have other work for thy skilful fingers."

"My duteous brother would, perhaps, employ them in puncturing his noble sire, at the field of Archembraye, but a maiden's needle wounds less deeply than a warrior's sword," said Adela, archly.

"Certes, thy tongue is sharper than thy needle," said Robert, reddening, "and thine eyes outdo thy tongue. On the field of Archembraye I did but wound my father's arm, while one bright shaft from thine eyes has pierced Count Stephen's heart."

"Methinks a heart so vulnerable, should be clad in armour," said Adela, reddening in her turn.

"Thy woman's wit doth run before my speech and prophesy my errand," said Robert. "The Count Stephen, of Blois, bids me entreat the fair Adela to bind him in *ring armour*, that the friend of Robert may be his brother in arms."

"*He* bids thee!" said Adela, dropping the embroidery. "Is the count, then, in Rouen?"

"Even so, *bien amie*," replied Robert. "Hast thou not marked a noble figure entering the church at twilight, and emerging at sunrise, his regards bent upon the ground except, perchance, when he steals a glance at my charming sister, accompanying her mother to matins or vespers."

"In truth, I marked such a youth," said Adela, blushing, "but wherefore frequents he not the court?"

"He holds his vigil of arms till twelfth day," replied Robert, "and the Conqueror has promised, that ere the Yule-clog, as Atheling calls it, has ceased to burn, he will himself lay the accolade of knighthood upon the shoulder of the young count. 'Tis my father's wish that his children assist at the ceremony."

"My father's wish!" said Adela, in a tone of deep surprise.

"Certes, sweet," replied her brother, "thinkest thou the Conqueror sees not the white flocks that range the green pastures of Blois, that he hears not the sound of the busy looms of Chartres, and loves not the sparkling wine, that flows from the blushing vineyards of Champaigne?"

"Robert, thou hast broken my needle," said Adela, striving confusedly to hide from the penetrating eyes of her brother, the influence which these considerations exercised over her own ambitious heart.

"I have broken thy needle of wool, that thou mightst thread a finer with floss of silk to embroider the scarf for thy gallant knight," said Robert, rising to withdraw. Adela followed him to the antechamber, and dismissing the attendants, concerted with him the arrangements for the pageant.

Scarcely confessing to herself the sweet hopes that for the first time agitated her bosom, she quitted the joustings and maskings of the holidays, and passed the festive season in the privacy of her own apartment, where assisted only by the faithful Maude, she wrought upon Tyrian purple the golden lions of Chartres, budded the shining damask with the *fleur de lis* of Champagne, and sewed the embroidered field azure with the pearly crescent of Blois. The deep tones of the turret clock tolling the midnight hour broke the stillness that reigned through the castle, just as Adela severed the last silken thread from the embroidery frame, and held up the gorgeous baldric in the light of the lamp before the admiring gaze of her friend.

"Hush!" said Maude, placing her finger on Adela's lip to repress a joyous exclamation, "we have a proverb in the north that, '*finished works bring prophetic dreams.*'—Hasten to seek thy pillow, but beware thy glance wander not from yon bright star that even now glimmers through the casement. Breathe not a word while I wreathe the silken scarf in the folds of thy canopy, and whisper the mystic charm of the morthwyrtha." With an incredulous smile Adela obeyed, and dismissing the tire-women, Maude left her to her solitary slumbers. The sun had scarce risen when Maude again entered the apartment.

"The visions of the future have visited thy rest," said she, glancing inquiringly at the thoughtful countenance of the princess.

"Question me not," replied Adela, "a promise and a fear have bewildered me—coming years can alone explain the mystery."

The great hall of the palace was fitted up for a brilliant ceremony. All the knights and nobles, bishops and clergy of Normandy, and the adjacent provinces, arrayed in the most gorgeous vestments of their several orders, with high-born dames and blushing maidens, sparkling in jewellery, lined the apartment, at the upper end of which stood the family of the Conqueror, beside an altar covered with cloth of gold.

The young princes Robert and William after attending Count Stephen to the bath clothed him in white garments, and covered him with a crimson cloak, the one symbolical of the purity of his soul, the other of his determination to shed his blood in the cause of heaven. Arrayed in this simple garb, after the celebration of the high mass, he entered the hall and approaching the altar, presented his sword to the bishop, who blessed and consecrated it to the service of religion and virtue.

Lanfranc then addressed him thus. "Thou seekest, Count of Blois, to become a knight—thou art of noble birth—of liberal gifts and high in courage.—Thou must be strong in danger—secret in councils— patient in difficulties—powerful against enemies—prudent in deeds. Lay thy hand upon this holy missal, and swear to observe the following rules." And Stephen laid his hand upon the clasped volume, and repeated slowly, after the priest.

"I do solemnly promise and swear to spare neither my blood nor my life in defence of the Catholic faith,—to aid all widows and orphans—to protect the innocent and oppressed—to be humble in all things—to speak the truth from the heart—to seek the welfare of my vassals—to regard the rights of my sovereign—and to live righteously before God and man."

Then rising from his knees and throwing off his cloak the neophyte stood with his head reverently inclined toward the priest, while Prince William buckled on the spurs of knighthood, and Edgar Atheling fastened the greaves, and Robert belted the corselet; gracefully he sank upon his knee, when Maude advancing adjusted the helmet upon

31

his closely curling locks, and Constance presented the spear with its drooping pennon; but his head bowed in conscious devotion, and the warm blood glowed eloquently on his manly cheek, while Adela, the lady of his love, tremulous with agitation, passed the scarf about his neck—fitted the silken folds across his breast, and belted the jewelled knot upon the ivory sheath of his sword.

Apparelled in his splendid armour the young count took the consecrated weapon from the altar, and presenting it to the king, knelt before the throne while the monarch rose and laid upon his shoulder three gentle blows, saying in a voice whose deep tones echoed to the farthest end of the hall, "In the name of St. Michael, and St. Stephen, I make thee knight. Be loyal, bold and true."

Following the example of the Conqueror, each knight advanced a step, drew his sword from the sheath, and while the hall gleamed with the flash of burnished steel, the man of God again took up the word, blessing him who had newly undertaken, and those who had long been engaged in holy warfare, and praying that all the hosts of the enemies of heaven, might be destroyed by Christian chivalry.

The trumpets sounded without, and the knights thronging around their brother in arms, conducted him to the court below, where vaulting upon their steeds, they rode through the admiring crowds, among whom Stephen scattered largesses with a liberal hand.

The banquet over, a gallant train of mounted knights and ladies emerged from the wooded park and wound along the banks of the Seine. There was rare sport that day, when the fox broke cover, and the hounds darted away upon his track, and the curvetting steeds bounded over the crisp green sward, in the wild excitement of the chase; but the proud barb of Stephen obedient to the rein, curved his glossy neck and moved with lofty step, by the dappled palfrey of Adela, while the young knight whispered words that the princess loved to hear; and thus in sweet converse the day wore away, and when the solemn night came on, beneath the blue cope of heaven, while the stars gazed from their sapphire thrones and the river mingled its low music with the murmur of their voices, Adela plighted her troth to Stephen Count of Blois.

But a ceremonial more joyous than a betrothal—more solemn than a burial, occasioned the removal of the court to Feschamp.

From the day of Harold's death, Cicely his betrothed, devoted herself to the cloister. Her father had bestowed a princely dower upon the convent of her choice, and fixed the day of her profession upon the high festival of Easter. At the close of the Lenten fast, she quitted the scene of her childish pleasures, gazed a last *adieu* on the hills, vales and streams, over which the early spring of that bright climate was casting its mellow sheen—distributed alms among the mendicant crowds that thronged her route, and bade a kind farewell to the multitudes, that flocked from every village and hamlet, to invoke the blessing of heaven upon her holy purpose.

Adela stood again in the old abbey of Feschamp, listening to the joyous sound of the *matin* chime, but neither the happy associations awakened by the place and hour, nor the warm breath of early love could charm the sadness from her heart.

She had entered the dark cloister, and conducted Cicely from her weary vigil beside the holy relics, to wreathe her dark locks with jewels and gold, and array her fair form for the last time in the garb of a princess. With the selfishness of affection, she suffered none but Maude to share the pious task.

Fast fell her tears as the whispered sounds of her sister's devotions forced upon her an appalling sense of the final separation.

The convent bell had scarce ceased its summons, ere a splendid concourse filled the galleries, and thronged the aisles of the abbey to witness the holy bridal.

Proudly and painfully beat the heart of the king, as his saintly daughter leaned upon his breast—twined her soft arms lovingly about his neck—and imprinted her last kiss upon his cheek; but sympathetic tenderness overmastered all other emotions, as with gentle force he drew her from the last fond embrace of her weeping mother, and the convulsive clasp of the almost frantic Adela, and resigned her in all her youthful beauty, to be immured in a living tomb. Her three young sisters less grieved at the parting, than pleased with the pageant, with hasty *adieus* prepared to take their place in the ceremony.

With a light step nicely modulated to the soft chanting of the nuns, the little Adeliza bearing a jewelled crucifix, led the procession, followed by Constance and Gundred, each carrying a lighted taper and bearing between them a lily-shaped basket of wrought silver, containing the vestal habit and veil which they laid upon the altar.

At the solemn call of the bishop, the fair Cicely entered, prepared as a bride adorned for her husband, and supported by the matron sisters passed up the long aisle, her white robes like a gathering mist floating about her fragile form, and her calm and serene countenance, beaming with such angelic sweetness from beneath the gossamer wreath which ornamented her head, that to Maude's fanciful vision she seemed already crowned with the radiant halo of the saints. A brilliant burst of jubilant melody, pealing from the organ, accompanied the nuns in their welcoming hymn, "*O Gloriosa Virginium*," and a breathless silence pervaded the holy courts as the soft voice of Cicely responded. "Receive me, oh Lord! according to thy holy word."

Kneeling before the bishop she begged his benediction and the name of Cecilia her patron-saint. The reverend Father gave her the consecrated name, signed her with the sign of the cross, and sprinkled holy-water upon her garments.

The high mass celebrated, and the *Kyrie Eleison* sung, a waxen taper was placed in her hand, and seated by the chancel, she listened with devout attention, while the archbishop portrayed the beatitude of that high vocation, which had called her from the pomps and vanities of earthly grandeur, to the durable riches of a heavenly kingdom; from the waning light of earthly affection to the ineffable love of the immortal bridegroom;—from the fading lustre of an earthly diadem, to the changeless glory of an eternal crown: and scarcely had he concluded with the gracious words, "Many daughters have done virtuously, but thou excellest them all," when the whole orchestra took up the note of commendation and "Gloria in Excelsis" sounded through the cloistered aisles, echoed along the vaulted roof, and breathed to the heart of the waiting novice the full reality of joy.

The sacred vestments were blessed and replaced in their silver shrine, and the children resuming their precious burden preceded their sister into an inner, apartment, where busy nuns disrobed her of her resplendent array,—despoiled her of her costly ornaments—and one by one shred away her long, bright locks, that never more might stir a thought of pride.

The solemn *bandeau* was bound about her brow, the black serge garment wrapped about her form, and when she again knelt before the bishop, saying, "I am the handmaid of Christ," an ill-suppressed shriek from Adela, told how changed was her appearance, and how gloomy was the fate that awaited her—but the votaress saw nothing, heard nothing, save the sacred mysteries in which she was engaged. Prostrated as if in deep abasement she lay upon the marble floor, while the choir chanted the litany; gently she inclined to the abbess, to be bound by the girdle of humiliation; reverently she bowed her head to receive the veil that should forever shut the world from her sight; joyfully she accepted the ring that sealed the irrevocable vow; and while the choir chanted, "Come, oh spouse of Christ, receive the crown," a coronal of mingled thorns and roses was placed upon her head—and Cicely was a nun.

Loud anthems pealed upward to the swelling dome, and every demonstration of joy welcomed the bride to her new home.

The royal guests sat down to a splendid repast in the great hall of the convent, and nuns and novices shared in the sumptuous entertainment; but between Cicely and her family was an impassable barrier of an iron grating, and four thick and cold stone walls separated her forever from the friends of her youth.

Chapter 6

What is't we live for? tell life's fairest tale—
To eat, to drink, to sleep, love, and enjoy,
And then to love no more!
To talk of things we know not, and to know
Nothing but things not worth the talking of.

Sir R. Fane, Jr.

"Methinks," said Adela, as she sat with Maude in the loved twilight conference, "it were a weary thing, to fast and pray as doth my sister Cicely, and look forever on those dull, cold images of stone or pictured saints, whose holiness we can never hope to reach."

"Thou thinkest so, dearest, because on the bright scroll of thy future is pictured a living form glowing with youth and beauty," said Maude; "but when death shuts out the light of hope, the pencil of love illumines the canvass ever with the image of a saint."

"I have never seen a Saxon saint but thee, best one," said Adela, affectionately kissing her cheek. "Cicely worships the memory of him who would have wrested the broad realm of England from her father."

"And Agatha died for one who loved that father," said Maude, half reproachfully.

"I cannot read aright the riddle of life," replied Adela, pensively, "less still the riddle of love. Doth not the heart seek happiness as the flower seeks the light? yet what men call the 'ends life lives for,' wealth and power and dominion, terminate in discontent, despair, and death. No duke of Normandy, since the days of Rou, hath been so successful as William the Conqueror, yet the meanest serf is happier than he: and this love that makes my heart flutter like a joyous bird, has consigned our Agatha to an early grave—immured Cicely in the abhorrent convent—and," she added, with a deprecating glance, "has plucked the last pale rose from the cheek of my lovely Maude."

"Thou speakest thus because thou knowest neither life nor love," replied the maiden. "Thou deemest wisely that a lofty purpose must call the strong man to effort, else lying dormant would his faculties perish with the rust of inactivity. Our pious bishop, Aldred, used to say; that any purpose so holy as not to need evil means to work its ends, like the consecration of the wafer, brings to the human soul the *real presence* of Christ."

"Thy riddle is too deep for my poor wit," said Adela. "Tell me of the love I know not—thy love."

"Thou fanciest thou lovest Count Stephen," said Maude, with a sigh, "but should he plight his love to another, thou wouldst regard him with hate and scorn."

"Aye, verily," replied Adela, her cheeks glowing, and her dark eye flashing, at the thought.

"So loved not Maude Earl Edwin. Thy father bade him give his hand to Agatha, and when I marked the undivided current of their lives, flowing on in a stream of bliss, Ambition and Hope were quenched in my heart, but Love went forth to light their pathway, and gilds with heavenly radiance their early tomb."

"Maude!" exclaimed Adela, enthusiastically, "thou wert not formed for this sinful world; thou shouldst dwell with the angels, for verily thou art one of them."

"Commend me not," said Maude, "thou little knowest the bitter repinings of my heart when I heard I might not enter the convent with Cicely, nor how my soul recoils from this unnatural alliance with Simon."

"And thou wouldst rather kneel upon the cold stone floor, and scourge thy tender flesh with knotted cords, than live almost a princess in thy merrie England!" said Adela, with unaffected surprise.

"Nay, rather would I work a weary pilgrimage to Palestine, and dwell an eremite in the lonely caves of Engaddi, had choice been left with me," answered Maude.

"A pilgrimage were not so sad a fate," said Adela; "the marvellous tales with which thou didst beguile my childhood hours, so wrought upon my fancy, that even to this day the very name of Jerusalem calls up visions bright as the bowers of Eden. Never have I wondered that pilgrims flocked to the Holy Land when they deemed the thousand years of prophecy accomplished, and expected to witness the azure gates unfolding above the holy sepulchre, and the Saviour descending upon the Mount of Olives amid all the terrific splendour of the final judgment."

"Scarce a century since," sighed Maude, "men looked for this heavenly kingdom, and verily believed they found in prophecy the confirmation of their hopes. My grandsire died upon the banks of the Jordan earnestly expecting the coming of his Lord."

"There is a flash of spears in the moonbeams," interrupted Adela, gazing from the arrow-slit of the turret. "Seest thou not a troop of horse, winding along the brow of the hill? Eye and heart alike deceive me if that be not Count Stephen's plume. Methought, ere this, he had reached the borders of Maine. And there is Robert by his side. Our lady grant their coming bode no ill."

"They pass beneath the shadow of the castle," said Maude. "They are not all mounted. Those men on foot, in the garb of friars, how wearily they follow, leaning upon their long staves."

"They are pilgrims!" exclaimed the maidens with one voice. "Let us descend to welcome them."

Prince Henry met them in the corridor. "Count Stephen has returned," said he, "and awaits my sister in the tapestry chamber."

"Come with me, Beauclerk," said Maude, leading away the young prince. "Thou shalt conduct me to these holy pilgrims."

"Adela," said Stephen, kissing the hand of his affianced as she entered, "thou art surprised, but I hope not ill-pleased at this unlooked-for return."

"I feared me some mischance had occasioned it," said Adela, "but seeing thee well, I am happy—yet wherefore art thou come?"

"Thy brother, Robert," replied Stephen, "vouchsafed to escort me with twenty lances to the town of mantes—but when we reached the banks of Eure, we found the bridges swept away, and the fords rendered impassable by the swollen waters. A band of pilgrims were encamped upon the other side, and at the sight of the Norman pennon, they sent forth a piteous cry for aid. We swam our steeds across the turgid stream, and each horseman mounting a palmer behind him, we brought them safely over. And what was my joy to find I had thus rendered some slight service to Ingulfus, the early tutor of my loved Adela."

"Our lady be praised, the good Ingulfus has returned. His pupil then shall thank his benefactor as she ought."

"He is wayworn and weary," pursued Stephen, "much toil hath he had in his long pilgrimage, and precious are the relics he has brought from Palestine. I craved from his gratitude a portion of the holy dust, for thy oratory. Should danger threaten the unworthy Stephen, the prayers of Adela, at such a shrine, would doubtless avail for his protection."

The princess started, and the colour fluctuated on her cheek, as with a look of surprise and recognition she regarded the beautiful crystal urn, with its amethystine entablature, on which were engraven the names of Adela and Stephen.

"Dost reject my gift, or hath some sudden illness seized thee?" said her lover, anxiously, remarking her strange emotion.

"A silly dream—a passing faintness," said Adela, convulsively grasping the urn, and pressing her pale lips upon the inscription. "The hour wears late, tomorrow we will meet again."

The young count imprinted a kiss upon her cold brow, and supporting her trembling steps to the antechamber, consigned her to the care of her attendants.

When the lovers met the following morning in the chapel to which all the inhabitants of the city repaired, to see the high altar decked with the palms of the pilgrims, and join in the general thanksgiving for their return, all traces of agitation had disappeared from the countenance of Adela. Relieved from his jealous fears, Count Stephen basked in the sunshine of her smiles, and protracted his stay during the festivities consequent upon the affiancing of Constance with Alan, Count of Bretagne. The young bride was dowered with the lands of Chester, once the possession of the unfortunate Earl Edwin. And William, at the same time, accorded his approbation to the love of Stephen and Adela. Every heart seemed filled with gaiety. Entertainment succeeded entertainment. The days were occupied with joustings, hunting, hawking, feats of archery and tournaments; the evenings were spent in games of hazard, or whiled away in listening to the wondrous tales of Ingulfus.

CHAPTER 7

Some upon penance for their sins,
In person, or by attorney ;
And some who were or had been sick;
And some who thought to cheat Old Nick;
And some who liked the journey;
And the staff was bored and drilled for those

38

Who on a flute could play;
And thus the merry Pilgrim had
His music on the way.

Southey.

"On my return to Caen with the remains of my dear lady Agatha," said Ingulfus, "I abandoned all thoughts of pilgrimage, till learning that the clergy of Germany had determined upon a visit to the Holy Land, the desire to worship at the tomb of the Saviour, returned again so strong upon me, that I was induced to unite with a Norman troop, which joined the company of the archbishop at Mentz. We were a goodly band," continued he, "out of every nation, kindred, tongue and people, of the Latin world—and heaven that moved us to this expiation of our sins, opened before us the way, and provided for our sustenance, both in the castles of princes, and in the cottages of peasants.

"The monasteries, of which many have been founded by pious men throughout all Germany, furnished resting-places for the weary, and hospitals for the sick. When we entered upon the kingdom of Hungary, which is 'a well-watered and fruitful country,' we found a strange people, whose nobles and warriors indeed live in walled towns, and castles strongly fortified among the rocks; but the common people, for the most part, dwell in tents like Abraham of old, and feed their flocks and herds upon the banks of the streams. These be the people, which the holy fathers thought were the Gog and Magog of sacred writ, and truly they came like a storm into Europe, and like a cloud they covered the land—both they and their bands. And because the time of their coming was near the end of the thousand years prophesied by St. John, many wise men did say, that they were the signs and forerunners of the end of the world. Howbeit since the end is not yet, there be not many at the present which hold this doctrine."

"Are there not some who say, that Gog and Magog are the heresies which vex the church?" inquired Robert.

"Even so," said Ingulfus; "but such are not led by the true and manifest words of Scripture, but following 'cunningly devised fables' have explained away even the promises of God. Now that these are the people is proved, in that they came from Persia and from the north quarters, and the name in which they most delight is Magyar, which plainly agreeth to Magog, and whosoever shall dwell in the latter days, will see 'wars and rumours of wars' in Hungary, according to my judgment. I have learned many things concerning them; for either for my sins, or the badness of the roads, the beast on which I rode fell lame, and therefore was I forced to leave the horsemen, and follow on foot, supporting the weariness of the way with pilgrim's staff. Among us were those, who from fear and love of adventure, and not from devotion, had undertaken the pilgrimage. Their vain talk and godless manners troubled me sore. There was one who having inserted a shepherd's reed in his staff, played thereon and sang with his voice, not the pious psalms of the church, but the unholy madrigals of the sinful and profane. And for that he saw it pleased me not, he delighted in it the more, and walked by my side, and when I could not rid myself of his company, I questioned him concerning his history.

"He was an Anglo-Dane of the north countrie, a born thrall of Earl Edwin, and had led a roving life from his youth. This man, whose name was Hardrager, was the false vassal who betrayed the young noble, and received from the justice of the Conqueror, the sentence of perpetual imprisonment. But the princes of this world are often compelled to use unworthy instruments in carrying forward their plans. When your royal father deemed it expedient for the peace of the realm to punish the treason of Earl Waltheof, and no man was willing to become his executioner, Hardrager purchased free pardon by beheading him."

"It was well he sought to expiate his offences by a pilgrimage," said Adela.

"Nay," said Ingulfus, "no thought of true penitence had ever entered his mind. Instead of profiting by the clemency of his sovereign, he applied himself anew to wicked practices, pursuing the hare and slaughtering the deer in the New Forest; till finally having suffered the loss of an ear for his crimes, and still continuing to set at naught the game laws, he was condemned to death; but as if the Almighty had raised him up for a 'thorn in the flesh' to his servants, Hardrager again escaped his doom. It pleased your noble sire, when he founded Battle Abbey, on the field of Hastings, and appointed monks to pray for the souls of the slain, to grant to the abbot the power of showing mercy to the guilty. It chanced accordingly when Hardrager was drawn from his dungeon, and carried toward the gibbet, that the worthy abbot meeting the cart, caused the procession to stop, and moved with pity for the criminal revoked his sentence, and laid on him the penance of pilgrimage.

"Hardrager lost no time in quitting England, and found means to join our company, upon the banks of the Rhine. He seemed well provided with purse and scrip, and often on days of fasting, purchased an indulgence from the bishop for himself and other vain persons, to regale themselves with meat and wine; and yet he seemed not to be without a sense of sin, and a certain reverence for the commands of the church. He rose early, and performed his devotions with the most scrupulous regularity, and every night scourged his naked shoulders with a knotted lash; and when I looked for a reformation in his life from this wholesome discipline, he told me he did not that for his own sins, but for the sins of another, who furnished him money for the expedition; for, by reason of his poverty, he had engaged to work out a three years' penance, that had been imposed on his benefactor; and he added, with a light laugh, 'I can better endure the smarting of my flesh by voluntary flagellation, than the loss of it by compulsory abstinence.'"

"By St. Stephen," exclaimed Robert, laughing, "the cunning knave is the true scapegoat of Scripture. It were no bad thought thus to expiate our sins by the vicarious suffering of some poor wretch."

"Heaven forefend," said Stephen, "that we should be compelled to raise our own exchequer by such means."

"The indulgences and requisitions of the church," gravely continued Ingulfus, "are too often perverted. I thank our blessed lady, who rather than continue me in the society of this wicked one, laid me upon a bed of sickness. For many days, I had with difficulty continued my journey, but Hardrager, who seemed insensible to fatigue, supported me by his strong arm, till coming to the lands of a powerful Hungarian, whose flocks and herds covered the hillside for many a league, we fell behind the other pilgrims, and my weariness increasing upon me, I sank exhausted and senseless upon the ground.

"What was my surprise when my consciousness returned, to feel myself upborne in the arms of Hardrager, who was attempting to place me upon the back of a horse which he had stolen from the adjoining pasture, and bridled with the scourge that he wore about his loins. 'Cheer up, holy father,' said he, 'heaven has sent thee help in time of trouble. I will walk by thy side, and we will soon prove to yonder heartless drones that the last shall be first.' In reply to my remonstrance, he added, with a misbelieving smile, 'Nay, is it not written, "The wealth of the wicked is laid up for the just," yon savage Magyar may rejoice in the happy chance which enables him to send a substitute to the holy city.'

"Upon my positive refusal to mount, he stood for a moment ir-

41

resolute, and then, with a smile, 'twixt jest and earnest, fell upon one knee before me, saying, 'Gra'mercy, good monk, I would crave thy blessing and absolution for this sin ere we part, for since thou wilt not accept the bounty of heaven, I must e'en take it myself.' Observing my hesitation, he rose hastily, saying, 'It boots not, 'tis but a few lashes more, and my shoulders are well able to bear them. *Adieu*, holy father, I grieve that thy conscience stands in the way of thy advancement,' and springing upon the restive beast, he was away with the swiftness of the wind."

"Nay, methinks I should have been less scrupulous," said William, laughing. "The fellow's dexterity merited absolution."

Ingulfus resumed, "Sick and alone, and much cast down in spirit, I stretched myself upon the grass, and looked only for death, but He who suffers not even a sparrow to fall without his notice, had compassion upon me, and sent a good Samaritan to my relief. Korshah, the noble Magyar, returning from the chase, came where I was, and seeing my low estate, gave his servants charge concerning me, to convey me to his own castle, where I tarried for above the space of a month, till my bruised feet were healed, and my broken health restored."

"It was a deed of Christian charity. I would fain learn something of this strange people," said Adela; "do they observe the rites of our church?"

"At the beginning of the present century," replied Ingulfus, "St. Stephen, the Alfred of his nation, divided the country into seventy-two counties and twelve bishoprics, but though the people have submitted to baptism, and observe the sacred canons, yet there prevails among them a strange mixture of barbarian fables, with the truths of holy writ; and their language is for the most part coloured with the extravagant, but beautiful expressions of the Orientals. And because my mind was intent upon the prophecies, and I would know concerning Gog and Magog and the chief princes of Mesech and Tubal, I questioned the noble Magyar of his country and the people of his ancient land.

"'My people,' said he, 'are numerous as the stars of night, and countless as the drops of falling showers. The smallest twig of yonder elm, that throws its shadow across the valley, is greater when compared with its trunk, than is the Hungarian branch, in comparison with the Scythian tree, whose roots strike deep into the soil of China, and whose boughs overshadow the Alps—extend beyond the sea of darkness on the north, and distil dews upon the broad and fruitful regions of Persia and Cathay. Beyond the possessions of our tribes to the eastward,' he continued, 'may no man go; for a desert and a land of darkness lasts from that coast, unto terrestrial Paradise. There are the mountains and hills which arose from Noah's flood, when the soft and tender ground was worn away by the waters, and fell and became valleys. Paradise is the highest part of the world, so high that it touches the borders of the moon.

"And there by a radiant way through the gates of the morning the angels were wont to descend to commune with our first parents; but that way was closed that Lucifer might return no more to the regions of light after he had tempted them, and thus with them was he driven forth from the garden. And Eve carried in her hand the seeds of the apple which she had given unto her husband, and wherever she wandered she cast them into the earth, and shed her tears upon them, and they sprang up and bore fruit, some good and some evil, and from those seeds came every green tree and herb that grow upon the earth. And this garden is enclosed all about by a wall, which seems not to be of natural stone—and the gate is of carbuncle flashing, with an incredible splendour, and shooting on every side its beams like flaming swords. Wherefore some visionary ones said it was fire, and many became worshippers thereof.

"And in the highest place in Paradise, exactly in the midst, is a well that casts out four streams, which run by divers lands throughout all the earth, and above the fountain of the streams, the four princes of the stars weave the semblances of what shall be, and cast them upon the waters, and whithersoever these flow there entereth a spirit into the nation or the people that dwell upon the banks, and they go forth conquering and to conquer. And thus were the tribes of Asia inspired to go toward the west, and establish their domain in Europe. Therefore wise men do study the stars, and read in the scroll of heaven the will of the Invisible. And all the sweet waters in the world above and beneath, take their rise from the well of Paradise. The drops of the morning-dew are gendered there, and thither the clouds return after the rain.

"There the light zephyrs gather rich odours under their wings, and from thence carry them abroad upon all the face of the earth, and give to every flower its perfume. And because of the abundance of precious things that are found therein, many have entered these rivers and essayed to pass by that land of chaos unto Paradise, but they might not speed in their voyage; for many died of weariness, by reason of rowing against the strong waves, and many were dashed in pieces against the dark rocks. And many vessels bound with iron were drawn aside by the shipman's stone, and held that they might never go thence.' I inquired concerning this stone," said Ingulfus, "and he told me there were in the eastern seas certain rocks of adamant which attract iron; and that men would break off pieces, and suspend them by a thread, and that one point thereof would turn to the north, and another to the south; and he said also that there are two stars fixed in the heavens, about which all the firmament turns as a wheel upon an axle.

"He said, moreover, that the earth and sea are of a round form, and that by this stone many mariners have passed the whole compass of the earth, and come again to the same point whence they set out. And these be not half the things that he told me, and there is none of them all but have some reason and understanding in them, and some good points of our belief. But though this man was both learned and devout, it grieved me to see in him the remains of his ancient superstition, for he was accustomed to worship before a hideous idol. And when he knew I was grieved concerning the thing, he said he worshipped not the image, but the virtue which was in it, even as we have images of our Lady and of the saints, which we set before us, to keep their holiness in mind. Howbeit the man showed me no little kindness; and when I was sufficiently recovered, he furnished me with a strong, well-appointed horse, replenished my purse, and accompanied me to the next town on my journey.

"I had hard riding to overtake my companions, which I should have failed in doing, had they not rested in Constantinople.

★★★★★★

"This city was first called Byzantium, which name is still preserved in the imperial money called *byzants*. It was by divine suggestion that its appellation was changed. For when Constantine the Great was pursuing his victorious course to the east, he lodged in that place; and in his dream he saw, and behold there stood before him an old woman, whose brow was furrowed with age; but presently clad in an imperial robe, she was transformed into a beautiful girl, and fascinated his eyes by the elegance of her youthful charms—and he waked and slept again; and there came one unto him and said, 'The woman thou sawest is this city worn down by age, whose walls thou shalt restore, and whose beauty shall signalize thy name to the end of time. Mount thy horse and give him the rein, to go whithersoever he will. Take the royal spear in thy hand, and its point shall describe the circuit of the wall upon the ground.'

"The emperor eagerly obeyed the vision, and employed the most skilful architects in building the city. By casting in masses of rock and sand, they straitened the ancient waters, and thus the sea wonders to see fields unknown before amid its glassy waves, and surrounds and supplies the city with all the conveniences of the earth. Constantine erected there the circus, statues of triumphal heroes, and tripods from Delphi. And all the saints whose bodies he was able to collect out of every country, were brought thither. In Constantinople is the fairest and noblest church in the world, called St. Sophia. It is of a circular form, domed in, and supported with pillars of gold and silver, hung about by lamps of the same precious metal. High mass is offered there on a different altar each day in the year.

"In its innermost part on the north side, is a large and beautiful apartment, wherein is a chest containing three pieces of our Lord's cross. Three times in a year this chest is brought out into the nave of the church, and placed upon a golden altar, where all the people are permitted to worship it. Howbeit I saw it not, which thing is a grief of mind to me. And they say concerning this cross, that when Adam was about to die, Seth went unto the angel that kept Paradise, to beg the oil of mercy for his father. But the angel gave him only three grains of the tree of life. And Seth buried them in the grave of Adam, and from these grains sprang up three trees, and from these were fashioned the cross on which our Saviour was crucified, as is contained in these words, '*In cruci fit palma cypressus oliva.*'

"Thus from the death of Adam came life into the world. And when our Lord had risen from the dead, the Jews moved with envy, took the crosses from Mount Calvary, and hid them in the earth. And thus St. Helena, the mother of Constantine, who was descended from the ancient kings of Britain, found them; and when she could not distinguish the cross of the Saviour from those of the thieves, she caused a dead body to be laid upon them, and when it touched the true cross it arose. St. Helena caused these relics to be conveyed to Constantinople; but the cross of Dismas the good thief, was carried to Cyprus, and men worship it there. There also she found the Saviour's seamless coat, and the four nails that pierced his hands and feet; and of one of these the emperor made a bridle for his horse to carry him in battle, and thereby he overcame all his enemies, and reigned from Persia to the British Sea.

"They showed me also a part of the crown of our Lord, made of the branches of Aubespine; and I had one of those precious thorns given to me as a great favour, and it hath this virtue; that whosoever beareth it about him, is secure from thunder and from tempest, and from the malevolence of evil spirits and demons. We tarried long at Constantinople, for there were many wonderful things to be seen. Every year the birthday of Jesus is celebrated with rejoicings; and on these occasions one may behold representatives of all the nations that inhabit different parts of the world; and the common people are amused with surprising feats of jugglery and dexterous motions of wild beasts, and birds of prey that have been trained to fight each other. And the emperor entertained the bishops right royally in the palace of the Blaquernel, in feasts and games, and gave them gifts of gold and silver, rich apparel and costly jewels, so that they were in no haste to depart, and many of the mixed multitudes that followed with us, remained there, and entered the service of the emperor."

Ingulfus was surprised the following day in the midst of his studies, by a secret visit from Adela.

"I am come," said she, "to obtain of thee, the precious thorn from the crown of our Lord."

The countenance of Ingulfus indicated at once his reluctance to part with the inestimable relic, and his strong desire to gratify the princess.

"Nay," said she, observing his hesitation, "I know its value, and am prepared to reward thee at whatsoever cost."

"Though it may have been the practice of some unworthy palmers, to trade in relics," said Ingulfus, "I cannot make merchandise of that which pierced the brow of my blessed Lord. It is thine without money, and without price."

Tears of gratitude beamed in Adela's eyes. "Good father," she answered, "I know right well, that by reason of thy holiness thou art safe from sudden danger, and therefore thou canst not need this talisman as does thy unworthy pupil; yet it grieves me to take without recompense that which is so dear to thee. Is there no gift in the power of Adela which Ingulfus would accept?"

"Thy father hath sometime suggested," returned the friar, modestly, "that he would reward my poor services with a benefice. It would please me well, to spend the few short days that remain unto me, in England. Near the monastery of Croyland was I born, and within the shelter of its walls would I die."

"Trust me for the accomplishment of thy wish," said Adela, bowing her head for his benediction. Then wrapping the holy thorn in a piece

46

of silver tissue, and placing it in her bosom, she departed.

CHAPTER 8: INGULFUS' STORY CONTINUED

When thou shalt see an old man bent beneath
The burden of his earthly punishment,
Forgive him, Thalaba!
Yea, send a prayer to God in his behalf!
                                    —Southey.

From Constantinople we proceeded across the Bosphorus through Asia Minor. Our route was tedious in the extreme, and after we entered upon the territory of the *infidels*, we were continually harassed by flying bands of Arabs; so that many were slain, and some being driven from the main body were lost among the mountains, and we saw them no more. At length with much toil, the pilgrims reached the village of Capernaum, where being hardly beset by the robbers, they were constrained to tarry, until they could obtain a safe escort from the *emir* at Antioch. Howbeit I only relate these things as they were told me in Jerusalem; for a strange adventure separated me from my fellows. There are two fountains, Jor and Dan, which flowing down from the mountain, are collected into one, and form the Jordan.

When we passed them in our route, I was constrained to linger among the shepherds, who fed their flocks in the green pastures which there abound, and several devout persons tarried with me; and on the morrow, when we had taken our leave, we journeyed on, and straightway we came to the conflux of these streams,—and when we saw the Jordan, each man hasted to divest himself of his garments, that he might bathe in that stream, in which our blessed Lord was baptized. So occupied were we with the holy ceremony, that we had not observed a band of Arabs, who assailed us with a shower of stones and javelins, and separated us one from another. What farther passed I know not, for a blow upon the temple felled me to the ground, and deprived me of sense.

When I unclosed my eyes, I thought myself among the fiends of hell; and feeling for my crucifix, I found myself wrapped in many folds of fine cloth, in which I was firmly but gently bound. As my senses gradually returned, I began to note the things about me. The apartment seemed a long, dark cavern, whose limits I could not distinguish, lighted by a fire at the farther extremity, round which half clothed, swarthy figures were engaged in roasting pieces of flesh. Others of the same appearance were seated upon mats, with a cloth spread before them upon the ground, cutting the meat with long, crooked knives, or tearing it with their white pointed teeth, with savage voracity. Apart from the rest, seated upon an elevated cushion with his legs crossed, was a tall, strong-built man, with hair and beard white as snow, hanging over his shoulders, and down to his breast.

He took no part with the revellers, but seemed to control by his look their wild, gibbering talk, to the end that it might not disturb my slumbers; for through excessive faintness, I seemed only to exist between sleeping and waking. His regards were fixed upon me, and his appearance recalled a dim recollection which I was vainly striving to trace, when at a word from him, the whole band disappeared behind an angle in the wall. The old man then lighted a torch and approached me, carefully removed the bandage from my head, anointed my wound with sweet-smelling balm, and gave me to drink of a fiery liquid, which spread like an elixir through my veins, and seemed instantly to reanimate me. With a smile at my puzzled look, he plucked away the false beard and hair, and revealed to my astonished sight, the swarthy countenance of Hardrager.

"Well met, holy father," said he, with his wonted laugh. "Hast come to bring a blessing to the habitation of Hardrager?"

"Is this thine habitation?" said I. "Then I was not so far wrong in thinking myself in purgatory!" (for I was ill-pleased with the strange place and bad company.) "But by what fatal mischance came I hither? Has the Saviour, for my sins, denied me at last the sight of his holy sepulchre?" and I sank back in despair.

"Nay," said Hardrager, "but for the mischance which thou deplorest, thou mightest indeed have been in purgatory."

"And where am I?" eagerly inquired I.

"Thou art in the strong-hold of the Old Man of the Mountain, and guarded by the assassin band of Mount Lebanon," replied he.

"The saints preserve me!" said I, ejaculating a prayer.

"In truth thou showest little gratitude," said Hardrager, "to one who hath saved thy life, (thanks to the good Hungarian steed that brought me to thy rescue). Knowest thou not the proverb? 'Speak well of the bridge that carried thee safe over!'"

Finding from his words, but more especially from the seriousness of his manner, that this wild man had really undertaken to render me an essential service, I began to regard him with more complacency, and finally brought myself to listen with interest to his story. Stung with remorse for his agency in the death of the noble Saxons, Edwin and Waltheof, he had determined, as soon as his pilgrimage was accomplished, to join the Varangians of Constantinople, and make perpetual war upon the Conquerors of England. On his route through Syria, he fell in with a band of Arabs, wild and reckless like himself, who, scorning allegiance to any leader, had established themselves among the ruined towers and rocky fortresses of Mount Lebanon, and thence carried on predatory warfare upon all who ventured to travel that way.

They wore the Mohammedan garb, and observed some of the institutions of the Koran, but were followers of Ali, uncle of the prophet. The superior abilities and learning of Hardrager, enabled him soon to master their language and their tenets, and by the fortunate solution of some timely mysteries, he impressed them with the belief that he was the prophet of Allah, and soon brought them to take oath to obey all his requirements.

But though he had thus apostatized from the faith of his fathers, he retained a copy of the New Testament, and religiously fulfilled his vows at the holy sepulchre, and with honesty worthy a better man continued his nightly flagellations. He had instilled into his wild followers his own hatred of the Norman race, and it was because of this that they fell upon us with such violence at the Jordan. I should have perished with my companions, for the Assassins were proceeding to rip open the bodies of the slain and wounded in search of coin, had not Hardrager recognized my Saxon countenance and interposed for my rescue. With the greatest care and tenderness, he had me conveyed in a litter to their nearest haunt, where, after protracted insensibility, I found myself stretched upon the couch of skins in the cavern.

As soon as I was sufficiently restored, he mounted me upon the good steed of the Magyar, which, being unable to walk, I was fain to ride, and accompanied me till we came in sight of the pilgrims encamped upon the Mount of Olives, for by his messengers, Hardrager had intelligence of their movements, and conducted me by the shortest route to join them.

"Benedicite, holy father," said he, as he lifted me gently from the horse, and reverently inclined before me, "a blessing in the Saxon tongue would be health to my guilty soul."

A tear glittered in his eye, and if it were a sin Heaven assoil me, for I yielded to his importunity and granted him the blessing. "*Adieu*, good friar," said he, "thou hast taken a load from my heart. Accept from the gratitude of Hardrager that which may stand thee instead, when thy fancied relics are of little avail." So saying, he gave me a small slip of parchment inscribed with Arabic characters, and rode slowly away. I thrust the scroll into my purse, little knowing its value, for my sight and sense were filled with Jerusalem, which I now saw for the first time.

As I walked along the brow of Olivet, like my Saviour, I beheld the city and wept over it, for the glory of Solomon's temple had departed; the holy prophets and apostles had passed away, and bands of *infidels* whose bright scimitars gleamed in the light of the setting sun dashed through her sacred streets, and encountered each other with barbarian clamour in her holy courts. The sound of the vesper-bell from the church of the Ascension invited us to prayer. With divine rapture we pressed our lips upon the stone imprinted with the last footsteps of our Saviour, and with pious theft we gathered some of the sacred dust from before the altar.

Descending from the mountain, we spent the night in fasting and prayer in the garden of Gethsemane, and at the first cock-crowing, arose to pass over the Brook Cedron. In the valley of Jehoshaphat we were met by the venerable patriarch, with the Latin and Syrian Christians of Jerusalem, who conducted us in solemn procession through the midst of the city to the church of the Holy Sepulchre.

There, amid the clangour of cymbals, and the sweet sounds of psaltery and harp, we bowed in worship and adoration, while through the cloud of ascending incense streamed the effulgence of innumerable lights, like the Shechinah of the ancient temple, and Jesus Christ the inhabitant of the place, alone knew the sighs we breathed, the tears we shed, the prayers we offered, and the thanksgivings we uttered.

Our vows were accomplished, and with the benediction of the patriarch upon us, we went forth, to climb the hill of Calvary, to visit the pool of Bethesda, and to mourn over all the pleasant places which the followers of Mohammed have laid waste. There was one among us, who, for the sins he had committed, and the compunctions of conscience that he suffered, was desirous to yield up his soul at the tomb of the Saviour.

This celebrated man, Fulk Earl of Anjou, had compelled two of his servants by an oath, to do whatsoever he commanded, and when we had completed our procession, and obtained absolution, he was by them dragged naked through the streets towards the Holy Sepulchre, one of them holding him by a twisted withe about his neck, the other, with a rod scourging his bare back, while the penitent cried out, "Lord, receive thy wretched Fulk, thy perfidious, thy runagate—regard my repentant soul, oh Lord Jesus Christ."

Howbeit he obtained not his request at that time. We were desirous to go down from Jerusalem to Jericho, to worship at Gilgal, and view that sea, whose black waters roll over the cities of the plain; but the wealth of the archbishops had been noised abroad, and the thieves that abound in those parts, fell upon all those who ventured that way, stripped and wounded them, and departed, leaving them to perish by the wayside. But our Norman bands accompanied by a party of Germans, arming themselves with swords determined to visit the Church of the Nativity, at Bethlehem.

We accomplished our purpose in safety, and were returning through the fields of the wood, when a band of mounted Saracens, with wild cries, dashed among us. Reluctantly, each man drew his sword and stood for his life. The attack fell heaviest upon the Normans, and despite our vigorous resistance, we should, doubtless, all have perished beneath their javelins, had not the frantic gestures, and more especially the green turbans of our assailants, reminded me of the cave of Hardrager, and recalled his parting words. Hastily opening my purse, I held up the Arabic scroll, before the eyes of a barbarian, whose drawn scimitar was flashing above my head.

At sight of it his demeanour instantly changed. He alighted, assisted me to rise, laid his hand upon his heart to express his concern for what had happened, and shouting, *Allah ackbar*, to his companions, drew them from their work of blood, and forthwith the flying band disappeared. Nearly half our number were slain, and the rest of us wounded and disheartened, slowly retraced our steps to Jerusalem, and relinquished all attempts to visit the other holy places with which the vicinity abounds. Though the patriarch, and the monks of the various monasteries gave us hospitable entertainments, yet, such had been the length, the weariness and discouragements of the way, and such the thinning of our ranks by famine, fatigue, disease, and hostility, that we were fain to choose the readiest means of return.

Learning that a fleet of Genoese merchantmen were anchored in the harbour of Joppa, we determined to purchase a passage overseas with them. The archbishops, therefore, gathered the pilgrims together, and numbered them, and of the seven thousand that had set out from Mentz, scarce three thousand remained; and on our way from Jerusalem to the place of embarkation through the rocky defiles which are the favourite haunts of the barbarians, we estimated that another thousand perished.

Our voyage to Brundusium was the most prosperous part of our journey. Thence we came to Rome; where I showed my life to our holy father the pope, and was absolved of all that lay on my conscience, concerning many grievous points, as men must needs have that travel in company with so many people of divers sects and beliefs. We then proceeded through Italy, and the archbishops took the route to Germany; and of our band that left Normandy, thirty well-appointed horsemen, twenty miserable palmers, only, repassed the Alps, and entered France on foot, ill, weary, and penniless; and had not a kind Providence sent the noble Earls Robert and Stephen to our relief, we might at last have perished on the banks of the Eure.

CHAPTER 9

Can piety the discord heal,
Or stanch the death-feud's enmity?
Can Christian lore, can patriot's zeal,
Can love of blessed charity?

The year 1077 opened with great rejoicing in Normandy. The royal family were reunited for the last time, to celebrate the marriage of Adela and Constance, with the wealthy and powerful husbands of the Conqueror's choice. The young Count and Countess of Blois, whose castles were numerous as the days in the year, determined to make a festive progress through their dominions, and the Earl of Bretagne, with his bride, with their young sister, Gundred, and her undeclared lover, the Earl of Warrenne, joined the happy party.

In the midst of her happiness Adela did not forget her promise to Ingulfus. The evening before her departure, she visited the cloister of the palmer, and acquainted him with his preferment to the Abbey of Croyland. The good friar's gratitude and pleasure were unbounded.

"Holy father," said the countess, "I have yet one boon to crave."

"Name it," said the priest. "If it lieth in my poor ability it shall not fail thee."

"Because it lieth in thy power do I intrust it to thee," continued she. "The body of Earl Waltheof, the father of our much-injured Maude, is interred at the four cross-roads, without the gates of Winchester; when thou takest possession of thy benefice, as soon as may be, thou wilt give him Christian burial, in the churchyard of Croyland, and cause daily masses to be said for his soul."

Ingulfus readily promised compliance.

52

Adela still lingered. "The lovely Maude goes with thee to England. Thou wilt be compelled to marry her to Simon. Soften, as much as possible, her hard fate, and watch over her interests, and comfort her with thy counsels."

"It shall be done," said Ingulfus, fervently.

"Father, I would confess."

And the young countess, in all her beauty and pride, knelt at the feet of the venerable man, and with the simplicity of a child, poured out her soul before him.

As Adela had predicted, the Conqueror, on his return to England, took with him Maude, as the bride of Simon. Robert sailed, also, in the same vessel, being commissioned by the king to establish Simon, now Earl of Huntingdon, in his new possessions.

William, too, accompanied his father, for he, more than any of the sons, comprehended the policy, and partook of the spirit of the Conqueror.

The remaining years of the Queen Duchess Matilda, were passed in splendid solitude, in the royal palace at Bayeux. The early death of the princess Adeliza, the failing health of Constance, together with fresh dissensions in her family, pressed heavily upon her mind, and occasioned the lingering illness that slowly conducted her to the tomb.

The loss of his beloved queen, and the undutiful conduct of his sons, aggravated the natural irritability and imperiousness of William, so that according to the English chroniclers, "He became, after her death, a thorough tyrant." He passed the four remaining years of his life in a constant succession of petty annoyances, and fruitless wars, with Philip of France.

In the stately castle of Chartres, sat the lovely Countess Adela apparently busy with embroidery, in that age almost the only home occupation of females. A shade of sadness was upon her brow, and an expression of anxious care indicated the mother's sympathy with the suffering child, that an attendant was vainly striving to soothe.

"Draw the couch of the little William to my side, Therese," said the countess, observing the tears in the girl's eyes. "Thou hast a tiresome task. Remove these frames," continued she to the maidens, "and go ye all to disport awhile in the pleasance, I will watch my boy's slumbers."

The feeble child stretched his hands to his mother, and laying his head upon her breast sank quietly to sleep.

"Poor suffering one," soliloquized Adela, "thou knowest naught but thy mother's love. Already thy younger brothers despise thy imbecility—the courtiers regard thee with indifference—and the very menials flout thee. No ducal coronet, or kingly crown will grace the head of my first-born."

The sound of heavy steps in the corridor disturbed the slumberer. He lifted his head, moaned heavily, and regarded with a vacant stare the warrior who entered.

"Robert, my beloved brother!" exclaimed the countess, the joy of former times flitting across her countenance.

With a moody and dissatisfied air the duke returned the frank greeting of his sister, and throwing himself upon a seat by her side, said in a tone of ill-concealed impatience,

"Adela, I have come to thee, for the prudent counsel of our mother dwells with thee. I am robbed of my rights and stripped of my heritage."

"Art thou not Duke of Normandy," inquired his sister with surprise.

"Aye, verily. Our father left me the duchy with a blessing that sounded marvellously like a curse. 'The dukedom of Normandy,' said he, 'I granted unto my son Robert, and having received the homage of his baronage, that honour given cannot be revoked: yet he is a foolish, proud knave, and will be punished with cruel fortune.'"

"The saints preserve thee," said the countess with a look of alarm, "and England"—

Robert interrupted.—"'Tis of that I would speak. The Conqueror bitterly bewailing the desolation and woe he had wrought in England, protested that he had so misused that fair and beautiful land, that he dare not appoint a successor to it, but left the disposal of that matter in the hands of God."

"Thou shouldst then have been king," said the countess, "since God made thee his first-born."

"So should I have been," said the duke, "but for the craft of William; but while I tarried in Germany, little thinking that my father's illness would terminate so suddenly, the red-haired usurper hastened over sea, and gaining Lanfranc to his interest secured the throne."

"Always unready," sighed Adela. "And while the elder sons were thus employed, the young Henry watched by the bed of his dying father. Is it not so?"

"Small watching had the Conqueror's death-bed," said Robert, with something between a smile and a sneer. "The filial Beauclerk set off to secure the treasures, and the attendants equally rapacious and inhuman, plundered the house of all the money, plate, and precious furniture, and even stripped the person of the monarch. And after Herlwin had succeeded in conveying the body to the abbey of St. Stephen's, and they were about to place it in the grave, there stood forth an insolent noble, and forbade the interment. 'This spot,' said he, 'was the site of my father's house, which this dead duke took violently from him, and here upon part of my inheritance founded this church. This ground I therefore challenge, and charge ye all as ye shall answer it at the great and dreadful day of judgment, that ye lay not the bones of the destroyer on the hearth of my fathers.'

"And there, exposed to the jeers of the assembled multitudes, was the body forced to wait, while Henry drove a sharp bargain with the owner of the soil, and purchased leave of burial for the paltry sum of sixty shillings. Oh Adela!" said Robert, rising and striding through the apartment in extreme perturbation, "I am weary of this greatness which makes enemies of brothers, and yields one scarce a grave at last."

The head of the countess was bent low over her sleeping child: and the duke continued, "I sometimes wish I were an eremite, and unless thy clear wit can devise some expedient by which I can obtain my rightful inheritance, and chastise the vanity of this presumptuous Rufus, I am resolved upon a pilgrimage."

"Thou saidst Lanfranc, assisted William: our uncle Odo hates Lanfranc," said Adela.

Robert caught at the suggestion. "My sister, I thank thee," he exclaimed eagerly. "Thou hast made me king. I will to Normandy, and summon my trusty squires to council. Simon of Huntingdon, Hugh of Norfolk, and William of Durham, are already disaffected and ready for revolt. Odo shall head the conspiracy in England."

Full of his new project the duke hurried away, scarcely waiting for the pecuniary aid, with which the countess, who knew the impoverished state of his finances, hastened to furnish him.

******

The well-concerted scheme of the conspirators failed, through the characteristic indolence and procrastination of Robert. Odo effected an inglorious escape from England, and the rebel earls gladly made terms with the king. Many of the insurgents repaired to Normandy, and suffered the confiscation of their estates; and while the Countess of Blois daily expected a summons to attend Robert's coronation, she was surprised by intelligence that William had crossed the sea with a numerous army, and by menaces, bribery or fraud, had obtained possession of almost every fortress, on the right bank of the Seine.

The barons who held lands under both brothers, laboured to effect a reconciliation through the mediation of the French monarch.

Robert still reckoning upon the liberal aid of his sister and her wealthy lord, resisted all overtures of peace; but Adela comprehending the hopeless defect of a character, that not even a crown could stimulate to promptitude, persuaded him to accept the terms of the treaty.

★★★★★★

As the splendid cortege attendant upon the Countess of Blois, and her young sons Thibaut, Stephen and Henry, swept along the great road from Chartres to Blois, the green arcades of a beautiful grove stretching down to the brink of a small stream that rolled its clear waters to the Loire, invited them to rest during the noontide hours. With loosened rein the steeds wandered at will cropping the tender herbage, or slaked their thirst in the rippling brook; while reposing upon the greensward, the party made a refreshing repast. The children, left to the unrestrained indulgence of their boyish glee, gathered wild flowers for their mother, hallooed to the echoes of the wood, or pursued each other along the banks of the stream.

Allured by the sound of their happy voices, the countess left the company and stole after them, catching occasional glimpses of their dancing plumes, as they bounded on before her, till coming to an opening in the glen, she stopped before an antique crucifix that some pious hand had reared upon the verge of a fountain. Occupied with the sweet thoughts suggested by the place, she scarcely noted the absence of her children, till the little Henry, pulling her by the robe exclaimed with a face all radiant with joy, "This way *ma mère*, Thibaut says we've found a hermit's cell, and Stephen is talking with the hermit." Yielding to his impetuosity the countess hastened forward and discovered sitting at the entrance of a sylvan lodge, just where the shadow of the cross fell longest at sunset, a youthful saint, if saint he was, reading his breviary, and telling his beads with affected sanctity.

"Beauclerk!" said the countess after a scrutinizing gaze at his half-concealed features.

"Thou knowest me then," said the pretended monk, in a tone of bitter reproach, rising and throwing off his gray friar's gown and cowl. "I thought myself forgotten by all my father's house."

"'Tis our uncle Henry," said Thibaut, amazed and chagrined at this transformation of his newly discovered hermit.

"And hast thou then doubted the affection of Adela?" said his sister.

"It were not strange that I should doubt the love of one leagued with my foes," replied the prince sorrowfully.

"How leagued with thy foes?" inquired the countess in great surprise.

"Thou surely dost not mock me," said Henry marking the tears trembling on her eyelids. "Thy countenance bespeaks thy sincerity. Have I then been the dupe, as well as the prey of my designing brothers?"

"If thou hast distrusted the love of Adela, yes," replied his sister, "but come thou with me. My lord awaits us at the castle of Blois. He shall investigate thy cause and redress thy wrongs."

"Come with us, dear uncle," reiterated the children observing his hesitation.

"Yield thyself, rescue or no rescue," said the young Stephen balancing a stick as a lance, and leading off the prince in triumph.

"And hast thou not heard of the siege of St. Michael's Mount?" said Henry as he rode by the side of his sister, at the head of the cavalcade.

"A passing rumour, and much I fear me, purposely perverted to restrain my interference, was all that reached me," replied Adela. "Tell me all."

"Thou knowest," continued Henry, "that by the will of our father, the duchy of Normandy fell to Robert, and the rich heritage of England was given to William. Henry had neither patrimony nor domains, some small treasure was all my share. This I gave to Robert in the hour of his need, for the lands of Cotentin, and then passed into England, to secure the dower of my mother. On my return, the prodigal having squandered the moneys received from me, seized and confined me in one of his fortresses. When Normandy was invaded, he released me from my imprisonment, and I did him good service in compelling William to raise the siege of Rouen. In the treaty to which thou didst persuade Robert, I was the principal sufferer, and therefore"—added he with warmth, "did I deem that the guileful duke, had stolen into the sanctuary of my sister's affections, and robbed me of thy love, my choicest treasure."

"My much-injured brother," said the countess, affectionately, "I knew not that thy interest was involved, else I had given far different counsel. But proceed with the story of thy wrongs."

"My traitor brothers united like Pilate and Herod of old," proceeded Henry, with increasing asperity, "seized my castles in Cotentén, and dogged my steps like sleuth-hounds on the track, till I took refuge in Mt. St. Michael, where the friendly tides kept them at bay; and there I had perished with thirst, had not Robert's tardy compassion ministered to my necessity, and finally effected my release. Since then, I have wandered a fugitive and an outcast, craving scant hospitality of my brother's vassals, and solacing my weary hours with clerkly studies."

"Courage, my good brother," said Adela, with enthusiasm. "Thou shalt wander no more. Count Stephen will put thee in the way to mend thy fortunes; and, perchance, thou wilt one day inherit the proud fiefs of both thy brothers. See! yonder gleams the spires of Blois. But what knightly train proceeds up the broad avenue of the castle. Listen! The warder sounds his bugle blast, and the drawbridge is lowered. Put thy horse to his mettle; these laggards may follow at their leisure." So saying the countess and her brother dashed forward, and entered the courtyard just as the retinue of the Duke of Normandy wound up the staircase, leading to the great hall.

At sight of Robert, Henry's eye flashed, and with an indignant gesture he turned to depart, but Adela, with a determined air, laid her hand upon his arm. "Remain," said she, "that portcullis bars all egress from the castle, and yon proud duke shall not escape till he has done thee ample justice."

Earl Stephen gave a cordial welcome to Robert, and greeted his countess with much affection, but the entrance of Henry threw him into evident perturbation, nor did it relieve his embarrassment to see his wife, with characteristic heroism, advance between the rival brothers, and fix her flashing eyes upon Robert.

The noble conduct of the repentant duke happily averted the gathering storm.

"Spare thy reproaches, sweet sister," said he, "and thou, my brother, forgive the grievous injuries thou hast suffered, and accept the only reparation that lieth in my power. I restore unto thee Cotentén, and would but for my poverty indemnify thee for thy losses. I have determined on a visit to the Holy Land; and I would dispose my worldly affairs, so that should I never return, man shall not accuse me before the throne of God."

The frankness of his confession, and the seriousness of his manner, allayed the resentment of Henry, and effected an apparent reconciliation. Harmony being thus restored, Robert proceeded at proper intervals to unfold the desires and purposes that had brought him once again to counsel with Adela.

Since the treaty which confirmed William in the sovereignty of England, not only, but secured to him several strong fortresses in Normandy, the duke had resigned himself to listlessness and luxury. In his aimless expeditions his attention had been frequently attracted by the appearance of a monk, who embodied in himself the spirit of a hermit, a pilgrim, and a soldier. His head was bare, his feet naked. His diminutive figure, attenuated by frequent abstinence, was wrapped in a coarse garment. His prayers were long and fervent, and the enthusiasm that gleamed in his eyes kindled the fires of holy zeal, in every town, village, and hamlet through which he passed. As he rode along, every street and highway was thronged with people, who worshipped the weighty crucifix he bore aloft, and listened with sighs and tears, while he depicted the sufferings of the Christians of Palestine, and with loud and frequent appeals to Christ and the holy mother, challenged the warriors of the age to defend their brethren, and rescue the tomb of the Saviour from the dominion of *infidels*.

Robert's curiosity was excited. He joined the eager crowds that followed the steps of the monk, and listened to the thrilling words till the latent desire of pilgrimage that had long slumbered in his mind awoke to life and activity, and he became a convert to the preachings of Peter the Hermit. But while he hesitated at the palmer's gown and staff, the united voices of chivalry and religion, bade him don his armour and draw his sword.

In the general council of the church, at Placentia, the ambassadors of the Greek Emperor Alexius Comnenus had portrayed the distress of their sovereign, and the danger of Constantinople, from the victorious Turks. The sad tales of the misery and perils of the eastern brethren, drew tears from the assembly, and several champions declared their readiness to march to the East.

The Greeks were dismissed with assurances of speedy and powerful succour. Pope Urban had given his sanction to the scheme, and summoned a second council to meet in Clermont the following November, to confer upon measures for sending armed forces into Asia.

It was to secure the concurrence of Adela, and the co-operation of Stephen, that Robert now came to Blois.

The representations of her brother, and the subject of his discourse renewed, in the memory of Adela, the fancy sketches of her childhood, and called up the half-formed purposes of her early youth. With the clear-sightedness peculiar to her character, she scanned the wide field thus opened to ambition, balanced the possible with the impracticable, determined for her brother the only course that would give free scope to his knightly abilities, and coveting for her husband a share in the glorious enterprise, persuaded him to embrace the scheme, and thus rendered herself really the *"Heroine of the First Crusade."*

Chapter 10

Onward they came, a dark continuous cloud
Of congregated myriads numberless.

"To dispose of his worldly affairs so that man might not accuse him before the throne of God," was a more serious and protracted work than the Duke of Normandy had anticipated. The patience of Stephen was in consequence nearly exhausted, in waiting his preparations, and it was not till the council of Clermont had been several days in session, that the nobles entered the district of Auvergne. As they approached the place of meeting, the highways were thronged by the eager crowds that flocked towards the city; and all the plains as far as the eye could reach, were dotted with tents and booths, that afforded temporary shelter for the thousands that could not find accommodation in the town.

On the morning of the eighth day, at an early hour, the reverend clergy, with the pope at their head, ascended a wooden pulpit, erected in the midst of the concourse, and declared to them the decrees of the synod, concerning the various matters at that time agitating the church. But ecclesiastical decisions and local interests were lost in the absorbing theme that occupied every heart. The blessing of Heaven was invoked upon their deliberations; and a stillness fell upon the waiting multitudes, like the hush of winds before the mighty storm, while the Monk of Amiens in a voice of persuasive eloquence and power, told them how terrible were the sufferings of their brethren in the East, and how burdensome was the tribute exacted by the inhuman Mussulmans.

He stated that lodging in the house of Simon, the patriarch of Jerusalem, he had become an eyewitness of these enormities, and had been commissioned to invite all the princes of the West, to contribute towards their remedy; that on a certain day filled with grief, he had entered the church of the Resurrection, and given himself to prayer, till at length sinking upon the cold stone pavement, there had breathed upon his senses,—first a soft strain like a shepherd's flute, swelling into a heavenly harmony, such as the advent angels sung, and then, triumphant anthems deepening into the trumpet's thunder tone, and the discordant clash of armour; that like Elijah of old he had afterwards heard a still small voice, saying, "Arise, Peter, make haste and fulfil without fear, what I have enjoined upon thee; for I will be with thee. It is time for the holy places to be purified, and for my servants to be succoured in their distress;" that immediately after the seraphic vision had beamed upon his sight, the brightness of the light awoke him; when he beheld lying upon the altar a letter containing the words of the Saviour; and his own pilgrim's staff transformed into a sword.

The hermit ceased; and held up the miraculous scroll before the eyes of all the people. A wailing swept over the vast throng, and the whole multitude bowed, as the forest bends before the first rush of the tempest.

Seizing upon the favourable moment, the pontiff arose and addressed the assembly:

My brethren and dearest children, whether kings, princes, marquises, counts, barons, or knights, all you who have been redeemed by the bodily passion, and shedding of the blood of our Lord Jesus Christ, hear the complaints of God himself, which are addressed to you concerning the wrongs and unlooked-for injuries, which have been done to him in Asia, where sprang the first germs of our faith, where the Apostles suffered martyrdom, and where at the present day, the persecuted Christians with stifled sighs, long for a participation in your liberties. Have compassion upon your brethren that dwell in Jerusalem, and in the coasts thereof,—check the insolence of the barbarians, and you will be extolled throughout all ages—let your zeal in the expedition atone for the rapine, theft, homicide, licentiousness, and deeds of incendiarism, by which you have provoked the Lord to anger,—turn against the enemies of Christ those weapons, which you have hitherto stained with blood, in battles and tournaments against yourselves.

To those present, I command this; to those absent, I enjoin it. For ourselves we will trust in the mercy of the Almighty God, and in virtue of the power He has given us, and by the authority of the blessed Apostles, Peter and Paul, we absolve all who engage in this holy war, from all the offences which they shall repent in their hearts, and with their lips confess, and in the retribution of the just we promise to the same an increased portion of eternal salvation. And this forgiveness shall extend also to those who contribute by their substance or counsel to its success. Go then, brave soldiers, and secure to yourselves fame throughout the world. God will accompany you on your march—the season of the year be propitious, both by the abundance of fruits, and by the serenity of the elements.

Those who shall die, will sit down in the Heavenly guest-chamber, and those who survive will set their eyes on the Saviour's sepulchre. Happy are they who are called to this expedition, that they may see the holy places in which our Lord conversed with man, and where to save them he was born, crucified, died;—was buried and rose again. Take then the road before you in expiation of your sins, and go assured that after the honours of this world have passed away, imperishable glory shall await you, even in the kingdom of Heaven.

Loud shouts of 'God wills it,' 'God wills it,' pronounced simultaneously in all the different dialects, and languages, spoken by the nations of which the multitude was composed, for a moment interrupted the prelate. Commanding silence by a motion of the hand, he resumed:

Dear brethren, today is shown forth in you, that which the Lord has said by his evangelist, 'When two or three shall be assembled in my name, there shall I be in the midst of them.' For if the Lord God had not been in your souls you would not all have pronounced the same words, or rather God himself pronounced them by your lips, for it was He who put them in your hearts. Be they then your war-cry in the combat, for those words came forth from God. Let the army of the Lord when it rushes upon his enemies, shout but that one cry, '*Deus vult*,' '*Deus vult*.'

Oh brave knights! remember the virtues of your ancestors; and if you feel held back from the course before you, by the soft ties of wives, of children, of parents, call to mind the words of our Lord himself, 'Whosoever loveth father or mother more than me is not worthy of me. Whosoever shall abandon for my name's sake, his house, or his brethren, or his sisters, or his father, or his mother, or his wife, or his children, or his lands, shall receive an hundred fold, and shall inherit eternal life.' Gird yourselves then, my brave warriors, for the battle, and let him who is ready to march, bear the holy cross of the Lord upon his shoulders, in memory of that precept of the Saviour, 'He who does not take up his cross and follow me, is not worthy of me.'

The agony of conflicting emotions that shook the assembled throngs, burst forth in a storm of sighs, groans, and tears, and as the trees of the forest fall prostrate in the blast, the agitated multitudes sank upon their knees, smote their breasts in sorrow, poured forth their confessions, and consecrated their persons and their property to the Holy Crusade.

CHAPTER 11

There the wild Crusaders form,
There assembled Europe stands,
Heaven they deem awakes the storm,
Hell the paynims' blood demands

The results of the council of Clermont were speedily felt throughout Europe. No nation was so remote, no people so retired, but, gaining the intelligence by common rumour, or miraculous revelation, commenced preparations for the mighty enterprise.

The Welshman forsook his hunting,—the Scot his native mountains,—the Dane forgot his wassail-bowl,—the Norwegian left his fishing-tackle on the sand. Whatever was stored in granaries or hoarded in chambers, to answer the hopes of the avaricious husbandman, or the covetousness of the miser, all was deserted, or bartered for military equipments.

Zeal and sympathy, and indignation and chivalrous feeling, and the thirst for glory, and the passion for enterprise, and a thousand vague, but great and noble aspirations, mingled in the complicated motive of the Crusade. It increased by contagion—it grew by communion—it spread from house to house—and from bosom to bosom—it became a universal desire—an enthusiasm—a passion—a madness.

Princes laboured like peasants at the forge or in the armoury. High-born dames abandoned their embroidery, and employed their delicate fingers in fabricating garments for the retainers of their lords.

The Countess of Blois laid aside the famous Bayeux tapestry, which her mother had left for her completion, and accompanied her husband from castle to castle, through all their wide domains, presiding over the labours of her maidens, while with pious zeal they stitched the red cross upon the surcoats of the warriors.

Robert pledged his ducal domains to the grasping Rufus, for a sum of money scarcely sufficient to meet the expenses of the expedition; and Edgar Atheling bestowing his orphan nieces in the nunnery of Wilton, joined the train of his friend.

Godfrey, Duke of Lorraine, a prince of the royal house of France, assembled his followers, from the banks of the Rhine to the Elbe; Raimond of Toulouse, and Adhemar, bishop of Puy, called the Moses and Aaron of the host, collected the Goths and Gascons, and all the mingled people between the Pyrenees and the Alps; Bohemond of Apulia commanded the tribes from the Tuscan sea to the Adriatic, while volunteers from all parts of Europe flocked to the standards of these noble leaders, or joined the band of the Hermit himself.

The long-looked-for time was now at hand, when the hoary garb of winter being laid aside, the world clad in vernal bloom, invited the pilgrims to the confines of the East. And in the beginning of March, 1097, the masses of European population began to roll. The first band that swept on through Germany into Hungary consisted of twenty thousand footmen, marshalled under Walter the Penniless. Then followed Peter the Hermit, with forty thousand men, women and children. Next a German priest headed fifteen thousand enthusiasts, and another band of two hundred thousand unarmed and disorderly people hurried on by the same path; and ere these desperate adventurers had reached the borders of the Grecian Empire, Europe glittered with mustering hosts of warriors arrayed in all the pomp and splendour of chivalry, and led by the greatest warriors of the age.

Few chieftains brought so many soldiers to the standard of the cross as Stephen, Count of Blois and Chartres. But notwithstanding the precipitate zeal of Robert, and the prompt and politic measures of Adela, the summer was wasted in idle delays; and it was not till the autumnal equinox that these distinguished nobles joined the forces of Hugh, Count of Vermandois, and crossed the Alps, intending to proceed by sea to the Holy Land. They found Pope Urban at Lucca, and received from him the standard of St. Peter. The autumn was passed in the gaiety and dissipation of Italy, where the earls disposed their troops for winter-quarters. Count Stephen returned once more to Blois, already dissatisfied with the prospects of the expedition. In the ensuing spring, one year after the time designated by the pope, with Robert

64

and Hugh, and their united forces, the husband of Adela embarked for Palestine. In the meantime numbers, disaffected by the first encountering of difficulties, returned to claim subsistence from the bounty of the Countess of Blois.

"Methinks, my beneficent sister," said Henry, observing her charity towards the miserable wretches, "if thou hadst seen yon beggars sell their flocks and herds for a few shillings, thou wouldst be better inclined to laugh at their folly than relieve their poverty."

"Adela counts it not folly for a man to sell all he hath for the kingdom of Heaven's sake."

"I fancy," said Henry, laughing, "that those self-sacrificers have an eye to the 'manifold more in this life,' rather than to the heavenly inheritance; and *some*, I trow, understand by the kingdom of heaven, a principality in Palestine."

"And were not the establishment of Christian powers in Asia a worthy purpose?" returned Adela, little pleased at her brother's insinuations.

"*Certes*, my beloved sister. But wherefore didst thou detain thy unworthy Beauclerk, is there not kingdom or duchy for him?"

"Nay! I scarcely claim the merit of detaining thee," said Adela, "since I suspect that a stronger tie than compassion for my lone estate has withheld thee."

"That a tender interest in the declining health of the Red King somewhat influenced my decision I cannot deny," replied Henry, evasively.

"And had the superlative beauty of the Red King's ward no influence?" said Adela, pressing her advantage.

"Nay, sister, since thou divinest my secret," said Henry, frankly, "I will e'en tell thee all. Perceiving that thy crusades would draw from the Norman power its military strength, I deemed it wise, in case of my brother's death, to entrench myself in the affections of the English people, by uniting my personal interest with the Saxon race. Accordingly, when Robert sent me to England to negotiate the mortgage of his duchy with Rufus, I visited the nunnery of Wilton, with Edgar Atheling."

"And thou sawest there the fair novice, Matilda," interrupted Adela.

"Call her not novice, she scorns the name, and hath a spirit like a queen. In presence of her uncle the Atheling, she tore the hateful veil from her head, and trampled it under her feet."

"And did the spirited damsel smile upon thy suit?"

"I proffered no suit save to her uncle."

"And what said the Atheling to thy visionary scheme?"

"He promised to give her to me with his blessing, on his return from the crusade."

"But here comes another son of Cushi, with tidings for the Countess of Blois. Judging from his tattered garments, and limping gait, his story must eclipse all that have gone before. My *'visionary schemes'* shall not claim the attention that should be devoted to this magnificent eastern ambassador;" and with a smile of irony Henry took his departure.

The appearance of the individual who entered the presence of Adela, and the tidings he brought, fully justified the sarcastic conjectures of Henry. He was a refugee from the party of Walter the Penniless, a band whose only recommendation for the Holy war was their poverty. Before setting out, each one was searched, and the man upon whose person was found the sum of two *sous*, was hooted from the camp. Animated by a blind fanaticism, they expected that rivers would be opened for their passage; that flesh would be miraculously supplied; manna rained from heaven upon them, and the smitten rock send forth its cooling stream.

The hospitality of the Hungarians confirmed their faith; but when they entered the kingdom of Bulgaria, the illusion vanished, and the famine-stricken multitudes, abandoning their presumptuous trust in heaven, resorted to carnage and plunder. The exasperated inhabitants fell upon them without fear or mercy. Many were slain, numbers fled to the forests, and a remnant of the disappointed devotees attempted to retrace their steps to their own land.

After listening to the account of the miserable fugitive, Adela remarked, that the misfortunes of the company doubtless proceeded from their forgetfulness of the last directions of the Saviour: "He that hath a purse let him take it, and likewise his scrip, and he that hath no sword let him sell his garment and buy one."

"Ah, lady!" said the wretched fanatic, "think not that our misfortunes arose from our want of money or arms, but rather through our impatience to be gone, that led us to set out on Friday, instead of waiting for the holy rest of the Sabbath."

The countess was residing with her family in Troyes, when she gave audience to another of her "eastern ambassadors," as Henry jocosely called them.

This man arrived at nightfall, on a sorry mule, the self-same animal that a few months before, under Peter the Hermit, had led greater hosts to battle than Bucephalus under Alexander, and which had enjoyed such a reputation for sanctity that even his very hairs were devoutly treasured as relics. Now, jaded and dispirited, with drooping head and pendant ears, the poor beast slowly paced his heavy way up to the gates of the castle. His rider seemed no less bowed with grief and fatigue, and wearily dismounting, he meekly waited among the servants, till summoned to the presence of his mistress.

"You behold, noble lady," said he, "one of those individuals whose fate it is to bring ruin upon every expedition in which he embarks."

"Miserable man," exclaimed Adela, "hast thou betrayed the army of the Lord?"

"God forbid that I should have been guilty of so foul a deed," said the pilgrim, devoutly crossing himself; "but the curse of Jonah rests upon me. Evil was the day when, impoverished by the wars of Duke Robert, I plundered the sacred vessels of a church, and melted and sold them, to obtain food for my starving family. The crime lay heavy on my conscience, and to expiate its guilt I joined the band of the Hermit. But my sinful love for my children prevailed over my devotion, and Satan tempted me with the thought, that were they permitted to accompany me, they at least might win the crown of martyrdom, though their father should suffer the punishment of his sins. With much difficulty and labour, we scraped together means to purchase a yoke of oxen and a cart, and the charity of my noble countess (heaven reward thee) provided raiment for my poor old father and helpless infants.

"Heaven pardon me, but my wicked heart was inflated with pride, as seating my precious ones in the vehicle, I walked by their side; and pleased was I as we reached any town or city, to hear the little ones inquire, if that were Jerusalem. Fool that I was not to remember the Saviour's words, 'He that forsaketh not all that he hath, cannot be my disciple.' There were many who, falling into the same error, cumbered the train with useless baggage, and many feeble and sick, both men and women, caused that our route was tedious and slow. The heat of summer came on, and the weariness of the way seemed to increase. My children forgot their innocent prattle, and stretched their tender limbs upon the floor of the cart. The old man, my father, slept, and we could not wake him; and my wife gave me the infant from her breast—it was dead—and we buried them by the wayside.

67

"This was the beginning of sorrows. But the *horrors* of my crime flashed upon me, when certain sons of Belial among our company, set fire to the houses, and commenced to plunder the people through whose villages we passed. The inhabitants armed against us, and I shudder to describe the bloody scenes which followed. Enraged at the wanton attack, they rushed out upon us, fell upon the rear of the army, glutted their wrath with the blood of all that opposed them, and destroyed that part of the multitude whom weakness left without defence. My wife and sons fell victims to their fury, and Therese, my lovely daughter, was torn shrieking from my arms, and carried away by a brutal ruffian."

"Unhappy Therese," said Adela, dropping a tear. "My poor William has pined for his patient nurse."

"In the extremity of my desperation," continued the pilgrim, "I rushed into the thickest of the fight, and sought for death; but in vain. My crimes were too great, and I was reserved to mourn the loss of those for whose dear sakes I had perilled my soul.

"Deploring the ruin that my sins, and the sins of such as me had brought upon the holy pilgrims, I determined to hide myself in a convent, and seek by a life of penance, the pardon I hoped to have found at the Saviour's tomb; and finding the deserted mule of our leader, wandering upon the border of a marsh, I mounted upon his back, and begged my way hither."

The countess gave him money for the remainder of his journey, to the monastery of Caen, and with a heavy heart dismissed him.

★★★★★★

A German monk of great sanctity resided in a solitary cell in the forest of Troyes. The fame of cures, effected by him, through the medium of invisible agents, led the countess to consult him with regard to her invalid son. Thibaut and Stephen, with a small train, accompanied her to the hermitage.

On their return their way was obstructed by a crowd, collected about a grotesque-looking figure clothed partly in armour, and partly in priestly robes. His head was ornamented with a cap like that of a merry-Andrew, at the top of which flourished a feather cut in the form of a cross. From his shoulders hung numerous thongs, to which were attached boxes and bags of various colours and dimensions, and a rosary of small human bones was suspended about his neck. This he occasionally shook with demoniac glee, as an accompaniment to songs, whose sentiment strangely alternated between piety and pro-

68

fanity.

"News from the wars," shouted he approaching the cavalcade.

Holy relics for sinners all,
The thumb of St. Peter, the tooth of St Paul.

"Yea more—Babylon has fallen—the Jews, the Jews—Shadrach, Meshach, and Abednego, are consumed in the burning fiery furnace— Ha! ha! How the flames crackled and sparkled—How the Long-beards winced and writhed—Ashes! Ashes!" said he, throwing the contents of one of the boxes into the faces of the spectators—"Yea more—

The crusaders followed the spirit divine,
And water and blood it turned into wine;
That made us strong for the slaughter.

Drink—heal—wassail,"—and he poured from a bottle a noisome liquid, from which the crowd shrank back in disgust.

"The demons shrieked in the forest—and the little fiends winked in the marshes—they showed us the way to the holy sepulchre— bridges of corpses—rusty armour—glaring eyeballs. How the wolves howled on our track—and the black ravens croaked over the dying— 'Twas rare sport to hear them groan.

The goat led his followers up the steep rock,
The goose flapped her wings, and headed the flock;
List to the sound of the martyrs' bones;

. . . and the lunatic broke into a wild fantastic dance, rattling his boxes and shaking his horrid rosary with demoniac frenzy.

The countess was here relieved from her involuntary attendance upon the frightful exhibition, by the approach of Prince Henry, who having consigned the madman to proper care, dispersed the crowd, and permitted the train proceed.

In reply to Adela's anxious inquiries, he informed her that the miserable creature whom she had seen, had belonged to a mad-rabble, that set off for the Holy Land without leader or guide, held together only by the strange infatuation of adoring a goat and a goose, which they believed to be filled with the divine spirit.

Their malignant zeal was directed principally against the Jews, whom they exterminated wherever they came. The Hungarians de- nied them a passage through the country. The fanatics attempted to force their way across the Danube. The nation rose to arms, and for several days smote them with such slaughter, that the fields were strewed with the slain, and the very waters of the river were hidden by the multitude of the corpses.

"Heaven punished their impiety with a loss of reason," said Adela, with a sigh.

"Their impiety began with a loss of reason," said Henry, drily. "Thy pardon, sweet sister, but the heralds of thy grand expedition and the tidings they bear, remind one of the evil messengers of Job, each man having escaped alone to tell thee."

"We have as yet gained intelligence only from the ill-appointed and barbarous hordes that encumbered rather than aided the expedition. When we shall receive news from warriors, whose heroic courage executes the plans of temperate wisdom, I trust that the disasters of our foes will form the theme of conversation," said Adela, with much spirit.

"Nay, I meant not to vex thee," returned Henry, soothingly, "and to prove my desire of peace, I have brought with me a flag of truce," and he handed her a letter from her husband.

******

Adela's letter from Stephen contained the most gratifying intelligence. Completely duped by the artful policy of Alexius, the count gave a glowing description of his reception at Constantinople, and the splendid ceremony by which the Latin chiefs did homage to the Greek emperor, for the cities they hoped to win in Palestine.

He described the magnificence of the city, and enlarged upon the advantages which the holy legions would derive from this allegiance, both in supplies of money and provisions. He stated that Alexius had already furnished ships to convey them across the Bosphorus, that a part of the army were already in Asia Minor, and expatiated upon the munificence of their Imperial host, who each week presented the leader of the expedition with as much gold as two slaves could bear upon their shoulders.

Delicately alluding to the favours bestowed upon himself, he closed the epistle by presenting the monarch's request to the mother, that her son Stephen should be sent to Constantinople, to receive princely nurture at the most refined and elegant court in the world.

Tears of affection and gratification filled the beautiful eyes of the countess, as gazing upon her blooming boy, she murmured, "My son may yet wear the diadem of the Cæsars. My father was styled The Conqueror, because he added a poor island to his duchy of Nor-

70

mandy, but what title shall he bear who restores a continent to the dominion of Christendom?"

★★★★★★

For the three following months the countess received no certain intelligence concerning the fate of the crusade. There were rumours of famine in the Christian camp, and stories of dreadful battles with the *infidels*; but the statements were vague and unsatisfactory.

Prince Henry had been absent for some time quelling an insurrection in Normandy, and the loneliness of Adela's situation, together with the anxiety of her mind, filled her thoughts with melancholy forebodings, and subdued the natural vivacity of her manners.

The prince upon his return, was alarmed by the pallor of her countenance, and the sadness of her tones.

"Cheer thee, my sister," said he, "thou wert, indeed, a prophet, to declare that the victories of the warriors would compensate for the disasters of the rabble crowds."

"Art thou the bearer of good tidings?" said Adela, a flush of hope irradiating her features.

"Aye, verity," returned the prince, with exultation, "a well-authenticated account of the victories of the cross, embellished with as pretty a Passage of Arms in Cupid's tilt-yard, as the Romancers could well desire."

"Sport not with my impatience," said Adela. "Tell me the name of thy messenger, and the news he brings."

"The messenger is Gilbert of Becket, a Saxon esquire of Edgar Atheling, and, therefore, direct from Duke Robert and Count Stephen. He sailed with them across the Ionian Sea, and carried the shield of his master at the grand parade, in Constantinople."

Adela interrupted him. "I know all to the time of their departure from that city. How have they sped in their encounters with the Infidels?"

"The first place of importance which they attacked," replied Henry, "was Nice, the chief city of Rhoum, occupied by the Seljoukian Turks, who exacted tribute from all the inhabitants of Asia Minor. The Sultan Soliman hearing of the coming of the crusaders, left his capital defended by a strong garrison, and hastened to the mountains levying troops in all directions. The first body of *croises* that reached the city, was led by Godfrey of Boulogne, and Hugh of Vermandois, who took up their position on the eastern side. Raimond of Toulouse, and the Bishop of Puy, encamped on the south, while Robert of Flanders, and

Bohemond of Tarentum pitched their camp upon the north.

"And of this Bohemond, the noble chief of Otranto, I must tell thee. Forty Norman gentlemen who had distinguished themselves in the wars of our father, returning from a pilgrimage to the Holy Land, disembarked in Italy. Learning that the Prince of Salerno was besieged by the Saracens, they threw themselves into that town, and being supplied with arms and horses, soon compelled the Infidels to retire. After their return home, deputies came to Normandy from the prince imploring their further assistance. In consequence of his promises and persuasions, several bodies of adventurers, at the head of whom was Robert Guiscard and his eleven brothers, emigrated together, cleared the south of Italy from the locust-like invaders, and established themselves lords of Apulia and Calabria.

"Robert Guiscard spent most of his life in wars with the Greek emperor, and was finally poisoned by Alexius. Bohemond, the son of this Guiscard, espoused the quarrel, and was preparing to avenge his father's death, but when he heard the crusade proclaimed, his chivalric spirit at once caught the flame. Dashing his armour to pieces with his battle-axe, he caused them to be formed into small crosses, which he distributed among his followers, and abandoning his possessions in Italy, joined the pilgrims with his cousin, Tancred, a youth distinguished for beauty, valour, generosity, enthusiasm—"

"I care not," said Adela, "though he were as beautiful as Absalom and wise as Solomon. There are two less distinguished chiefs, who possess far more interest for me than all the warriors in Italy."

"Of those thou shalt hear anon," said Henry. "When this Bohemond was in Constantinople, the emperor sought to win his friendship."

"Return not to Bohemond again," interrupted the countess, "'tis of Stephen and Robert I would hear."

"Now, sister," said Henry, playfully, "thou knowest not what thou refusest. Will it not please thy woman's curiosity, to hear of the magnificent rooms of the Blaquernel, filled with stores of money and jewels, costly garments, and rich silks of unheard-of value, that Alexius gave Bohemond to secure his allegiance."

"Nothing will please me," said Adela, "but to know what is the fortune of my husband."

"And that will please thee well," said Henry, breaking into a playful laugh. "Stephen, triple Count of Blois, Chartres, and Champagne, the husband of my gifted sister," bowing to the countess, "son-in-law of

72

William the Conqueror, father of earls, and I doubt not of kings, the most beautiful, accomplished, eloquent, and *prudent* man of the times, was chosen president of the council of chiefs."

"Heaven bless thee for thy news," said Adela, in a transport of joy; "and Robert?"

"Justifies his youthful soubriquet of 'unready.' He came last to the siege of Nice. His troops, however, were fresh and vigorous, and when he approached the city by the west, which position had been left for his encampment, he scanned, with a fearless eye, the double walls, defended by three hundred and fifty towers, filled with bowmen, and spearsmen of the most determined valour. He drew up the warriors of Normandy, with those of Blois and Chartres, and a band from Boulogne, where a great part of the people led by Walter the Penniless and Peter the Hermit had been defeated and slain. The *infidels* in mockery had formed here a great pile of their bones, and covered them with earth; so that when Robert arrived with his forces, he pitched his tent just beside the green sepulchre of those who had found martyrdom on that very spot.

"Peter the Hermit, with the remnant of his forces, soon after joined the besiegers, and the army, as they were then numbered, consisted of 600,000 infantry and 100,000 mailed cavalry. Each man confessed his sins, and the sacrifice of mass being offered, they commenced the erection of engines, and other preparations for the siege. Soliman himself was encamped upon the mountains, scarcely ten miles off, watching in what manner he might best free his city from the enemies that clustered around it. Two of his messengers were intercepted by Godfrey. They confessed that they were sent to concert with the besieged a double attack upon the Christian camp. The crusaders immediately prepared for the conflict. By break of day the Moslems began to descend from the hills, and issue from the town.

"The Christians received them everywhere with determined valour, repulsed them on all points, became in turn the assailants, and all the plain around Nice grew one general scene of conflict. This attack was twice repeated with the same result, and the sultan was at last compelled to retire, astonished at the lion-like courage of the Franks, who with a thousand lances, could charge, and easily put to flight twenty thousand Turks. But amidst these splendid achievements, which the Saxon Gilbert described, with great vividness, he said it was mournful to see the pilgrims at nightfall collecting the dead bodies of their companions and bearing them in sad procession to the cypress groves adjacent, where by the melancholy glare of the torches they buried them without coffin or shroud.

"To intimidate the besieged, the *croises* cut off the heads of the fallen Moslems, and shot them from their engines into the city.

"The Turks invented a horrid method of retaliation. Long iron hooks were let down from the walls, by which the bodies of the slaughtered Christians were seized and drawn up through the air, and after being stripped and maimed were again cast forth upon the ground.

"Young Gilbert being wounded and lying insensible, was grappled and drawn into the city in this manner, but finding that life was not extinct, they delivered him over to the care of Soliman's physicians, who tended him as a prisoner of note. The siege had been protracted to some length and the Christians had succeeded in undermining a huge tower at the north-eastern angle of the wall. The *sultana*, alarmed at the loss of this important defence, determined upon flight. Several boats were prepared, and the queen, with her train, among whom was young Gilbert, attended by a dark-eyed daughter of an *emir*, beautiful as an *houri*, attempted to make her escape at night by way of the lake. As the little fleet moved stealthily in the shadow of the overhanging cliff, Becket seized a bow, and dexterously discharged an arrow towards the nearest outpost of the Christian camp.

"The twang of the bow-string attracted the attention of the Moslems, but Zaida perceiving the danger of her favourite smote the strings of her harp, and thus, ingeniously reproducing the sound, made the whole appear the result of accident.

"Becket afterwards learned, that the dart fell at the very feet of the sentinel dozing by the watch-fire, who started up, aroused his comrades, and soon the knights of Duke Robert swarmed along the shore.

"The Paynims plied their oars in vain, the Normans intercepted their flight. The *sultana* was taken prisoner, and only the boat of the *emir* with the disappointed Gilbert escaped capture.

"The Christians having thus discovered the means, by which the city was supplied with provisions, procured boats from Constantinople and converted the siege into a blockade. All hope now abandoned the Turks, and about the time of the summer solstice they offered terms of capitulation.

"The necessary negotiations were in progress, when Tatius, the lieutenant of the subtle Alexius, entered into a private treaty with the besieged, and while waiting for the gates to be opened, with indignation and astonishment the Christians discovered the imperial ensign floating upon the walls of Nice. Alexius endeavoured to appease their wrath by distributing rich bribes among the chiefs, and largesses among the private soldiers, but dissatisfied and exasperated they struck their tents, and departed without setting foot within the city they had conquered.

"Meanwhile, the captive Becket, was conveyed to the army of the *sultan*, and though his ardent spirit chafed at restraint, and panted for the fight, his impatience was soothed by the tender attentions, and sweet songs, of the *emir's* daughter.

"Soliman, with the whole of his force, amounting to 200,000 men, hung upon the rear of the crusading army, concealing his own evolutions, by his perfect knowledge of the country, and watching those of the *croises* with the keen anxiety of a falcon hovering over its prey. By some mischance, Robert and Bohemond were separated from the main body of the army. They encamped nevertheless on the banks of a beautiful stream, in the valley of the Gorgon, and passed the night in repose. Scarcely had they commenced their march, on the following morning, when the immense army of the *sultan* appeared upon the hills. From his station upon a lofty eminence, Becket had opportunity to watch the progress of the contest, and from Christian captives that were brought to the camp, he learned many particulars concerning his companions.

"Our brother Robert, with a vigour and promptitude foreign to his character, drew up his forces, formed a rampart of wagons and baggage, and exhorted his men to meet with bravery the overwhelming shock. The terrific cries of the Turks, as they bore down upon the little band, the tramp of cavalry—the ringing of armour—the clash of shields—the trumpets of the Christian hosts—the shouts of the chiefs and heralds, raised so fearful a din that none could distinguish the war-cry of friend from foe. Becket perceived, however, that the Christians dropped the points of their long lances, and prepared to receive the heavy charge upon their swords, when suddenly each Moslem raised his bow, as he galloped forward, a thick cloud seemed to hide all objects from his sight, and two hundred thousand arrows dropped death among the followers of the cross."

An involuntary shudder shook the frame of the countess, and she pressed her hands upon her eyes, as if to shut out the dreadful vision.

Her brother continued, "The European chivalry spurred up the hill against their assailants. The Turks, as was their habit, yielded ground on every side, avoiding by the fleetness of their horses, the lances of the knights, and like the Parthians of old, continuing their fearful archery, even as they fled. Again they wheeled, and with fiendish yells, fell upon the diminished band, encompassing them within the valley; and fast as the *infidels* fell beneath the tremendous blows of the Norman battle-axes, new foes stepped into their places. Borne back by the growing multitude that pressed upon them, the knights gave way before the Saracens, and were driven struggling against the very pikes of the foot-soldiers, that were advancing to their support. The Christians wavered.

"At this critical moment, Robert revived all the courage of his heart, and baring his head in the midst of the fray, seized his banner, and clear and far above all the roar of the conflict, Becket distinguished his cry of, Normandy! Normandy to the rescue! The crusaders rallied, and stood again to their arms, and the Turks were driven back. Again the Saracens bore down upon them, giving them not a moment of repose. Thick and fast was mown the flower of Christian chivalry, soldier beside soldier, and knight beside knight. In the glimpses granted by the rapid evolutions of the Arab cavalry, Becket could see the women of the camp bringing water from the river to the fainting troops, and bathing the wounded and dying. Thus the battle lasted for many hours, when the eye of the Saxon soldier perceived a cloud of dust rising behind the hills.

"Then came banner, and pennon, and lance, and glittering armour, and the Red Cross fluttering on the wind. In scattered bands spurring on their horses for life, on came the western division of the *croises*. None waited for the others, but each hastened to the fight, and rank after rank, troop after troop, shouting, 'Deus vult,' 'Deus vult,' rushed over the mountains to the valley of the battle. The Christian war-cry thrilled the heart of the heroic Gilbert, and he panted once more to join the standard that bore the emblem of our holy religion. Tearing off the white turban that Zaida had bound about his brow, he held it up aloft, vainly hoping to attract the attention of his countrymen, and regain his liberty. But all were too intent upon the rout of the *infidels*, to notice the signal, and his heart sunk within him, as the *emir*, fearing total discomfiture, commanded the slaves to carry away the women and prisoners to a strong fastness in the mountains.

"As they led him along the brow of the hill, he still kept his longing eye fixed upon the scene of conflict, and distinctly discerned at the head of the division of Raimond and Godfrey, the forms of two canonized martyrs, in armour glittering above the brightness of the sun; and he could perceive that their presence struck terror into the heart of the enemy. But farther particulars concerning the battle he could not learn, except from the Saracens themselves, who seemed sadly discomfited, and hurried on in advance of the Christian army, through Phrygia and Cilicia, laying waste the villages, and making a desert of the country through which they passed.

"At Tarsus he was separated from his faithful Zaida, and lodged alone in a Paynim tower, overlooking the Cydnus. Here he pined in loneliness day by day, gazing through the arrow-slit upon the never-varying hills, or watching wearily the waterfowl sporting upon the bosom of the stream. The Christian host passed beneath the very walls of his tower. He distinguished the forms of Robert, and Stephen, and the Atheling, and the armourial bearings and ensigns of the various detachments of European chivalry, and he struggled like an imprisoned bird to be free. He shouted the honoured names of the leaders, and the potent war-cry of the Christians; called on the Saviour, and Mary, and every saint in the calendar for release; but in vain. The walls of his prison alone echoed his cry; no ear heard his voice; no eye was lifted towards his lonely turret. He watched till the last cross disappeared in the distance, and overwhelmed with despair, sank in agony upon the floor.

"The moon was riding high in heaven when he was awakened by the light touch of a delicate hand, and the soft voice of Zaida whispered, 'Gilbert! England!' the only Saxon words he had taught her. He started up, and an exclamation of joy mounted to his lip. But Zaida, with a warning motion, imposed silence, and beckoned him to follow her. Silently he tracked his stealthy way through the mazes of the castle, guided by the vision that glided on before him, more like a spirit of the air, than a being of earthly mould, and the young Englishman had dizzy work to follow her down a rude stone stair, winding to the base of the cliff, where a little skiff was moored. She motioned him to embark. He obeyed, and turned to place her by his side. She was gone. Far up the steep he saw the last flutter of her white robe. He sprang to follow, but a strong arm dashed him to the bottom of the boat. The rowers bent to their oars, and the little bark glided noiselessly down the stream."

"Did he rejoin the Christian army?" said Adela.

"All along the banks of the river," replied Henry, "he beheld, with torturing gaze, the watch-fires of the Christian camp, and heard the pass-word repeated by familiar voices, but the pirates, for such they were, permitted him neither to speak nor move. Reaching the sea of Cyprus, they put him on board a vessel, and he was conveyed to Brundusium."

"And were these pirates *infidels?*" inquired Adela.

"Saracens they were not," said her brother, "but to what extent they believed in our holy religion Becket was not prepared to state. They spoke several dialects of the Europeans, and at the commencement of the crusades, turned their course towards the Holy Land, in the pleasant hope of serving both God and mammon with the sword."

"And what farther chanced to the Saxon?" inquired the countess.

"He returned through France, and when I saw him at Feschamp, had engaged his passage to England. And now, dear sister, I have come to take my leave of thee, in order to accompany him."

"The news thou hast brought has removed a burden from my heart, and nerved me to my duties," said his sister. "But wherefore wouldst thou to England?"

"I have learned that the Duke of Bretagne is pressing his suit with the fair Matilda, and I must away to see that the prize be not riven from my grasp."

"Hast heard aught of the Countess of Huntingdon?" inquired Adela.

"Aye, and strange news concerning her have I for thine ear. Thou knowest 'tis scarce a twelvemonth since the death of her husband Simon; and she has again entered the holy estate of matrimony."

"Impossible!" exclaimed Adela. "She who so longed for the quiet of conventual life!"

"She was forced to forego her own inclinations to escape the tyranny of Rufus," returned Henry.

"Poor Maude!" said Adela, "her life has been a continual sacrifice to the selfish interests of others."

"Her patient meekness disarms even her cruel fate," said Henry. "Simon always regarded her with the most devoted affection, and made her sole heir to all her father's former possessions. It is said that our brother Rufus had fixed his eye upon the charming widow, and that to avoid his addresses, she accepted the hand of David, prince of Scotland."

"She will then be thy best advocate with David's sister, Matilda."

"Truth," said Henry. "The future Queen of Scotland shall aid to place the crown on the head of the future Queen of England. Farewell. When I come again I hope to present thee my lovely bride."

"Heaven speed thy purpose," said the countess, fervently, and thus they parted.

CHAPTER 12

I rather tell thee what is to be feared,
Than what I fear.

The administration of the affairs of her domains, rendered it difficult for the Countess of Blois, in the absence of the most vigorous part of the population, to provide for the numerous families, left dependent by the wars; and the increasing helplessness of her idiot son, added greatly to the burden of her cares. 'Twas Christmas morning, the anniversary of her betrothal. A crowd had assembled in the grand cathedral of Chartres, to unite in the sacred solemnities of the day, and to witness the christening of Lucy, the infant countess. So occupied was Adela with the impressive scene, that she did not observe the entrance of several knights, on whose noble forms and toil-worn habiliments, the eyes of the multitude were riveted with the most intense curiosity; nor did she notice, while the bishop sprinkled the babe with the holy-water, and consecrated it to God, that their leader had advanced to the altar and knelt beside her at the font: but when the warrior stretched out his arm to receive the white-robed cherub from the hands of the priest, she turned to see her *husband* gazing with unutterable tenderness upon his infant daughter, whom he now beheld for the first time.

The unexpected return of their lord gave an additional impulse to the festivities of the day among the numerous retainers of the count.

When the joyous greetings and congratulations were over, and Adela and Stephen were left to the free interchange of their own thoughts, the countess, who suspected that some misadventure had occasioned this unannounced arrival, led the way to an explanation. "And wherefore comes not Robert with thee?" she inquired.

"Methinks thou mightest spare thine asking," said Stephen, looking fondly upon her. "Robert has not those ties that draw me to my native land. Adventure and war are wife and children to him."

"Did wife and children draw my husband from the paths of glory and the cause of God?" replied the countess, apprehensively.

"Those paths which thy imagination invests with glory," said Stephen, "are but the tracks where reptiles and savage beasts have found their way, among craggy rocks and thorny bushes, bleeding deadly venom. We followed them through deplorable suffering, and were conducted to disaster and defeat. And as for the cause of God, if thou hadst seen the vices of these *holy croises*, and the hardships they endured, thou wouldst have deemed either that they were not the people of God, or that the Almighty took little note of the sufferings of his faithful servants."

"'Tis the faint heart that feels the toils of the way, and distrusts the care of Providence," said Adela, reproachfully. "Did not the vows of knighthood alone forbid thee to abandon the holy cause?"

"To abandon a cause forsaken by God and man, were the dictate of prudence," retorted Stephen, stung by the censure of his beloved countess.

"Prudence is born of cowardice," replied she, with unabated warmth. "I have hitherto heard of deeds of valour, not of desertion; of victory, not of defeat."

"Thine ignorance then excuses thy violence," said Stephen; "but if thou wilt listen patiently to thy lord, thou mayest perchance become better informed."

"I will listen to nothing that brands my Stephen with cowardice!"exclaimed Adela. "My heart exulted in the thought that the president of the chiefs would counsel them to worthy deeds!" and the haughty woman burst into tears of mingled tenderness and mortified pride.

"By the crucifix at Lucca!" exclaimed Stephen, rising in wrath, "an thou wilt not listen to reason, 'twere vain to talk."

"And if reason determined thy return, wherefore comest thou alone?" said Adela, striving to conquer her emotion.

"Alone!" replied the count. "Of the multitudes that left Europe at the preaching of Peter, three fourths have returned already or fallen victims to their folly. The hermit himself has fled from the sight of miseries that he was impotent to relieve and unable to endure. Baldwin has joined a piratical band that ravage the coast of Cilicia. Raimond, of Toulouse, languishes the victim of a pestilential fever. Godfrey, the soul of the expedition, torn and lacerated, in an encounter with wild beasts, lies prostrate with his wounds; nay, the Count Melun, and Tatius the lieutenant of Alexius, have withdrawn their forces; and when sickness compelled me to retire for a season from the siege of Antioch, fifteen thousand Turks, from the heart of Asia, were on their way to join the myriads that surround the Christian camp."

"And what kind hand tended thy illness?" said the countess, her

80

tenderness returning at the thought of his suffering.

"The bivouac of the soldier admits few of those attentions so grateful to an invalid," replied her husband, much softened. "However, my indisposition was of short duration, and I should have rejoined my companions, had not intelligence reached me that caused me to abandon all hope for the success of the enterprise.

"I tell thee that the project of subduing Asia is utterly foolish and vain. The Greek Empire, the barrier of Europe on the east, is little less *infidel* than the sons of Islam; and every conquest of the Christians is claimed by Alexius as feudal lord. He wrested from us the city of Nice in the very hour of victory. On my return, I met him at the head of his army on the way to take possession of Antioch, and by representing the power of the Turks turned him from his purpose."

"But do not the people of God always triumph in the battles with the *infidels?*" inquired Adela.

"In single encounter or in a fair field," replied Stephen, "the *croises* are uniformly victorious: but valour wields no weapon against famine and disease. Our army, at such a distance from their own land, must be dependent for supplies upon the grace of Alexius, each victory, therefore, but lays the foundation for another contest, and were Palestine delivered from the Turk, it would require still greater exertion, to wrest it from the Greek."

The countess was silenced by reasoning which she could not answer, but against which all her feelings revolted. Yet though she apparently acquiesced in her husband's decision, her heart was keenly alive to every rumour that might reflect upon his fame. Nor were her feelings soothed, by hearing that the pilgrims besieged in Antioch, enfeebled by disease and wasted by famine, reproached Count Stephen, as the cause of all their miseries; since he had withdrawn his own forces, not only, but turned back the armies that were hastening to their relief.

Her pride and ambition were deeply wounded by these reports, and when she learned that the Christians, at the very point to die of starvation, had bound themselves never to abandon the cause, till they had pressed their lips upon the Holy Sepulchre; that visions of saints and apostles, had reawakened energy and activity in their wasted ranks, that the lance that pierced the side of the Saviour, had been discovered and that a "bright squadron of celestial allies," had closed in with the battalions of the Christian army and pursued the Saracen legions from the vale of the Orontes, she felt that her husband had not only tamely resigned an earthly crown, but had by the same cowardly act forfeited an heavenly inheritance. In the agony of her disappointment and chagrin, she vowed she would give him no rest till he returned to the Holy Land, to wipe out with his blood if need be, the foul stain upon his honour.

In this state of mind Stephen found it impossible to interest her in any of their accustomed occupations and amusements. News from the Crusade alone restored her wonted animation, and as these tidings, generally, reflected little honour upon himself, he suppressed as much as possible all intelligence from the East, and contrived to pass his time in distant parts of his domains. The torturing suspense of the countess at length induced her secretly to dispatch a messenger to Italy. He returned bearing a transcript of an official letter, which the chiefs of the Crusade had sent to Pope Urban. After giving the details of the march from Antioch along the sea-coast past Tripoli, through the country of Sidon to Ramula, the letter went on:

> Thence our troops continued their route to the village formerly called Emmaus, and like the disciples of old 'our hearts burned within us,' when there came to us certain brethren from Bethlehem to comfort us, after all our fatigues, and to welcome us to this holy and beautiful land. Sleep was banished from every eye, and ere midnight was well passed, every man animated by the fervour of hope and the intensity of desire, had girded on his armour and come forth from his tent, prepared for the last conflict.
>
> We wandered along the highways and fields, in darkness; but at length the heavens blushed with the glorious suddenness of eastern dawn, and as the sun shot his level rays across the sacred brow of Olivet, the holy city lay before our eyes. 'Jerusalem! Jerusalem!' was repeated with tumultuous wonder, by a thousand tongues.
>
> Every fatigue, every danger, every hardship, was forgotten, and the warrior became at once a simple pilgrim; his lance and sword were thrown aside, and the passion which stirred every heart, was clothed with divers gestures. Some shouted to the sky—some wept in silence—some knelt and prayed—some cast themselves down and kissed the blessed earth—'all had much to do to manage so great a gladness.' Taking off our shoes, we trod the sacred ground with naked feet, and thus proceeding,

came in front of the city and pitched our camp upon the north, between the gate of St. Stephen and the tower of David. It was early summer, the harvest was upon the ground, the grapes were ripe upon the vines, and before the waters of the autumnal equinox, dropped upon us out of heaven, the ensign of the cross was floating upon the walls of Jerusalem.

For having long assailed the bulwarks in vain, we prepared movable towers of great strength, which we rolled to the walls, commenced the assault, not as in former times at the sound of drums and trumpets, but with the inspiring melody of hymns and psalms, while the priests bowed on Mt. Zion and prayed for the aid of heaven on the ensuing conflict.

The *infidels*, to manifest their rage, erected the symbol of our holy religion, and cast dust upon it, but the Lord was with us, and the sacrilegious insult was well atoned by their blood, for while Godfrey and Baldwin leaped from a tower and planted a banner upon the battlements, Tancred and Robert burst open one of the gates, Raimond and his followers scaled the walls, and thus we have freed the city from the dominion of the *infidels*, and avenged the cause of heaven.

We laid down our arms, washed our hands from the bloody stains, put on the habiliments of repentance, and in the spirit of humility, with uncovered heads and reverent feet, walked over all those places which the Saviour had consecrated by his presence.

The ghost of the departed Adhemar came and rejoiced with us, and the spirits of the martyrs who perished on the road from Europe to Jerusalem, appeared and shared in the felicity of their brethren. The whole city was influenced by one spirit, and the clamour of thanksgiving was loud enough to have reached the stars.

Thus in the year of our Lord 1099, was the city of Jerusalem added again to the dominion of Christendom, on the very day and hour of the crucifixion of the Saviour. At this auspicious time, Pope Urban second sits in the Roman see; Henry is emperor of the German, and Alexius of the Grecian empire. Philip reigns in France and William Rufus in England, whilst over all men and all things, reigns our Lord Jesus Christ forever and ever, to whom be honour and glory for endless ages.

CHAPTER 13

I have deeply felt
The mockery of the shrine at which my spirit knelt.
Mine is the requiem of years in reckless folly passed,
The wail above departed hopes on a frail venture cast.

Whittler

Acting upon the hint of Adela, Prince Henry repaired immediately to Huntingdon and secured the good offices of Maude and her husband, in effecting a communication with the beautiful novice Matilda. He was thus enabled to counteract the efforts of his powerful rival Warrenne, Earl of Surrey, to whom Rufus had promised her hand. Deeming it unsafe however to quit England, he tarried at court and passed his time in hunting and hawking, according to the manners of the age. The New Forest was the constant scene of dissolute pleasures. The sweet solemnity of the deep woods was daily disturbed by the Bacchanal revel, and the pure echoes of the dell were forced to answer the loose laugh and thoughtless imprecation. Godly men lifted up their voice against the corruptions of the age, and saintly priests warned by omens and dreams, admonished the Red King on a certain day, to avoid the glen in which Prince Richard was supposed to have contracted his fatal disease. But the impious Rufus, with studied contempt led the chase that way, diverting his attendants with ribald jests upon the warnings he had received.

"Come, Deer's foot," said Warrenne, tauntingly to Prince Henry, "yonder bounds the stag. The fair hand of Matilda to him who brings the antlered monarch down."

"I have broken the string of my arblast, and must repair to the hut of this forrester to replace it," replied Henry coldly.

"Come on, ye laggards. Ho! Tyrrel, thou and I alone will be in at the death," cried Rufus, putting spurs to his horse. As Henry entered the cottage, a weird wife rose up as if from the ground before him, chanting in Norman French,

Hasty news to thee I bring—
Henry, thou art now a king.
Mark the words and heed them well,
Which to thee in sooth I tell.

The closing words were interrupted by hurried cries of alarm and distress. The prince turned, and the horror-stricken Tyrrel, whose err-

84

ing shaft had slain the king, dashed past the door. Comprehending the whole affair at once, Henry remounted his horse and rode full speed to Winchester, forced the keys from the keeper, and took possession of the regalia and royal treasure. The people thronged round him in the streets, and while the nobles and prelates were debating on the claims of Robert, the populace, whose allegiance he secured by the promise of English laws and an English queen, made the city resound with loud shouts of "Long live King Henry." Within three days he was crowned at Winchester, by the bishop of London.

Scarce a month after the Countess of Blois was apprized of these events, the tardy Robert arrived at Chartres. He had lingered in Apulia to woo Sybilla, the fair cousin of Bohemond,[1] and now returned to claim his inheritance, after his younger brother was securely seated on the throne. The countess received him with the greatest joy, and honoured his peerless bride with the most distinguishing attentions; but when she learned that he depended upon her good offices with Stephen to secure assistance in a meditated invasion of England, her love for her favourite brother Henry, and her apprehension of the unsteady rule of Robert, moved her to dissuade him from the scheme, and she secretly hoped that he might be made instrumental in inducing her husband to return again to the Holy Land. She learned from Robert the various success of the leaders of the crusade. While some were still carving their way with the sword, Bohemond was Prince of Antioch, Baldwin of Edessa, and Godfrey enjoyed the enviable distinction of being King of Jerusalem.

"The voice of fame has spoken oft to me of the prowess of my brother Robert," said she. "Did not his peers deem him worthy a principality in Palestine?"

"Nay, it needed not the suffrages of the chiefs, since heaven itself preferred my poor claims above all others," replied Robert. "When a king was to be chosen, the bishops gave to each leader a waxen candle, and directed us to walk in procession to the Holy Sepulchre. As we advanced within the sacred place, a sudden flame kindled upon the taper I held in my hand, but at that moment a whisper of Rufus' death swept across my spirit, and remembering the throne of England I dashed out the light."—

"Unhappy man!" exclaimed the countess. "Thou hast refused the call of heaven. Look not for success in any future enterprise. Hope not

1. *Bohemond I, Prince of Antioch: a Norman Soldier of Fortune and Crusader 1050-1111* by Ralph Bailey Yewdale is also published by Leonaur.

that divine sanction will back thine endeavour, and expect not aid or succour by thy sister's intervention."

"By the Holy Rood," shouted Robert in wrath, "thou queen'st it well for a woman whose craven husband was the first to desert his standard. It were indeed the part of a madman to expect assistance from the dastard earl."Before the anger of the countess gave her voice to reply, he strode from her presence.

Meantime, Henry hearing that Robert had arrived in Normandy, strengthened his power by conciliating the English nation, and took prompt measures to redeem his promise of giving them an English queen. But for some unaccountable reason the Saxon princess seemed averse to quitting her gloomy convent, nor would she consent to bestow her hand upon the handsomest and most accomplished sovereign of his time, till he had promised to confirm to the nation all the ancient laws and privileges established by her great ancestor Alfred, and ratified by Edward the Confessor. When a digest of these rights and immunities had been made, and a hundred copies committed to the care of the principal bishoprics and monasteries of England, she consented to become "the bond of peace to a divided nation—the dove of the newly sealed covenant between the Norman sovereign and her own people."

The efforts of Robert, delayed till Henry's power was thus consolidated, of course proved ineffectual. He wasted the munificent dower of his beautiful Sybilla, in idle feasting, and having buried his lovely wife the third year after their marriage, he gave up Normandy to Henry, for an annual pension, and was finally taken in a revolt, conveyed to Cardiff Castle, where in a sort of honourable captivity he passed the remainder of his useless life.

The spirit of crusade was still active in Europe, and combined with this spirit, was the hope of gain, springing from vague and exaggerated accounts of the wealth and principalities which the leaders of the first expedition had acquired. The devastated lands of Palestine were soon settled by families who immigrated from pecuniary or pious motives, and not long after the death of Godfrey, and the election of Baldwin I. to the throne of Jerusalem, several bodies of armed men set out to join their brethren in Asia. Count Stephen, wearied with the incessant importunities of his ambitious wife, shamed by the example of Hugh, Count of Vermandois, and stimulated, perhaps, by the hope of obtaining easier conquest, and less dangerous honours, consented to return to the Holy Land. At Constantinople they met with Raimond of Toulouse, who was returning for assistance, and proceeded under his guidance. On their way through Asia Minor, they encountered the Turks, lost one hundred thousand men, together with Hugh of Vermandois, who died of his wounds, at Tarsus. Raimond of Toulouse was slain at Tripoli, but Stephen, Count of Blois, with the rest of the leaders proceeded straight to Jerusalem; and having by the completion of his pilgrimage, wiped out the disgrace of his first desertion, embarked on board a vessel to return to Europe.

The heart of the countess dilated with pride and joy, as from time to time she heard of his noble deeds, and with feelings akin to the romance of her youthful admiration, she hourly expected his return. One evening, sitting thus alone, a servant announced, that a monk in the anteroom craved permission to speak with her. The countess ordered him to be instantly admitted, and her heart sickened with a sad foreboding, as a diminutive figure veiled in palmer's weeds stood before her.

"Speak thine errand quickly," said she, pale and breathless with agitation. "What of my lord?" He replied only by an upward motion of the hand, and Adela knew that her husband was dead. She sank back in her seat and clasped her hands, but kept her eyes fixed with the intensity of the keenest emotion upon the face of the monk. "Tell me all, good father," said she, in a voice nervously firm.

"I know little, noble lady," replied the palmer, "and though I have come all the way from Palestine to bring thee tidings, my story will be brief. Thou hast, doubtless, heard of the poor services of Peter the Hermit, in awakening the attention of Europe to the low estate of Jerusalem. When by Divine favour I had been so blest as to conduct the greatest warriors of the age to the conquest of the Holy Sepulchre, and had seen the Christians thus relieved from Turkish oppression, fall at my unworthy feet, and call down blessings upon my head, I felt to exclaim like Simeon of old, 'Lord, lettest now thy servant depart in peace, since mine eyes have seen thy salvation.'

"With the deepest humiliation, for having in a moment of temptation, wavered in faith, I thought to found a monastery upon the shores of Lake Gennesareth, where I might have the example of the sinking Peter ever before mine eyes. One evening, as I walked upon the shores of the sea, revolving these things in my thoughts, I felt myself suddenly seized from behind. A bandage was thrown over my eyes, I was forcibly lifted from the ground, placed upon a mule and hurried forward. I attempted to cry out, but a hand was laid upon my mouth, and a voice whispered in Anglo-Norman, 'Fear not, old man, thou art among friends, and bidden only to labour in thine holy calling.' Thus assured, I ceased my struggles. How far I was conveyed, I know not, but when the bandage was taken from my eyes, I found myself in a wild cave of the mountain, by the side of a dying crusader, and recognized in the pale countenance before me, the lineaments of Stephen Earl of Blois. 'Take courage, noble count,' said the voice that had before spoken in mine ear, 'I have caught a priest whose ghostly counsels will speedily prepare thee for the long journey, which all must sooner or later take.'

"With a tenderness which one would scarcely look for in such a savage, the chief raised the dying earl, and gently supported him while I received his directions concerning certain affairs, and ministered the last rites of our holy faith. The count pressed me to promise that I would, myself, bring to thee the epistle, which he had with much pain and difficulty indited. And when I hesitated, by reason of the monastery which I had resolved to found, he summoned all his remaining strength, and while I guided his trembling hand, drew for me a deed of the vale of Montier, and bade me bring it to thee for thou wouldst ratify it, and endow the abbey by thy bounty. Scarcely had he finished it, when his wounds bleeding afresh, a deadly faintness seized him. The chief laid him back upon the cushions. I held up the crucifix before his eyes, and murmuring a prayer in which were mingled the names of wife and children, he expired.

"That night I gave him Christian burial beneath one of the cedar-trees of Mount Lebanon, the swarthy barbarians holding torches, and looking with reverent awe upon the solemn scene. Before morning I was again blindfolded, and conducted to the sea-coast, and put on board a vessel bound for Italy." So intent had the hermit been on his narration, that he had not observed the countess, pale and rigid as though turned to stone; and when she clutched with convulsive eagerness the parcel he extended, he bowed and withdrew.

She tore off the envelope, and the scarf which her girlish hand had wrought in the hours of her first sweet love, soiled and bloodstained, fell across her lap, and crept accusingly to her feet. She opened the letter and read—

To Adela, my best and only beloved, thy Stephen sends this last token of affection. In this my dying hour it is my sweetest consolation to feel that with my sword I have pierced the cloud that has so long been between us, and that could I see my Adela, she would smile upon me as the loved and honoured husband of her youth. I have bathed in the Jordan, and worshipped at the sepulchre; but it was the *human love* and not the *Divine*, that baptized my soul with joy, and whispered pardon to my wounded spirit. I have sought for glory in the land of patriarchs and prophets, and I have found it; but in the accents of fame my ear has heard only the voice of Adela.

The Eternal saw mine idolatry and punished it. Adverse winds drove back the vessel that was to bear me to my native land. The King of Jerusalem called upon us again for aid. We fought in the plains of Ramula, seven hundred knights against the whole force of the Turkish Army. Hemmed in on every side, we fell, bravely defending the standard of the cross. Fainting from loss of blood, my dull ear heard the cry of '*Allah ackbar*.' Like one dreaming I called upon the name of Hardrager. Immediately the *old man* came to me and stanching my mortal wound, bound it tightly with the scarf which I had thrown across my breast to animate me, for the conflict. I was conveyed away, and awoke as did Ingulfus, in the cave of the assassins.

I know that I shall die. I cannot long sustain the pressure of the ligament, and when once 'tis loosened my last blood will flow. Hardrager has promised me Christian burial, and sent for a priest to shrive my parting soul. Think of me kindly, proudly, my best beloved. Teach my sons to honour their father's name, for he died fighting in the Holy Land. Kiss my darling Lucy, the sweet babe who unconsciously smiled upon my return. Darkness gathers upon my sight. The forms that gladdened my youthful days pass before me, and the fairest among them all is my bride, my Adela.

A few more words were indistinctly traced, the page seemed blotted with tears, and the name of Stephen was scarcely legible.

Years passed over the spirit of the countess in the intense agony of that one night. Her heartstrings strained to their utmost tension by the power of this mighty woe, thenceforth gave no response to the light fingering of ordinary circumstance. The tender solicitude of friendship, the sweet prattle of childhood, the hilarity of mirth, the consolations of religion, and the schemes of ambition, were endured and accepted with the same passionless apathy. She made a journey to Normandy, and arranged a reconciliation between her brother Henry and the primate Anselm with her accustomed wisdom. She visited Boulogne, and presided at the nuptials of her son Stephen with her wonted grace. She gave her Lucy to the Earl of Chester, with a mother's blessing, and saw her depart in the fatal white ship without emotion.

But when she again stood at the door of the abbey of Feschamp to welcome Maude once more to Normandy, the curtain of retrospection was lifted, and the whole drama of her life passed before her. Adela and Maude! The disparity between the happy child and the sad captive was less striking than the contrast between the elegant and stately Countess of Blois, and the serene and gracious princess of Scotland, who now met after life had gathered the bloom of their youthful beauty, and left the indefinable shades which character traces upon the human countenance. Fixed and calm were the features of Adela, once radiant with vivacity, but their repose was the death of emotion, and their calmness was not resignation, but submission to inexorable fate. The face of Maude, still fair and beautiful in the strength of its repose, beamed with the serene benignity of ineffable peace, and she seemed one, the joyousness of whose inner life found occasion for an overflow of beneficence in every outward occurrence.

Again they journeyed together through the scenes that witnessed the triumphal progress of William the Conqueror. But it was now the task of Maude to soothe the spirit of her friend, bound with the chain of remorseful regret. Cicely, celebrated for her piety, had become lady abbess of the convent of Caen, and it was the intention of the countess to enter the nunnery under her care. In fitting up her dormitory Adela had laid aside all her accustomed magnificence, and the only relic of her former state was a gorgeous curtain that divided her oratory from the cheerless apartment, chosen as the home of her future years.

"Maude," said she, as they sat together there, "rememberest thou the riddle of life and love that once formed our theme of converse in an hour like this? How thy heart pined for the convent, and mine shuddered at its gloom."

"Aye," said Maude, "well do I remember it, and often have I smiled at the presumption which made me attempt to solve the greatest mystery of human existence, and arrogate to myself the choice of the future; when the highest wisdom leads only to the faithful performance of daily duties."

"I mind me now," replied the countess, "that thy gentle admonition pointed to that effect.—But I scorned control, and when I saw the cruel policy by which my father strengthened his dominion, I determined that my hand should never seal the bond of a political alliance, and it was not till after years that I learned that the meeting between Stephen and myself resulted from a preconcerted plan to bind me to one whose mild virtues would counteract my unholy aspirings. Thy instructions had taught me the power of a righteous purpose, and I sought its aid to compensate for what I considered a defect in my husband's character, vainly hoping that ambition, sanctioned by religion, would secure its reward. With fatal skill I wrought upon his generous affections till he relinquished the dear delights of his family, to seek barren laurels, and find a lonely grave on a foreign shore."

"Reproach not thyself," said Maude, tenderly.

The countess heeded not her interruption. "Thou and I," said she, "have wrought for different ends, and the results for which I toiled have come to thee unsought."

Maude would have replied, but the passionate woman proceeded. "Nay, let me speak; for since my great grief has fallen upon me, I have unburdened my heart to no one. As a captive thou didst bring a blessing to the household of the Conqueror; thy sweet spirit moulded the rude Simon into a benefactor of his dependents, and I know well that it was thy benevolent wisdom which instructed Matilda to secure the liberty of England, and the stability of Henry's throne. Thy silent sacrifices have made the rich current of thy life one stream of beneficence, while my erring spirit has converted the bounties of heaven into fountains of misery.

"My wicked pride found occasion in the imbecility of my first-born William for ceaseless repining, and sowed the seeds of sorrow in the hearts of my other noble beautiful children. Thibaut is in arms against his sovereign, Stephen a pensioner on the fickle humours of a king, Henry seeks preferment through the church, and my lovely Lucy, the darling of her father, lies entombed in the sea. Oh! Maude! Maude! my best and truest friend, pity her whose only occupation through long years has been 'to write bitter things against herself.' But I might have known it all," continued she impetuously, "for heaven through thy intercession deigned to warn me of my fate, and I would not tell thee lest thy gentle love should win me from it."

She drew aside the curtain of the oratory, and led the princess within the shadow. Through the oriel windows the mellow light of the autumnal sun fell softly upon the altar, where stood beside the crucifix the crystal urn containing the hallowed dust of Palestine. The scarf of Stephen, with its golden embroidery rusted, and its bright pearls dimmed with his blood, was wound round the precious love-gift, and fastened with the thorn obtained from Ingulfus.

"It seems but yesterday," said she, tenderly detaching the baldric, "since I held this up before thee with pride and pleasure, and in careless wonder saw thee wreathe it in the canopy of my couch. But that dream, now that my whole life looks a dream, seems the one reality of my existence. I shall tell it thee, for my spirit already feels the balm of thy gentle sympathy.

"My slumbers were at first broken and disturbed. I seemed with Stephen and Robert in an eastern land, hurrying over rocks and sands, a tiresome, weary way, in pursuit of a crown which constantly tempted, but eluded the grasp. First I missed Stephen from my side, then Robert disappeared, and at last I sank down among myriads of wretches perishing of thirst. I woke in terror, and it was long ere I could compose myself again to rest. Whether I slept again I know not, but as I lay gazing into the depths of the heavens, my vision seemed to pierce beyond the stars; and from the uttermost distance came one winging his way past the bright orbs, till he stood within the casement, the impersonation of my lover.

"My scarf lay upon his breast, and his right hand held out to me an urn, pure as though formed of consolidated light, upon whose amethystine entablature was engraven *Human Love*. As I extended my hand, and clasped the precious treasure, the shattered inscription fell to dust in the vase. I raised my eyes,—he threw a pitying smile upon me, and immediately there sprang up from the ashes a celestial flower, and as each living petal unfolded, there floated off a radiant line of light bearing the sacred words *Divine Love*, till the whole air was filled with redolence and beauty.

"The ringing of the *matin* chimes recalled me to consciousness, and my bright vision was absorbed by the flood of glory which the morning sun poured into the apartment.

"Thou saidst truth!" exclaimed Maude. "Thy dream is a reality; for in the ashes of *Human Love*, the *Divine* plants the sweetest hopes of existence."

The long sealed fountain of Adela's tears began to flow, and as the gracious drops distilled from her surcharged heart, and her paralyzed sensibilities felt once more the bliss of emotion, the strong, proud woman, became gentle and humble as a child.

"Maude," said she, clasping her hands in gratitude, "there was ever a mystery about thee. I had thought to wear out my life in sad penance, and thou hast opened to me a source of happy contemplation: henceforth my desert future, fertilized by the sweet waters that have gushed from the rock at thy magic touch, shall blossom with the flowers of Paradise."

The Abbess Cicely here entered, and summoned them to the hall of general reception, where Maude embraced her son and received the ambassadors sent by her husband to conduct her to Stirling, the place appointed for her coronation, as Queen of Scotland.

"Go," said Adela, with affectionate joy, as she saw her depart. "Go to thy bright destiny. Thou art a living illustration of the truth of scripture, *'Be thou faithful over a few things, and I will make thee ruler over many things.'*"

ELEANOR OF AQUITAINE.

Eleanor

CHAPTER 1

In the midst was seen
A lady of a more majestic mien,
By stature and by beauty marked their sovereign Queen.

The southern provinces of France, Poitou, Saintogne, Auvergne, Perigord, Limousin, Angoumois and Guienne, received of the Romans the classic appellation of Aquitaine. This beautiful land, watered by the Garonne and Loire, whose clear and sparkling streams, flowing from vine-clad hills, stretched their silvery arms to irrigate the fairest fields and to enclose the finest harbours in the world, was in the twelfth century, inhabited by the most civilized and polished people on the face of the earth. The arts, and the idealities, and the refinements of life, like the native flowers of its sunny vales, seemed wakened and nourished by the genial airs of a climate, softened by the proximity of the sea, and rendered bracing by the mountain breeze.

The numerous and independent sovereigns, whose feudal sway extended over this fair territory, imbibed the spirit of chivalry, and caught the enthusiasm that precipitated the armies of Europe upon Asia. Count Raimond of Toulouse, was one of the first who took the cross, at the council of Clermont. He was styled *par excellence* the Moses of the expedition. Before leaving for Palestine, on his returnless voyage, he ceded his dominions to his daughter, wife of William IX. of Poitou. The grand-children of William IX. were Eleanor and Petronilla. The father of these fair sisters, William X., left Aquitaine in 1132, with their uncle Raimond, who was chosen prince of Antioch.

The poetical taste of Eleanor was early cultivated and developed by the unrestrained freedom she enjoyed in the queenless court of her minstrel grandfather in Gay Guienne. The language that prevailed all over the south of France, was called Provençal. It was the mother-tongue of Duke William, the grandfather of Eleanor, who was one of the most liberal patrons and earliest professors of that style of composition in which the Troubadours celebrated the feats of love and arms. The matchless charms of Eleanor were enhanced by all the accomplishments of the south. Her fine genius found ample exercise in composing the *sirvantes* and *chansons* of Provençal poetry, and her delicate fingers wiled the spirit of music from the echoing harp to accompany her voice adown the tide of song. She inherited from her grandfather the political sovereignty of her native dominions not only, but the brilliant talents and ancestral superiority that made her Empress in the realm of Taste, and Queen of the courts of Love.

When the gay and licentious Duke William felt the infirmities of age coming upon him, he determined to seek the readiest means to rid himself of the burden of his sins. Accordingly, he resolved to resign the most potent sceptre in Europe to the unpractised hand of his youthful granddaughter, and devote the rest of his days to prayer and penitence in a hermitage of the rocky wilderness of St. James de Compostella. Eleanor had not attained her fifteenth year when her grandfather commenced his career of self-denial, by summoning the baronage of Aquitaine to transfer their allegiance to herself; and the child-sovereign exercised the royal functions of her new dignities while the duke visited the court of Louis le Gros and offered her hand to the young prince.

The wise lawgiver of France readily accepted the proposal—for the rich provinces which constituted the dower of Eleanor, held allegiance to the crown, only by feudal tenure; and the son, equally impatient for the possession of his fair prize, set off with a noble train for Bordeaux. The light heart of Eleanor was easily won by the unrivalled attractions of Louis le Jeune, whose courtly graces were illuminated by the prospect of the crown of Charlemagne; while the damsels that composed her court, exercised their blandishments with cruel skill upon the too susceptible hearts of the cavaliers that came in the train of the bridegroom. The parliament of Love deliberated day by day in mock solemnity upon the pretensions of the fair rivals, and the discreet decisions of Eleanor, the presiding genius of the conclave, inspired the songs of Trouveres and Troubadours, who vied with each other in celebrating her charms.

A succession of long, bright days, closed the month of July, and on the last evening the court of Love continued its session till the brilliant twilight had faded from the western sky, and the mellow harvest-moon poured a silver flood upon fountains that sprang as if instinct with life to catch and fling the shining radiance upon the gay company that still lingered in the Rose Pavilion. The queen of the court, attired like Venus, sat upon a throne, canopied with Acaeia, through whose trembling leaves the light fell playfully contending with the envious shadows that seemed striving to hide her smiles.

At her feet sat her favourite page, with wings framed of gauze attached to his shoulders, holding a lyre, fashioned to resemble the bow of Cupid, upon which he occasionally struck a few notes to announce a change in the evening's entertainment. Lovely maidens arrayed as Nymphs and Graces reclined upon verdant couches around the fair arbitress of these amorous debates. Groups of light-hearted girls, representing heathen goddesses, listened encouragingly to their favourite minstrels, and strove, by various subtle arts, to win the meed of praise to the verse that celebrated their charms. *Sirventes* and *chansons* had been recited and sung, still the assembly listened with an air of impatience, as if anticipating matters of more general interest. With a smile that at once excited and baffled curiosity, the queen touched the cheek of her page with her flowery sceptre, saying, "Why slumbers the harp of my pretty Peyrol? Has he no song for the ear of his lady?"

"Peyrol cannot sing in the Romance Walloon," said the youth, casting down his eyes with jealous pique.

"Proud one," replied the queen, "thou knowest that though the lord of *oui* and *non* delights our eye, his language charms not our ear. We would hear a pretty *faibleaux* of Grenada, or wilt thou give us a fitting apostrophe to the court, where Gaiety and Innocence preside."

"Nay, honoured lady," said the page, "since Gaiety and Innocence parted company on the plains of Pleasure, harmony hath forsaken the lyre, and not even the goddess of Love can heal the discord."

"Thou pratest, pert boy," replied the queen, with a stolen glance at Petronilla.

Perceiving from her tone, that he had presumed too far, the page bent over his harp and rapidly swept his fingers across the strings, saying apologetically,

"If my lady will accept a lay of Bretagne, Peyrol is ready to do her bidding."

"The sweet tones of the *langue d'oc* little befit the rugged legends of the northern clime," said the queen, "but tune thy lyre without further parley." The page needed no second command, but sang:—

In a province fair of sunny France,
Beside a winding river,
Over whose waves in joyous dance,
The sunbeams gleam and quiver,
Stood a castle tall, a goodly sight,
With its broad and rich domain,
And therein dwelt a noble knight;
I ween he had a lady bright
And three sweet babes withouten stain.

A generous heart, an open hand,
To courtlie companie,
And eke as any in the land
For beggars of low degree.
So gentle his mien in lady's bower,
So full of courtesie,
Yet valiant was he in tournament,
And a good bow in the greenwood bent,
I wot right dextrously.

He had been blest in his earthly state
With such fair prosperity,
That his heart beat high with pride elate,
Forgot he the giver good and great
And Christian humility.
Whereat to punish his arrogance,
Our Lady sent him sore mischance,
And dire adversity.

Sir Isumbras to the hunt has gone,
Riding so gallantly,
With hawk and hound in the dewy morn,
When a vision bright above him born,
Appeared in the clear blue sky.
He saw a maiden meek and fair,
An angel I wist was she,
A messenger sent to bid him prepare
For chill calamity.

A woful man was the knight that day,
He turned him home in sore dismay,
When his good steed fell and died,
And hawk and hound of life bereft,

98

Sir Isumbras in the forest left,
With no living thing beside.
When to him there came his little foot page,
As fast as he might hie.
My noble master, a sad message,
It is that I bear to thee.
"Thy proud castell lies in ruins low,
Thy lady and children escaped the blow,
But and with jeopardy."

The knight bowed meekly to heaven's decree;
A wiser and sadder man was he,
And with his lady and children, three,
Sir Isumbras boune him o'er the sea—
A penitent pilgrim he would be
To holy Palestine.
Through seven weary lands they went—
The strength of the babes was wellnigh spent,
For charity, cold was their nourishment.
They came to a wood, with flowers besprent—
To a rapid river of broad extent,
Where never the sunbeams shine.

His eldest born, Sir Isumbras bore
With tenderest care to the farther shore;
But ere he returned again,
A lion fierce from the thicket sprang—
The little one tore from that cruel strand,
Nor him might they regain.

He found his lady weeping, full lorn,
For in his absence a leopard strong,
With a fell and bloody unicorn,
The others from her arms had torn.

The lady wished that she might die,
Or ever this sore calamity,
She should have been preserved to see;
But the knight with meek humility,
To Mary mother a prayer 'gan say,
That his penance might soon have end—
When wandering through the weary land,
The Sultan's captives they were ta'en

99

Before his face to bend.

I trow the Sultan had rarely seen
A lady so lovely, in form or mien,
Or a knight so bold and true.
"Sir knight, I will give thee gold and fee,
As much as thou might wish to see,
If thou wilt renounce Christianity,
And fight for the banners of Paynimrie,
And sell thy lady bright to me;"
His form to its height he drew.

"Our Lady forefend that I should e'er
In infidel ranks a standard bear,
Or the holy cross betray;
And for weal or woe my lady fair,
I wed in the face of day;
A recreant knight I be when e'er
This right I shall gainsay."

They have putten off his scarlet mantell
Within the goldis shred;
They drove him from that land of Baal,
And left him as he were dead.
The lady was sent to a far countrie,
The bride of the Sultan she should be,
When from the wars of Chrisendie
In triumph he returned.

Asleep in the forest the good knight lay
And when he awoke at dawn of day
He saw his treasure borne away,
By an eagle strong in search of prey—
No longer he there sojourned.
To the Virgin he made a fervent prayer
Invoking for aye her watchful care.
Then to Palestine he turned.

Through ten long years the knight pursued
His weary pilgrimage;
Then buckled he on his armour bright,
With heart beating free and light,
He hath boune him for the fight,
A gallant and unknown knight

100

Withouten heritage.

Much they marvelled then to see
A warrior, unknown as he,
Such deeds of valour do.
They wist he was no mortal wight,
But some weird magician sprite,
When in the thickest of the fight
The Sultan dread he slew.

They have broughten him to the Christian king
With gladness and great welcoming,
And honour and praise had he;
But his object fell he did obtain,
For his mighty enemy he hath slain.
He donned his pilgrim weeds again,
And his wanderings pursued.

The scorching sun, with a feverish glare,
On the burning sands cast radiance clear;
When weary and faint the knight drew near,
Where stately and tall a castle fair
From a green oasis rose.
The cool palms waving in golden light,
With music of murmuring fountains bright,
Beckoning called the fainting knight
To bowers of repose.

He passed the portals of the hall,
And stood 'mong squires and good knights tall,
Holding it seemed high festival.

A lady beautiful to see,
Sat 'neath a gorgeous canopy.
She was queen of that countrie,
Lady of generous chivalry,
And eke of lowly charity.
The holy Palmers with reverence,
Welcomed she to her residence;
Gentle and kind was she.

But the knight would not be comforted,
For restless recollection shed
A sadness over all.
In silent mood he wandered

Through tower and lofty hall.

It fell on a day the Queen with her guest
Were seated at the mid-day feast,
When entered her favourite page in haste.
In the early morning he went in quest
Of eaglets' eyries, and on the crest
Of a lofty mountain he found a nest,
With golden treasure hid in its breast,
Wrapped in a scarlet mantel.

No sooner beheld she the page's prize,
Than the tears o'erflowed the ladie's eyes.
My true and loyal knight she cries,
(The palmer looked on with mute surprise.)
Hast thou Sir Isumbras seen?
One moment they gazed in silent survey,
The mists of memory rolled away;
And locked within his arms she lay—
The lost one found again.
And there was feast and festival;
Resounded then through bower and hall,
The lute and joyous madrigal;
And joustings there were in tournament,
And breaking of lances in compliment,
To the beauty of ladies bright;
Then over the Sultan's fair domain,
In peace the knight and lady reign;
Till the king in all sincerity,
Strove with pious zeal to free
From the bonds of Infidelity,
His Paynim lieges hight.

But no one there his cause upheld,
Save God and the Queen, I trow;
And were they e'er so valourous,
Never could they withstand
An armament so numerous,
As the unbelievers' band.

Then by a chance miraculous,
The tide of war was turned.
As they might be sent in our Lady's name,

Three knights came pricking o'er the plain,
As if the ground they spurned.
Came the first on a lion strong;
On a leopard the second was borne—
The third bestrode a unicorn.
Tall men and brave were they;
The hosts of the Saracens fled in dismay,
And repenting of their disloyalty,
Returned they then to their fealty;
And the knight and lady peacefully
Together with their children, three
Restored to them so happily,
Reigned in tranquillity,
Prosperously and long.

They lived and died in good intent;
Unto Heaven their souls went.
When that they dead were,
Jesus Christ, Heaven's king,
Give us aye his blessing,
And shield us aye from care.

Rousing herself from the abstraction that had prevented her hearing the song of her page, the queen remarked, "Thy story is somewhat long, and for ourself we would have preferred that the husband had won the holy estate of martyrdom 'neath the sword of the Soldan. But thou hast rhymed it right dextrously, and we opine that the moral of thy lay accords well with the ascetic manners of the north." She extended her wand. The herald then stood forth, and sounding a few notes on a *chalumeaux*, cried,

Comes there no cause of Arrets d'amour,
Our gracious liege and sovereign before,
From lady, knight, or troubadour?

The flute-like call was thrice repeated, and then a low response to the challenge issued from a mimic grotto, curiously roofed with overhanging vines.

"The minstrel of our sister Petronilla has leave to present her cause before our court," said the queen encouragingly, as the troop of the young princess advanced from the shadow into the clear light, and knelt at the footstool of justice.

"The Lady Petronilla," began the troubadour, "arraigns before the court her recreant knight, Count Rudolph of Vermandois. Cold greeting gives he for her fair looks, scant courtesy for her warm smiles; his ungloved hand returns not the pressure of her slight fingers, and the banderol she sent him flutters not from his gleaming lance." A slight pause followed this accusation, and the herald again stood forth and demanded if any minstrel or troubadour could say aught in extenuation of the offence of the accused. Not a voice answered, not a harp string stirred. At the third call the page of Eleanor arose, and with a graceful obeisance begged to be heard.

"Rudolph of Vermandois," said he, "witnesseth by me, that since he set lance in rest to do his devoir for the fair Adelais of Champaigne, his eye and smile, and heart and hand, as loyal husband and true knight, are due and devote to her alone."

A general murmur attested the disapprobation of the assembly at this new and strange defence; for it had already become a proverb in Guienne, that "*True love cannot exist between married persons.*" The importance of the action, however, elicited a brilliant contest among the rival Troubadours, and never was a case more warmly argued, more skilfully enveloped with the subtleties of logic, or more thoroughly transpierced with the sallies of wit, than that which arose from the efforts of the wily granddaughter of Philippa of Toulouse, to fascinate the husband of the granddaughter of Adela, Countess of Blois. The fair jurors finally, like their successors in modern days, rendered their verdict in accordance with preconceived opinions, independent of justice or argument. The defence being thus found invalid, the culprit was put under ban of the court, and all true ladies were forbidden to smile upon him, except by the grace of his slighted lady-love.

The fairy camp then adjourned its sitting to receive the royal guests, who were already on the way to meet them. As Eleanor accepted the assistance of her lover to climb the terraced pathway leading to the castle, she said with her most bewitching smile, "We consign our young sister, Petronilla, to the care of our noble cousin of Vermandois." The count dissembling his reluctance bowed and offered his hand to the sprightly sorceress, and the queen whispered her sister, "The hawk is hooded, it must be thine to bind his jesses."

CHAPTER 2

Where is the antique glory now become,
That while some wont in woman to appear?

Where be the bold achievements done by some?
Where be the battles, where the shield and spear?
And all the conquests which them high did rear
Be they all dead, or shall again appear?

Spenser.

The first of August, 1137, rose upon a brilliant ceremonial. The princely capital of Bordeaux glittered with all the splendour that Guienne, and its dependent fiefs could supply; for on that day the native subjects of Eleanor assembled to accept the resignation of Duke William, and to give the hand of their liege lady in marriage to the heir of France. Though Eleanor was sufficiently dazzled by the prospect of ruling in the court of Paris, she had the sagacity to accept the proposal of her barons and refuse her consent to the arrangement, till by charter and deed she had secured inviolate the laws and customs of Aquitaine, and the administration of the government to herself alone. Upon the conclusion of the ceremony the duke laid down his robes and insignia of sovereignty, and in presence of his loving subjects and weeping grandchildren, took up the hermit's cowl and staff and departed on his lonely pilgrimage.

The royal cortege set out the following day for the north, resting only at the principal towns, where the young duke and duchess received the homage of the feudal lords.

At Blois, the Count of Vermandois, who had by circumstances that seemed to him wholly accidental been forced to give his constant attendance upon the artful Petronilla, embraced once more his beautiful Adelais, and pleading her ill health, obtained permission of the prince to absent himself for a time from court. The disappointed Petronilla could scarcely conceal her chagrin at this unlooked-for interruption in her proceedings, and from that moment conceived the most violent hatred of her innocent rival.

On their entrance at Paris, instead of the enthusiastic greeting and splendid festivities which Eleanor had anticipated, the bridal party was escorted through silent streets by weeping attendants, who conducted them to the death-bed of Louis VI. The great legislator of France gazed with a look of solemn benignity upon the youthful pair that knelt to crave his parting blessing, and reminding them, that their recent union involved not only their individual happiness, but the peace and prosperity of both the north and the south, added with his expiring breath, "Remember, royalty is a public trust, for the exercise of which a rigorous account will be exacted by Him who has the sole disposal of crowns and of sceptres."

On the conscientious mind of Louis, the words of his dying father made a deep impression; but his thoughtless partner was no sooner crowned Queen of France, than she entered upon her career of folly, exerting all her talents, and exercising all her influence in the exciting games of court intrigue. The impassioned verse in which Abelard celebrated the beauty and love of the gifted but frail Heloise, furnished employment for Eleanor's Provençal minstrels, and formed the topic of general remark among the minions of the court. She assisted the persecuted monk in his defence before the Council of Sens, and after his death caused his body to be conveyed to the chapel of the Paraclete, and consigned to the care of the melancholy Heloise.

She persuaded Louis that the services of his prime minister Vermandois, were indispensable at Paris, and thus, again, brought that nobleman within the charmed sphere of Petronilla's attractions. She contrived, at the same time, to secure for herself a devoted admirer in the Count of Ponthieu, who became the agent of her slightest wish. Through his gallantry she succeeded in involving the beautiful Adelais in some matters of court scandal, and thus by exciting the jealousy of the Count of Vermandois, and exposing him to the bewitching spells of her sister, she finally persuaded him to divorce his lovely and amiable wife, and espouse the designing Petronilla.

Adelais sought to hide her sorrow and her wrongs in the seclusion of a convent; but her brother, the valiant Count Thibault of Champagne, was not inclined to suffer the indignity in silence. Such, however, was Eleanor's power over the plastic mind of her husband, that the count appealed in vain to the sympathy or justice of the king. Finding that his remonstrance could not reach the royal ear, he presented his cause before the pope, who compelled Vermandois to put away the guilty Petronilla, and take back the injured sister of Champagne. The repudiated wife enraged at her own dishonour, and incensed at the undissembled joy with which Vermandois exchanged her dazzling graces, for the long-regretted charms of the weeping recluse, again had recourse to Eleanor.

The queen, not less vindictive than her sister, and more practised in diplomacy, succeeded in fanning an ancient feud between Louis and Count Thibault, into the flame of war. The king invaded Champagne at the head of a large army, and commenced a devastating progress through the province. The town of Vitry, strongly walled and fortified, for a long time resisted the royal forces; but the queen, whose apprehensions of the temperate counsels of Suger, prompted her to accompany her husband upon every occasion, privately commissioned a body of Gascons to set fire to the town at the very moment of its surrender. The flames spread from house to house, and finally extended to the cathedral, and thirteen hundred persons who had taken refuge there, were burned to death. The king stung by the cries of his perishing subjects, exerted himself for their rescue, but in vain; and the horrors of the scene made such a fearful impression on his mind, as seriously to affect his health. The vision of his lamented father, repeating in solemn tones, "Remember, my son, that royalty is a public trust, for the exercise of which a rigorous account will be exacted by Him who has the sole disposal of crowns and of sceptres," haunted his slumbers and destroyed his rest.

Queen Eleanor journeyed with him from one holy place to another, to entreat the prayers of pious monks in his behalf, but the dejection of his mind increased to such an extent, that even her insinuating blandishments failed to recall him from his gloomy contemplations. Wearied with fruitless endeavours, she petulantly remarked to Petronilla, who now triumphed in the possession of a new lover, the young Count Maurienne, "Fate has given me the name of queen with the destiny of a nun. Would we were again in our native realm, for I tire of this dull life. Instead of the gay minstrelsy of the sweet southwest, I am jaded with perpetual psalmody, and my attempts to beguile the weary hours with the 'joyous science,' are mocked with the mummery of muttered prayers. I have married a monk rather than a monarch;" and the mortified queen burst into tears.

While this state of feeling subsisted between the conscience-stricken Louis and his discontented consort, news of the fall of Edessa and the conquests of Noureddin reached Europe, and the sagacious Eleanor saw, in the general sympathy which the intelligence excited, the means by which she might make the melancholy of Louis the instrument of her own pleasure. She forsook at once her gay amusements, joined her husband in alms, deeds and prayers, expressed the greatest pity for the misfortunes of their royal cousins, and constantly wished that she might be permitted to lead her brave Provençals to restore the gallant Courtenays to their lost principality of Edessa.

The gracious change in the character of Eleanor delighted the penitent monarch, and he began to listen with interest and pleasure to her oft-repeated suggestion, that a pilgrimage would prove an acceptable penance for the misdeed at Vitry. Animated by a renewed hope, he called a council of the clergy and nobility of his kingdom to deliberate on the propriety of an expedition to the Holy Land, and by their advice despatched deputies to gain the sanction of Pope Eugenius. The vicar of Christ entered readily into the design, and commissioned the famous St. Bernard, abbot of Clairvaux, to preach the *Second Crusade.*

Louis and his queen, and all their court, attended on the ministry of the holy man, and such crowds flocked to listen to the eloquent saint that no cathedral, however large, could contain them. His auditors were impressed by his sanctity, persuaded by his enthusiasm, and carried away by his zeal. "The cross!" "The cross!" was echoed from every tongue. Louis and his queen were the first to adopt the holy symbol, and as the multitudes that pressed forward to follow their pious example soon exhausted the supply already prepared, the reverend orator tore his monkish garment into small pieces and fixed them to the shoulders of his kneeling converts.

Encouraged by his success, St. Bernard passed into Germany, and every city and village from Constance to Carinthia responded to the call of war. Those who understood not even the language which he spoke, were awed by his gestures, and the dignity of his demeanour, and the miracles that accompanied his presence. The mind of the emperor Conrad III. was moved by his startling delineations of the judgment day, when punishment should be inflicted upon the idle, and heavenly rewards showered upon the faithful, and openly professed that the Lord of the Germans knew and would perform his duty to the church.

The romantic purpose of becoming a female crusader now completely occupied the light head of Eleanor, and as she was in the very plenitude of her charms, and possessed sufficient wealth to practise any extravagance, she soon made it the fashion among all the vain sentimentalists of her court. The absurd arrangements which she made for the campaign, gave little promise of rational conquest. The female recruits sent their useless distaffs and embroidery-frames to all the knights and nobles who had the good sense to suppose that Heaven would be better pleased with their remaining in peace at home, than by their going abroad to destroy their fellowmen; and this ingenious taunt had the desired effect upon the doughty knights, who, fearing a woman's raillery, joined an expedition to Syria to prove their valour. The fair warriors clothed themselves in helmet and hauberk, having golden crosses tastefully embroidered upon the left shoulder; gilded slippers, glittering spurs, and silver-sheathed falchions suspended from the side completed the equipment, and mounted on richly-caparisoned steeds, they formed a brilliant squadron, caracoled about Paris and performed a thousand fantastic follies in public, calling themselves the bodyguard of the *Golden-footed Dame.*

CHAPTER 3

A voice, a flute, a dreamy lay,
Such as the southern breeze
Might waft, at golden fall of day
O'er blue transparent seas.

Louis took the cross in 1146, and in the following year, having received from the pope the consecrated banner as a warrior, and the staff and scrip as a pilgrim, set out for the general rendezvous at Mentz with his queen and her grotesque cavalcade. Here they were joined by an immense number of nobles and knights and soldiers, among whom were crusaders from England and the remote islands of the northern sea. After the lapse of half a century, the second crusade, consisting of two hundred thousand people, tracked their way along the banks of the Danube by the whitening bones of those who had fallen victims to the blind fanaticism of the first expedition. Manuel Comnenus, who now sat on the throne of Constantinople, adopted the same policy that had distinguished the councils of his grandfather, Alexius.

His envoys, bearing letters filled with flattery and fair speeches, met the advancing warriors, but the imperial guides were instructed to conduct the soldiers of the west by difficult and circuitous routes, and the purveyors had secret orders to furnish them with sacks of flour mixed with chalk and lime. Conrad, who was the brother-in-law of Manuel, was so indignant at this breach of hospitality, that he crossed the Bosphorus without meeting or conferring with the emperor—but the splendid city of Constantinople presented too many attractions to the female adventurers to be passed in so hurried a manner.

The wily Comnenus soon perceived that the readiest means to divide the forces of the crusade would be to amuse the fickle Queen of France. All the voluptuous refinements of the Greek court were accordingly put in requisition to detain his unwelcome visitors, and if the avaricious Bohemond was bribed with the contents of a treasure-chamber in the palace, Eleanor might well be excused if her frivolous

109

fancy was captivated by her splendid suite of rooms adorned with all the luxury of eastern magnificence, and the richly-attired slaves that waited her slightest bidding, and when at last they set forward, the Damascene silks, costly jewels, and precious gifts, which Manuel showered upon the finery-loving Amazons, added not a little to the cumbrous baggage with which the thoughtless queen loaded the expedition.

Louis, lulled into security by the flattering assurances of Manuel, had lingered in the Greek empire till the defeat of Conrad at Iconium, when convinced by the report of the discomfited Germans, of the treachery of his royal host, he set forward with his troops along the coast of Asia Minor. They passed Thyatira, Sardis, and Philadelphia without accident, defeated the Turks on the banks of the Meander, and arrived in safety at Laodicea. The freaks of Eleanor and her female warriors were the cause of all the misfortunes that afterwards befell the French army. On the second day after leaving Laodicea, their way led up the mountains, by a winding and difficult ascent. The prudent king sent forward the queen and her ladies, escorted by his choicest troops, under the guard of Count Maurienne, charging them to entrench themselves upon the wooded heights that overlooked the valley of Laodicea. Himself followed slowly with the rearguard, encumbered by the useless baggage, and harassed by the Arabs.

The Count Maurienne, with Petronilla by his side, rode gallantly up the steep, and halted at the place appointed, but when Eleanor reached the spot she was so attracted by the appearance of an adjacent valley, cooled by waterfalls, and shaded by thickets, which seemed to beckon them on with an inviting grace, that she insisted upon pressing forward, and forming the bivouac there. The Count Maurienne endeavoured to dissuade the queen from her purpose, by representing the danger of abandoning the commanding position designated by the king, but opposition only increased her pertinacity, and aided by the light artillery of Petronilla's eyes, she soon brought the discomfited knight to terms.

The scene that opened before them as they descended into the valley, was sufficient to charm away all fatigue and fear. The rocky heights at the west, behind which the sun was just sinking, veiled their bold fronts in the misty fringes of the opal clouds; the blue Mediterranean circled the horizon on the south; and far to the east stretched every variety of woodland, meadow, and glade, till the Taurus ridge, melting into the sky, shut out the sands of Syria. The happy party soon entered the valley. The sumpter mules were speedily unloaded, the light spars planted, the white canvass of the tents stretched upon them, and a cold collation spread out for their refreshment. When the repast was finished Eleanor caused her couch to be placed at the door of the tent, so that wild roses nodded at its pillow, and flinging herself upon it, as the brilliant stars of that eastern clime looked down upon her, she exclaimed, "Petronilla, my sister, seems not this like our own dear Provence? I could almost fancy myself once more in the Rose Pavilion."

"*Certes*," said Petronilla, "and were it not a fitting time and place to hold the festival of our Court of Love? Methinks yon, count," with a mischievous glance at Maurienne, "withstood our entreaties to enter this delightful retreat beyond the limits of gallantry."

"Gra'mercy, fair ladies," said the count, with mock gravity, "that I fear the frowns of this august tribunal more than the displeasure of my royal master, is perhaps my sin, and it is with unfeigned apprehensions that I surrender to the court."

"I accuse the count—" began the princess.

Maurienne interrupted her, "Petronilla my accuser! Then am I lost indeed. I had hoped to hear her eloquent lips plead my excuse."

"Nay! nay!" said Eleanor, striking the velvet turf with her tiny foot. "The court forbids these disorderly proceedings. Henry de Blois, arrest thou the Count Maurienne at the complaint of the princess, bind his hands with this string of pearls, and confront him with his accuser. Our brave Warrenne, take thy spear and stand sentinel by yon copse. A prowling Saracen would make an awkward addition to our goodly company. Knights and ladies, recline at ease upon these verdant cushions. When the cause of this culprit shall have received verdict, perchance your own delinquencies may pass review."

"Heaven forefend!" exclaimed a chorus of voices, mingling ejaculations with merry laughter and gay *pasquinade*.

The queen, now in her element, succeeded in quelling the tumultuous mirth, though an occasional titter was elicited by the solemn visages of Maurienne and Petronilla, who played their part to admiration.

"Where is the petulant Peyrol?" inquired the queen, looking round the circle, "we can no more proceed with our important affairs without the aid of song than could the prophet without the inspiration of music."

"Peyrol, my liege, attends upon the king," replied a Spanish cavalier, who had recently rode so constantly by the side of the queen that the courtiers dubbed him her saddle-*beau*.

"Gonzalvo," returned Eleanor, "we have heard that thou stringest a lute upon occasion. Let not our pastime be marred by the defection of this truant boy. Give us a Moorish ballad, if thy memory serves thee with nothing better. Our royal spouse will be here *anon* and summon us to prayers."

"I am but a poor pilgrim, and little skilled in the 'Joyous Science,'" said the Spaniard, with affected modesty; "but the command of my queen must give me the fitting inspiration." He touched a melodious prelude, and sung in a clear, manly voice:—

"I a minstrel of Grenada, Gonzalvo Bercio hight,
Once wandering as a pilgrim, found a meadow richly dight,
Green and peopled full of flowers, of flowers fair and bright,
A place where many a weary man would rest him with delight.

"And the flowers I beheld all looked and smelt so sweet,
That the senses and the soul they seemed alike to greet,
While on every side ran fountains through all this glad retreat,
Which in winter kindly warmth supplied, yet tempered summer's heat.

"And of rich and goodly trees there grew a boundless maze,
Rich grapes and apples bright, and figs of golden rays,
And many other fruits beyond my skill to praise,
But none that turneth sour, and none that e'er decays.

"The freshness of that meadow, the sweetness of its flowers,
The dewy shadows of the trees that fell like cooling showers,
Renewed within my frame its worn and wasted powers,
I deem the very odours would have nourished me for hours."

An arrow that pierced the tent, and fell among the strings of the minstrel's harp, interrupted the symphony, and called forth discordant screams of terror. A moment after the Earl of Warrenne, breathless and bleeding, rushed into the assembly, and communicated the startling intelligence, that the Turks had taken possession of the heights allotted for their encampment, and that the king, unaware of his danger, was proceeding to the snare, spread for his whole army. Maurienne hastily cast away his mimic fetters, and counselling his lovely charge to remain as close as possible beneath the shadow of the trees, stationed a small guard to defend them, and hastened back to the assistance of his sovereign.

The Syrian moon now rose broad and clear in the east, and the frightened females, huddling together like a flock of timid sheep, could distinctly see the heavy-armed troops on which rested all their hopes, toiling slowly up the mountain, in the face of a tremendous shower of arrows and loose masses of stone which the Moslems threw upon them from above. Men, horses and baggage, overborne by the sudden attack, rolled down the precipitous steep, and the expiring cries of familiar voices could be distinctly heard through the still air. Maurienne soon succeeded in putting to flight the Arabs that had attacked the vanguard, but the most dreadful havoc was made among the followers of Louis, and the king himself was only saved by the greatest efforts of personal valour. Seven thousand of the flower of French chivalry paid with their lives the penalty of the queen's caprice. The baggage containing the fine array of the lady-warriors, was plundered by the Arabs, and the fragments of their dainty supper was the only provision left for their sustenance.

The further progress of the French was beset with dangers and privations. The discipline of the army was broken, and they marched or rather wandered, for they knew not the roads, along the coast of Pamphilia, purchasing or plundering food of the frightened inhabitants; and famine thinned the ranks with such rapidity, and so many horses and other beasts of burden perished by the way, that it was finally determined to turn aside from these scenes of desolation and proceed by sea to Antioch. But upon reaching the coast, a new difficulty occurred.

A sufficient number of ships could not be procured to transport them all, and the brave peers of France, with honourable pride, agreed that the simple pilgrims, with the women and children, should alone make their passage with the king, while themselves should continue their route on foot. Louis distributed what money he had among the soldiers, who were left to surmount the higher difficulties of the land route, and engaged a Greek escort and guide to conduct them, and taking leave of the miserable beings who had followed him to their own destruction, went on board the ships. The escort soon deserted the French soldiers, the guide betrayed them, and but few if any ever reached Syria.

The royal party arrived at Antioch in a condition little short of beggary; but Prince Raimond, the uncle of Eleanor, opened his hospitable gates to them, and by the beautiful stream of the Orontes, the distressed warriors of the cross refreshed themselves after their fatigues, and the thoughtless queen regained once more her roses and her smiles. Recent experience had greatly cooled her military ardour, and the gaiety of the court of Antioch presented greater attractions to her fancy than a journey over the sandy plains of Syria. Prince Raimond, wishing to avail himself of the panic which a new arrival of crusaders had spread among the Turks, to extend the limits of his own territories, set himself at once to prevent the immediate departure of Louis for Jerusalem.

The prince was the handsomest man of his time, and directly began to pay the most assiduous court to his lovely niece. The queen, flattered by his attentions, commenced such a series of *coquetries* with him as greatly scandalized and incensed Louis; but it was not till she attempted to persuade her husband to join Raimond in an expedition against Cesarea that she found she had at last irritated the kind monarch beyond the limits of forbearance. Louis left her in anger, and departed with his forces for Jerusalem, where he was received with the greatest joy. Crowds of ecclesiastics and laymen going out to meet him, conducted him within the holy gates, singing, "Blessed is he that cometh in the name of the Lord."

Disappointed in the assistance of Louis, Raimond determined to secure an ally in Saladin, a young *emir* of the *sultan*. Eleanor, who was at this time moping with chagrin at the desertion of her husband, first saw the handsome barbarian at a Passage of Arms given by Raimond for her amusement, in which the dark-browed Saracen drove a javelin through the target with such skill and grace as completely pierced her heart. She immediately conceived the idea that if she should convert this powerful *infidel* to the Christian faith, she should achieve a greater conquest than all the forces of Christendom. Prince Raimond, who gladly availed himself of any attraction that should detain the Arab chief within the walls of Antioch, smiled upon her pious project.

But to bring a follower of the Prophet devoutly to consider the tenets of the Latin church, required more familiar intercourse and a greater exercise of personal influence than the ceremonious observances of Eastern society permitted, or the strictly virtuous deemed quite discreet. The zealous queen, however, scorned to be controlled by such fastidious considerations. Her apartments opened upon a terrace which conducted to a garden filled with every variety of odouriferous shrub and fragrant flower, at the foot of which a clump of olive-trees spread abroad their arms to hide a mossy seat from the intrusive rays of the sun. A little wicket concealed by vines led from the garden

114

into the street, and Eleanor kept the key. Through this wicket she admitted her young disciple, and in this retreat, with missionary zeal, commenced her efforts for the conversion of the Mussulman. It was some time before the European and Asiatic succeeded in coming to a perfect understanding; for though Saladin was tolerably well versed in the *Lingua Franca*, his vocabulary comprehended little else than those terms used in common intercourse or war.

Whether the philosophers of that day had taught that though some languages may be deficient in expressions of abstract ideas, all are replete in the dialect of love, certain it is, that both teacher and pupil became aware of the fact in their own particular case. But it was no part of Eleanor's religious plan to entangle herself in a *mésalliance*, and when the fascinated *emir* began to stammer forth his admiration, she playfully told him she could understand love only in the Provençal tongue. The Saracen took his departure, and though she watched anxiously for the arrow tipped with the eagle feather, by which he was wont to announce his coming, she saw him not again for twenty days. When the long-wished-for token at length appeared, and the handsome youth in his crimson robe and green baldric stood again before her, his face radiant with joy, and his dark eyes sparkling with delight; when she heard him pour forth his eloquent passion in the loved Provençal, with all the fluency and ease of a native, she almost fancied a miracle had been wrought, and felt convinced that not to lead such talents to the bosom of the church would be a grievous sin.

The Saracen soon persuaded her that love for her alone had endowed him with supernatural powers, and the delicate flattery determined her to exercise to the fullest extent the influence that could produce such wonderful effects. The young *emir* belted his tunic with a silken girdle several yards in length. Upon this ribbon Eleanor, still intent upon her design, embroidered a cross which the youth accepted with his accustomed gallantry, saying, "I worship the Divinity it represents." The next day he brought her a casket of diamonds, and an ivory box filled with the sweetest perfumes. As he reclined at her feet she opened the box, and twining his raven hair about her fingers poured the precious liquid upon his head.

Peyrol who from his childhood had regarded the queen with the impassioned devotion of the south, had hardly consented to share her heart with Louis. Since her marriage, her ambition for conquest had kept him constantly in a state of jealous excitement. His interested eyes had been the first to discern her stolen interviews with Saladin; and on the day of her acceptance of the diamonds, he contrived to secrete himself in the garden, and thus witnessed the whole affair. Convinced of her danger, he set off direct for Jerusalem, to advertise Louis of her conduct, and while Eleanor fancied herself doing God service in her efforts to convert the lord of the Saracens, though at some slight sacrifice of personal delicacy, the king arrived at Antioch, and hurried her away with small leave-taking of her uncle, and without even allowing her a parting interview with her heathen convert.

Eleanor submitted to this unaccustomed harshness of her husband, with a very ill grace. She attempted to explain to him that she was doing more for the preservation of the Sepulchre than King Baldwin himself. She expressed the most violent anger at being the object of unfounded suspicion, and entered the Holy City in a most indignant mood. The upright mind of Louis could not be made to comprehend the piety that led to such an ebullition of temper, nor could he well appreciate the purity of a motive that induced a wife to exchange presents with a lover; and from this time all confidence between them was at an end. The Queen of France was, notwithstanding, received and entertained at Jerusalem, with all the honours due her rank; but Peyrol was instructed to watch her movements, and prevent any further communication with Raimond.

A council was held at Ptolemais, composed of the Christian powers of Syria and Palestine, and the crusaders from Europe, and though the restoration of the Courtneys to their lost principality was the object of the expedition, it was decided that Damascus was a far more dangerous neighbour to Jerusalem than the remote city of Edessa. The decree to march to Damascus was accordingly passed, and the kings Louis VII., Baldwin III., and Conrad III. brought their troops into the field.

The best disciplined parts of the army were the Knights of the Temple, and of St. John.[1] In the early days of pilgrimages, an institution for the care of the sick had been established in Jerusalem. In this friendly hospital the wounded and dying of the first crusade were received and tended with the greatest care. King Godfrey with affectionate gratitude rewarded their pious labours by the gift of an estate in Brabant, whence they derived a steady revenue. The association acquired importance, and finally formed a religious house under the tutelage of St. John the Baptist. They took the usual vows of chastity,

1. *Knights of St John: a History to the Siege of Vienna, 1688* by Augusta Theodosia Drane is also published by Leonaur.

poverty, and obedience, and the patriarch of Jerusalem invested them with a black robe, having a white linen cross of eight points upon the left breast.

In *A.D.* 1113, the Hospital was put under the protection of the Holy See, and their revenues increasing beyond the demands of charity, about *A.D.*1130, they determined to draw the sword against the enemies of the faith. The Hospitallers were accordingly arranged into three classes, nobility, clergy, and serving brothers, who divided their duties between making deadly war upon the *infidels*, healing the wounds of the Christian soldier, and praying for the souls of the departed. The admirers of valour and piety either joined their standard or enriched their coffers. Great men sent their sons to them for instruction, and the Knights Hospitallers soon became a powerful monastic and military order.

A few years later, some French gentlemen founded the equally honourable institution of the Red Cross Knights. The original design of this order, was to watch the road and keep open the communication between Europe and the Holy Land. At first they were fed and clothed by the Hospitallers, and to indicate their poverty, adopted a seal with the figures of two men on one horse. They bound themselves to the three great monastic virtues, and added some austerities, which were supposed to give them power with God and man. They were originally styled *Milites Christi,* but when Baldwin I. assigned them a residence in the royal palace, adjacent to the Temple of Solomon, they assumed the title of Templars,[2] or Knights of the Temple. They wore linen coifs with red caps close over them, shirts and stockings of twisted mail, sapra vests and broad belts with swords inserted, and over the whole was a white cloak touching the ground. This order, too, rose into dignity and power; and the military friars of the Hospital, and the Red Cross Knights of the Temple, soon became the bulwark of Christendom, "the nurse of manly sentiment and heroic enterprise."

Acquainted with the roads, the Templars led the way to Damascus, and accustomed to succour the weak, the Hospitallers brought up the rear of the Christian army. The eastern and southern quarters of the city of Damascus were defended by impregnable walls; but the north and west were faced by fields and gardens, and protected only by towers and ditches. Here the crusaders pitched their camps; and numerous and long-continued were the engagements between the Christians

---

2. *The Military Religious Orders of the Middle Ages: The Knights Templar, Hospitaller and Others* by F. C. Woodhouse is also published by Leonaur.

and Moslems. They succeeded in driving in the outposts of the *infidels* and seizing several fortifications looked upon Damascus as their own. But now a more serious contest arose. Should Damascus become an appanage of Jerusalem, a fief of the French crown, or a German principality? Days and weeks passed away in fruitless disputes among the crusaders, and at length it was determined that the prize should be given to the Count of Flanders, because he had twice visited the Holy Land. This decision only increased the dissatisfaction.

There were rumours of treason in the camp, and the Templars were accused of accepting bribes. A proposition was made to remove the camp to Ascalon, and while debate fostered delay the Saracens had time to repair the fortifications of Damascus, and to summon assistance from the *sultan*. The German emperor, terrified with the report that the *emir* of Mosul was marching to the city, was the first to abandon the siege; and the other leaders, discontented with themselves and with each other, gloomily retraced their steps to Jerusalem. Conrad, with the shattered relics of the German host, immediately returned to Europe; but the king of the French lingered several months, visiting the holy places, and seeking opportunities to do military service worthy the expedition; till at length learning from Peyrol that Eleanor, through the connivance of Petronilla, had exchanged letters with Saladin, and was meditating a flight to Antioch; he gathered together the miserable remnant of his army, amounting to three hundred persons, and accompanied by his enraged queen and her crest-fallen Amazons, embarked for Constantinople. Here Eleanor found some small consolation in repairing the sad inroads made upon her wardrobe at the defeat of Laodicea. From Constantinople the dissatisfied pair sailed for France.

It was the intention of Louis to put away his wife immediately on his return, but the sagacious Abbot Suger dissuaded him from this course, since he would thus detach from the crown the great duchy of Aquitaine, the probable inheritance of the young Princesses Mary and Alix. She was, however, closely watched, and forbidden to visit her southern domains. In *A.D.* 1150, Geoffrey Plantagenet, the Count Anjou, came to the court of Louis VII., with his son Henry, a youth about the age of Saladin, whose fine person and literary attainments made him an object of attraction to all the ladies of Paris. To Geoffrey Eleanor confided her troubles, one of the greatest of which was, the refusal of the king to adopt the courtly adornings of the times, particularly the long-toed shoes, fastened to the knee by golden chains; and she was especially vexed that he had, at the suggestion of the clergy, parted with his long curls, handsome beard and *mustachios*.

"Already," said she, "he wears the shaven chin and the serge robe, and he needs only the tonsure and cowl to make him a priest."

The duke repaid her confidence by delineating his own domestic afflictions arising from the haughty demeanour of his consort the Empress Matilda, whose irritable temper had not been improved by her ineffectual struggles with Stephen for the throne of England. Altogether they had a very sympathizing meeting.

Two years after, Henry of Anjou once more visited Paris to do homage for his domains, and the queen with a facility acquired by practice, transferred to him the partiality she had entertained for his father. The young Plantagenet was a noble, martial-looking prince, with a fair and gracious countenance, and eyes that sparkled with intelligence and energy. In the light of this new attachment, Eleanor discovered that King Louis was her fourth cousin, and farther that the divorce he had threatened was a matter of conscience and propriety. Louis for the first time in many years seemed to find happiness in the same plan that pleased his queen. A council of the church was called at Beaugencie, and in the presence of Eleanor and Louis, and a numerous circle of relatives, the marriage was declared invalid on account of consanguinity.

Leaving her daughters in the care of their father, the liberated princess joyfully departed with her sister Petronilla and her Provençal attendants to her own country. On her way southward she stopped some time at the castle of Blois, where the old Count Thibaut, father of Adelais, whose domestic peace she had so selfishly invaded, became enamoured of the great Provence dower, and offered his hand to his fair guest. Unabashed by the lady's prompt refusal, the venerable suitor determined to detain her a prisoner in his fortress till she should comply with his proposition; but Peyrol accidentally learning the design, disguised his mistress and her sister in his own apparel, conducted them through the postern by night, and procuring a fisherman's boat, escaped with them down the Loire.

Here a new danger awaited them. Geoffrey of Anjou, the young brother of Henry Plantagenet, captivated by the charms of the princess, stationed himself with a strong guard, at the Pont de Tas, with the intention of carrying her off. Before the fugitives reached the spot they perceived the ambush, and the royal ladies, each seizing an oar, concealed their faces by bending to their tasks, while Peyrol ingeniously evaded the questions of the sentinel, by displaying the fishing-tackle and turning the boat into a little creek, as if preparing to commence the morning's sport. Hidden by the willows that shaded the stream, the party pursued their way with the utmost rapidity, and before the count had discovered their escape, they were beyond the reach of capture.

The enthusiastic greetings with which the Provençals hailed the return of their beloved duchess, had scarcely subsided into the quiet demonstrations of affectionate obedience, when the young Henry Plantagenet followed her to Bordeaux, and in that wealthy city, with all the pomp that the luxurious Provençal could command, they were married the first of May, *A.D.* 1152. Thus the sweet provinces of the south became the appanage of the English crown, and a foundation was laid for those desolating wars that for centuries drained the best blood of both France and England.

CHAPTER 4

Imperial being! E'en though many a stain
Of error be upon thee,
There is power in thy commanding nature.

Henry immediately conveyed his bride to Normandy, and installed her in the palace at Bayeux, once the residence of the family of William the Conqueror. The marriage of Eleanor, but little more than a month after her divorce, astonished all Europe. Especially was the King of France incensed by a union which made his already too powerful vassal lord of seven more beautiful and wealthy provinces.

He immediately entered into an alliance with Stephen to deprive Henry of Normandy, and incited the baffled Geoffrey to make war upon his brother.

"Let the stupid king do his worst," said Eleanor to her husband, as she despatched Peyrol to order the vessels of Bordeaux into the English Channel. "The barons of *oc* and *no* will raise the banner of St. George and the golden leopards far above the *oriflamme* of France, and rejoice at having such fair cause of quarrel with the suzerain and jailer of their princess."

The Provençal fleet that was thus brought to guard the coast of England, was of essential service to Henry in quelling the agitations excited by Louis not only, but in securing his peaceful accession to the throne of his grandfather, Henry I. During the six weeks that elapsed after the death of Stephen, before he was ready to assume his crown, the maritime power anchored in the English harbours preserved the public tranquillity, and kept all foreign enemies in awe. Henry and Eleanor, with a brilliant train, landed on the coast of Hampshire, at the beginning of December, *A.D.* 1154, and proceeded direct to Winchester. The prelates and nobles gathered round them from every part of the kingdom, and their journey from Winchester to London was a continual triumph.

Their coronation, which took place in Westminster Abbey, was without parallel for magnificence. The silks, brocades, and velvets shot with silver or embroidered with gold, which the new queen had brought from Constantinople, and the jewels which she had hoarded as mementoes of her self-denying efforts in Palestine, served to illuminate this august ceremony. The dark beauty of the south wore her long, black hair closely braided, and bound about her head, like an eastern tiara, from which flashed the diamonds of her Paynim lover like jewels set in jet. Her snowy kirtle, of the finest Indian fabric, confined at the throat by a collar of gems, and fastened by a jewelled belt at the bodice, fell in an amplitude of drapery to her feet, and the same transparent vesture covered, without concealing, the exquisite roundness of her arms. Over this was thrown an elegant *pelisson*, bordered with fur, having full loose sleeves, lined with ermine. In fine contrast with his sparkling queen, stood Henry, the first monarch of the warlike Plantagenets.

The Saxon lineaments predominated in his face and person, the wealth of his brown locks, and his thick, curling mustachios gave an air of manliness to his somewhat boyish visage, but his calm youthful countenance was not at that period marked with the strong and violent passions that afterwards kindled in his eye, and darkened in his frown. He wore a doublet of crimson damask, and a short Angevin cloak, which gained for him the soubriquet of Courtmantle. The ecclesiastics who graced this ceremony also appeared in gowns and cassocks of silk and velvet, another importation of Eleanor from Constantinople. After the celebration of the Christmas festivities, the royal pair took up their residence in Bermondsey, a pastoral village, nearly opposite London, where was an ancient Saxon palace and a priory.

While Eleanor remained in this quiet retreat, Henry devoted his energies to settling the affairs of his government, with a prudence and discretion beyond his years. In one council, he appointed the great officers of the crown; in another he confirmed to his subjects, all the rights and liberties secured under the famous charter of Henry Beauclerk, in a third he induced the barons to do homage to his eldest son

William, and in the event of William's death, to his second son Henry, a child in the cradle. He demolished many of the castles reared by the rebellious barons under Stephen, dismissed the foreign mercenaries or Brabancons, that had long infested the kingdom, and compelled Malcolm, grandson of David and Maude, to exchange three northern counties for the earldom of Huntingdon, which the King of the Scots claimed as the descendant of Earl Waltheof.

During the stormy period of Stephen's reign, the ecclesiastical tribunals had acquired an authority above the judicial courts; and it was the ardent desire of the monarch to reform this abuse. He owed so much, however, to the friendship and constancy of Theobald, archbishop of Canterbury, that he found it difficult to work any innovation upon the jurisdiction of the church so dear to the heart of his venerable friend. Eleanor occupied in her own pleasures, and it is charitably to be hoped in the duties of a mother, took little interest in these affairs; for the death of her eldest boy, and the birth of a daughter, had in some sort awakened her mind to maternal responsibilities. She was particularly solicitous with regard to the tutor to be chosen for her son Henry, and herself made a visit to the archbishop to confer upon the subject. A few days after the king entered her apartments in an unusually facetious mood.

"The good Theobald," said he, "who suffered banishment for my mother, has parted with his right hand to benefit her son. He has sent us his own archdeacon as a tutor for Henry."

"And how looks the candidate for our favour; is he fair and wise?" asked Eleanor.

"Nay, for that," said Henry, "the archbishop, with his wonted sagacity, has shown due regard for the tastes of the family, since the man he has sent is half Saxon, half Saracen."

"A Pullani," exclaimed Eleanor, her curiosity at once excited. "I met many of this class in Palestine. Comes he direct from the Holy Land?"

"Nay, he was born in London, and except some of the characteristics of his wily race, is as good a Christian as ever attended mass. His father, Guilbert Becket, was taken captive in the first crusade, and confined in the palace of an *emir*. The daughter of the *infidel* fell violently in love with the young Christian, liberated him by night, and pawned her jewels to a band of roving pirates, to engage them to convey him safe to Europe. Thither she followed him through a great variety of dangers, replying only 'London,' 'Guilbert,' to all who questioned her.

These two magic words brought her to the metropolis, where she found the object of her search. She was baptized by the Saxon name of Matilda, and Becket rewarded her devotion by marrying her. Thomas à Becket was their only son. He passed his childhood under the care of the canons of Merton; he has studied in the schools of Oxford and Paris, frequented the lectures on Philosophy at Bologna, been bred in a thorough knowledge of the civil and canon law, has visited Rome, stands high in the favour of pope and primate, and with all these qualifications," added Henry, in a tone of exultation, "*he is not a priest.*"

Eleanor was delighted with the story, and Becket was immediately installed as tutor of Prince Henry. Becket's romantic origin, affable manners, but more especially his nice tact in exhibiting intelligence or ignorance, according to the demands of delicate emergencies, recommended him at once to the favour of both king and queen. The principal residences of the royal family were Westminster palace, Winchester, and the country palace of Woodstock, the favourite abode of Henry Beauclerk and Matilda the good. In this charming retirement, Eleanor amused herself and the ladies of her court, with mysteries and mummeries, contrived and acted by the priests and parish clerks. Even the miracles of the holy volume were degraded from their sacred character, and made the subjects of clumsy efforts at merriment. Eleanor, who delighted in scenic amusements, on one occasion instructed the master of ceremonies to dramatize the miraculous trials of St. Dunstan.

So many characters were necessary for this important play, that new recruits of abbots, clerks and scholars were imported from the neighbouring priory, and the queen's *dames d'honneur* were enlisted in the choir, and faithfully drilled in the chanting of most unearthly melodies. The usual services in the chapel were for several days omitted. The carpenters displaced the priests, and instead of the sound of matins and vespers, the walls echoed with the noise of workmen's hammers, preparing a false floor for the mimic purgatory. The trees of the park were robbed of their leafy honours, to fit up a forest over the high altar, which by the removal of a panel, and the addition of dry leaves, pebbles and mosses, answered very well for the hermit's cave.

The eventful night arrived, and expectation, so long on tiptoe, quietly settled itself upon the temporary benches to enjoy the intellectual treat, while an imaginary moon broad as the shield of their Saxon fathers, reflected the light of a supposed invisible torch placed behind a window shutter. Owing to the imperfection of the machinery there was some difficulty in raising the curtain, but the queen was privately informed that the creaking was not intended as part of the play. The learned and gifted Provençal must be pardoned if she exchanged some sly criticisms and satirical smiles, with the witty Peyrol, at the expense of the well-meaning performers.

The scene opened disclosing a barren heath, in the centre of which was a mound of rubbish, strewed with grass and surmounted with a huge stone, which had been transplanted with much care and labour, from an adjacent cromlech. By its side stood a youth, who bashfully hanging his head and awkwardly twirling a wand, thus unfolded the plan of the drama:—

Here you see this hill and stone,
For that you may know anon.
The story of the blest St. Dunstan:
For dun is hill, and stone is stane,
That is what this here shall mean.
To the holy Saint was trouble sent,
As we here shall represent—

When young harlequin had concluded his prologue, he paused in great embarrassment staring up at the curtain, till finding that it refused to fall he stepped to the side of the stage and assisted its descent with all his strength.

A considerable bustle then ensued behind the scenes, during which the audience amused themselves as is usual in such cases, by suppressed titters and whispers.

The reluctant curtain again rose, and instead of the notable hill and stone, the individual typified thereby, St. Dunstan himself appeared, a burly Saxon priest wedged into his altar-cave; an appropriate arrangement admirably adapted to the tradition, since he could neither sit, stand, nor lie down at ease in it. The holy man was professedly engaged at his devotions, rattling off *credos* and *ave maries* in a style showing a lamentable want of familiarity with Latin. The arch tempter was a little behind his time, for the saint had evidently exhausted his stock of prayers, and had commenced a repeat when Lucifer appeared in the disguise of a labourer with spade in hand. Approaching the cave, he held out a bag of gold and invited the holy Father to follow him. The hermit impatiently waved his hand and turned his eyes resolutely away from the glittering lure, while the baffled demon walked off the stage. Confused groans and shrieks from the imps beneath followed his departure, while the choir of unseen angels sung with great emphasis—

With gold he doth the saint assail,
But not with this can the devil prevail.

The next scene was of a more striking character. The monk was this time interrupted by the advent of a beautiful damsel, who, gliding like an apparition of light from the greenwood, stopped before the cave, showered roses upon his missal, and in the most enticing manner sought to win him from his devotions. The saint, however, remained firm, and when she laid hold of his arm, he snatched a pair of pincers, conveniently heated for the occasion, and zealously seized the sorceress by the nose, who first cried piteously and then bellowed most lustily—but the heart of the pious priest was not to be moved. In the struggle, the glittering mask unfortunately fell off, carrying with it the whole apparatus of the flimsy disguise, and a saucy-looking page, thus unexpectedly revealed, scampered off the stage, much to the discomfiture of the players and greatly to the amusement of the spectators. This *contre-temps* produced a most uncommon roaring among the demons below, while the choir sung with renewed vehemence—

With love he doth the saint assail,
But not with this shall the devil prevail.

Hardly had the cheering and laughter subsided, when the curtain rose the third time. A sulphurous vapour filled the apartment, and from a trap-door in the staging, amid mimic thunders and faint attempts at lightning, rose his Satanic majesty, in *propria persona*, with the usual adjuncts of horns, hoofs and tail. As if to strengthen the trembling saint for the final conflict, the choir reiterated with great excitement—

With fear he doth your heart assail,
But not with this shall the devil prevail.

The fiend advanced with diabolical grimace, and the whole staging trembled beneath his tread, while the terrified devotee shrank to the farthest corner of the cell, and throwing his huge arms round the wooden crucifix, told his beads with startling volubility. It was evidently the fiend's object, to detach St. Dunstan from the cross; but the broad-shouldered priest was more than a match for the sturdy boor, encumbered as he was with the trappings of his new dignities. A terrible struggle ensued, but such was the desperate energy with which the saint grasped the holy symbol, and so intimately was it connected with the whole design of the performance, that in attempting to drag the priest from its protection, the stout yeoman tore the crucifix from the altar, the forest from its foundations, and while the choir were preparing to vociferate a splendid song of triumph, friar and fiend, angels and apparatus were precipitated into the yawning purgatory beneath.

At the same moment, the man with the moon abruptly set, leaving the chapel in total darkness. The musical pitch wavered and quavered, and terminated in shrieks of affright, and the audience, apprehensive that the devil had not yet his due, fled in most undignified haste. It was not until the queen had reached her own apartments, and her tire-women one after another came hurrying to her presence in ludicrous disarray, that she forgot her fright and gave way to a genial burst of merriment. The forlorn damsels at length found it impossible not to join in her mirth, and every fresh arrival was hailed with irrepressible peals of laughter.

"Welcome, my *angeliques*," cried the queen. "I feared that your late promotion would unfit you for mortal duties; but I perceive, with pleasure, that a foretaste of the punishment that awaits the unfaithful, has rendered you more than usually alert this evening. For ourself, we feel the necessity for repose, and will gladly be disrobed for our couch."

Notwithstanding the unsuccessful efforts of her Saxon clerks, Eleanor was not discouraged. She summoned from Blois a celebrated abbot named William, who, under her patronage, and assisted by her genius, brought out his tragedy of Flaura and Marcus, the first appearance of the regular drama in England.

Chapter 5

For close designs and crooked counsels fit,
Sagacious, bold, and turbulent of wit;
Restless, unfixed in principle and place,
In power unpleased, impatient in disgrace.

Thomas a Becket had risen rapidly in the royal favour. His calm discrimination and cool judgment had made him the chosen counsellor of his patron, his sedulous attention to his pupil had won the heart of Eleanor, while his courtly qualities and knightly address made him popular with all classes of people. The king conferred upon him the honours of Eye, the wardenship of the tower of London, and made him chancellor of the realm. The versatility of his accomplishments enabled him to adapt himself to Henry's various moods, and he thus became the monarch's inseparable companion. The rapidity of his rise was equalled only by the splendour of his course. He rivalled the king in the appointments of his household, exercised the most unbounded hospitality towards those who visited the court, and became the medium through which the subjects communicated with their sovereign. The king was his frequent guest, and the monarch and the favourite seemed bound by ties of real friendship.

Queen Eleanor had removed her court from Woodstock, to the palace of Beaumont, in Oxford, where the celebrated Cœur de Lion was born, *A.D.* 1157. On the receipt of this pleasing intelligence, the king set off with his chancellor and train to join his family. As they rode along, conversing upon terms of the most easy familiarity, a miserable beggar followed them asking an alms. The king carelessly bestowed a few pence, and the chancellor observing the tattered garments of the mendicant, facetiously remarked, that the command was not to feed the hungry alone, but to clothe the naked.

"Thou sayest truth," said the king, "and art thyself worthy to illustrate thy own doctrine."

So saying, he seized the chancellor's cloak, and began pulling it from his shoulders. The favourite resisted this charitable impulse, and put spurs to his horse. The king, however, retained his grasp, and urged his steed to keep pace with that of the close-fisted courtier, and betwixt their struggles and laughter, both had nearly been rolled in the dirt. Becket, finally, released his hold, and the wondering beggar wrapped his shivering limbs in the finest mantle in the kingdom.

As their road wound through the rich meadows of Evenlod, they caught occasional glimpses of the nunnery at Godstow, half-hidden among the trees, and before they reached the outer line of the convent walls, they saw at a short distance before them, crossing a rustic bridge, the figure of a beautiful girl, mounted upon a coal-black steed. The ease and grace with which she reined the mettlesome animal, the exquisite symmetry of her form, set off by the rich drapery of her robe, first attracted the king's notice. Her hair of a golden brown escaping from a turban-like riding-cap, floated like a veil over her shoulders, and air and exercise imparted a brilliant bloom to a face of lily fairness, and gave additional lustre to eyes, whose mirror-like depths seemed formed to reflect the light of heaven. Henry instinctively drew rein as the beautiful being dashed across their way and struck into a bridle-path, followed by a venerable-looking serving man, in green livery.

"What dazzling vision is this?" said Henry, pausing as if to recall a half-forgotten memory. "I have seen that face before, or my eye is, for the first time, at fault."

"The appointments of the servant are those of the Clifford's," said Becket, coldly.

"And what is the name of the fair creature with the golden locks?" pursued Henry.

"If it be the daughter of Lord Walter de Clifford, her name is Rosamond," said Becket, little inclined to satisfy the monarch's inquiries.

"Walter de Clifford!" said the king, with a thrill of recollection. "I mind me now, when the King of Scotland laid the sword of knighthood on my shoulder, it was the Lord de Clifford that buckled on my spurs; and this fair girl, then a child of exquisite beauty, sat among the maids of the queen, who presided at the tournament. A king bred in a foreign land must needs be a sad stranger in his own realm. Canst thou point me to the home of this fair damsel?"

Becket, who perceived that the impetuosity of the monarch would not brook evasion, answered; "Clifford castle is some two days' distance, on the banks of the Wye. The Lord de Clifford has been a crusader in Palestine this many a year, and his daughter, who after her mother's death, was in care of the nuns of Godstow, is haply on her way to the convent. The serving man, I see, is old Adam Henrid, her seneschal."

"Let us push on," said Henry, "tonight we sup at Godstow. Much I wonder," he added, musingly, "if the sweet girl holds in recollection the image of the boy knight."

"Becket," he added, aloud, "there is little about me to betray the king. I will be tonight, the simple Duke of Maine. Be thou my squire. Our men in attendance may proceed to Oxford." So saying, the impatient monarch put spurs to his horse, and galloped forward followed by his reluctant courtier, and alighted at the nunnery just after Rosamond had been received within its walls. The sound of the bell brought to the great gate of the convent the portress, summoned from her evening meal, and still holding in her hand the bunch of leeks and slice of brown bread, which formed the repast.

"And what wouldst thou, sir knight?" she inquired, gruffly.

"Rest and refreshment," said Henry, in French. "We are weary travellers, and seek shelter for the night."

"Ye are from beyond the sea," replied the portress, "and we will none of your outlandish tongue. Yonder lies the way to Oxford."

"Becket," whispered the king, "let thy ready wit serve us in this time of need, and thou shalt not find thy lord ungrateful." The wily chancellor, who never lost the opportunity of laying the monarch under obligation to himself, instantly rejoined in Saxon to the nun,

"Open to us, good mother. The Duke of Maine is a zealous patron of the church, and perchance thine own convent will be none the poorer for granting him entertainment."

The mollified portress immediately admitted them, muttering apologetically, "The wayfarer and benighted are ever received with Christian charity, by the sisters of the blessed St. Bernard."

★★★★★★

The infant Richard was a child of great promise, and his ambitious mother began, at once, to plan for his future advancement. She besought her husband to bestow upon the prince the dukedom of Aquitaine, and to permit her to convey him thither, to receive the homage of the barons, and to arrange a betrothment between him and Philippa, the infant daughter of her sister Petronilla and Raymond of Arragon. To her great joy and surprise Henry acceded at once to the proposal, and co-operated in her scheme for remaining some time as regent in her southern dominions.

Louis VII., King of France, had given his two daughters by Eleanor, in marriage to the Counts of Blois and Champagne; and after the death of his second wife Constantia, conferred the crown matrimonial upon their father's sister, Adelais of Champagne, widow of the famous Rudolph of Vermandois. He also bestowed upon the Count of Champagne the office of seneschal of his kingdom, which of right belonged to Henry, as Duke of Anjou, who, enraged at this measure, made war upon his liege lord. The affair was finally compromised by the affiancing of Henry's eldest son with Louis's third daughter Marguerite. Henry and Eleanor repaired to Normandy to celebrate the nuptials, and Becket was sent to Paris to bring the young bride to Rouen. On this important occasion the chancellor travelled in the greatest state.

When he entered a town two hundred and fifty boys singing national airs led the procession, while from wagons covered with skins and protected by guards and dogs the populace were regaled with draughts of English beer. Other wagons, each drawn by five horses, led by servants in splendid livery, followed with the furniture of his chapel, bed-chamber and kitchen, his plate, wardrobe, and attendants. Then came twelve sumpter horses each carrying a groom and monkey; then the esquires, gentlemen's sons, falconers with hawks upon their wrists, officers of the household, knights and clergymen, and last of all Becket himself in familiar converse with a few friends. The French, when they saw an ambassador affecting a magnificence greater than their own sovereign could command, exclaimed, "What manner of man must the King of England be, when his chancellor travels in such state." The King of France received Becket with the most distinguishing courtesy, and committed the infant Marguerite to his care. Becket conveyed the little princess to Rouen, where the contract of marriage was solemnized, and the juvenile bride and bridegroom were committed to him for education, and Louis gave to Henry three cities as the dower of his daughter.

But a misunderstanding arising with regard to the matter, a fresh compromise was effected by another match. The death of the little princess of Arragon had left the hand of Richard again at liberty. This hand was given as a pledge of amity to Alice, the infant daughter of France, who was also conveyed to England for education. It was the policy of Henry to strengthen his government by powerful alliances: and these early marriages were followed in quick succession by similar unions between Geoffrey his third son and Constance the heiress of Bretagne, and his eldest daughter Matilda with Henry the lion Duke of Saxony.

In the midst of these domestic and political arrangements Theobald, Archbishop of Canterbury, died; and the king entered upon his long-meditated design of reforming the abuses of the church. He had loaded Becket with every demonstration of favour and affection, and counting confidently upon his co-operation, offered him the vacancy. The chancellor objected that he was not a priest, but Henry insisted that the time required to take orders was only a few hours. Still the chancellor seemed to decline the dazzling gift. He protested that were he once a bishop he must uphold the rights of the church, and solemnly told the king the night before his consecration that the mitre would interpose an eternal barrier between them. Henry persisted, and Becket at last modestly accepted the first office in the kingdom.

Directly on his investment the new archbishop became as much distinguished for his austerity as he had before been for his ostentation. He resigned his office of chancellor, dismissed his knightly train, clothed himself in sackcloth, fed upon the coarsest fare, drank water nauseous with fennel, and daily upon his knees washed the feet of thirteen beggars, whom he afterwards dismissed with alms. On all occasions he defended the rights of the church in opposition to those of the crown. As he was the most learned man in the kingdom, the most eloquent and the best beloved, he possessed unbounded influence with all classes, and Henry soon found in the man whom he trusted as an ally a most powerful adversary.

But the king did not on this account relinquish his plans for reform. A parish priest had been guilty of murder under circumstances that peculiarly aggravated the crime. The judicial courts sought to try the criminal. The bishop contended that degradation from office was the highest punishment that could be inflicted upon a son of the church. The affair created great sensation throughout the kingdom, and Henry finally convened a general council of the nobility and clergy.

Several articles, were drawn up called the Constitutions of Clarendon, the drift of which was that no churchman should be entitled to privileges greater than those enjoyed by his peers among the laity. Becket at first refused to sign the articles and the other bishops followed his example. Being threatened with exile or death he at length yielded; but afterwards, learning that the pope did not approve his course, he retracted his consent. The king incensed at the conduct of his favourite, ordered a succession of charges to be prepared, on which the archbishop was cited to trial. Becket declined the jurisdiction of the court and appealed to the pope, finally escaped across the sea and made his way to the King of France.

Troubles in Aquitaine had made it necessary for Eleanor to take up her abode there, where, in company with her children, she remained some time exercising the functions of regent with great ability. To detach Prince Henry, who was enthusiastically fond of his tutor, from the party of Becket, the king sent for him to be crowned at Westminster, and admitted to a share of the government. But when the princess Marguerite found that Becket, the guardian of her youth, was not to place the diadem upon her head, she trampled upon the coronation-robes, and perversely refused to leave Aquitaine for London. King Louis took up his daughter's quarrel, and entered Normandy at the head of an army.

Henry hastened to defend his domains, and hostilities were commenced, but the two monarchs had a private conference, and Henry finally promised to seek an immediate reconciliation with his exiled primate. The archbishop of Rouen and the bishop of Nevers were authorized to arrange an interview, and the King of England awaited the arrival of his rebellious subject in a spacious meadow, on the borders of Touraine. As soon as Becket appeared Henry spurred on his horse, with his cap in hand, thus preventing any formal recognition, and discoursed with all the easy familiarity of former days. At the gracious words of his master, the archbishop descended from his horse, and threw himself at the feet of his sovereign; but Henry laid hold of the stirrup, and insisted that he should remount, saying,

"Let us renew our ancient affection for each other,—only show me honour before those who are now viewing our behaviour." Then returning to his nobles, he remarked, "I find the archbishop in the best of dispositions towards me; were I otherwise toward him I should be the worst of men." The king, however, adroitly avoided giving the kiss of peace, a circumstance which the primate observed, and made the subject of the most gloomy presage. Having waited in vain for the money which Henry had promised him, Becket borrowed a sum sufficient to defray the expenses of the journey, and contrary to the advice of his friends, returned to his diocese. He despatched a letter to the king at Rouen, which closed thus:—

It was my wish to have waited on you once more, but necessity compels me, in the lowly state to which I am reduced, to revisit my afflicted church. I go, sir, with your permission, perhaps to perish for its security, unless you protect me; but whether I live or die, yours I am, and yours I shall ever be in the Lord. Whatever may befall me or mine, may the blessing of God rest on you and your children.

★★★★★★

Before the meeting between Becket and the king, the pope had issued letters of suspension against those who had assisted at the coronation of the young prince, and Becket returned to England with those letters upon his person, and immediately proceeded upon the work of excommunication. These tidings were conveyed to Henry by the first ship that sailed for Normandy, and the outraged monarch exclaimed in a fury of passion, "Of the cowards who eat my bread is there not one to rid me of this turbulent priest?" Four knights, at the head of whom was Reginald Fitzurse, immediately set out for England, and proceeding straight to Canterbury, entered the house of the archbishop, and required him, in the king's name, to absolve the excommunicated prelates.

Becket refused, and repaired to the church with the utmost tranquillity to evening vespers. The solemn tones of the organ had ceased, and the archbishop had opened the book and commenced the lesson of the martyrdom of St. Stephen, "Princes sat and spake against me," when the knights, with twelve companions, all in complete armour, burst into the church. "Where is the traitor? Where is the archbishop?" inquired Fitzurse.

"Here am I," replied Becket, "the archbishop, but no traitor." He read his doom in the eyes of his pursuers."Tyrant king," muttered he, "though I die I will be thy undoing." He wrote hastily upon a tablet, "*Woodstock*," and giving it to his only attendant, whispered, "Deliver this to Queen Eleanor. Tarry not till thou find her." Then turning calmly to the knights,

"Reginald," said he, "I have granted thee many favours, what is thy object now? If thou seekest my life, I command thee, in the name of God, not to touch one of my people."

"I come not to take life," replied Reginald, "but to witness the absolution of the bishops."

"Till they offer satisfaction I shall never absolve them," said the prelate.

"Then die!" exclaimed the knight, aiming a blow at his head. The attendant interposed his arm, which was broken, and the force of the stroke bore away the prelate's cap, and wounded him on the crown. As he felt the blood trickling down his face, he joined his hands and bowed his head, saying, "In the name of Christ, and for the defence of his church I am ready to die." Turning thus towards his murderers, he waited a second stroke, which threw him on his knees, and the third prostrated him on the floor, at the foot of St. Bennett's altar. He made no effort towards resistance or escape, and without a groan expired. The assassins instantly fled, and the people, who had by this time assembled, crowded into the cathedral.

The priests with pious reverence took up the body of the dead archbishop, and laid it in state before the high altar. They tore his garments in pieces, and distributed each shred as a sacred relic. The devout wiped up his blood and treasured the holy stains, and the more fortunate obtained a lock of hair from his honoured head. Becket was interred with great solemnity in Canterbury cathedral, and all the power he had exercised in life was but a trifle to the influence of the miracles wrought at his tomb.

Henry was celebrating the holidays in Normandy, when the news of this event threw him into the deepest melancholy. The train of calamities, which would inevitably follow the curse of the church, made him tremble for his throne, and the natural horror of the crime alarmed his imagination and partially disordered his reason. He knew not how to receive the murderers, nor yet how to treat with the pope, and finally concluded to give the matter over to the judgment of the spiritual courts. The assassins in consequence travelled to Rome, and were sentenced by way of expiation to make a pilgrimage to Jerusalem. To evade meeting the legates of the pope, Henry determined to seize this opportunity for his long meditated invasion of Ireland.

The same month that witnessed the splendid coronation of Henry and Eleanor, had been signalized by the succession of Nicholas Breakspear, to the throne of the Vatican. This prelate, consecrated under the name of Adrian IV. was the only Englishman that ever sat in the chair of St. Peter; and his partiality for his native sovereign had led him to bestow upon Henry, a grant of the dominion of Ireland. Now when troubles arose in that province and circumstances rendered absence from his own dominions desirable, the king led an army into Ireland.

From the time of the marriage of her daughter Matilda with the Lion of Saxony, Eleanor had not visited England. The arrival of Becket's messenger in Bordeaux, conveyed to her the first intelligence of the prelate's death; and the mysterious word *Woodstock*, immediately revived a half-forgotten suspicion excited by the stratagems of Henry, to prevent her return to her favourite residence. Her woman's curiosity prevailed over her love of power, and she intrusted the regency to her son Henry, repaired to England, and lost no time on her way to Woodstock. As she approached the palace, her keen eye scanned every circumstance that might lead curiosity or lull suspicion, but with the exception of a deserted and unkept look, the appearance of the place indicated no marked change. Though she came with a small train and unannounced, the drawbridge was instantly lowered for her entrance, and the aged porter received her with a smile of unfeigned satisfaction.

The state rooms were thrown open and hastily fitted up for the reception of the royal inmates, and the servants, wearied with the listless inactivity of a life without motive or excitement, bustled about the castle and executed the commands of their mistress, with the most joyful alacrity. Under pretence of superintending additions and repairs, Queen Eleanor ordered carpenters and masons, who under her eye, visited every apartment, sounded every wall, and tore off every panel, where by any possibility an individual might be concealed. She did not hesitate even to penetrate the dungeons under the castle; and whenever the superstition of the domestics made them hesitate in mortal terror, she would seize a torch and unattended thread her way through the darkest and dampest subterranean passages of the gloomy vaults. All these investigations led to no discovery. The pleasance offered little to invite her search. It had been originally laid out in the stiff and tasteless manner of the age, with straight walks and close clipped shrubbery, but so long neglected it was a tangled maze, to which her eye could detect no entrance.

Below the pleasance the postern by a wicket gate communicated with a park, which was separated only by a stile from the great forest of Oxfordshire. Mounted on her Spanish jennet, Eleanor galloped through this park and sometimes ventured into the forest beyond, and she soon discovered that the attendants avoided a thicket which skirted the park wall. Commanding the grooms to lead in that direction, she was informed that it was the ruins of the old menagerie, located there by Henry I., overgrown by thorns and ivy and trees, that shut out the light of the sun. The aged porter assured her that no one had entered it in his day, that wild beasts still howled therein, and that the common people deemed it dangerous to visit its vicinity. He added, that one youth who had charge of the wicket, had been carried off and never again seen; and that all the exorcisms of the priests could never lay the ghost.

The old man crossed himself in devout horror and turned away; but the queen commanded him to hold the bridle of her horse, while she should attempt the haunted precincts alone. The thick underwood resisted all her efforts, and she found it impossible to advance but a few steps, though her unwonted intrusion aroused the beetles and bats, awakened the chatter of monkeys and the startled twitter of birds, and gave her a glimpse of what she thought were the glaring eyeballs of a wolf. A solemn owl flew out above her head as she once more emerged into the light of day, and the timid porter welcomed her return with numerous ejaculations of thanksgiving to the watchful saints; but he shook his head with great gravity as he assisted her to remount saying;

"I would yon dismal bird had kept his perch in the hollow oak. Our proverb says, '*Woe follows the owl's wing as blood follows the steel.*'"

Disappointed in the wood, Eleanor relinquished her fruitless search. But by dint of questioning she learned, that though the palace wore the appearance of desertion and decay, it had been the frequent resort of Henry and Becket, and since the favourite's death, her husband had

135

made it a flying visit before leaving for Ireland. Farther than this all inquiries were vain. The unexpected return of her husband, and his look of surprise and anxiety at finding her at Woodstock, again awakened all her jealous fears. His power of dissimulation, notwithstanding, kept her constantly at fault, and during the week of his stay, nothing was elicited to throw light upon the mystery. Henry had been negotiating with the pope to obtain absolution for Becket's murder, and was now on his way to Normandy to meet the legates.

The morning before his departure, Queen Eleanor saw him walking in the pleasance, and hastened to join him. As she approached she observed a thread of silk, attached to his spur and apparently extending through the walks of the shrubbery. Carefully breaking the thread she devoted herself by the most sedulous attention to her husband, till he set out for France, when she hastened back to the garden, and taking up the silk followed it through numerous turnings and windings till she came to a little open space near the garden wall, perfectly enclosed by shrubbery. The ball from which the thread was unwound lay upon the grass. There the path seemed to terminate; but her suspicions were now so far confirmed that she determined not to give up the pursuit.

A broken bough, on which the leaves were not yet withered, riveted her attention, and pulling aside the branch she discovered a concealed door. With great difficulty she opened or rather lifted it, and descended by stairs winding beneath the castle wall. Ascending on the opposite side by a path so narrow that she could feel the earth and rocks on either hand, she emerged into what had formerly been the cave of a leopard, fitted up in the most fanciful manner with pebbles, mosses, and leaves. She made the entire circuit of the cave ere she discovered a place of egress: but at length pushing away a verdant screen, she advanced upon an open pathway which wound, now under the thick branches of trees, now through the dilapidated barriers that had prevented the forest denizens from making war upon each other, now among ruined lodges which the keepers of the wild beasts had formerly inhabited; but wherever she wandered she noted that some careful hand had planted tree, and shrub, and flower in such a manner as to conceal the face of decay and furnish in the midst of these sylvan shades a most delightful retreat.

At last she found herself inextricably involved in a labyrinth whose apartments, divided by leafy partitions, seemed so numerous and so like each other as to render it impossible for her to form any idea of the distance she had come, or the point to which she must proceed. The sun was going down when by accident, she laid her hand upon the stile. Following its windings, though with great difficulty, she emerged into the path that terminated in the forest. The low howl of a wolf-dog quickened her steps, and she arrived at the palace breathless with fear and fatigue.

Sleep scarcely visited her pillow. She revolved the matter over and over again in her mind. "Where could Henry find balls of silk? For whose pleasure and privacy was the labyrinth contrived? What hand had planted the rare exotic adjacent to the hawthorn and the sloe? Was this tortuous path the road to a mortal habitation? And who was the fair inmate?" She could hardly wait for the dawn of the morning, and when the morning came it only increased her impatience, for heavy clouds veiled the sun, and a continued rain confined her for several days to her apartments.

When she next set out on her voyage of discovery she took the necessary precaution to secure a hearty coadjutor in the person of Peyrol, who silently followed her with the faithfulness of early affection, wondering to what point their mysterious journey might tend. At the secret door she fastened a thread, and with more celerity than she had hoped, traced her former course to the labyrinth; with much difficulty she again found the stile, and after a diligent search perceived a rude stair, that winding around the base of a rock assumed a regular shapely form, till by a long arched passage it conducted to a tower screened by lofty trees, but commanding through the interstices of the foliage a view of the adjacent forest. Here all effort at concealment was at an end.

The doors opened into rooms fitted up with all the appliances of wealth, and with a perfection of taste that showed that some female divinity presided there. Vases of fresh-culled flowers regaled the senses with rich perfume. A harp lay unstrung upon the table, a tambour frame on which was an unfinished picture of the Holy Family leaned against the wall, while balls of silk and children's toys lay scattered around in playful disorder. Everything indicated that the tower had been recently occupied, but no inmate was to be found. Retracing their steps into the forest they proceeded by a well-beaten path along the banks of a little stream, to a pebbly basin in which the waters welled up with a faint murmur that spoke of rest and quiet.

A sound of music made them pause, and they heard a low gentle voice followed by the lisping accents of a child chanting the evening hymn to the Virgin. Stepping stealthily along they saw, half shaded by a bower inwoven with myrtle and eglantine, a beautiful female kneeling before a crucifix hung with votive offerings. Her face was exquisitely fair, and her eyes raised to the holy symbol seemed to borrow their hue from the heavens above. A soft bloom suffused her cheek, and her coral lips parted in prayer revealed her pearly teeth. The delicate contour of her finely rounded throat and bust were displayed by her posture, and one dimpled shoulder was visible through the wavy masses of bright hair that enveloped her figure, as though the light of the golden sunset lingered lovingly about her.

An infant, fairer if possible than the mother, with eyes of the same heavenly hue, lay by her side. He had drawn one tiny slipper from his foot, and delighted with his prize laughed in every feature and seemed crowing an accompaniment to her words. Startled by the sound of footsteps, the mother turned, and meeting the dark menacing gaze of Eleanor, snatched up the baby-boy, which clasped its little hands and looked up in her face, instinctively suiting the action of entreaty to the smile of confident affection. The elder boy before unnoticed advanced as if in doubt, whether to grieve or frown.

The deep earnest gaze of his hazel eyes and his soft brown hair, clearly indicated his Norman extraction, and when he passed his arm half-fearfully, half-protectingly around his mother's neck, and the eloquent blood mounted to his cheek Eleanor recognized the princely bearing of the Plantagenets.

"False woman," said she, darting forward and confronting the trembling mother with flashing eyes, "thou art the paramour of King Henry, and these your base-born progeny." To the paleness of terror succeeded the flush of indignation not unmingled with the crimson hue of shame, as the fair creature raised her head and repelled the accusation.

"Rosamond de Clifford is not King Henry's paramour. My lord is the Duke of Maine; and when he returns from the wars will acknowledge his babes before the nobles of the land."

"Aye, the Duke of Maine," retorted Eleanor, in scornful mockery, "and of Anjou, and of Normandy, and through his injured queen lord of the seven beautiful provinces of the south. Thy white face has won a marvellous conquest. The arch-dissimulator boasts many titles, but one that bars all thy claims. He is the *husband* of Eleanor of Aquitaine!"

"Becket! where is Becket, why comes not my friend and counsellor?" exclaimed Rosamond in the accents of despair, as a conviction of the truth flashed upon her mind.

"Dead," replied the infuriated woman, approaching nearer and speaking in a hoarse whisper. "Henry brooks no rival in his path, nor will Eleanor." The implied threat and fierce gestures warned Rosamond of her danger, and clasping her frightened children to her breast, she sank down at the feet of the queen in the utmost terror and abasement. "Heaven assoil thee of thy sin," said Eleanor, turning to depart, "at dawn we meet again."

CHAPTER 6

Oh! think what anxious moments pass between
The birth of plots, and their last fatal periods;
Oh! 'tis a dreadful interval of time,
Fill'd up with horror, and big with death.

The first conference of Henry with the legates proved unsatisfactory, but at the second, in the presence of the bishops, barons and people, with his hand on the gospels, he solemnly swore that he was innocent both in word and deed of the murder of Becket. Yet, as his passionate expression had been the occasion of the prelate's death, he promised to maintain two hundred knights for the defence of the Holy Land; to serve in person against the *infidels* three years, either in Palestine or Spain, and to restore the confiscated estates of Becket's friends. Pleased with the successful issue of this negotiation, Henry was preparing to return with joyful haste to England, when his peace was disturbed by quarrels originating in his own family. For some unaccountable reason his children seemed all armed against him. His son Henry demanded immediate possession of either England or Normandy, and on being refused appealed to his father-in-law Louis VII.

Before three days had elapsed, Richard and Geoffrey followed their brother, and soon after Henry learned to his dismay that Queen Eleanor had herself set off for the court of her former husband. Remembering the perilous vicinity in which he had left the queen, it at once occurred to him that she was the original instigator of the plot. By a skilful manoeuvre, he intercepted her flight, and sent her back to Winchester a prisoner. Immediately his undutiful sons, adding their mother's quarrel to their own grievances, bound themselves by oath to the King of France that they would never make peace with their father except by Louis's consent. The Duke of Flanders joined the league of the parricides, and the King of Scotland poured into the northern counties his strongest forces. Never was the crown of Henry in such danger.

While repelling the attacks of the insurgents in Normandy, he received a visit from the Bishop of Winchester, who entreated him to return once more to England, as his presence alone could save the kingdom. Henry at once set out. His countenance was gloomy and troubled, and his mind seemed deeply affected by the rebellion of his children, the perfidy of his barons and general combination of the neighbouring princes, and above all, by his fearful uncertainty with regard to the fate of those whom he had so long and so carefully guarded. To ease the torment of his mind, he secretly determined to make a pilgrimage to the tomb of the recently-canonized martyr St. Thomas à Becket. He landed at Southampton, and without waiting for rest or refreshment, rode all night towards Canterbury.

At the dawn of the morning, he descried the towers of Christ's Church. Dismounting from his horse, he exchanged the garb of the king for that of a penitent, and walked barefoot towards the city, so cruelly cutting his feet with the stones that every step was marked with blood. He entered the cathedral, descended to the crypt, knelt before the holy relics of his former friend, confessed his sins; and then resorting to the chapter-house, bared his shoulders, and submissively and gratefully received three stripes from the knotted cords which each priest, to the number of eighty, applied for his spiritual benefit. Bleeding and faint, he again returned to the crypt, and passed the night in weary vigils upon the cold stone floor. The following morning he attended mass, and then mounted his horse and rode to London, where the fasting, fatigue and anxiety he had undergone threw him into a fever.

Scarcely had he recovered, when he learned that his enemies had abandoned the idea of invading England and were concentrating their efforts upon his continental dominions, and that an army more numerous than any which Europe had seen since the expedition of the crusades, was encamped under the walls of Rouen. These circumstances made it necessary for him to embark again for France.

In two successive campaigns he foiled the attempts of his rebel sons and their foreign allies, and finally brought them to demand a general pacification. The three princes engaged to pay due obedience to their father, the King of the Scots agreed to hold his crown as a fief of England, and this made it necessary for all parties to proceed to York.

Peace being again restored, after a great variety of detentions and delays, Henry at last found himself at liberty to obey the promptings of his heart, and visit Woodstock. He endured with such patience as he could the enthusiastic greetings of the household, and at the imminent jeopardy of his secret, took his way through the pleasance. He was first alarmed by finding the concealed door in the wall wide open, and every step of his advance added to his apprehensions.

There were marks of a bloody struggle at the entrance to the tower, and everything within indicated that the occupants had been disturbed in the midst of their daily avocations. The rocking-horse of Prince William stood with the rein across his neck, as if the youthful rider had just dismounted, the pillow of the little Geoffrey still retained the impression of his cherub head; the thimble and scissors of Rosamond lay upon the table, but the embroidery was covered thick with dust, and rust had corroded the strings of the harp.

The scene by the Hermit's Well was yet more desolate. Withered herbage and leaves had stopped the welling fountain, and entirely choked the current of the stream. Rosamond's bower, once invested with every attraction, now neglected and deserted struck a chill upon his soul. Rank weeds had overrun the verdant seats, the eglantine struggled in vain with the ivy, whose long and pendulous branches waved and flapped in the night-breeze like the mourning hatchments above a tomb. A bevy of swallows took wing at his entrance, the timid rabbit fled at his intrusive step, and a green lizard glided from beneath the hand with which he supported his agitated frame against one of the columns. Rosamond was gone.

But by what means had she been conveyed from the retreat where she had so long dwelt content with his love, and happy in the caresses of her children? Was she a wanderer and an outcast, with a bleeding heart and a blighted name? Had she made her couch in the cold, dark grave? Had her indignant father returned from the Holy Land, and immured her in the dungeons of Clifford castle to hide her shame? Or had some other hand dared to blot out the life so dear to him?

The thought was madness. He ran, he flew to the palace. The old porter was summoned and closely questioned. He remembered the time of the queen's last visit, her anxiety to penetrate the wood and search the castle. The night before her departure three of her French servants suddenly disappeared, but as several horses were missing at the same time, and the queen had been employed in writing letters, it was supposed that they were couriers. There were lights seen, and cries heard in the wood. One of the grooms affirmed that the ghost of the youth who some years before was spirited away, appeared in the stable, and a boy belonging to a neighbouring peasant had never since been heard of. Though Henry traced this story through all the interpolations and additions that ignorance and credulity could give it, neither his utmost inquiries nor his subsequent researches could elicit any further fact.

Satisfied that nothing could be learned at Woodstock, the king hurried to Winchester. The passionate queen, amidst upbraidings and revilings, acknowledged that she had discovered the retreat of his mistress, and that, stung by jealousy, she had threatened to take her life by the poniard or poison; that to prevent the escape of her fair rival, she had stationed two of her Gascon servants, a guard at the tower-stair. But she declared that when she returned on the following morning to execute her fell purpose, she found the grass dripping with gore, and not far distant the dead bodies of her servants, and the corpse of another whom she had known in her early days as Sir Thomas, guarded by a wolf-dog just expiring from a sword-wound; and that, assisted by Peyrol, she had dragged the bodies into the thicket, and then vainly endeavoured to trace the fugitives. Notwithstanding all the threats that Henry employed to extort further confession, she persisted in affirming her ignorance of the fate of Rosamond.

Little crediting her asseverations, he increased the rigor of her confinement, and installed Alice, the affianced of Richard, with almost regal honours, in the state apartments. This sudden partiality of his father roused the jealousy of Richard, and he demanded the hand of his bride in terms not the most respectful nor conciliatory. Henry felt that the bond between his son and France was sufficiently strong, and ingeniously delayed the nuptials.

Then ensued another rebellion led by young Henry; but before the day fixed for battle arrived, anxiety and fatigue threw the prince into a fever, from which he never recovered. On his death-bed his soul became agitated with fear and remorse. He sent messengers to his father to implore forgiveness for his unfilial conduct, and ordered the priests to lay him on a bed of ashes, where having received the sacraments, he expired. The king was about the same period called upon to part, in a more hopeful manner, with his second daughter, Eleanor, who had been for some time betrothed to Alphonso, King of Castile. Henry's affection for his children in their early years, was of the most tender character; and Eleanor's fondness for him for some time subsequent to their marriage, partook of the passionate devotion of the south, but when her fickle attachment was assailed by the demon of jealousy, her love was changed to hate: and as Henry justly imagined, the rebellion of his sons was the consequence of her instructions.

His domestic afflictions aggravated the melancholy occasioned by the mysterious disappearance of Rosamond, and he lamented in bitterness of spirit that the tempting lure of wealth and dominion offered in the alliance of Eleanor, had bribed him from his boyish purpose of placing Rosamond on the throne of England. He cursed the ambition that had nurtured foes in his own household, and deplored the selfish passion that had remorselessly poured sorrow into the young life that ventured all upon his truth. The calm heroism of his early character was changed into petulant arrogance. He frequently spent whole days hunting in the forests, or riding alone in different parts of his dominions.

In the simple garb of a country knight, he had often sought admittance to the ancient seat of the Cliffords, and the nunnery of Godstowe, but without success. The sight of a crowd of people collected round a returned pilgrim at length suggested another mode of disguise. Procuring a palmer's weeds, he repaired to Herefordshire, and craved an alms from the servants, at Clifford castle. He was at once admitted, and the curious household gathered round the holy man to listen to his story.

It had been, he said, a long time since he had left the Holy Wars. He had been a wanderer in many lands, but his heart had led him to his native country, to seek for those whom he had known in his youth. He would fain see, once more, the good Lord de Clifford, for he had saved his life in Palestine. The servants replied that the Lord de Clifford had not been heard from for many a year. "Might he gain a moment's audience of the Lady de Clifford?" The lady died soon after her lord's departure. "Could he speak with Adam Henrid?" The good *seneschal* had been long dead.

His voice faltered as he inquired for Rosamond. An ominous silence was the only reply. "And Jaqueline, the lady's maid?" She, too, lay in her grave. He ran his eye along the group, and said with a look of embarrassment and pain, "There is none to welcome my return. It was not so in the good days when my lord and my lady rode forth to the chase with their gallant train, and the sound of feasting and wassail resounded in the castle hall. Remains there none of Lord Walter's kin to offer welcome or charity in our lady's name?" A proud boy stepped forth among the listeners, and with princely courtesy extended his hand.

143

"Come with me, holy father," said he, "it shall never be said, that a pilgrim went hungry and weary from the castle of the Cliffords." With a step that accorded better with his impatience than his assumed character, Henry followed the lad to an inner apartment, where a repast was soon spread before him. As soon as the servants had withdrawn he entered into conversation with his young host. "Thou art a De Clifford," said he, as though it were an undoubted fact. "What is thy name?"

"William," replied the youth; "and this clerk," pointing to a fair boy who sat reading in the deep embrasure of the window, "is my brother Geoffrey."

"And how long have you dwelt at the castle?"

"Some winters," replied the boy, after a moment's hesitation.

"Who brought you hither?"

"We came with Jaqueline, from our cottage in the wood."

"And where is your mother?" said Henry, making a desperate effort to speak with calmness.

"She went with Jaqueline so long ago, that Geoffrey does not remember her."

"And your father?" said Henry, with increased agitation.

"Jaqueline said our father was a king, and we must never leave the castle till he came for us."

"And why did Jaqueline leave the castle?"

"She went to the convent for confession; and there was where she died: but it is a long way."

The heart of the father yearned towards his sons, as he gazed from one to the other, and compared their features with the miniature that their infant charms had set in his memory, but with the sweet certainty that he had at last found the objects of his search, was born the thrilling hope that their mother yet lived. Then a struggling crowd of thoughts, emotions, and purposes rushed through his mind, and foremost among them all was the idea that Eleanor might be divorced, Rosamond's wrongs repaired, the diadem of England placed upon her brow, and his declining years solaced by the affection of these duteous sons who should take the places and titles of the rebel princes. Yet even in the midst of the tumult of his feelings his wonted self-control taught him not to risk the safety of his new-found joys by any premature discovery. Rising from the table with an air of solemnity, he pronounced his parting blessing in a tone of the deepest fervour, and hurriedly took his leave. Retaining his disguise, but occupied with thoughts that ill-became a palmer's brain, he bent his steps towards the nunnery of Godstowe.

Near the close of the second day he entered the confines of Oxfordshire, and found himself, little to his satisfaction, in the vicinity of a country fair, with its attendant junketing, masquerade, and feats of jugglery and legerdemain. To avoid the crowd, he determined to seek lodging in a booth that stood a little apart from the main encampment. The weary monarch had stretched himself to rest, when the sound of uproarious mirth disturbed his slumbers, and a Welsh balladsinger, whom he remembered to have seen in the service of Giraldus Cambrensis, the tutor of John, commenced in a voice of considerable power and pathos, the following song:—

When as King Henry ruled this land,
The second of that name,
Besides the queen, he dearly loved
A fair and comely dame;
Most peerless was her beauty found,
Her favour and her face;
A sweeter creature in this world
Did never prince embrace.

Her crisped locks like threads of gold
Appeared to each man's sight,
Her sparkling eyes like orient pearls
Did cast a heavenly light;
The blood within her crystal cheeks
Did such a colour drive,
As if the lily and the rose
For mastership did strive.

Yea, Rosamond, fair Rosamond,
Her name was called so,
To whom dame Eleanor our queen
Was known a deadly foe.
The king therefore for her defence
Against the furious queen,
At Woodstock builded such a bower,
The like was never seen.

Most curiously that bower was built
Of stone and timber strong,
One hundred and fifty doors

145

Did to this bower belong;
And they so cunningly contrived
With turnings round about,
That none but with a clew of thread
Could enter in or out.

And for his love and lady's sake
That was so fair and bright,
The keeping of this bower he gave
Unto a valiant knight.
But Fortune, that doth often frown
Where she before did smile,
The king's delight, the lady's joy
Full soon she did beguile.

For why, the king's ungracious son
Whom he did high advance,
Against his father raised wars
Within the realm of France.
But yet before our comely king
The English land forsook,
Of Rosamond, his lady fair,
His farewell thus he took.

"My Rosamond, my only Rose
That pleasest best mine eye,
The fairest flower in all the world
To feed my fantasy,
The flower of my affected heart,
Whose sweetness doth excel,
My royal Rose, a thousand times
I bid thee now farewell.

"For I must leave my fairest flower,
My sweetest Rose a space,
And cross the seas to famous France,
Proud rebels to abase.
But yet my Rose, be sure thou shalt
My coming shortly see,
And in my heart, when hence I am,
I'll bear my Rose with me."

When Rosamond, that lady bright,
Did hear the king say so,

146

The sorrow of her grieved heart
Her outward looks did show,
And from her clear and crystal eyes
Tears gushed out apace,
Which like the silver pearled dew
Ran down her comely face.

Her lips erst like the coral red,
Did wax both wan and pale,
And for the sorrow she conceived
Her vital spirits did fail.
And falling down all in a swoon,
Before King Henry's face,
Fell oft he in his princely arms
Her body did embrace.

And twenty times with watery eyes,
He kissed her tender cheek,
Until he had revived again
Her senses mild and meek.
"Why grieves my Rose, my sweetest Rose?"
The king did often say.
"Because," quoth she, "to bloody wars
My lord must pass away.

"But since your grace on foreign coasts,
Among your foes unkind,
Must go to hazard life and limb,
hy should I stay behind?
Nay, rather let me, like a page,
Your sword and target bear,
That on my breast the blows may light,
That should offend you there.

"Or let me in your royal tent
Prepare your bed at night,
And with sweet baths refresh your grace
At your return from fight.
So I your presence may enjoy,
No toil I will refuse;
But wanting you my life is death,
Nay, death I'd rather choose."

"Content thyself, my dearest love;

Thy rest at home shall be,
In England's sweet and pleasant soil;
For travel suits not thee.
Fair ladies brook not bloody wars;
Sweet peace, their pleasures breed
The nourisher of heart's content,
Which Fancy first did feed.

"My Rose shall rest in Woodstock's bower,
With music's sweet delight,
Whilst I among the piercing pikes
Against my foes do fight.
My Rose in robes of pearl and gold,
With diamonds richly dight,
Shall dance the galliards of my love,
While I my foes do smite.

"And you, Sir Thomas, whom I trust
To be my love's defence,
Be careful of my gallant Rose
When I am parted hence."
And therewithal he fetched a sigh,
As though his heart would break,
And Rosamond, for very grief,
Not one plain word could speak.

And at their parting well they might,
In heart be grieved sore,
After that day fair Rosamond
The king did see no more.
For when his grace had passed the seas,
And into France was gone,
Queen Eleanor with envious heart
To Woodstock came anon.

And forth she calls this trusty knight,
Who kept this curious bower,
Who with his clew of twined thread,
Came from this famous flower;
And when that they had wounded him,
The queen this thread did get,
And went where Lady Rosamond
Was like an angel set.

But when the queen, with steadfast eye,
Beheld her heavenly face,
She was amazed in her mind
At her exceeding grace.
"Cast off from thee these robes," she said,
"That rich and costly be;
And drink thou up this deadly draught,
Which I have brought to thee."
Then presently upon her knee,
Sweet Rosamond did fall;
And pardon of the queen she craved,
For her offences all.
"Take pity on my youthful years,"
Fair Rosamond did cry,
"And let me not with poison strong,
Enforced be to die.
"I will renounce my sinful life,
And in some cloister bide,
Or else be banished if you please,
To range the world so wide.
And for the fault which I have done,
Though I was forced thereto,
Preserve my life and punish me,
As you think good to do."
And with these words, her lily hands
She wrung full often there,
And down along her lovely face,
Proceeded many a tear.
But nothing could this furious queen
Therewith appeased be;
The cup of deadly poison strong,
As she sate on her knee,
She gave this comely dame to drink,
Who took it in her hand,
And from her bended knee arose,
And on her feet did stand,
And casting up her eyes to heaven,
She did for mercy call,
And drinking up the poison strong,

149

Her life she lost withal.

"Help! ho! Have done with your foolish madrigal," cried a stout yeoman, who had watched the terrible agony depicted upon the face of the king, during this rehearsal; "the holy palmer is well nigh suffocated with your folly."

"Give him a taste of one of the psalms of David," hiccoughed a little man from the opposite side of the booth, "the pious aye thrive upon the good book," and he laughed at his own profanity.

"A horn of good English beer will do him better," roared a Yorkshire man, pouring out a bumper of ale. "Build up the body, mon, and the soul will do weel eneugh."

"Gramercy!" cried the minstrel, going nearer and gazing upon his distorted features. "Some evil demon possesses him. 'Tis a terror to look upon his bloodshot eyes."

"An if the evil demon is in him 'twere best to cast him out," interposed the owner of the booth. Suiting the action to the word, he dragged the senseless king from the couch of fern leaves, to a more refreshing bed upon the dewy grass. The cool air at length revived the miserable monarch, and the very torture of returning recollection gave him strength to rise and pursue his course. On he sped through the night, insensible to fatigue and regardless of rest. As he struck into the bridle path where his eyes were dazzled by the bright vision that first led his feet to Godstowe, the faint sound of the convent bell fell upon his ear. He thought it the ringing of the *matin* chime; but approaching nearer, the solemn toll smote heavily upon his heart, for he recognized in it the knell of a parting soul. He quickened his steps, and by reason of his friar's gown, gained ready admittance to the convent.

The messenger that had been despatched for a priest to shrive the dying nun had not yet returned, and Henry's services were put in requisition to perform the holy office. Without giving him time for question or explanation, the frightened sisters hurried him through the long passages of the dormitory and introduced him into a cell, where stretched upon a pallet of straw, lay the pale and wasted form of Rosamond. The faint beams of morning struggling through the open casement, mingled with the sickening glare of waxen tapers, which according to the rites of the church, were placed at the head and foot of the bed. The couch was surrounded with objects intended to familiarize the mind with the idea of death, to fit the soul for its final departure. A coffin half filled with ashes stood near, whereon was placed the crown and robe, in which she had professed herself the bride of Christ, now ready to adorn her for her burial, and the necessary articles for administering extreme unction, were arranged upon a small table, above which hung a cross bearing an image of the dying Saviour. With a despairing glance at these terrible preparations, Henry approached the bed, and gazed upon the unconscious sufferer.

Unable to command his voice, he waved his hand and the attendant devotees retired from the room; the lady abbess whispering as she passed, "I fear our sister is too far gone to confess." Hastily throwing back his cowl, he bent over the sleeper, raised her head, clasped in his own the attenuated hand that had so often returned his fond pressure, and in the accents of love and despair, whispered her name. The dying one languidly lifted the snowy lids that veiled her lustrous eyes, and looked upon him, but in the vacant gaze was no recognition.

"My Rosamond!" cried Henry, passionately pressing a kiss upon her ashy lips. A thrill ran through her frame, her slight fingers quivered in his clasp, and the world of recollections that rushed back upon her brain, beamed from her dilating eyes. Her palsied tongue assayed to speak, but Henry caught only the low sound, "My children!"

"My children"—reiterated the monarch—he said no more—her breast heaved—her lips trembled with the last faint sigh, and a smile of ineffable joy rested on the features of the dead.

CHAPTER 7

Ingratitude! thou marble-hearted fiend,
More to be dreaded when thou showest thee in a child,
Than the sea-monster

The protracted imprisonment of Queen Eleanor infuriated her Provençal subjects. The southern court, deprived of its most brilliant gem, no longer attracted the gifted and the gay from all parts of Europe. The troubadours in effect hung their harps on the willows, and the faithful Peyrol, banished from the presence of his beloved mistress, attempted to console the weary hours of her captivity, by tender *Plaintes*, in which with touching simplicity he bewailed her misfortunes. Wrote he:

Daughter of Aquitaine, fair fruitful vine, thou hast been torn from thy country, and led into a strange land. Thy harp is changed into the voice of mourning, and thy songs into sounds of lamentation. Brought up in delicacy and abundance, thou enjoyedst a royal liberty, living in the bosom of wealth, delighting thyself with the sports of thy women, with their songs, to the sound of the lute and tabor; and now thou mournest, thou weepest, thou consumest thyself with sorrow. Return, poor prisoner—return to thy cities, if thou canst; and if thou canst not, weep and say, 'Alas! how long is my exile.' Weep, weep, and say, 'My tears are my bread both day and night.' Where are thy guards, thy royal escort?—where thy maiden train, thy counsellors of state? Thou criest, but no one hears thee! for the king of the north keeps thee shut up like a town that is besieged. Cry then—cease not to cry. Raise thy voice like a trumpet, that thy sons may hear it; for the day is approaching when thy sons shall deliver thee, and then shalt thou see again thy native land.

But the warlike chiefs of Guienne did not confine themselves to expressions of tenderness. Richard and Geoffrey, though often hostile to each other, were always ready to lead the barons of the south to battle, and for two years the Angevin subjects of Henry and the Aquitaine subjects of Eleanor, incited by her sons, gave battle in the cause of the captive queen, and from Rochelle to Bayonne the whole south of France was in a state of insurrection. The melancholy death of Geoffrey added to the afflictions of his already wretched mother. In a grand tournament at Paris he was thrown from his horse and trodden to death beneath the feet of the coursers. He was distinguished for his manly beauty and martial grace, and Eleanor had regarded him with an affection as intense as was the causeless hatred she bore to his wife Constance.

His infant son Arthur, for whom Eleanor's namesake had been set aside, inherited the dower of his mother both in possessions and enmity. Not long after the death of her favourite son Eleanor was called upon to part with her youngest daughter Joanna, who became the bride of William II. King of Sicily. Thus deprived of all affection, Eleanor dragged on a monotonous existence during Henry's protracted search for Rosamond.

The innocence of his queen being fully proved, the softened monarch began to regard her with more complacency: but the vindictive spirit of Eleanor, incensed by the indignities she had suffered, and enraged by being the victim of unjust suspicions, could not so easily repass the barriers that had been interposed between their affections, and though she accompanied her lord to Bordeaux, she set herself to widen the breach between him and Richard, and he soon found it necessary to remand her again to the seclusion of Winchester palace.

When Henry received absolution from the pope for the murder of Becket, he solemnly swore to visit the Holy Land in person, and the day had been fixed for his departure with Louis King of France. The death of that monarch prevented the expedition, and Henry had delayed it from time to time, though the patriarch of Jerusalem and the grand-master of the knights Hospitallers, had made the long and difficult journey to England, and in name of Queen Sibylla, had delivered to him as the successor of Fulk of Anjou, the royal banner and the keys of the Holy City and Sepulchre. Now impressed with a sense of the vanity of human hopes, and the fading grandeur of earthly distinction, he determined if possible, to divert his mind from the endless train of sad recollections, by plunging into the excitement of novel scenes and rekindling his wasting energies at the fane of Religion.

The eyes of all the European nations were at this time directed, with peculiar anxiety to the distresses of the Christians in Palestine. At the death of Baldwin III. the sceptre passed to the hands of his brother Almeric, who wasted his subjects and treasure in a fruitless war with the Vizier of Egypt. The crown from Almeric descended to Baldwin IV., his son by Agnes de Courteney, heiress to the lost principality of Edessa. Baldwin IV. was a leper; and finding that disease incapacitated him for performing the royal functions, he committed the government to his brother-in-law Guy de Lusignan, a French knight whom Henry had banished for murder. At the death of Baldwin his sister Sibylla and her husband Guy became King and Queen of Jerusalem, but the Count of Tripoli refused to do them homage.

At last he consented to proffer his allegiance to the queen, on condition that she should be divorced from Lusignan and choose a partner who should be able to protect the kingdom. Sibylla was a woman of great beauty, majestic person and commanding talents. She consented to the proposal of the Count of Tripoli, only requiring in return the oath of the barons that they would accept for sovereign whomsoever she should choose. The terms were settled, the divorce obtained, and the ceremony of her coronation took place. As soon as she was crowned, turning proudly to the rebel lords, she placed the diadem on the head of Lusignan, saluted him as her husband, bent the knee to him as king, and with a voice of authority, cried aloud, "*Those whom God has joined together let not man put asunder.*" The simple truth and affection of the queen, and the grandeur of the spectacle awed the assembly; and the astonished barons submitted without a murmur.

The famous Saladin, about the same time, began his career of conquest in the East. Tiberius, Acre, Jaffa, Cesarea and Berytus were the trophies of his victories. One hundred thousand people flying from the sword of the Turks crowded into Jerusalem, and the feeble garrison was not able to defend them. Saladin, unwilling to stain with human blood the place which even the Moslems held in reverence, offered the inhabitants peace on condition of the surrender of the city, and money and lands in Syria; but the Christians declared that they would not resign to the *infidels* the place where the Saviour had suffered and died. Indignant at the rejection of his offer, Saladin swore that he would enter the city sword in hand and retaliate upon the Franks the carnage they had made in the days of Godfrey de Boulogne. For fourteen days the battle raged around the walls with almost unexampled fury.

The Moslem fanatic fearlessly exposed his life, expecting that death would give him at once to drink of the waters of Paradise,—the Christian, hoping to exchange an earthly for a heavenly Jerusalem, poured out his blood in protecting the Holy Sepulchre. When it was found that the wall near the gate of St. Stephen was undermined, all farther efforts at defence were abandoned; the clergy prayed for a miraculous interposition of heaven, and the soldiers threw down their arms and crowded into the churches. Saladin again offered favourable conditions of peace. The miserable inhabitants spent four days in visiting the sacred places, weeping over and embracing the Holy Sepulchre, and then, sadly quitting the hallowed precincts, passed through the enemy's camp, and took their disconsolate way towards Tyre, the last stronghold of the Latins in Palestine.

Thus after the lapse of nearly a century, the Holy City that had cost Europe so much blood and treasure, once more became the property of the *infidel*. The great cross was taken down from the church of the Sepulchre and dragged through the mire of the street, the bells of the churches were melted, while the floors and walls of the mosque of Omar, purified with Damascene rose-water, were again consecrated to the worship of the false prophet. The melancholy tidings of this event occasioned the greatest sensation throughout the Christian world. The aged pontiff died of a broken heart. The husband of Joanna put on sackcloth and vowed to take the cross. Henry, Philip, the new King of France, the Earls of Flanders and Champagne, and a great number of knights and barons resolved to combine their forces for the redemption of the Holy City.

Immediately upon the death of Rosamond, Henry had made all the reparation in his power to her injured name, by acknowledging her children and placing them at Woodstock to be educated with his son John. The boys grew up to manhood, and developed a perfection of personal elegance and strength of character more befitting the sons of a king than any of the children of Eleanor. He promoted them to offices of honour and trust, and made Geoffrey chancellor of the realm.

Everything was now ready for the king's departure. In a general council held at Northampton it was enacted that every man who did not join the crusade should pay towards the expense of the expedition one tenth of all his goods; and the Jews were fined for the same purpose one fourth of their personal property. Henry wrote letters to the emperors of Germany, Hungary and Constantinople, for liberty to pass through their dominions, and receiving favourable answers, passed over to France to complete the arrangement with Philip, when the whole plan was defeated by that monarch's demanding that his sister Alice should be given to Richard, and that the English should swear fealty to the prince as heir-apparent to the throne. Henry refused; and his son Richard, in the public conference, kneeling at the feet of the French monarch, presented him his sword, saying, "To you, sir, I commit the protection of my rights, and to you I now do homage for my father's dominions in France."

The king, amazed at this new act of rebellion, retired precipitately from the council, and prepared with some of his former alacrity, to meet the combination against him. But Fortune, that had hitherto smiled upon him, seemed now to forsake him. He was defeated in every battle, driven from city to city, his health became impaired, his spirits failed, and at last he submitted to all the demands of his enemies, agreeing to pay twenty thousand marks to Philip, to permit his vassals to do homage to Richard, and above all, to give up Alice, the cause of so much domestic misery.

He stipulated only for a list of the disaffected barons who had joined the French king. The first name that caught his eye was that of John, the idolized child of his old age. He read no further, but throwing down the paper, fell into one of those violent paroxysms of rage to which of late years he had been so fearfully subject. He cursed the day of his birth, called down maledictions upon his unnatural children and their treacherous mother, flung himself upon the couch, tore the covers with his teeth, and clutched the hair from his head, and swooned away in a transport of anger and grief. A raging fever succeeded; but in his lucid moments he superintended an artist, who, at his command, painted upon canvass, the device of a young eaglet picking out the eyes of an eagle. Day after day the monarch lingered and suffered between paroxysms of pain and grief, and intervals of lassitude and insensibility; and when others forsook his bedside in weariness or alarm, Geoffrey, unconscious of drowsiness or fatigue, stood a patient watcher by his dying father.

The feeble monarch recognized in the voice of this son the tones which his ear had loved in youth, and obeyed its slightest bidding; and the only alleviation of his agony was found in gazing upon the face that revived the image of his lost Rosamond. Taking the signet-ring from his finger, he placed it upon the hand of Geoffrey; "Thou art my true and loyal son," said he. "The blessing of heaven rest upon thee for thy filial service to thy guilty sire. Commend me to thy brother William and his beautiful bride. As for the others, give them yon parable," pointing to the picture of the eagle, "with my everlasting curse." He leaned his head upon the breast of his son, and supported in his arms, expired.

★★★★★★

Eleanor survived her unhappy consort more than twenty years, and in that time made some amends for the follies and vices of her early life. The first step of her son Richard on his accession to the throne, was to release his mother from her confinement, and make her regent of the kingdom. She employed her freedom and her power in acts of mercy and beneficence, making a progress through the kingdom, and setting at liberty all persons confined for breach of the forest-laws, and other trivial offences, and recalling the outlawed to their homes and families. During the absence of Richard in the Holy Land, she administered the government with prudence and discretion, and after the accession of John, resumed the sceptre of her own dominions, slowly and painfully gathering, in the crimes and miseries of her children, the fruit of the evil counsels she had given them in their childhood. At the age of eighty she retired into the convent of Fontevraud, and three years after died of sorrow, when the peers of France branded her son John as the murderer of Arthur.

BERENGARIA OF NAVARRE.

Berengaria of Navarre

Chapter 1

What thing so good which not some harm may bring?

E'en to be happy is a dangerous thing?

"Sing no more, for thy song wearieth me," exclaimed the impatient daughter of Navarre, tossing upon her couch with the heavy restlessness of one who courts slumber when nature demands exercise. The Moorish maiden, accustomed to the petulance of the beautiful Berengaria, arose from her cushion and laying aside her lute, murmured despondingly, "The proverb saith truly, *'Tis ill-pleasing him who is ill-pleased with himself.*" Abandoning further attempts to soothe her mistress, the attendant retired to the extremity of the long apartment and gazed listlessly from the casement. "Art vexed that my ear loved not the sound of thy lute, peevish child?" inquired the youthful princess. "Read me a riddle, or tell me a marvellous tale of the *genii*, such as thou hast learned in thy southern land." With the air of one who performs an accustomed task while his thoughts are far away, the girl resumed her seat, and recited

A Tale of Araby

Once upon a time three *genii*, returning from their missions to mortals rested beside the well Zemzem. And as they sat recounting to each other the things that they had seen, behold they fell into conversation concerning the Eternal One (whose name be exalted), the destinies that reign over the fate of men, the characteristics of the world, and the misfortunes and calamities which happen unto all, both the righteous and the wicked. And one said to another, "Declare unto us now what is thine opinion, and what knowest thou concerning this thing. What is that, diffused in air, dissolved in water or concealed in earth, the subtle essence of which, being bestowed upon one of human mould, shall bring him nearest to the throne of Allah, (blessed be his name), and give him right to eat of the tree that standeth in

158

the seventh heaven by the garden of the Eternal Abode?" And the first said, "It is Beauty," and the second, "It is Love," and the third, "It is Happiness." And there arose a contention among them; and when they found that neither could convince the others, they agreed to depart each on his way, to search the elements of all things for that concordial mixture with which he would nourish a human soul into immortality. So they went their way. And after the lapse of a cycle of years, they returned again and sat by the well Zemzem. And each bore in his hand a phial purer than crystal, sealed with the seal of Solomon the wise, the magnificent.

Then spake the first, saying, "Earth hath no form of beauty from the flash of the diamond hidden in its deepest caves, through all the brilliant variety of gems and sands of gold; no delicate pencilling from the first faint tinge upon the rose-bud's cheek to the gorgeous dyes of the flowers and fruits that deck the vale of Cashmere; water hath no shade of colouring from the sea-green lining of its coral caves, to the splendid iridescence of its pearly shells; air hath no tint of the virgin stars, no ray of parted light; vapour beareth no beauty in its morning clouds and rainbow hues, from which I have not ravished the subtlest source. Whatever form of Beauty can become apparent to the sense, either as breath of fragrance, sweetness of sound, or grace of motion, sublimated to its purest element, lieth here enclosed for the endowment of whomsoever we shall choose." And he held up the phial, and lo! it contained a liquid having a faint colouring of the rose.

Then spake the second and said, "The Almighty (blessed be he) hath given unto me that mysterious power by which I read the thoughts and purposes of men, even as the Holy Prophet (on whom be benedictions) was wont to read the *Book of Life*.

"From the heart of the child that turneth ever to watch the movements of its mother, from the heart of the servant that seeketh the favour of her mistress, from the heart of the sister that exults with pride in the glory of her brother, from the heart of the maiden that beateth bashfully and tenderly at the sound of the footsteps of her lover, from the heart of the bridegroom that yearneth with strong desire towards his bride, from the heart of the father that expands in the fullness of joy at the sight of his first-born, from the heart of the mother that watcheth ever the steps of her child, whether he sporteth in innocence by her side or wandereth with vice in foreign parts; I have gathered the sweetest and purest and truest thought of Love. Its impalpable essence lies hidden in this phial," and he placed it before

159

them. And lo! it seemed filled with a vapor which flushed in their gaze with the hue of the dawn.

Then spake the third and said, "It is not permitted unto me the servant of Ifraz the Unknown, to declare unto you in what outward manifestations of human hope or desire, in what inward workings of thought and feeling, I have detected and imprisoned the elusive spirit of Happiness," and he held up his phial before them. And with one voice they exclaimed, "It is empty." And they laughed him to scorn.

Then spake he in anger and said, "Truly the fool proceedeth upon probability, and the wise man requireth proof." And they replied, "Go to, now, we will abide the proof."

And forthwith they took their way to the land of Suristan. And as they passed by the well of Israel, Ben Izak (on whom be peace), they saw a maiden bearing a pitcher of water. And the first said, "Behold, now, immortality is given unto man by the Almighty the Ordainer of fate and destiny (whose name be exalted), but unto woman it is not given except as her *beauty* shall delight the heart of man." But the second said, "Except as *love* gives her a seat by the Well of Life;" and the third, "Except as *happiness* translates her to Paradise." Then said the first, "Let us contend no more, but let us take this damsel and bestow upon her, each our separate gift, and she shall be a sign and a testimony concerning these things." And thus they agreed together.

And when the maiden retired to her couch, and the angel of sleep had laid his finger upon her eyelids, the first *genii* calling upon the name of God the All-perfect (blessed be he) broke the seal of his phial, and poured a portion of the liquid upon her lips. And the three *genii* watched her slumbers till the dawn; and thus they did evening by evening. And they beheld her form developing in loveliness, tall and straight as the palm, but lithe and supple as the bending branch of the oriental willow. Her smoothly rounded arms gleamed like polished ivory beneath the folds of her transparent *izar*, and the tips of her rosy fingers were touched with the lustre of henna. Her lips had the hue of the coral when it is wet with the spray of the sea, her teeth were as strings of pearl, and the melting fullness of her cheek was suffused with the soft bloom of the peach.

In her eyes was the light of the stars, and her eyelids were adorned with *kohl*. Her hair was glossy and black as the plumage of the raven, and when she covered it with her veil, her countenance beamed from it comely as the full moon that walketh in the darkness of the night. Her speech was as the murmur of the waterfall and the clear tones of the nightingales of the Jordan. She was a wonder unto herself and unto her neighbours. Her step had the lightness of the gazelle and the grace of the swan; and when she went forth abroad, the eye that beheld her beauty exclaimed, "Glory be to him who created her, perfected her, and completed her." But the *genii* beheld with sorrow and mortification that she became vain, and that foolish thoughts sprang up in her heart; so that it was said of her, "Hath God the High, the Great, put an evil spirit in the perfection of beauty?" Then said the second *genii*, "Ye shall see what the elixir of *love* shall do."

And he entered into her chamber, and he broke the mystic seal which was the seal of Solomon Ben David (on both of whom be peace), and a sweet odour was diffused through the apartment. And the lips of the sleeper moved as with a pleasant smile, and there beamed upon her countenance the nameless charm with which the *houris* fill with delight the dwellers in the Garden of Eternity. And it came to pass that all who looked upon her loved her and said, "There is none among the created like her in excellence of beauty, or in charms of disposition. Extolled be the perfection of the Creator of mankind." And they strove one with another which should possess the inestimable treasure. And contention and strife arose daily among them; and her heart inclined unto all, and she feared to unite herself with one, lest grievous wars should follow.

Therefore her soul was filled with grief, and she ceased not to weep by day and by night, and the tears were on her cheeks. Then said the third *genii*, "Behold sorrow is of earth, and the beauty and love ye have bestowed have gathered with them the noxious principles inwoven in the basis of human things. Ye shall behold the power of happiness." Then he took the colourless phial, and he broke the seal thereof, calling upon the name of Ifraz the Unknown, and lo, hour after hour the invisible, impalpable elixir seemed to permeate her being, and the light of her eye was tempered to a holy ray, the colour blanched on her cheeks, and the vivacity of love gave place to the serenity of content. And as she walked forth the voluptuous and the wise said, "Behold she is too pure for earth, the Terminator of delights and Separator of companions will soon call for her. Extolled be the perfections of the Eternal in whose power it lieth to annul and to confirm."

And when the two *genii* saw that Beauty and Love availed not, they were filled with envy, and they seized the damsel and conveyed her away to the cave of enchantment. And the third *genii* being transported with grief and disappointment, broke the phial, and that which remained of the elixir of Happiness returned to its primeval source, and entered again into the combinations of human things. But the seal being broken it became known to mortals that the elixir of Life existed in the elements, and hence it is, that those who are skilled in the mysteries of nature have searched its grand Arcanum with the powerful agencies of alchemy, and tortured the *genii* with spells and incantations to wring from them the mighty secret.

Berengaria had listened to the story with unwonted interest, and at its close started up from her couch and eagerly inquired, "What has been the result? Have they discovered the long-sought principle? I have heard wondrous tales concerning these alchemists. Men say they deal in the black art; but were there one in Navarre, I would brave the imputation of sorcery to question him concerning the elixir of beauty."

"A Moorish physician dwells in the suburbs of Pampeluna," replied Elsiebede, measuring her sentences with timid hesitation, "whom I have often seen in the byways, gathering herbs, it is said he readeth the fates of mortals in the stars."

"Let us go to him," exclaimed the princess, "bring me my *pelisson* and veil."

The girl obeyed with a trembling alacrity, that to a less occupied observer, would have betrayed that the expedition was the unexpected accomplishment of a long-cherished desire.

"This way," said Elsiebede, drawing her mistress from the public street, now beginning to be thronged with labourers returning from their toil, "the alchemist brooks not impertinent intrusion, and we must beware that no officious attendant, nor curious retainer find the place of his abode." Silently and swiftly the two maidens threaded a narrow alley, leading through an unfrequented part of the town, turning and winding among buildings more and more remote from each other, till it terminated on a grassy heath, surrounding a dilapidated mansion. The sun had already set, and Berengaria, never too courageous, began to shudder at the loneliness of the place.

With instinctive fear, she clung tremblingly to the arm of her resolute dependent, whispering, "Whither dost thou lead me? There is here no sign of human life. Let us return." But the spirited slave bent the weak will of the mistress to her purpose; and with alternate assurances of safety and incitements to curiosity, led the way to the rear of the ruined pile, where descending a stone stair, she gave three raps upon a low door. The grating of rusty bolts was heard, the door was cautiously opened, and Berengaria felt herself suddenly drawn within the portal. A glare of dazzling light blinded and bewildered her, and a stifling vapour added to her former terror, almost stupefied her senses.

The voice of Elsiebede somewhat reassured her, and as her eyes became accustomed to the light, she took a survey of the scene before her. The apartment seemed to have been originally the kitchen of the castle, one end being occupied by a wide, large chimney, now built up except in the centre, where a furnace, covered with crucibles, glowed with the most intense heat. A white screen with a small dark screen before it, nearly concealed one side, of the apartment, while on the other side from three serpent-formed tubes connected through the wall with retorts, gleamed tongues of coloured flame. Various gallipots, alembics, horologues, diagrams, and dusty manuscripts were deposited upon shelves in angles of the wall.

The principal occupant was a man of a lean, haggard figure, bowed less by age than by toil and privation. A few black, uncombed locks escaping from the folds of a turban, once white, now begrimed with smoke and dust, straggled over a swarthy forehead, marked with lines caused by intense thought, and abortive speculations. He was dressed in Moorish garments, the sleeves tucked above the elbows, revealing his emaciated arms, while his talon-like fingers grasped an immense triangular crystal, through which he was casting refractions upon the screen. His deep, cavernous eyes seemed to gleam with the fires of insanity, yet he spoke in a tone of deep abstraction, though with something like the voice of affection. "Disturb me not, my daughter, but stand aside till I have completed my experiment."

The maidens remained silently by the door, and Berengaria had leisure to note the motions of a dwarf African, who sat diligently blowing the bellows of the furnace, rolling his eyes, and saluting the ladies with smiles which served at once to exhibit his white teeth and his satisfaction at the interruption.

Notwithstanding her fears at finding herself in so strange a situation, the curiosity of Berengaria was so excited by the novelty of the scene, that she waited patiently while the philosopher experimented first with one light and then with another, till apparently becoming dissatisfied with the result, he attempted to change the position of the tubes. Scarce was his purpose accomplished, when a deafening explosion rent the air, followed by sounds as of the falling of the ruin overhead. Profound darkness ensued, and the groans of the wounded alchemist mingled with the demoniac laughter of the African, and the echo of her own shrieks increased the terror of the princess almost to agony. Elsiebede alone retained any share of self-possession. "A light, a light, Salaman," exclaimed she.

Instantly a line of blue flame crept along the wall, and a tiny torch in the hand of the dwarf mysteriously ignited, revealed again his malevolent countenance, and threw his misshapen and magnified image in full relief upon the screen. An odour of brimstone that seemed to accompany the apparition, did not serve to allay Berengaria's apprehensions. Elsiebede for once forgot her mistress. Hastily snatching the torch from the negro, she lighted a lamp and raising her father from the stone floor, began to examine his wounds. The blood was oozing from a contusion upon the back of his head, one side of his face was dreadfully burned, and his right hand lay utterly powerless. Giving hurried directions in Moorish to the grinning Ethiope, Elsiebede with his assistance placed her father upon a couch behind the screen, and bathed the painful wounds with a balmy liquid from one of the dusty phials, accompanying her soothing appliances with the soft and gentle expressions of affection.

Their language was foreign to the ear of Berengaria, but she discovered by the tones of the father, and the tears of the daughter, that he was chiding her as the cause of his misfortune. At length overcome by his upbraiding, Elsiebede drew from her bosom a silken purse, and taking thence a jewel kissed it fervently, and like one resigning her last treasure at the call of duty, put it into his extended hand. The black meanwhile had prepared a cordial, which he intimated would soon give her father rest. The alchemist eagerly swallowed the draught, and soon sank into a heavy sleep.

Berengaria, whose impatience had scarcely brooked the delay necessary for this happy consummation, hurried the reluctant Elsiebede away. "I knew not, Elsie," said she, when they were at a safe distance from the ruin, "that thy father dwelt in Pampeluna. I thought thou wert an orphan, when my father moved by thy beauty and distress purchased thee of the rude Castilian. Tell me thine history."

"My father," replied Elsiebede, "was when young the physician of the Moorish prince, and occupied himself in separating the hidden virtues of nature from the impurities with which they are combined. When walking abroad to gather plants for the prosecution of his inquiries, he met every day a young flower girl, carrying her fragrant wares to the palace of the Alhambra. Attracted by her beauty, he purchased her flowers, and interested himself in her history. He learned that she belonged to a band of Saracens or Gyptianos, that had recently settled in Grenada. He loved her and she became his wife.

"I was their only child. My youth was spent in listening to the wondrous tales of the East, with which my mother delighted me, or in acquiring the elements of science with my father. The sudden illness and death of my mother destroyed all my happiness. My father betook himself again to the most abstruse studies, spent whole nights in watching the stars, practised incantations to the spirits of the air, and pondering continually upon the mystery of death, commenced the search for that mighty principle which is said to prolong human existence.

"Many wonderful secrets of nature were in this process revealed to his sight; but he became so sad and gloomy, and his eyes beamed on me with such an unwonted fire, that I feared lest grief should dethrone the angel of reason. To divert his mind, I began to lead him forth in his accustomed walks. One day when we had lingered rather later than usual beyond the walls of Grenada, a band of armed Castilians fell upon us, and carried us away captives. The noble Sancho found me singing songs for my cruel master, and redeemed me from my fate."

"And what became of thy father?" inquired Berengaria. "He was enabled by some of his medicines to heal a long-established malady of his captor, and thus obtained his freedom: since which, until within a few months, he has wandered through Spain in search of his lost child."

"And wherefore didst thou commit to a dying man the precious jewel which I saw in thy hand?"

The tears of Elsiebede began to fall fast, and with a choking voice she replied, "Question me not, I entreat thee. Oh, my mistress, concerning the ring, at another time I will tell thee all." Touched with the instinctive reverence that nature always pays to genuine sorrow, the princess forbore further inquiries, and the two maidens completed their walk in silence.

The terror that Berengaria had suffered took away all desire to prosecute her inquiries with the alchemist, but with unusual consideration, on the following day, she dismissed Elsiebede at an early hour, giving her permission to pass the night with her father. The poor girl returned in the morning overwhelmed with grief. The alchemist was dead. From her self-reproaches and lamentations Berengaria learned,

165

that in his scientific researches he had consumed all his property, and melted every valuable belonging to his daughter, except her mother's ring. This gem she had steadily refused to give him, both on account of its being a memento and a charm, and the failure of his experiment with its fatal results he had in his dying hour attributed to the lack of the potency of the precious gem.

Stung with remorse, Elsiebede declared that if the ring could not save her father's life, it should at least procure him a grave, and telling her mistress that she could never again look upon the jewel without a shudder, begged her to accept it, and to assist her in burying him according to the rites of the Mohammedan religion. In catholic Navarre this was next to an impossibility; but through the generosity of the princess, and the ingenuity of Salaman, the corpse was secretly conveyed to the Moorish cemetery in Grenada.

CHAPTER 2

O, such a day
So fought, so followed, and so fairly won,
Came not till now, to dignify the times.

It was a gala-day in Navarre. Sancho the Strong, the gallant brother of Berengaria, had proclaimed a tournament in compliment to his friend Richard Plantagenet, Count of Poitou. In the domestic wars which had vexed the south of France since the marriage of Eleanor of Aquitaine with Henry of Anjou, these valiant youths had fought side by side, and from a friendship cemented by intimacy as well as similarity of tastes and pursuits, had become *fratres jurati*, or sworn brothers, according to the customs of the age. Both were celebrated for their knightly accomplishments and their skill in judging of Provençal poetry, and each had proved the prowess of the other in chivalric encounter, and provoked the genius of his friend in the refined and elegant contests of minstrelsy and song. The brave Sancho had arranged the lists, giving to his friend the first place as knight challenger, reserving the second for himself, and bestowing the third upon their brother in arms, the young Count of Champagne.

The gay pavilions were set, a splendid concourse assembled, and Berengaria, proclaimed Queen of Beauty and Love, had assumed her regal state attended by all the beauties of Navarre, when to the infinite disappointment and mortification of the prince, Count Raimond of Toulouse arrived to say, that Richard, having received letters from his mother, had found it necessary to depart suddenly for England; but that the festivities of the day might not be marred by his absence, he entreated that the bearer of the message, Count Raimond, might occupy his pavilion, bestride his war-steed, and do his devoir in the lists. With a courtesy that ill-concealed his chagrin the noble Sancho accepted the substitute, and conducting him to the tent glittering with green and gold, consigned him to the care of the esquires; while himself went to acquaint his sister with the mortifying fact that the spectacle, for which they had prepared with such enthusiastic anticipations, was yet to want the crowning grace expected from the presence of that flower of knighthood, Richard Plantagenet.

To conceal from the spectators the knowledge of this untoward event, their father, Sancho the Wise, who held the post of honour as judge of the combat, decided that Count Raimond of Toulouse should assume the armourial bearings of Richard, and personate him in the lists. These preliminaries being satisfactorily arranged, the heralds rode forth and proclaimed the laws of the tournament, and the games proceeded. The Count of Champagne and the royal Sancho, better practised in the exercises of the lance than the Spanish cavaliers who opposed them, won applause from all beholders; but the crowd seemed to take especial delight in the prowess of Count Raimond, shouting at every gallant thrust, and every feat of horsemanship, "A Richard, a Richard! A Plantagenet!"

Notwithstanding the unfavourable auspices under which the tournament commenced, the sports of the day were as gay and animated as the most sanguine could have hoped. The three challengers had overborne all opponents. With a heart fluttering with pride and pleasure, the young Blanche of Navarre had seen her sister confer a golden coronet upon the Count of Champagne, and Sancho had also received from Berengaria a chaplet in honour of his knightly achievements. But the first in honour as in place, was the warrior who had personated Richard. When, however, he laid aside his visor, to receive the well-won laurel as leader of the victors, the multitude discovered that the hero whom they had greeted with such enthusiastic applause was Count Raimond of Toulouse, and new bursts of acclamations rent the air, while the marshals, and squires, and heralds, forgetting for a moment their duties, gathered round the throne of Love and Beauty to interchange congratulations with the gratified count.

In the general excitement no one had noticed the entrance of a *knight adventurous*, one of those wandering cavaliers who, to perfect themselves in feats of arms, travelled from province to province, challenging the skill of all comers in chivalrous combat. The appearance of this knight-errant was such as attracted all eyes. He was mounted on a bay horse of spirit and mettle that hardly yielded to the strong rein; his helmet was surmounted with a crest of the figure of a red hound, while his erect form shielded in brown armour, and the firmness with which he maintained his seat gave him the appearance of a bronze statue, borne along in the procession. Disregarding the indications that the fortunes of the day were already decided, the stranger knight rode directly to the pavilion emblazoned with the arms of Richard, and struck his spear with such force upon the shield, as to summon at once the attendants to duty.

"Whom have we here?" exclaimed Sancho, with a hearty laugh. "By our Lady, Count Raimond, this day's sun shall not set till the heathen hound on the crest of yon crusading knight hath bit the dust. Pardieu, I almost envy thee thy good fortune to tilt against so fair a foe." The interest which this newcomer gave to the flagging sports was evinced by the eager inquiries and hurried whispers that went round among the spectators. A breathless silence ensued, as Count Raimond couched his lance and started forward to meet his strange challenger. "A Raimond! A Raimond!" cried the crowd, as the two combatants dashed upon each other.

"Long life to the Red Knight," "Success to the Crusaders," was echoed by the fickle multitude, with increased satisfaction, as the hero of Toulouse, overthrown by the violence of the shock, struggled beneath his fallen charger, while the stranger applying rein and spur, caused his gallant steed at one bound, to leap over the prostrate horse and rider, then dexterously compelling the animal to caracole gracefully in front of the queen's galley, and lowering his lance, the victorious knight courteously bowed as if laying his honours at the feet of Love and Beauty. The prizes for the day were already bestowed; but the enthusiastic Berengaria found it impossible to let such prowess go unrewarded. Hastily untying her scarf, she fastened it to the end of his spear, and the Crusader, with the armorial bearings of Navarre streaming from his lance, rode slowly and proudly from the lists.

The squires meanwhile had extricated the vanquished Raimond from his perilous position, and conducted him to his tent, where his bruises were found to require the skill of the leech. All were busy with conjectures concerning the unknown, many sage surmises very wide of the truth were hazarded by those best acquainted with heraldic devices, and arguments were rapidly increasing to animosities, when the slight tinkling of a bell again drew the attention of the concourse.

"A champion! A champion," exclaimed they again as a second knight, strong and broad-shouldered, sheathed in shining black armour, entered the arena. Glimpses of a ruddy complexion and sparkling eyes, were visible through the jetty bars of his visor, and a raven with smooth and glossy plumage, its beak open, and a bell suspended from its neck, was perched upon his helmet. His coal-black steed was a war-horse of powerful make, deep-chested and of great strength of limb; his red nostrils distended by his fiery impatience, glowed like the coals of a furnace, while the gauntleted hand that with matchless skill controlled his speed, looked as though it might have belonged to a giant of the olden time.

The impetuosity of the black knight left the spectators not long in doubt of his purpose. Count Henry of Champagne was summoned to reassume his armour and make good his claim to his recently won laurels. "Pray heaven thine eye and hand falter not, Count Henry," exclaimed Sancho, as he personally inspected the armour of his friend, and cautioned the squires to see that each ring and buckle was securely fastened. "The issue of this combat should depend upon thine own right arm, not upon a weak spring or careless squire."

The courtesy of the black knight seemed proportioned to his strength and skill. Reining his horse to the left, he gave the count the full advantage of the wind and sun, and instead of meeting him in full career, eluded the shock, parried his thrusts with the most graceful ease, and rode around him like a practised knight conducting the exercises of the tilt-yard in such a manner, as to develop and display the prowess of an ambitious squire; and when at last Count Henry lost his saddle, it was rather the effect of his own rashness, than from any apparent purpose of his antagonist; for exasperated to the last degree at being thus toyed with, he retreated to the extremity of the lists, put his horse upon its full speed and dashed upon his opponent.

The black knight perceiving the intent of this manoeuvre, brought his well-trained steed at once into an attitude of perfect repose, and sitting immovable as an iron pillar, received the full shock upon his impenetrable shield. The horse of the count recoiling from the effect of the terrible collision, sank upon his haunches, and the girth breaking, the rider rolled in the dust. Something like a smothered laugh broke from beneath the bars of the stranger's visor, as he rode round his vanquished foe, and extended his hand as though inviting him to rise. But his demeanour was grave and dignified, when he presented himself before the admiring Berengaria, who in default of a better chaplet stripped her tiny hand of its snowy covering, and bestowed the embroidered glove as the guerdon of his skill.

"Part we so soon, sir knight?" said Sancho, reining his steed, so as to keep pace with that of his unexpected guest. "I would fain set lance in rest against so fair a foe." Without deigning a reply, the knight put spurs to his horse, and leaping the barriers disappeared in the wood. Rejoining his two friends in the pavilion who were condoling with each other over their inglorious defeat, Sancho burst into a stream of invective. "Ungrateful cravens," cried he, "to repine at heaven's grace. I would have given the brightest jewel in the crown of Navarre, for leave to set lance in rest against either of yon doughty knights."

"Thou shouldst have been very welcome," exclaimed Raimond, laying his hand upon his wounded limb. "Our Lady grant henceforth that dame Fortune send all such favours to thee," and he laughed in spite of his discomfiture. A startling blast from the wood interrupted the colloquy, and Count Raimond petulantly exclaimed, "Methinks the foul fiends have congregated in the forest! That hath the sound of the last trumpet."

"Aye, verily," replied Count Henry, reconnoitring from the door of the pavilion, "and yonder comes Death on the pale horse. Prince Sancho, thine hour has come, prepare to meet thy final overthrow." There seemed a terrible significance in the words, for upon a snowy charger, whose mane and tail nearly swept the ground, just entering the lists, was seen a knight, dressed in a suit of armour of such shining brilliancy as almost to dazzle the eyes of the beholders. His crest was a white dove with its wings spread, and conspicuous upon his right shoulder appeared a blood-red cross. He carried neither lance nor spear, but an immense battle-axe hung at his saddle-bow.

"By my troth," said Sancho, "be he the angel of death himself, I will dispute his empire, even though he bring twelve legions of his mysterious retainers to back him. It shall not be said that the chivalry of Spain, aye, and of France to boot," casting a glance at his crest-fallen friends, "are but trophies of the prowess of these unknown demigods."

"Heaven grant thou mayest make good thy boast, for truly these demi-gods wield no mortal weapons," said Count Raimond, with a bitter smile, as the prince anticipating a challenge rode forth to meet the white champion.

Unpractised in the use of the mace, Sancho, whose ire was completely roused at seeing the honours of the day borne off by strangers, disregarded the laws of the tournament (which required the challenger to use the same weapons as his adversary), and seizing his spear, attacked his opponent with a fierce energy, which showed that he fought for deadly combat, and not for trial of skill in knightly courtesy. The brilliant figure, at the first rush, bowed his head, till the plumage of the dove mingled with the flowing mane of his courser, and suffered the animal to sheer to the right, thus compelling the prince, in his onward career, to make a similar involuntary obeisance as the result of his ineffectual thrust.

Completing the *demivolte*, the two champions again returned to the onset; and now the mace of the white knight describing shining circles round his head, received upon its edge the spear of the prince, clave the tough oak wood asunder, and sent the spear-head whirling through the air almost to the feet of the spectators. A second, a third, and a fourth spear met with the same fate. The welkin rang with the applause of the beholders. "Bravo, sir white knight!" "Glory to the Red Cross!" "Honour to the crusader!" "Death to the Paynim," accompanied the flourish of trumpets and the shouts of heralds, which, together with the flutter of pennons and the waving of signals from the galleries of the ladies, showed the exciting interest of the scene.

At length the dove-crested warrior, by a skilful manoeuvre, brought himself into such proximity as to be able with one blow to strike the helmet from the head of his antagonist; at the same moment, however, he extended his hand and prevented the unbonneted prince from falling prone beneath the feet of his horse. The gallant Sancho thus compelled to yield, with knightly grace accompanied his vanquisher to Berengaria's throne.

"Thy best guerdon, my sister, for thy brother's Conqueror," said he. "Beside the arm of Richard Plantagenet, I thought there was not another in Christendom that could break the bars of my visor and leave my skull unscathed. Why dost thou hesitate?" exclaimed he, observing her embarrassment. "The daughter of Sancho the Wise is not wont to be tardy when called upon to honour the brave. Has the same blow that still keeps the blood dancing in the brain of thy brother, paralyzed thy hand?"

"Nay," said Berengaria, while a brilliant blush suffused her cheeks, "but I would fain see the countenance of the brave knight, who carries off the honours of the field from such a competitor," and drawing

171

the ring of Elsiebede from her finger, she bestowed it upon the victor. Rising from his knees, the knight inclined courteously to the squires, who with a celerity lent by curiosity, unlaced his casque and unfastened his gorget, revealing the face of Richard Plantagenet, beaming fair and ruddy from the bright yellow curls that clustered round it, and eyes that sparkled in the full appreciation of the surprise and merriment that his unexpected apparition occasioned.

"*Mon cher frère*," exclaimed Sancho, grasping his hand, "I am conquered by Richard, then am I victor. Give me joy, knights, ladies, and squires."

The heralds taking up the word, sounded the tidings through the field, while the spectators shouted, "A Richard! a Richard! Long live the gallant Plantagenet!" The Counts of Toulouse and Champagne, assisted by their attendants, hastened to the scene, and discovering the scarf and glove of Berengaria resting beneath the loosened hauberk, recognized each his Conqueror, and found in that circumstance a greater balm for their wounded pride, than all their bruises had experienced from the mollifying appliances of leechcraft. The knights challengers thus all vanquished by the single arm of Richard, left the field with the highest sense of satisfaction, and the ready wit of their champion, pointed the sallies and directed the mirth of the banquet, which followed, and continued long into the night.

CHAPTER 3

Beshrew your eyes,
They have o'erlooked me, and divided me;
One half of me is yours, the other half yours,
And so all yours.

In the general excitement attendant upon the discovery of Richard and the breaking up of the tournament, Berengaria had remarked the agitation of Elsiebede, and seized an early opportunity to learn the cause.

"Where hast thou known Count Richard?" said she in a tone of feigned indifference.

"I have never seen him till today," replied the attendant.

"But thou didst start and turn pale when the White Knight disclosed the features of Plantagenet?"

"Aye, because I saw my lady bring a curse upon his head."

"A curse upon him? How meanest thou, silly child?" replied the princess, growing pale in her turn.

172

"Pardon, my dear mistress," continued Elsiebede, falling upon her knees, "I should have told you, the ring bestowed upon a knight, is a fatal gift."

"And why fatal?" inquired Berengaria, somewhat relieved that she had no greater cause for disquiet.

"I know not why. The jewel of the ring has been in the possession of my mother's tribe for many generations, and whenever man has called it his own, sorrow and distress have followed, till this tradition has become a proverb.

'Twill thwart his wish, and break his troth,
Betray him to his direst foe,
And drown him in the sea.

"Thou art too superstitious," said Berengaria, as her attendant recited the malediction, with an appearance of the most profound sense of its reality; "but to please thee, foolish child, I will regain the toy." Berengaria secretly determined to lose no time in relieving Richard from his dangerous possession, and accordingly lost no occasion for conversing with the prince; but though he treated her with the most distinguished courtesy, the term of his visit to Navarre expired before their acquaintance had ripened into an intimacy that would warrant her venturing upon the delicate task of reclaiming her gift. Months elapsed before Berengaria again saw the knight who had made such an impression upon her youthful imagination, and she began to fear that the ring had, in reality, conducted him to his predestined sepulchre in the sea, when her brother Sancho returning from a tour in France, brought intelligence of the most gratifying character.

"Rememberest thou, my sister," said he, "the valiant Plantagenet, who so gallantly bore off the honours of our tournament?"

"Aye, verily," replied the princess, casting down her eyes.

"He has been wandering through Germany, challenging all true knights to chivalrous combat, and has met with many strange adventures," continued Sancho.

"Recount them," said Berengaria, "I listen with attention."

"Thou who didst reward his valour, as red, and black, and white knight in one day, canst well appreciate his partiality for disguises," resumed her brother:"and it seems, that during this expedition, one had nearly cost him his life. Passing through the dominions of the King of Almaine, he assumed the dress of a palmer, but being discovered, was cast into prison. Ardour, the son of the king, learning that a knight of remarkable strength and prowess was confined in a dungeon, brought him forth and invited him to stand a buffet. Richard accepted the challenge, and received a blow that laid him prostrate. Recovering himself, he returned the stroke with so much force, that he broke the cheek-bone of his antagonist, who sank to the ground and instantly expired.

The king awakened to fresh transports of fury, at the loss of his son, gave orders that the prisoner should be closely fettered and returned to the lowest dungeon of the castle. But the monarch had, also, a daughter, a princess of great beauty, who became exceedingly interested in the man that had so dexterously slain her brother. Learning that a plan was on foot to make the bold knight the prey of a lion, she found means to enter his cell, and acquaint him with his danger. The bold heart of Plantagenet did not fail him in this extremity. Rewarding the solicitude of the tender Margery with a kiss, he desired her to repair to him in the evening, bringing forty ells of white silk, and a supper with plenty of good beef and ale. Thus fortified in the outer and inner man, he calmly awaited his fate.

The next day, as soon as the roar of the monster was heard, he wrapped his arm in the silk, and evading the spring of the animal, gave it such a blow in the breast, as nearly felled it to the ground. The lion lashing itself with its tail, and extending its dreadful jaws, uttered a most hideous yell; but the hero suddenly darted upon the beast, drove his arm down the throat, and grasping the heart tore it out through the mouth, and marched with his trophy, yet quivering with life, to the great hall of the palace, where the king with a grand company of dukes and earls, sat at meat. Pressing the blood from the reeking heart, Prince Richard dipped it in the salt, and offered the dainty morsel to the company.

The lords rose from the table, and declaring, that since the days of Samson, no mortal had achieved so wonderful an exploit, dubbed him *Cœur de Lion*, on the spot. The barbarian finding it impossible, longer to detain a prisoner who seemed to enjoy the especial favour of Providence, bestowed upon him gifts and presents, mounted him on a fleet horse, and with great joy, saw him depart. A herald has this morning arrived, to say that he wends his way hither; therefore, prepare, my sister, to receive the lion-hearted prince, with a state becoming his new honours."

Berengaria needed no second bidding. She was already more interested in the gallant Plantagenet than she dared confess, even to herself, while the conduct of Richard, upon his arrival, intimated plainly the attraction that had drawn him to Navarre, and the flattering attention with which both the elder and younger Sancho treated him, prom-

174

ised fair speed to his wooing. He was exceedingly fond of chess, and this game served to beguile many hours when the weather precluded more active sports. Though a practised, Richard was often a careless player, and his fair antagonist gained many advantages over him, while he pertinaciously declared himself vanquished by her beauty rather than her skill. The ready blush that followed his compliments gave occasion for renewed expressions of admiration, and often in the midst of triumph the victor found herself covered with confusion.

Many gages of trifling value were lost and won between the amicable rivals, but it was not till after repeated defeats that Richard began to suspect there was some article in his possession that his beautiful opponent was particularly anxious to win. He playfully proposed to stake his head against one lock of her hair, and when he lost the game, gravely inquired whether she would accept the forfeit, with its natural fixture, or whether like the vindictive daughter of Herodias, she would require it to be brought in a charger, as was the head of John the Baptist. Rearranging the pieces before she could interpose a remonstrance, he declared the stakes should next be his heart against her hand.

The game was terminated in his favour. Gallantly seizing her hand, pressing his lips upon it, he protested that in all his tournaments he had never won so fair a prize; then suddenly exclaiming, "What magic game is this, in which a man may both lose and win?" he laid his broad palm upon his side, and with an appearance of great concern, continued, "By the blessed mother my heart is certainly gone; and I must hold thee accountable for its restoration."

Making a strong effort at recovering her composure, Berengaria asserted that she had neither lost nor won the game, since he had arranged the pieces unfairly, and proceeded to capture her queen almost without her knowledge, and certainly without her consent.

The sportive colloquy finally ended in a compromise, Richard agreeing that the affair could justly be accommodated by Berengaria's staking her heart against his hand, and she playfully avowing that a gamester so unprincipled might expect to lose both body and soul, if he did not commit the arrangements to one of greater probity. The keen eye of Plantagenet soon discovered that this game possessed an interest for his fair rival far beyond the preceding ones, and in doubt whether it arose from her anxiety to gain his hand, or from her desire delicately to assure him that he could never win her heart, he suffered himself to be beaten. The result only increased his perplexity; for the princess, though evidently elated by her success, seriously proposed to relinquish her claim upon his hand, in consideration of the ring that glittered upon his finger. Too much interested any longer to regard the game, Richard pushed aside the chessboard, and fixing his eyes upon her, inquired, "Wherefore wouldst thou the ring?"

The princess more than ever embarrassed by the seriousness of his voice and manner, stammered forth, "The jewel is a charm."

"True," said Richard, with unaffected warmth, "Berengaria's gifts are all charms."

"Nay, nay!" said she, with uncontrollable trepidation, "I mean—I mean—it is a fatal possession."

"Of which I am a most undoubted witness," interrupted he, "since by its influence I have lost my head, my heart and my hand."

"Have done with this idle jesting, and listen to me," said Berengaria, earnestly. "It will thwart thy dearest wish, and betray thee to thy direst foe."

"None but Berengaria can thwart my dearest wish," said Richard, steadily regarding her, "and from my direst foe," he added, with a gesture of defiance, "this good right arm is a sufficient defence."

Tears shone in Berengaria's eyes, and she added, "Why wilt thou misunderstand me? I tell thee it will break thy troth."

"Our Lady grant it," responded he, with a shout of exultation. "Since the day I first received it, I have not ceased to importune King Henry to cancel my engagement with Alice of France."

The baffled princess having no further resource burst into tears.

"Nay, weep not, my sweetest Berengaria," said Richard, tenderly, "the gem is indeed a talisman, since by its aid only have I been able to discover the treasure thou hadst so effectually concealed from my anxious search. Fear no evil on my behalf, my poor life has double value since thou hast betrayed an interest in my fate." He stooped to kiss the tears from her cheek, and passing a chain with a diamond cross about her neck, left her alone to recover her composure.

CHAPTER 4

Ah me! for aught that I could ever read,
Could ever hear by tale or history,
The course of true love never did run smooth.

"A long and secret engagement, replete with hope deferred, was the fate of Richard the Lion-hearted and the fair flower of Navare." The vexatious wars in which Eleanor of Aquitaine constantly involved her husband and children occupied Richard in combats more dangerous than those of the tourney. The heart of Berengaria was often agitated with fears for his safety. She was also compelled to reject the addresses of numerous suitors, attracted by her beauty and wealth, and she thus subjected herself to the imputation of caprice, and the displeasure of her father, when her thoughts were distracted by rumours that Richard was about to consummate his marriage with Alice.

An occasional troubadour who sang the exploits of her gallant lover sometimes imparted new life to her dying hopes, and again when a long period elapsed without tidings of any kind, she bitterly reproached herself for permitting him to retain an amulet which she was so well assured would change the current of his affections; and notwithstanding the general frankness of his character, and the unfeigned earnestness of his manner, which more than his words, had convinced her of his truth; she was often tortured with the suspicion that Richard had only amused himself with the artlessness of a silly girl, and had no intention of demanding her of her father. Her only confidant in the affair was her brother Sancho the Strong, who consoled her by violently upbraiding her for the unjust suspicion, and resolutely vindicating the honour of his absent friend.

While the mind of Berengaria was thus cruelly alternating between hope and fear, her sister Blanche was wedded to Thibaut, brother of Count Henry of Champagne. On the festive occasion Richard accompanied the bridegroom: and when Berengaria once more read admiration and love in every glance of his speaking eyes, and listened to his enthusiastic assurances of devotion, and above all, when she heard his wrathful malediction against those who interposed the claims of Alice, she wondered how she could ever have distrusted the sincerity of his professions. But though her heart was thus reassured, the first intelligence that she received from Champagne through the medium of Blanche, overwhelmed her with new apprehensions.

It was asserted, that an alliance had been formed between Richard and Philip, the young King of France, to wrest Alice from the custody of Henry, and that the two princes, to prove that they looked upon each other as brothers, exchanged clothing, ate at the same table, and occupied the same apartment. The confident Sancho even, was somewhat shaken by this report; particularly as the Gascon subjects of Richard began to prepare for war. Instigated by his own doubts, but more especially by the mute appeals of Berengaria's tearful eyes, Sancho made a journey to the north to prove the guilt or innocence of his friend. At Bordeaux he learned that Richard had gone to Poictiers.

At Poictiers it was said he might be found at Tours.

At Tours the rumour was confirmed, that Richard had transferred his allegiance from Henry to Philip, and that Henry, in consequence of his son's rebellion, had fallen sick at Chinon, and that Richard had been summoned to that place to attend the monarch's death-bed. Without delay, therefore, Sancho posted forward to Chinon. As he ascended an eminence commanding a view of the road for some distance, he saw a band of armed horsemen riding in advance of him, and thought he discerned, in the van, the crest of Richard Cœur de Lion. Putting spurs to his horse, he joined the rear of the cavalcade, which proved to be the funeral procession of Henry II., led by his erring son to the abbey of Fontevraud. The mournful tones of the bell mingled with the clanging tread of the mail-clad nobles, as solemn and slow they followed the prince up the long aisle of the church.

The air was heavy with the breath of burning incense, and the strong and ruddy glare of the funeral torches, revealed with fearful distinctness the deep furrows made by age, and care, and grief in the noble features of the deceased monarch. The walls draped with the sable habiliments of woe, returned the muffled tones of the organ, while drooping banners, that canopied the bier, shook as with a boding shudder, at the approach of the warrior train. One solitary mourner knelt beside the altar, a fair-haired youth, whose features of classic purity, seemed to have borrowed their aspect of repose from the dread presence before him.

It was Geoffrey, the younger son of Rosamond. The solemn chanting of the mass was hushed, and the startled priests suppressed their very breath in awe, as heavy sobs burst from the great heart of Cœur de Lion, and shook the steel corselet that was belted above his breast. Geoffrey silently rose, and moving to the head of the bier, left the place of honour to his repentant brother. "My father!" exclaimed Richard, bending over the dead, and lifting the palsied hand, "My father! oh canst thou not forgive?" He stopped in speechless horror, for *blood* oozed from the clammy lips that till now had always responded to the call of affection.

The sensitive heart of Sancho, wrung with a kindred agony, could no longer brook the terrible spectacle. He left the abbey, and was followed by one and another of the crowd till the self-accusing parricide was left alone with the body of his sire.

★★★★★★

When the Prince of Navarre returned to Pampeluna, he forbore to

178

pain his sister's heart by a recital of the melancholy circumstances that had so affected his own, but he carried to her an assurance that *Richard would wed only Berengaria*, sealed with the mysterious jewel now reset as the signet ring of the King of England. He described the splendid coronation of his friend, the wealth of his new realm, and the enthusiastic rapture with which his new subjects hailed his accession to the throne. He also informed her that Richard, previous to his father's death, had taken the cross for the Holy Land, and that all his time and thoughts were now occupied in settling the affairs of the realm for this object; and that the alliance with Philip, which had caused her so much anxiety, was an engagement, not to marry Alice, but to enter with the French monarch upon the *Third Crusade*.

The prospects of her mistress awakened all the enthusiasm of Elsiebede. She dreamed by night and prophesied by day of long journeys on horseback and by sea, and she interspersed her prognostications with agreeable tales of distressed damsels carried off by unbelieving Afrites, and miraculous escapes from shipwreck by the interposition of good *genii*. But though her tongue was thus busy, her hands were not idle. She set in motion all the domestic springs to furnish forth the wardrobe of her mistress and herself with suitable splendour, and amused the needle-women with such accounts of eastern magnificence that they began to regard the rich fabrics upon which they were employed as scarcely worthy of attention.

In the beginning of the autumn of 1190, Queen Eleanor arrived at the court of Navarre to demand of her friend Sancho the Wise the hand of his daughter for her son Richard. The king readily accepted the proposal, for beside being Berengaria's lover, the gallant Plantagenet was the most accomplished, if not the most powerful sovereign of Europe. Under the escort of the queen dowager the royal *fiancée* journeyed to Naples, where she learned to her mortification and dismay that her intended lord was not yet released from the claims of Alice, and that the potentates assembled for the crusade were in hourly expectation of seeing the armed forces of Christendom embroiled in a bloody war to decide her title to the crown matrimonial of England.

The forebodings of Elsiebede did not increase her equanimity. "It is all the work of the fatal ring," said the superstitious maiden. "Did I not tell thee it would thwart his dearest wish?" Berengaria could reply only by her tears. Other circumstances made her apprehensive concerning the fate of the expedition. The Emperor Frederic Barbarossa was among the first of those whose grief arose to indignation at the fall of Jerusalem. He wrote letters to Saladin demanding restitution of the city, and threatening vengeance in the event of non-compliance. The courteous *infidel* replied, that if the Christians would give up to him Tyre, Tripoli and Antioch, he would restore to them the piece of wood taken at the battle of Tiberias, and permit the people of the west to visit Jerusalem as pilgrims.

The chivalry of Germany were exasperated at this haughty reply, and the emperor, though advanced in age, with his son the Duke of Suabia, the Dukes of Austria and Moravia, sixty-eight temporal and spiritual lords, and innumerable hosts of crusaders, drawn out of every class, from honourable knighthood down to meanest vassalage, set out from Ratisbon for the East. The virtuous Barbarossa conducted the march with prudence and humanity. Avoiding as much as possible the territories of the timid and treacherous Greek emperor, Isaac Angelus, he crossed the Hellespont, passed through Asia Minor, defeated the Turks in a general engagement at Iconium, and reached the Taurus Ridge, having accomplished the difficult journey with more honour and dignity and success than had fallen to the lot of any previous crusaders.

When the army approached the river Cydnus, the gallant Frederic, emulating the example of Alexander, desired to bathe in its waters. His attendants sought to dissuade him, declaring that the place had been marked by a fatality from ancient times; and to give weight to their arguments, pointed to this inscription upon an adjacent rock, "*Here the greatest of men shall perish.*" But the humility of the monarch prevented his listening to their counsels. The icy coldness of the stream chilled the feeble current in his aged veins, and the strong arms that had for so many years buffeted the adverse waves of fortune, were now powerless to redeem him from the eddying tide. He was drawn out by the attendants, but the spark of life had become extinct.

The tidings of this melancholy event came to Berengaria, when her heart was agitated by the perplexity of her own situation not only, but by the intelligence that Richard's fleet had been wrecked off the port of Lisbon, and that he was himself engaged in hostilities with Tancred. Cœur de Lion was indeed justly incensed with the usurper of his sister's dominions. Upon the first news of the fall of Jerusalem, William the Good had prepared to join the crusade with one hundred galleys equipped and provisioned for two years, sixty thousand measures of wine, sixty thousand of wheat, the same number of barley, together with a table of solid gold and a tent of silk, sufficiently capacious to accommodate two hundred persons. Being seized with a fatal disease, he left these articles by will to Henry II, and settling upon his beloved Joanna a princely dower, intrusted to her the government of the island. No sooner was he deceased, than Tancred, an illegitimate son of Roger of Apulia, seized upon the inheritance and threw the fair widow into prison.

The roar of the advancing lion startled Tancred from his guilty security, and he lost no time in unbarring the prison doors of his royal captive. But Richard required complete restitution, and enforced his demands by the sword. He seized upon Messina, but finally through the intervention of the French king, accommodated the matter by accepting forty thousand ounces of gold, as his father's legacy and his sister's dower. He also affianced his nephew Arthur of Brittany, to the daughter of Tancred, the Sicilian prince agreeing on his part to equip ten galleys and six horse transports for the crusade. Completely reconciled to the English king, Tancred, in a moment of confidence, showed him letters in which Philip had volunteered to assist in hostilities against Richard.

This treachery on the part of Philip brought matters to a crisis. Seizing the evidences of perfidy, Richard strode his way to the French camp, and with eyes sparkling with rage, and a voice of terrible power, upbraided him with his baseness. Philip strongly asserted his innocence, and declared the letters a forgery, a mere trick of Richard to gain a pretext for breaking off the affair with his sister. The other leaders interposed and shamed Philip into acquiescence with Richard's desire to be released from his engagement with Alice. Some days after the French king sailed for Acre.

But though the hand of the royal Plantagenet was thus free, the long anticipated nuptials were still postponed. It was the period of the Lenten fast, when no devout Catholic is permitted to marry. Eleanor finding it impossible longer to leave her regency in England, conducted Berengaria to Messina, and consigned her to the care of Queen Joanna, who was also preparing for the voyage. The English fleet, supposed lost, arrived in the harbour of Messina about the same time, and arrangements were speedily made for departure.

As etiquette forbade the lovers sailing together, Richard embarked his sister with her precious charge on board one of his finest ships, in the care of the noble Stephen de Turnham, while himself led the convoy in his favourite galley *Trenc-the-mere*, accompanied by twenty-four knights, whom he had organized in honour of his betrothment, under a pledge that they would with him scale the walls of Acre. From their badge, a fillet of blue leather, they were called knights of the Blue Thong.

Thus with one hundred and fifty ships and fifty galleys, did the lion-hearted Richard and his bride hoist sail for the Land of Promise, that El Dorado of the middle ages, the Utopia of every enthusiast whether of conquest, romance or religion.

CHAPTER 5

The strife of fiends is on the battling clouds,
The glare of hell is in these sulphurous lightnings;
This is no earthly storm.

Trustfully and gaily as infancy embarks upon the untried ocean of existence, the lovers left the harbour of Messina, and moved forth with their splendid convoy, upon the open sea. By day the galley of Berengaria chased the flying shadows of the gallant *Trenc-the-mere* along the coast of Greece, or followed in its rippling wake among the green isles of the clustering Cyclades; by night, like sea-fowl folding their shining wings, the vessels furled their snowy canvass, and with silver feet keeping time to the waves, danced forward over the glassy floor of the blue Mediterranean, like a charmed bride listening to the sound of pipe and *chalumeaux* that accompanied the spontaneous verse with which the royal troubadour wooed her willing ear.

The treacherous calm that had smiled upon the commencement of their voyage, at length began to yield to the changeful moods of the stormy equinox, which like a cruel sportsman, toyed with the hopes and fears of its helpless prey. Clouds and sunshine hurried alternately across the face of the sky. Fitful gusts of wind tossed the waves in air or plucked the shrouds of the ships and darted away, wailing and moaning among the waters. Then fell a calm—and then—with maddening roar the congregated floods summoned their embattled strength to meet the mustering winds, that, loosened from their caves, burst upon the sea with terrific power.

The females crept trembling to their couches, dizzy with pain and faint with fear. The sickness of Berengaria increased to that state of insensibility in which the body, palsied with agony, has only power to assist the mind in shaping all outward circumstances into visions of horror. She was again in the cell of the alchemist; saw lurid flames, heard deafening explosions, with unearthly shrieks and groans proceeding from myriads of fiends that thronged round her with ominous words and gibing leer. She felt herself irresistibly borne on, on, with a speed ever accelerated, and that defied all rescue, and with all there was an appalling sense of falling, down, down, down, into interminable depths.

The fantasy sometimes changed from herself, but always to her dearer self. Richard contending with mighty but ineffectual struggles against inexorable *genii*, was hurried through the unfathomable waters before her, the fatal ring gleaming through all their hideous forms upon her aching sight; and the confused din of strange sounds that whirled through her giddy brain could never drown the endless vibrations of the whispered words,

> 'Twill thwart his wish and break his troth,
> Betray him to his direst foe,
> And drown him in the sea.

The capricious winds at length sounded a truce between the contending elements. The baffled clouds, like a retiring enemy, discharging occasional arrows from their exhausted quivers, hurried away in wild confusion, while the triumphant sea, its vexed surface still agitated by the tremendous conflict, murmured a sullen roar of proud defiance.

The Princess of Navarre, relieved from the thraldom of imaginary horrors, became aware of the actual peril which the fleet had encountered. It was in vain that the anxious attendants interposed, she persisted in being conducted to the deck, whence with longing eyes she gazed in every direction for the bark of her lover. Not a vessel was in sight.

A wild waste of waters mocked her anxious scrutiny. Her own galley was so far disabled, that it was with much toiling and rowing, the mariners brought it into Limousa, the capital of Cyprus, and no sooner had they cast anchor, than Isaac Comnenus, the lord of the island, assailed the stranger bark with so much violence, that they were forced to row again with all speed into the offing. While the ship lay thus tossing at the mercy of the waves, dismantled fragments of shattered wrecks floated by, the broken masts and spars contending with the waters, like lost mariners struggling for life.

While Berengaria gave way to the harrowing conviction that the *Trenc-the-mere*, with its precious freight, had foundered in the storm, Richard, whose ship had been driven into Rhodes, was collecting his scattered fleet and scouring the sea for his lost treasure. Arrived off

Cyprus, he beheld the royal galley, and learning that it had been driven from the harbour by the pitiless despot, he landed in great wrath, and sent a message to Isaac, suggesting the propriety of calling his subjects from the work of plundering the wrecks to the exercise of the rites of hospitality.

The arrogant Cypriot answered that, "whatever goods the sea threw upon his island, he should take without leave asked of anyone."

"By Jesu, Heaven's king, they shall be bought full dear," retorted Richard, and seizing his battle-axe, he led his crusaders to the rescue, and soon drove the self-styled emperor, with his myrmidons, to the mountains. Without loss of time, Richard pursued him thither, and guided by the heron of burnished gold that gleamed from the imperial pavilion, penetrated the camp in the darkness, made a great slaughter of the enemy, and brought away all the treasure; Isaac again escaping with much difficulty. Two beautiful Arab steeds, Fanuelle and Layard, fell to the lot of the Conqueror.

In the world was not their peer,
Dromedary nor destrère.

With this magnificent booty King Richard returned, and taking possession of his enemies' capital, made signals for the entrance of the galley that had so long kept unwilling quarantine without the port. Berengaria, almost overcome with fatigue and fear, and fluttered with joy, was lifted on shore by the strong arms of the conquering Cœur de Lion. As he assisted her trembling steps towards the palace, a Cypriot of beggarly appearance threw himself on his knees before them, and presented to their astonished eyes the talismanic ring! Richard felt his gentle burden lean more heavily upon his arm, and saw in her colourless face, that all her apprehensions were reawakened. Gently whispering her words of encouragement, he turned to the stranger, and bursting into a hearty laugh, exclaimed, "Ha! knave, where got'st thou the bauble? Hast news of my chancellor?"

The mendicant replied, that a number of bodies had floated upon the beach, and that from the hand of one he had drawn this ring, which he brought to the English monarch in the hope of ransoming his wife and family, who had been taken prisoners. Richard, rejoiced at the recovery of the valued jewel, readily granted the request of the petitioner, adding as a bounty, a broad piece of gold. Slipping the signet upon his finger, he turned to his fair charge, saying, "Cheer thee, sweet-heart, thy ring has accomplished its destiny. The poor chancellor is 'drowned in the sea,' and thou mayest henceforth look upon it with favour, for today it shall *consummate* my 'dearest wish,' since the good bishop now waits to crown thee Richard's queen."

Relieved, that the ring, after all, boded no evil to Richard, and reassured by his words, Berengaria yielded to the sweet emotions that crowded upon her heart, and joyfully permitted him to conduct her into the presence of the archbishop, who, with the knights and nobles, awaited their coming. "And there," according to an ancient writer, "in the joyous month of May, 1191, in the flourishing and spacious isle of Cyprus, celebrated as the very abode of the goddess of love, did King Richard solemnly take to wife his beloved lady Berengaria." The allied crusaders, with the consent of the Cypriots, insisted that Richard should be crowned King of Cyprus, and a double coronal of gems and *Fleur-de-lis*, was placed upon the head of the bride, as Queen of Cyprus and of England. The daughter of Isaac came soon after to crave the grace of the new sovereigns, and the father, resigning his dominions, was bound in silver chains, and presented a captive to Berengaria.

It was now early summer, and the fleet of Richard, refitted and refreighted from the rich harbours of Cyprus, sailed once more for Acre. As they approached the bay, they descried a large ship laden to the water's edge, and despatched a light vessel to inquire whither she was bound, and what was her cargo. They were answered by an interpreter, that she came from Apulia, and was laden with provision for the French army. Perceiving only one man, they insisted on seeing the rest of the crew. Suddenly a multitude of Saracens appeared upon deck, and replied by a general shout of defiance. Immediately Richard gave orders to board the stranger.

The officers of the light-armed galleys felt some hesitation in assailing the lofty sides of the Turkish vessel. "I will crucify all my soldiers if she escape," cried Plantagenet. His men, dreading more their sovereign's wrath than all the arrows of the enemy, bent to the oars with all their strength, and drove the sharp beaks of their galleys into the sides of the foe. After a short contest the *infidels* surrendered, and the English found upon the prize great quantities of provision, barrels of Greek fire, arms, and treasures of gold and silver, which they had hardly unloaded when the vessel, scuttled by its despairing crew, sank like lead in the mighty waters.

Elated by this important capture, the Christians proceeded on their way. Just without the port of Acre they were met by a spy, who reported that the harbour was rendered inaccessible by a vast chain of iron, which the Saracens had stretched across the entrance. This formidable obstacle lent new vigour to Richard's arm. Selecting the largest and strongest galley in the fleet, he filled it with the stoutest rowers, took his station on the bows of the vessel, ordered it to be directed against the middle of the chain, and watching the moment of utmost tension, struck it so violently with his battle-axe, that it gave way, and the whole fleet passed triumphantly into the harbour.

Chapter 6: Selected From the Chronicle of Vinsauf, 1191

On the Saturday before the festival of the blessed Apostle Barnabas, in the Pentecost week, King Richard landed at Acre with his retinue, and the earth was shaken by the acclamations of the exulting Christians. The people testified their joy by shouts of welcome, and the clang of trumpets; the day was kept as a jubilee, and universal gladness reigned around, on account of the arrival of the king, long wished-for by all nations. The Turks, on the other hand, were terrified and cast down by his coming, for they perceived that all egress and return would be at an end, in consequence of the multitude of the king's galleys.

The two kings conducted each other from the port, and paid one another the most obsequious attention. Then King Richard retired to the tent, previously prepared for him, and, forthwith, entered into arrangements about the siege; for it was his most anxious care to find out by what means, artifice, and machines they could capture the city without loss of time.

No pen can sufficiently describe the joy of the people on the king's arrival, nor tongue detail it. The very calmness of the night was thought to smile upon them with a purer air; the trumpets clanged, horns sounded, and the shrill intonations of the pipe, and the deeper notes of the timbrel and harp, struck upon the ear; and soothing symphonies were heard, like various voices blended in one; and there was not a man who did not, after his own fashion, indulge in joy and praise; either singing popular ballads to testify the gladness of his heart, or reciting the deeds of the ancients, stimulating by their example the spirit of the moderns. Some drank wine from costly cups, to the health of the singers; while others mixing together, high and low, passed the night in constant dances.

And their joy was heightened by the subjugation of the island

186

of Cypruss, by King Richard; a place so useful and necessary to them, and one which would be of the utmost service to the army. As a further proof of the exultation of their hearts, and to illume the darkness of the night, wax torches, and flaming lights sparkled in profusion, so that night seemed to be usurped by the brightness of the day, and the Turks thought the whole valley was on fire.

CHAPTER 7

Out upon the fool! Go speak thy comforts
To spirits tame and abject as thyself;
They make me mad!

Baillie.

From the port of Acre, the great plain of Esdraelon stretches east to the Lake of Gennesareth, dividing the country into two parts. This plain has been the Aceldama of the nations that have warred in Palestine. There the stars in their courses fought against Sisera, there Saul and his sons fled and fell down slain before the Philistines, there the good King Josiah was conquered by the Egyptians, and there the Christians and Moslems with deadly enmity contended for the sovereignty of the Holy Land. The city of Acre was the possession of the *infidels*. Around it the besiegers, gathered out of every nation in Europe, lay in countless multitudes; splendid pavilions, gorgeous ensigns, glittering weapons, and armorial cognizances of every hue and form that individual fancy and national peculiarity could suggest, studding the plain, with all the varied colours that light weaves upon the changing texture of autumn foliage.

Beyond the beleaguering forces were encamped the sons of Islam, Turks, Tartars, Egyptians, and Bedouins, covering mountains, valleys, hills, and plains, with white and shining tents, while the black banner of Saladin floated above all in proud defiance of the crimson standard of the cross. The arrival of the English increased the camp of the crusaders, so that it stretched in a semicircle round Acre, from sea to sea, precluding all intercourse between the *soldan* and the city, while the Pisans with their light galleys cut off all supplies by sea.

Richard with the money he had brought from Cyprus, liberally rewarded the valour of the soldiers and diffused new courage among the troops. The King of England on the coast of Palestine, did not acknowledge himself the vassal of the King of France. In the council of the chiefs he had equal, if not greater influence, and in matters of general interest the rival sovereigns were usually found upon opposite sides. Sybilla, wife of Guy de Lusignan, was dead. Conrad of Montserrat, Prince of Tyre, having married her sister Isabella, claimed the ideal crown of Jerusalem. Philip supported the pretensions of Conrad, while Richard lent his powerful aid to Lusignan.

The Genoese and Templars sided with Philip, the Pisans and Hospitallers with Richard. Philip strove to seduce the vassals of Richard in right of his suzerainship, and offered three pieces of gold a month to each of the Norman knights that would join his standard, while Richard, more wealthy and less parsimonious, offered four pieces to such French feudatories as would be induced to fight under the banner of England.

These factions destroyed the unanimity so essential to success, and embarrassed every enterprise. In this posture of affairs, both monarchs were attacked with the fever incident to the climate, and thus though the garrison of Acre were suffering from famine, the besiegers were not in a condition to press their advantage.

★★★★★★

King Richard lay tossing upon his couch, consumed with fever and impatience, and scarcely enduring the gentle endeavours of his beloved queen to win him from the vexing thoughts that disturbed his repose. "Drink, my lord," said Berengaria, presenting him a cooling draught, "and compose thyself to rest. The leech saith that sleep is the best medicine for these Syrian maladies."

"Talk of sleep to the steed that hears the war trump, but speak not of rest and quiet to Richard while the banner of Islam floats in sight of the Christian camp. But for this cursed fever I should have stood beside the noble Alberic, and my gallant Knights of the Blue Thong on the walls of Acre."

Berengaria repressed an involuntary shudder. "Nay then, must I thank God for the fever, since else, we had this night to bewail not the loss of the French count alone, but the destruction of the bulwark of Christendom."

"Thou reasonest like a woman, as thou art," said Richard, in a petulant tone. "Thinkest thou the English curtel axe no better weapon than a Gascon's spear?"

"My woman's reason follows the fears of my woman's heart," said the queen, her eyes filling with tears, "and teaches me were Richard gone, both Palestine and Berengaria would lie at the mercy of the French king."

"By my halidome thou speakest truth," said Richard, tossing uneasily upon his side. "Therefore it chafes me to lie here inactive, lest perchance the crafty Philip first plant his standard upon the towers of Acre."

Feeling her utter inability to select topics in which the irascible monarch would not find causes of irritation, Berengaria summoned his favourite Blondel with the lute. But scarcely had Richard consented to listen to a Provençal chanson when the Earl of Salisbury entered.

"Ha! Longespee," exclaimed the monarch, "thou hast tidings from the leaders of the Christian host."

At the first entrance of Richard's warlike brother Berengaria had retired so as to be invisible to her lord, and motioned to silence. Hastily returning Richard's salutation, William conferred apart for a few moments with the queen and Joanna.

"The malady increases," said she, in much agitation. "Chafe him not with ill tidings, I do beseech thee. Already the fever burns to the verge of madness. Life depends upon his repose."

"What whisper ye?" exclaimed Cœur de Lion, startling them by his energy. "I tell you I will know all. Longsword, shamest thou the blood of the Plantagenet by counselling with women and leeches? Speak, man, I command thee."

Not daring farther to irritate the imperious invalid, the son of Rosamond came forward and stated that the Turks, perceiving the Christian army very much dejected at the loss of Count Alberic and his scaling party, had sent to beg a truce of eight days, promising at the same time, if the Soldan did not send them speedy assistance, to give up the city, on condition that all the Turks might be allowed to depart with their arms and property. In consequence of the severe indisposition of Richard, the chiefs had deemed it prudent not to disturb him with these matters; and hence the King of France and the Duke of Austria had taken the responsibility of returning a favourable answer to the proposition.

"By my father's soul," exclaimed Richard, "the son of France is more craven than I deemed. To give up the prize when just within our grasp is not to be thought of. Send the ambassadors to me. They shall find that Cœur de Lion will not barter glory for a deserted city. Go," added he, observing the hesitation of Longsword, "and venture not into my presence again without the envoys."

"But the leech said—" interposed Berengaria. "The curse of sweet

Jesus upon the leech! Am I to be subject to nurses, dosed with physic, and soothed with lullabys, like a muling child? Away! or my chamberlain shall enforce thy absence," said he, darting his first angry glance at his trembling queen.

Finding all remonstrance vain, the discomfited females yielded to his impetuosity, only obtaining for themselves the grace of being present at the interview. Ill as he was, the monarch was clothed in his robes of state; and with a cheek glowing with fever and eyes sparkling with unwonted brilliancy, was supported by cushions upon a settle, hastily arranged to answer the purpose of a throne. Scarcely were these preliminaries arranged, when the chamberlain ushered in Longsword with the envoys. The swarthy Egyptian Mestoc, with his splendid *caftan* and white turban, particularly attracted the admiration of the silent females, and seemed to exercise a fascinating power upon Elsiebede, who perused his countenance as though she discerned in it the familiar features of a friend.

The anger which Richard had testified towards his attendants, was modified into a haughty courtesy as he conversed with the noble Saracens. He cut off at once all parley concerning the proposition for permitting the Turks to leave the city without ransom, but he graciously accorded his assent to the truce. Berengaria observed with terror that though Caracois exhibited as lively an interest in the negotiations as the gravity of the Turks ever allowed, Mestoc seemed more occupied in scanning the person of the monarch, and regarded with wonder and curiosity the signet that glittered upon his finger.

The conference was scarcely over, when Richard sank back pale and exhausted from his recent exertion, and the leech being speedily summoned, insisted that the king should be left alone with him for the remainder of the night. Preparing a sleeping draught, and almost forcing it down the throat of his refractory patient, he moved the light into the anteroom of the tent, and giving the chamberlain strict orders not to admit any one, upon whatever pretext, sat down to watch the effect of his remedies. After a few uneasy tossings and muttered ejaculations of vexation and disquiet, the monarch sank into a heavy slumber, broken only by occasional imprecations against the *infidels*, whom he battled in sleep with an animosity that would have done credit to his waking vengeance.

As the twilight deepened into darkness, the coolness of the Syrian evening shed the grateful dew of slumber upon the weary eyelids of those who had answered the constant demands of the royal invalid, and brought the happy oblivion of rest to those who had engaged in the more warlike duties of the arblast and mangonel. The sounds of life gradually decreased, and a profound silence reigned throughout the Christian camp uninterrupted, save by the tread of the patrol who took his weary round upon the outposts, like the sentinel of a beleaguered city.

★★★★★★

In her protracted efforts to quiet the sobbing queen, Elsiebede learned a curious and inexplicable fact, namely, that a greater draft is made upon the patience and energy of the nurse by the over-excited feelings of the sensitive wife, than by the real wants of the sick man himself. Thus the leech had long been dozing upon his watch, ere the anxious Moorish girl had found it possible to leave the bedside of her mistress. At length the incessant calls upon her sympathy subsided into sighs which gradually relaxed into the regular breathing of healthy slumber, and the impatient attendant stealing noiselessly from the apartment sought among the attendants for the wily Salaman.

"Awake, Salaman," she whispered, softly. The black instantly arose, without salutation or remark, and stood before her rolling his eyes in perfect self-possession, as though to repel the suspicion that a person of his active vigilance could have been detected in the weakness of slumber. Laying her finger upon her lip, Elsiebede led the way among sleeping guards to the little enclosure in front of the tent. "Bring me," said she, "the signet-ring from the hand of the king."

Salaman, who had long laboured under the hallucination that no feat could be beyond his ability, looked absolutely sober at this unheard-of proposition, ejaculating, "It is to put my head into the lion's mouth!" but instantly recovering his self-complacency, he added, "Nothing can be easier. Remain here till I come." Skilfully avoiding the tent ropes, he wormed himself under the folds of the pavilion into the outer apartment, where the chamberlain and guard were snoring in melodious concert, and carefully lifting the curtain entered the royal presence. But through the darkness that reigned, he could not readily discern the precise location of the monarch's couch.

Creeping stealthily over the floor, he first laid his hand upon the foot of the physician, which with an instinctive kick warned him of his dangerous vicinity. Finally, as his eyes became accustomed to the darkness, he discovered the sparkle of the jewel upon the hand of the monarch, hanging over the side of the bed. To withdraw the ring from the somewhat attenuated finger was the work of a moment, but the touch, however slight, was sufficient to disturb the slumbering lion.

"Ha! the foul fiend!" ejaculated the dreamer, clutching the woolly hair of the negro. "The talisman is safe—cheer—thee—Berengaria—" Inarticulate sounds followed, which finally died away in silence; when Salaman, with practised caution, extricated his head from the lion's paw, and effected his retreat by the same stealthy and tedious process. Elsiebede awaited his coming with torturing impatience. Grasping the ring, she muffled her face in the veil usually worn by eastern females, and bidding him follow her took her way towards the city. The moon, just dipping its silver rim in the Mediterranean with its parting beam, threw the lengthened shadow of the patrol full across their way.

Cowering behind the awning of a tent they paused breathless and terrified, while the sentinel, turning his face towards Jerusalem, shouted above their heads in a tone rendered clear and startling by the stillness of the midnight, "Help! Help! Help for the Holy Sepulchre!" The adjacent sentinel took up the cry, repeating the words to his neighbour, who passed the watchword on, till "Help! Help! Help for the Holy Sepulchre!" echoed in all the languages of Europe, smote upon the ear of every sleeper in the Christian camp. When the sounds died away in the distance, the patrol continued his round. The terror of Elsiebede afforded infinite amusement to Salaman, whose irrepressible laughter added to her fears of being discovered, and increased her trepidation.

After this adventure they pursued their course with renewed speed, and arrived without molestation at the outpost, where the guard challenged their advance. Elsiebede presented the monarch's signet saying, "Delay not our errand," and the guard muttering, "There is ever some woman's prank in the light head of the queen," suffered them to pass.

As they took their solitary way between the camp and the walls of Acre, Salaman ventured to inquire, "Whither goest thou, Elsiebede?"

"I scarce know," replied the girl, in a husky voice, "but this evening there came before King Richard, one who looked upon me with my mother's eyes; and as he left the pavilion, he whispered me in the language of the Gyptianos, 'Meet me when the moon sets, at the tower of Maledictum.'"

"This way lieth the tower," said Salaman, drawing her to the right. They now approached the black and frowning walls of Acre, and turning an angle came close upon a small party of Turks sleeping upon the earth, and were challenged in the Moorish tongue. Salaman readily answered in the same language. Mestoc immediately advanced, and

192

taking the hand of Elsiebede led her apart, and a long and earnest conversation ensued. When she returned to Salaman, tears were on her cheek, and hiding her face in her veil, with no other explanation than, "He is the brother of my mother," she led the way back to the royal tent. "Haste thee," said she, thrusting the ring into his hand. "Should the prince awake, we are lost." Salaman sped on his errand, and repeated his perilous adventure with success. Not daring, however, to place the ring upon the monarch's finger, he laid it upon the covering near his hand, and effected a retreat, as far as the anteroom, where he unluckily stumbled against the settle on which rested the guard. The chamberlain instantly started to his feet, and Salaman quick as thought overturned the light, and escaped into the sleeping apartment of the common attendants, but here his progress was arrested by a half-awakened soldier, who seized his ankle and held him fast.

Hither as soon as the lamp could be relighted, he was pursued by the chamberlain, but such was the confusion, betwixt the muttering of those unwilling to be disturbed, and the blunders of those who fancied themselves broad awake, such was the cursing of devil, Turk and *infidel*, that no one had the faintest idea of what had happened. Scarcely had the chamberlain fixed his eyes upon the real culprit, when with the angry and important air of a responsible person, most unceremoniously wakened, Elsiebede entered, and advancing straight to Salaman, seized and began to shake him with the greatest violence, thus freeing him from the grasp of the guard. "Waken, minion," said she, "waken, I say. What gambols art thou playing again in thy sleep? I warrant me, thou hast an unquiet conscience. My lady will send thee from her service, if thou dost not confess thy sins, and rest in peace." The black rubbed his eyes, and stumbling about like one but half awake, succeeded in gaining his pallet, and joyfully ensconced himself beneath the covering.

"Thou seest," said Elsiebede, turning to the chamberlain, "the knave hath a trick of sleep-walking. Order these that they may remain quiet, for I would not that my mistress should be disturbed." Thus saying, she quitted the apartment.

"A trick of walking, he certainly hath," grumbled the chamberlain, "but whether sleeping or waking, misdoubts me. The misshapen unbeliever can bring no good to a Christian household."

In the royal tent, there was still greater clamour. The monarch roused by the first unlucky step of Salaman, and finding himself in darkness, vociferated loudly for a light; but gaining no answer waxed wroth, and seizing the medicine cup as the readiest missile, hurled it in the direction of the snoring physician. The silver coming in contact with the skull of the doctor, animated him to a remarkable degree; betwixt the darkness and the pain, he plunged about the room without knowing for what intent, till he fell prostrate across the couch of the king, who mistaking him for an invading Turk, beat him terribly with the pillows; and roaring for sword, spear and battle-axe, in the name of all the saints in the calendar, defied him to mortal combat.

At this juncture the chamberlain returned with the light, and seeing the king thus inflicting summary justice upon the leech, despite his own vexation burst into a hearty laugh, in which Richard, having already expended the superabundance of his choler, as soon as he comprehended the state of the case, joined with the greatest glee. The doctor meanwhile failed to see the point of the joke, and rubbing his head, declared with professional authority that nothing could be worse for the patient than such immoderate exercise and laughter. Picking up the cup, with a rueful countenance he mixed a fresh potion, which the facetious monarch drank to his health, and so composed himself again to rest.

Cœur de Lion received his ring when it was found upon the floor, without any sign of surprise, and readily accounted for its loss, saying, "Our royal signet is scarcely safe upon this emaciated hand, especially since we are liable to do battle for Christendom without gauntlet or sword." The castigation which he had given the doctor put him in such high good humour, that he swallowed the necessary nostrums with great facility, and the worthy leech fully appreciating this part of the joke availed himself of the king's unwonted condescension, to administer those nauseous restoratives which the monarch had before obstinately refused.

CHAPTER 8

Ah, never shall the land forget
How gushed the life-blood of the brave,
Gushed warm with hope and courage yet
Upon the soil they fought to save.
Bryant.

The eight days' truce was over, and Philip, recovered from his illness, again led the assault to the walls of Acre. Richard, also slowly convalescing, was borne to the scene of conflict, where he directed the operations of his warlike engines, offering a reward for every stone the soldiers dislodged from the tower Maledictum. The French had a machine of great power which they called "Bad neighbour," and the Turks, on their side, opposed to it a similar one named "Bad brother." These engines were plied day and night, and the tower became the scene of every variety of fierce attack and resolute defence, both by single combat and united effort. One morning a gigantic Turk, wearing the armour of Count Alberic, showed himself upon the wall in an attitude of defiance, when Richard, who had yielded to the representations of the chiefs, so far as to refrain from personal encounter, seized an arblast and sent an arrow winged with death to the heart of the Infidel. The exasperated Turks ran together to avenge his fall. The Christians met them with equal alacrity, and a slaughter ensued which continued till the darkness of night separated the combatants.

The Christians had commenced undermining the tower, and had proceeded to some distance under the wall, when they encountered a party of Turks who were mining for egress in the opposite direction. The noise of the digging and the uncertain light had prevented each from discovering the other, till the earth, suddenly giving way between them, the foes stood face to face, mattocks and shovels in hand. But when the astonished Turks saw that they had thus assisted the Christians to enter the city, they fled with great precipitation, and at once closed up the entrance. That night a part of the tower Maledictum fell, and the Saracens perceiving that all further resistance would be vain, offered conditions of peace.

They agreed to give up the city of Acre with all the treasures contained in it, both in money, arms, and clothing, to pay over two hundred thousand Saracenic talents, and restore the true cross which had been taken by the Moslems in the Battle of Tiberias. After much debate the council of chiefs acceded to these proposals, and all the Paynim noblemen in the city were given up as hostages till the conditions should be fulfilled. The preliminaries arranged, the gates were thrown open, and the Turks with grave but cheerful countenance and undaunted demeanour passed out of the city through the Christian camp towards Tiberias.

SELECTED FROM VINESAUF

At last when all the Turks had departed, the Christians with the two kings at their head, entered the city without opposition through the open gates with dances and joy, and loud vociferations, glorifying God, and giving Him thanks, because he had magnified His mercy to them, and had visited them and redeemed His people. Then the banners and various standards of the two kings were raised on the walls and towers, and the city was equally divided between them. They also made a proportionate division of the arms and provisions they found; and the whole number of captives being reckoned, was divided by lot. The noble Caracois, and a large number fell to the lot of the King of France; and King Richard had for his portion Mestoc and the remainder. Moreover, the King of France had for his share the noble palace of the Templars, with all its appurtenances; and King Richard had the royal palace, to which he sent the queens with their damsels and handmaids; thus each obtained his portion in peace. The army was distributed through the city, and after the protracted contest of so long a siege, gave themselves indulgence, and refreshed themselves with the rest they needed.

★★★★★★

No sooner were the Crusaders settled in the city than new troubles arose. Leopold, Duke of Austria, being a relative of Isaac Comnenus, who had joined the Templars, insisted that the Cypriot lady should be transferred to his custody; but Berengaria having become tenderly attached to her, refused to give her up. The quarrel ran high, and the exasperated Richard, in a moment of wrath, tore down the banner of Austria from the walls of Acre. This indignity gave rise to a mortal enmity, which hindered the arms and embarrassed the counsels of the *croises* during the whole campaign. The Christians, however, repaired the shattered walls and dwellings of the city, the clergy rebuilt and consecrated the altars, and the army watching for the fulfilment of Saladin's promises, rested from their fatigues in the enjoyment of security and luxury.

Before the expiration of the period granted for the redemption of the hostages, Philip Augustus, feigning illness, but in reality suffering with a consuming jealousy of the superiority of his rival, declared his intention of returning to Europe. The chiefs assembled in council protested against this unworthy desertion of the common cause, since Saladin, depressed by the fall of Acre, was in no situation to contest their route to Jerusalem. When Richard heard of Philip's determination, he outdid himself in the curses and maledictions he called down upon the recreant prince, and peremptorily refused to hold any communication upon the subject: but at last having expended the violence of his anger, he compromised by giving his consent to the measure on condition that the Duke of Burgundy and a large part of the French should remain in Syria, and that Philip should make oath to leave the realm of England unmolested, till forty days after Richard should himself return to his dominions. The French monarch then left Acre amidst the hisses and imprecations of the spectators. He stopped at Tyre, and resigning to Conrad his claim upon the conquered city, and the ransom of the Turkish captives, sailed for Europe. The term fixed for the redemption of the hostages had well nigh expired, and still Saladin protested his inability to find the true cross, and under different pretexts excused himself from redeeming the prisoners.

The palace of the *emir* in Acre, with its sheltered verandahs, cooling fountains, and richly cultivated gardens afforded a delightful residence for the household of Cœur de Lion. Elsiebede, in whom it revived the recollections of her childhood in the Alhambra, revelled in luxuries, each of which was endeared by happy associations.

A safe retreat being thus provided for his tender charge, Richard, intending as soon as practicable to commence his route to Jerusalem, ordered the *petrarias, mangonels,* and other warlike engines to be packed for transportation. He also despatched messengers to Conrad, Prince of Tyre, requiring him to repair with his hostages and army to Acre, to receive his share of the ransom, and to be ready to march against the *infidels.* The *marquis* refused; declaring that he dared not venture into Richard's presence, and that if the true cross were ever recovered, he was to receive half of it for the King of France, and until that time he should not give up the hostages.

A longer period having elapsed than that which had been assigned for the treaty, the council of chiefs was called to deliberate upon the fate of the captives. To leave three thousand prisoners without a sufficient guard, would be to surrender the city again to the Turks. To attempt to convey them with the army would be an inconceivable burden, attended with infinite danger. To provision such a multitude, whether in the city or camp, would be an intolerable tax upon the rapidly exhausting finances; and to set them free would be to add that number of active warriors to the ranks of their vigilant foe, and so to defeat the very end of the expedition. It was therefore determined that the hostages, on the following day, should be led forth upon an adjacent hill, and executed for the discomfiture of the Mohammedans, and the edification of all true Christians.

The noble Mestoc, considered as one of the most important and valuable of the hostages, received distinguishing marks of favour. He was lodged according to his rank, and enjoyed a freedom beyond that extended to the other prisoners, and thus Elsiebede obtained frequent interviews without giving rise to a suspicion of the relationship between them.

On the evening of the council of the chiefs, Salaman had managed, by means best known to himself, to hear all that passed, which he faithfully reported to Elsiebede.

The following night, as Mestoc was quietly reposing unconscious of the fate that menaced the Turkish prisoners, he was surprised by a visit from his niece, who, informing him of the purposes of the Christians, besought him to make his escape in a disguise she had prepared for the purpose.

The noble Egyptian refused, but moved by her pleadings, said to her, "Hadst thou a messenger by whom I might transmit a token to the *soldan*—but no, the gray of night already foretelleth the dawn. It is too late. Had the *soldan* valued the poor services of his servant, he had not left him to die by the hand of a Christian dog. Allah be praised, Death is the key that opens the gate of Paradise."

Finding further importunity vain, Elsiebede with many tears took her departure, revolving in her mind other methods of procuring a release.

At early morning, the prisoners were conducted in mournful procession through the gates of the city, by a great multitude of the most devout and warlike Christians, who, according to a contemporary writer, "marched forward with delight to retaliate with the assent of Divine Grace, by taking revenge upon those who had destroyed so many of the Christians with missiles, bows, and arbalests."

A report from an unknown source was in circulation among the soldiers, that fresh promises of ransom had been received from Saladin, and that if the execution could be delayed till evening, messengers would arrive with the treasure. By this artifice the chief *emirs* were preserved till long past noon. But no sign of rescue then appearing, those who looked for the downfall of Mohammedanism by the utter annihilation of its followers, caused the work of vengeance to proceed.

The calm indifference with which the Turks regarded the terrific preparations for their execution, elicited even the admiration of the Christians. It was not in the heart of a chivalrous knight like Richard, to look unmoved upon the destruction of his brave and gallant foes. "By the holy saints," exclaimed he, "this is a hangman's work. It were enough to tempt the sword of a Christian knight from its scabbard, to see yon lion-hearted warriors slaughtered like a parcel of silly sheep held in the butcher's shambles. Wore they but the cross upon their shoulders, I would sooner reckon them among my followers than the stupid boors of Austria or the tilting squires of France. Longsword, summon our good bishop of Salisbury, with the symbols of our holy religion. Peradventure, Divine Grace may turn the hearts of these brave men to the acknowledgment of the true faith."

In obedience to the order of the king, the bishop came forward, and holding up the cross, proclaimed life and liberty to all those who would renounce their heathen superstitions, and reverence the holy symbol. Not a voice replied to the offer of pardon, and as the priest, followed by the executioner, like the destroying angel of the Passover, moved among the ranks of the doomed and presented the crucifix, each man answering, "God is God and Mahomet is his prophet," bent his head to the fatal stroke, till of the whole number the noble Mestoc alone remained. King Richard regarded him with a troubled look, as the priest approached, and involuntarily raised his hand to stay the blow. The executioner paused; and the soldiers gazing in silent wonder, turned their eyes doubtfully from their sovereign to his captive, who stood unmoved among the headless bodies of the heroic band, that had with him defended the city to the last extremity, and that now lay stretched around him, the bleeding holocaust upon the altar of a strange faith.

The death-like silence that prevailed was broken by the faint sound of a trumpet, and at a distance was seen the flutter of a truce flag borne by a herald riding at full speed. The messenger advanced to the field of blood, hastened to the royal presence and presented a letter. The king cutting the silk with his sword, rapidly ran his eye over the contents, and then advancing, frankly extended his hand to the rescued Mestoc, saying, "Thy *soldan* has at length fulfilled the conditions of thy ransom. I grieve that he so little valued the lives of thy brave companions. His tardy measures forced me upon an evil work. Heaven grant that one day I may, upon his own person, be able to avenge their death."

Then, ordering the squires to prepare the Cypriot horses, he held the stirrup while the gallant *emir*, with the same grave and tranquil air, that had characterized him through the whole of that eventful day, mounted Lyard, and himself vaulting upon the saddle of the beautiful

Fanuelle, led the way to the palace.

On the morrow, therefore, of St. Bartholomew, being Sunday, the army was drawn up, early in the morning, to advance along the sea-coast, in the name of the Lord. Oh! what fine soldiers they were! You might there see a chosen company of virtuous and brave youth, whose equals it would have been difficult to meet with, bright armour and pennons, with their glittering emblazoning; banners of various forms; lances with gleaming points; shining helmets, and coats of mail; an army well regulated in the camp, and terrible to the foe! King Richard commanded the van, and kept the foremost guard.

The Normans and English defended the standard, the Duke of Burgundy and the French brought up the rear, and by their tardy movements and long delay incurred severe loss. The army marched from the seashore, which was on its right, and the Turks watched its movements from the heights on its left. On a sudden the clouds grew dark, the sky was troubled, when the army arrived at the narrow roads impassable for the provision wagons; here, owing to the narrowness of the way, the order of march was thrown into confusion, and they advanced in extended line, and without discipline.

The Saracens, observing this, poured down suddenly upon the pack-horses and loaded wagons, slew both horses and men in a moment, and plundered a great deal of the baggage, boldly charging and dispersing those who opposed them, as far as the seashore. Then there took place a fierce and obstinate conflict; each fought for his life. Oh, how dreadfully were our men then pressed! for the darts and arrows thrown at them broke the heads, arms and other limbs, of our horsemen, so that they bent, stunned to their saddle-bows; but having quickly regained their spirits, and resumed their strength, and thirsting for vengeance, like a lioness when her whelps are stolen, they charged the enemy and broke through them like a net.

Then you might have seen the horses with their saddles displaced, the Turks fleeing and returning, and the battle raging fiercer than before; the one side laboured to crush, the other to repel; both exerted their strength with the utmost fury, till King Richard hearing that the rear was put into great confusion, rode at full gallop to their assistance, cutting down the Turks right and left like lightning with his sword. And quickly, as of yore the Philistines fled from Maccabeus, so were the Turks now routed, and so did they fly from the face of King Richard and make for the mountains; but some of them remained amongst us, having lost their heads.

This extract is a facsimile of all the chances and changes that occurred to the Christians on their passage from Acre to Jaffa.

CHAPTER 9

He that hath nature in him, must be grateful;
'Tis the Creator's primary great law,
That links the chain of beings to each other.

At Jaffa a new contention arose. The French barons, fatigued with marching and fruitless skirmishing, advocated the policy of remaining a time in the city and rebuilding its fortifications; while Plantagenet, anxious to press his advantage, was desirous of proceeding to Ascalon. The soldiers remembering with regret the "loaves and fishes" of Acre, inclined to the counsel of the Duke of Burgundy, and Richard was forced to submit his better judgment to the unanimous voice of his followers.

It was in vain that the king urged the soldiers to a rapid completion of the works. The summer faded into autumn, and the fortifications were still incomplete. The Moslems began to collect in the vicinity of Jaffa, and all parties of Christians, whether of foraging or falconry, were subject to frequent surprise and attack. On one occasion, a party of Templars fell into an ambuscade of the Turks, and Richard, hearing of their danger, rushed out with a few troops to their assistance. The conflict was dreadful. Hordes of *infidels* fell upon the little band, who, struggling in the midst of their foes, with great loss carved their way to the city. On their return, William Longsword remonstrated with the monarch for this useless exposure of life, to which the generous Cœur de Lion, changing colour with indignation, replied, "Richard Plantagenet knows not the prudence that weighs safety against glory, and for the rest it is the office of a king to defend his subjects, and the business of a crusader to destroy the enemies of the cross."

The defences of Jaffa being complete, Richard prepared to prosecute the war with vigour. Leaving the city with a small garrison, he led his troops as far as Ramula, and made their camp on the bloody field where Stephen, Earl of Blois, received his mortal wound. A winter of extraordinary inclemency aggravated their hardships. The winds tore up the tents, and the rain spoiled the provisions, and rusted the arms. Through the hovering myriads of Saracens the Christians pressed their way almost in sight of Jerusalem. Richard was animated by the most ardent expectation. But the Templars, Hospitallers and Pisans, represented the impossibility of capturing the city, with their army in its present condition, the impracticability of garrisoning it against the Turks in the neighbourhood, and the certainty that the soldiers as soon as the sepulchre was recovered, would return to Europe, leaving the rest of Palestine in the hands of the *infidels*.

Influenced by these unanswerable arguments, the disappointed king gave orders to fall back upon Ramula, and continued to retrograde with his murmuring and discontented army to Ascalon, a city of great consequence, being the link between the Turks in Jerusalem, and the Turks in Egypt. The pains and perils of this backward march eclipsed all former sufferings, and when the dismantled walls of Ascalon at length received them, Famine stared upon them with her hollow eyes, and Faction with its sharpened fangs tore asunder the remaining cords that bound together the wasted body of the *croises*.

The Duke of Burgundy deserted the standard of Richard, part of the French soldiers retired to Jaffa, others to Acre, and others to Tyre; and while the proudest nobles and the most dignified of the clergy were employed like the meanest vassals, in repairing the ruined fortifications, Leopold wrapped in haughty selfishness surveyed the works with contemptuous sneers, and remarked, "The father of Austria was neither a carpenter nor a mason."

The Turkish *soldan* aware of the distress of his enemies, considered the war as nearly at an end, and dismissed a portion of his troops. He even extended the courtesies of civilized life to the valiant Richard, furnished his table with Damascene pears, peaches, and other delicacies, and with a liberal hand supplied the snow of Lebanon to cool his wines.

The chief *emirs* who, attracted by curiosity or admiration, visited the court of the British Lion, returned with the most exaggerated accounts of the urbanity and prowess of the gallant "Melech Ric."

One morning, at an hour somewhat earlier than his usual levee, Richard was surprised by a visit from Mestoc, accompanied by a female closely veiled. "Welcome, my noble Moor," exclaimed the king, as the Saracen advanced and bowed with the ceremonious obeisance of eastern courtesy. "Heaven bless the chance that hath brought thee hither. Next to a trusty friend, Plantagenet holds in honour a worthy foe."

The Saracen gravely replied, "The Melech Ric wrongs the errand of his servant, if he discern not in his ransomed captive, one whom he hath made his friend."

"I doubt not the truth of thy saying," replied the king, "since reason and experience teach that ingratitude is incompatible with true courage."

"The chief of the Egyptians is, indeed, thy friend," continued Mestoc;"but were he twice thy foe, he brings a passport to the heart of the king, for 'from the place of the beloved, a zephyr hath blown, and thou seest one whose presence is as the breath of the heliotrope.'" Turning to his companion, he lifted her veil, and disclosed the features of Elsiebede.

"Elsiebede!" exclaimed the monarch, in astonishment and alarm. "What of my queen? of Joanna? of England?"

"My royal mistress is in health," replied Elsiebede, "and by this token," handing him a casket, "commendeth her love to her absent lord: and peace resteth upon the household."

"And wherefore comest thou hither? and why under such convoy?" inquired Richard.

"The errand of my mistress required a faithful messenger; and the chief will explain the mystery of my coming," replied the girl.

With a puzzled look, Richard turned to Mestoc. "It is, perhaps, unknown to the prince of the west," said the chieftain, "that this damsel, Elsiebede, is the daughter of my sister."

"How?" exclaimed Richard, gazing with astonishment upon the Moorish girl."Our fair queen has long blinded our eyes to other beauty, or we should have seen what the most careless observer could not fail to note, that she has the countenance and bearing of a princess."

"The family of the Prophet (blessed be he)," said Mestoc, his swarthy cheek reddening with a touch of pride, "boasts not a more noble origin, than the Gyptianos slave of the Frankish queen."

"But by what means hath she discovered herself to thee in this strange land?" inquired Richard.

"What saith the proverb?" replied the Saracen. "'The heart thrills at the sound of the kinsman's voice.'When the Melech Ric gave audience to the ambassadors of Saladin, the ring upon his finger, once the talisman of our tribe, arrested my gaze; but the maiden's eyes, brighter than the jewel, moved me to speak to her in the Egyptian tongue. She comprehended my words, and met me that night at the tower Maledictum, where I learned her history and made her acquainted with her kindred. She visited me in prison, and when I refused to fly, despatched Salaman to the Sultan to beg my life. For the rest, thou knowest that I thank the brave leader of the Franks no less than the timely ransom for my rescue. Before leaving the camp of the Latins I gave the zealous Ethiope a passport, commanding all true Mussulmans to bring him wherever found, safe to my presence.

"When, therefore, thy queen, distressed by the enemies in thine own household, sought for means to communicate with thee, Salaman conducted Elsiebede to my tent; and I have hasted to convey her to my deliverer. For what saith the proverb? '*In the sky it is written, on the pages of the air, he who doeth kind actions will experience the like.*' Notwithstanding, let the damsel, I pray thee, depart with me; in the tent of my women she shall have careful attendance. If thou wouldst confer with her, the cunning Ysop knows her place of rest." Richard assented, and the Saracens withdrew.

The letters from the queen contained intelligence of the most startling character. The Genoese and Pisans, rivals for the carrying trade of the East, had made Acre their seaport, and to give dignity to their commercial animosities had espoused, the one the party of Conrad, the other that of Guy de Lusignan. Their feuds had kept the residents of the city in a constant state of apprehension, and Berengaria entreated her lord to return to Acre, or to cause her immediately to be transported to Jaffa. In the same package were despatches from England, of a nature equally alarming. No sooner had Philip reached Italy than he applied to Pope Celestine for a dispensation from his oath to leave Richard's domains in quiet.

When that request was denied, he proceeded in a covert manner to detach Prince John from his allegiance, promised him Alice in marriage, and offered to make him lord of all Richard's possessions in France. The prompt measures of Queen Eleanor had in some degree counteracted this design. Forbidding John, under the penalty of a mother's curse, to invade his brother's rights, she conveyed the hapless Alice to the strong castle of Rouen, where she subjected her to an imprisonment more rigorous than she had herself suffered in Winchester. The principal barons had leagued with John, or against him, and the whole realm was in a state of ferment.

The political troubles of England, the treachery of the French king, the solicitude of his beautiful queen, and the dubious prospects of the crusade, raised a tumult of agitating thoughts in the mind of the king, and he passed the night in a state of sleepless excitement. Scarcely waiting for the dawn, he summoned Salaman and despatched him for Mestoc. Impelled by the pressing exigencies of the case, he intrusted the generous foe with a knowledge of the embarrassments of his position, and entreated his good offices in bringing about an accommodation with Saladin, stipulating only for the possession of Jerusalem and the restoration of the true cross.

The Saracen undertook the commission, and after three days returned with the answer. With the stateliness of eastern formality the Mussulman declared his strong desire of peace, and his admiration of the courage and abilities of Plantagenet; but he asserted that he could never resign Jerusalem, since the sacred city was as dear to the Moslem as the Christian world, and that the principles of his religion forbade his conniving at idolatry by permitting the worship of a piece of wood. Thwarted in this negotiation, Richard again employed Mestoc to propose a consolidation of the Christian and Mohammedan interests by the establishment of a government at Jerusalem, partly European and partly Asiatic, which should secure to the pilgrims free access to the Holy Sepulchre, and feudal rights to all Christians who should choose to settle in Palestine.

Mestoc returned from this embassy accompanied by a young *emir* named Saphadin, a brother of the Turkish emperor. The overture of Cœur de Lion had been favourably received by the sagacious Saladin, but foreseeing that a stronger bond than a political alliance would be necessary to bind the two nations together, he had added to the articles the proposition of a union between his brother and the fair sister of Melech Ric. Saphadin was also commissioned to conduct the English king and his followers in safety to Acre.

CHAPTER 10

A pen—to register; a key,—
That winds through secret wards;
Are well assigned to Memory,
By allegoric bards.

When Richard arrived at Acre, he found affairs in the greatest confusion. The dissensions between the rival parties had terminated in open hostilities, more pressing messages urging his return had arrived from England, and he was forced to the conclusion that without

205

some concession on his part, the whole crusade would prove an entire failure. The military abilities of Guy, were inferior to those of Conrad. Richard thus found it easy to satisfy his claim by bestowing upon him the rich and beautiful island of Cyprus, while he conciliated the Genoese, by consenting to the coronation of the Marquis of Tyre.

Matters being thus accommodated between the jealous mercenaries, the mind of the king recurred to the original project of identifying the interests of the east and west, by uniting the heir of the thousand tribes, with the daughter of Henry Plantagenet. But Joanna, less susceptible of romantic enthusiasm than her mother, steadfastly rejected the offer of her Paynim lover, and the bishop of Salisbury, with other zealous priests sustained her decision, and Cœur de Lion overborne by their clamour, was forced to relinquish his cherished project. As some slight compensation to the disappointed Saphadin, he conferred upon him the honour of knighthood, and dismissed him with the strongest expressions of favour. Cœur de Lion then despatched a band of nobles to bring Conrad, the newly elected king, with all due honour to Acre.

Delighted with his splendid prospects, Conrad ordered magnificent preparations to be made for the ceremony of coronation, and gave himself up to the most extravagant joy. But returning one day from an entertainment given by the bishop, he was suddenly seized and stabbed by two assassins, followers of the Old Man of the Mountain.

His sudden death threw affairs again into confusion. The French who were encamped outside of Tyre, to the number of ten thousand, called upon the widow to give up the city for the service of King Philip. This she steadily refused to do; declaring that her lord had commanded her with his dying breath to resign it to no one but Richard, or whosoever should be elected King of Palestine. The French at once commenced hostilities, and the siege of the city had been some time in progress, when Count Henry of Champagne arrived in the camp. He was one of the most powerful vassals of the King of France; his mother was the half-sister both of Richard and Philip; his father had twice visited the Holy Land, and he was himself faithful to the interest of the crusade, and a general favourite among the warriors.

The French leaders besought him to accept the crown of the kingdom, marry the widow of the marquis, and heal the dissensions that embarrassed the movements of the *croises*. Richard's consent to this measure was easily obtained. The nuptials were solemnized with royal magnificence, and the new king immediately published an edict, calling upon all his subjects to arm for the ensuing campaign, and join the English forces at Acre. Before they were ready to set out for the final conquest of the Holy City, fresh accounts were received from England of the increasing power of Prince John, and the treachery of Philip Augustus, but Richard disregarding these pressing calls, determined to strike one more blow for the Holy Sepulchre. Hymns and thanksgiving testified the popular joy, and so sanguine were the soldiers of the speedy accomplishment of their wishes, that they carried with them only a month's provisions.

When they reached Bethlehem, the heats of summer had already commenced, and Richard began to feel that his force was not sufficient to encounter the hardships of the siege, and keep up communication with the stores upon the coast. It was therefore agreed that a council should be held, consisting of twenty persons; five Templars, five Hospitallers, five French nobles, and five native Christians of Syria, to decide upon the measures to be adopted. They ascertained that the Turks had destroyed all the cisterns within two miles of the city, that the waters of Siloa would be insufficient for the use of the army, and as the siege was therefore utterly impracticable, they gave it as their unanimous opinion that the most eligible plan, would be to proceed direct against Babylon. The French stoutly opposed this project, declaring that they would march nowhere else than to the siege of Jerusalem. The debate grew so warm that the Duke of Burgundy withdrew his forces from the main body of the army, and took up a separate position.

Harassed by conjectures concerning the condition of his English subjects, discouraged at the disaffection of his soldiers, grieved at the sight of sufferings which he could not alleviate, and mortified with the prospect of a final failure of his enterprise, Richard strolled from the camp to the brow of an adjacent eminence. Occupied by sad and gloomy meditations, he walked, with his eyes fixed on the ground, unaware of the extensive prospect that spread out before him, nor was he conscious of companionship, till William Longsword taking his arm, disturbed his revery by saying, "This way, sire, from yonder point can be seen where the setting sun gilds the towers of Jerusalem."

Instinctively the lion-hearted monarch raised his broad shield to shut out the view, while tears forced themselves from his manly eyes. "Nay, my brother," said he, "since God forbids to my unworthy arm the redemption of his Holy Sepulchre, I may not bless myself with a sight of his sacred city." He turned away, and silently retraced his

207

steps.

That night as he lay tossing upon his couch unable to sleep, he was surprised by a stealthy visit from Salaman. The officious black had gained permission of Mestoc to conduct the king to the cell of a hermit, who dwelt in one of the rocky caves with which the wilderness of Judea abounds. The devout man, whose venerable countenance and solemn appearance gave a strong guaranty for his truth, received the king with the deepest respect, and declared to him that a long time ago he had concealed a piece of the Holy Cross, in order to preserve it until Palestine should be rescued from the *infidels*. He stated that Saladin had often pressed him with the most searching inquiries concerning it, but he had faithfully guarded the secret, and to the King of England he now committed the precious relic, for the adoration of those brave men who had so valiantly fought in defence of the Christian faith. Reverently wrapping it in a cloth of gold, Richard conveyed it to the camp, and the following day the whole army were permitted to press their lips upon the sacred wood.

The troops had then orders to retire towards Jaffa, but civil rancour and fierce dissensions prevailed to such an extent among the forces, that but little discipline or order could be preserved. When they arrived before the place, they found it closely besieged by the Saracens, and on the point of surrender. The conflict which ensued was the most hotly contested of any that occurred during the Third Crusade. Richard performed prodigies of valour. His battle-axe gleamed everywhere in the van of the fight, opening for his followers bloody paths through the centre of the Turkish divisions. The gallant Fanuelle, ploughing her way through the serried ranks, bore him proudly on, while the arrows and javelins of the Saracens, rattled idly upon his iron vest, till at length a fallen foe, pierced with a spear the breast of his favourite, and amid the exulting yells of the barbarians, horse and rider fell to the ground.

Instantly starting to his feet, he drew his sword, and continued the combat undaunted as before. The generous Saphadin, who from a distance had watched the prowess of the valiant European, despatched a groom to his rescue with a splendid Arabian barb. Remounting, Richard continued the contest till the going down of the sun, when darkness separated the combatants. Jaffa was rescued, and the joy of this signal victory in some measure compensated the English for their bitter disappointment in abandoning Jerusalem. On reviewing his troops, Richard saw from their diminished numbers the utter hopelessness of attempting any further conquest, and this sad conviction strengthened the motives which determined his return to Europe. His late success gave him the vantage-ground in soliciting an honourable peace with the *soldan*, who, now that Richard was preparing to depart, was better able to estimate candidly, and appreciate fairly the knightly qualities and heroic courage that had distinguished his career in the Holy Land.

The Emperor Saladin and Richard Plantagenet, each with a brilliant train of attendants, met near Mount Tabor, to confer upon the momentous interests that clustered round the Holy City, and to arrange a protracted truce. The preliminaries occupied some days. The Saracens insisted upon the destruction of the fort of Ascalon, the Christians negotiated for the restoration of Jerusalem. It was at last settled, that Joppa and Tyre, and the country between them should be ceded to Henry, Count of Champagne, that Ascalon should be dismantled, and that the Christians should have free access to the Holy Sepulchre without molestation or tribute. The presence of Mestoc and Saphadin contributed not a little to the harmonious adjustment of these intricate affairs.

The treaty was to remain in force three years, three months, three weeks, three days, and three hours, a number of mysterious sanctity with the people of the East, and a space which Richard thought sufficient for him to compose the factions in England, and return to complete the conquest of Palestine.

Since her expedition to Jaffa, Elsiebede had remained in care of her uncle; and Richard was now informed that Saphadin, disappointed in his suit with the lady Joanna, had transferred his affections to the bewitching Gyptianos. The crosses which Cœur de Lion had borne in the crusade had somewhat moderated the imperiousness of his temper, and taught him the policy of a seeming acquiescence in inevitable necessity; and thus though vividly impressed with an anticipation of Berengaria's frowns, he gracefully acceded to the request of Mestoc, and bestowed the Moorish girl and her swarthy attendant upon his noble friend.

The *soldan* had arranged the pavilion of the Christian monarch with the utmost magnificence, at the southern extremity of the encampment, while his own sable tent had been pitched opposite on the north. Near the close of a bright Syrian day, as Richard sat listening to the strains with which Blondel beguiled the tedium of the listless hours, his chamberlain entered to announce the emperor. The illustrious *soldan* came without the usual attendants of his rank, and Richard surprised and not ill-pleased by this mark of friendly familiarity, received him with the frank cordiality characteristic of his nature. The face of the noble Kurd wore a seriousness that seemed the result of thought rather than the habitual gravity of his nation and religion, and Richard, with instinctive delicacy, dismissed the minstrel, and waited in silent wonder for the communication of his honoured guest.

But what was his surprise when the gifted Saracen, instead of employing the common *Lingua Franca*, addressed him easily and fluently in the liquid Provençal. "The Melech Ric," said he, "wonders to hear his mother-tongue in a foreign land, but not stranger to thee than to me are my words. Forty and three times have the constellations described their circles in the heavens since my lip assayed this language; but thy presence has been to my heart like the beams of the rising sun that causes the statue of Memnon to speak."

Astonishment prevented reply; but every feature of Cœur de Lion evinced the intensest curiosity. "Know then," said Saladin, answering the mute interrogation, "that as the warmth of our Eastern clime flushes the grape with a deeper hue than the temperate north, so it earlier awakens and strengthens the passions in the human breast. Hence was it that though but a youth I saw and loved a beautiful daughter of Frangistan. Her eyes—God said to them, Be—and they were, affecting my heart with the potency of wine. Her voice—it made me forget the spirits that stand about the throne of Allah (blessed be his name), and had not the Prophet ordained that she should suddenly be torn from me, I might have become a convert to the faith of the Nazarene."

"Would to heaven thou hadst!" ejaculated Richard, "for Godfrey of Boulogne could not more worthily fill the throne of Jerusalem."

Without appearing to note the enthusiasm of Richard, the Saracen slowly unfastened the scarf that bound his caftan, and exhibited the embroidered cross of Aquitaine.

"Thou art a Christian in thy secret heart," said Richard, starting up at the sight and grasping the hand of the *soldan*. "It solves the mystery of thy victories. I knew that no unbaptized Infidel could have so prevailed against the armies of the Lord."

"Nay," said the Mussulman, smiling gravely, "think not the prince of the thousand tribes worships a symbol as do the Franks, though for the memory of her whose slender fingers wrought the emblem, I have sometimes spared the lives of those whom our laws hold accursed—but there is no God but one God, and Mohammed is his Prophet."

Somewhat abashed Richard sat holding the scarf in his hand and murmuring half aloud, "The Provençal tongue; the cross of Aquitaine; a daughter of Frangistan." Then raising his eyes he said, with a look of painful embarrassment, "Noble Saladin, thy generous interest in the English crusader is sufficiently explained. Destroy not, I pray thee, the gratitude of the son of Eleanor by alluding to the follies of the mother."

"Nay," said Saladin, satisfied that he had correctly interpreted the hereditary peculiarities, which his observant eye had detected in Richard, "the name of the beloved is secure from reproach; but my memory still looks upon her as she was, and I would fain teach my imagination to regard her as she is. Dwells she in the trembling tent of age? or has the angel Azrael drawn around her silent couch the curtain of perpetual night?"

"She lives," returns Richard, proudly, "regent of my noble realm. Thousands receive benefits from her hands, which as thy poet saith, *'are the keys of the supplies of Providence.'*"

"I am content," replied the Saracen. "For the rest, hitherto, I have kept my secret in a house with a lock, whose key is lost, and whose door is sealed. So let it be henceforth between us. The peace of Allah rest upon Melech Ric, and may he die among his kindred." As he arose to leave the tent the voice of the *muezzein* was heard through the camp calling, "To prayer, to prayer." The noble chief paused upon the threshold, and turning his face toward Mecca, bowed his forehead to the dust, and reverently repeated the Mohammedan blessing.

Early on the subsequent day, the Latins prepared for departure, and there remained only the last formalities of ratifying the treaty. As the two monarchs, disdaining the common obligation of an oath, advanced to the centre of that fair and flowery meadow, and extended their hands above the parchment, they seemed the representatives of Mohammedan superstition and Christian enthusiasm, and a prophetic eye might have read in the appearance of these leaders of the belligerent powers, that for a century had caused the earth to tremble beneath their tread, the character and the destiny of the nations which they represented.

The form and countenance of the Saracen, erect and calm, but lithe and wary, with a certain air of majesty and repose, indicated a consciousness of the decay of youthful vigour, but a sense of compensation however in the resources of wisdom and skill laid up in the storehouse of experience, for the necessities of declining years.

In the compact and muscular frame, and sparkling eyes of Richard, were expressed that reckless spirit of pursuit, that ardour of passion, enthusiasm of love, romance, and religion, that steady self-reliance, born of conscious strength and indomitable will, which characterized the growing nations of Europe, and finally gave the dominion of the world to the Anglo-Saxon race. Grasping each other's hands, these two exponents of Oriental tactics and European chivalry mutually pledged their faith to the treaty, and parted less like deadly foes, than faithful friends, who hoped to meet again.

CHAPTER 11

He that can endure
To follow with allegiance a fallen lord,
Doth conquer him that did his master conquer,
And earns a place i' the story.

On his arrival at Acre, Richard learned that the friends of Conrad accused him as the instigator of the assassination, and that reports had been conveyed to Europe impeaching his honour as a king, and his fame as a warrior. Deeming it unsafe to attempt the passage in the *Trenc-the-mere*, he committed Berengaria and her ladies again to the care of Stephen de Turnham and his faithful Blondel, and saw them safely embarked for Navarre, Sept. 29, 1192. The following month, having provided for the safe return of the soldiers and pilgrims who had accompanied him on his fruitless expedition, he himself last of all, in the disguise of a Templar, sailed from the port of Acre.

As the rocky heights of Lebanon and the lofty summit of Carmel faded from his view, he stretched his hands towards the receding shores, and while tears streamed from his eyes, prayed aloud, "Oh Holy Land, I commend thee to God; and, if his heavenly grace shall grant me so long to live, I trust that I shall return according to his good pleasure, and set thee free from all thine enemies."

The voyage proved more disastrous than was common, even in those days of unpractised navigation. Many of the English vessels were wrecked upon the shores of Africa, others fortunately reached friendly ports whence the warriors returned by land to Britain. Six weeks after his departure from Acre, the vessel of Richard encountered a pirate ship off the coast of Barbary. Learning from the commander that his misfortunes had become known, and that the French lords were pre-pared to seize him as soon as he should land in Marseilles, he determined, as his ship was already unseaworthy, to pass up the Adriatic, and make his way through Germany. Landing not far from Venice with six companions, he pursued his route to the north. But news of the dispersion of his fleet had already reached Germany, and orders had been issued, that all travellers should be closely interrogated.

His companions were arrested; but the monarch escaped, attended only by a boy who understood the language of the country, and conducted him to houses of entertainment, unfrequented by persons of rank. Thus resting by day and travelling by night, they reached the borders of the Danube. Secure in his disguise, the king began to enjoy the frank hilarity and hearty cheer of the inn kitchen, and with a good nature appropriate to his assumed character, assisted in the preparations for the evening repast. A loitering spy observing a costly jewel upon the finger of the pretended friar, at once reported the suspicious circumstance to the governor.

A company of soldiers were immediately despatched to arrest him, the leader of which was an Austrian who had served under him in Palestine. The house was searched, and the landlord subjected to a close scrutiny concerning harbouring a man of the description of the hunted monarch. "There be no such person here," indignantly exclaimed the boor, "unless it be the Templar in the kitchen roasting fowls." The officers immediately followed the hint, and surprised the fictitious palmer with the spit in his hand.

The Austrian cavalier recognized, at once, the herculean frame and ruddy countenance of the king. "It is he. Seize him," cried he to his minions. Notwithstanding a valiant resistance, Richard was overborne by numbers and conveyed to the castle of Tenebreuse, where for several months all trace of him was lost.

★★★★★★

Meanwhile the vessel containing the princesses arrived safely at Naples, whence they journeyed to Rome. The enmity of Philip, and vague reports concerning the shipwreck of her husband, so terrified Berengaria that she remained here under the protection of the pope till the ensuing spring. During the carnival, the services of the royal ladies were in requisition for a brilliant masquerade. The affair, involving an uncommon call for *bijouterie*, the queen found no little amusement in searching the shops of the jewellers in pursuit of appropriate decorations. On one of these excursions her attention was attracted by the appearance of a boy clad in mean apparel who was offering a valuable jewel for sale.

The eagerness and suspicion with which the shopman regarded it excited her curiosity, and stepping forward she recognized the signet ring of Richard. Hastily purchasing the precious talisman she ordered the youth to follow her, intending to question him further concerning his master; but when she reached her apartments, he had disappeared. She sent messengers in every direction, and caused the most searching inquiries to be made, but all in vain; he was nowhere to be found. Her anxiety for the fate of Richard, found vent in fruitless exertions and floods of tears. The mysterious circumstances reawakened all her superstitious apprehensions.

She was convinced that the fatal ring which she had so foolishly given and so weakly allowed him to retain, had finally accomplished his prediction, "betrayed him to his direst foe, or drowned him in the sea." At one moment she bewailed him as dead, at the next upbraided her friends for neglecting to deliver him from the dungeon in which she was positive the Duke of Austria had confined him. Blondel, whose devotion to his royal friend equalled her own, set off at once under the character of a wandering minstrel in search of his master.

At length the pope, moved by Berengaria's distress, placed her under the escort of Count Raimond of Toulouse, the hero of the tournament, who, with a strong guard, conducted the queens across the country to Navarre. The valiant Raimond soon found it an easier and pleasanter task to soothe the mind of the lovely Joanna, than to listen to the unavailing complaints of the despairing Berengaria, and so resigned did he become to his grateful duties, that before they reached the end of their journey he had become a candidate for the office during life of sympathizer and protector.

In the joy of welcoming her youngest daughter, Queen Eleanor forgot her hereditary enmity to her cousin of Toulouse, and Count Raimond received the hand of Joanna with the resignation of the contested claim to that splendid fief, which had so long filled the south of France with strife and bloodshed. Deprived of the society of the tranquil and considerate Joanna, Berengaria was more than ever lonely and disconsolate, and the death of her father, Sancho the Wise, not long after, added another weight to the sorrow that oppressed her.

Eleanor's detention of the Princess Alice had drawn upon Normandy a fierce invasion by Philip Augustus, and the noble domain might have fallen a prey to his rapacity had not Sancho the Strong, moved by the pleadings of his sister, traversed France with a choice band of knights, and compelled his grasping sovereign to abandon the siege of Rouen.

★★★★★★

Meantime the faithful Blondel traverses many a weary league in search of the lion-hearted king. His harp gives him ready entrance to the castles of the great and the cottages of the lowly. Warriors mingle their rude voices with the chorus of his soul-stirring tensons, and light-hearted maidens weep pitying tears at the sound of his tender *plaintes*. Stern jailers, like the Furies that guarded the lost Eurydice, leave their dismal avocations, and "listening crowd the sweet musician's side." The lyre of Orpheus draws back the rusty bolts and opens wide the ponderous doors, and many a hapless prisoner is charmed with the strains of light and love that for years had only visited his dreams.

But Richard is not among the minstrels; his voice echoes not in the chorus of the warriors; his sad complaint is not heard among the wail of the captives. The troubadour turns away disappointed from each new trial, but restless affection prompts him to repeated endeavours, and ephemeral hopes continually lead him on.

He wanders along the banks of the Danube, he sits beneath the dark shadow of the Tenebreuse, from whose portals no ransomed captive has ever yet come forth to the free light of day. He assays his most thrilling strains, but the guards, insensible as the granite effigies that frown upon him from the lofty turrets, remain unmoved. He throws down his lyre in despair, and hot tears gush from his eyes. The image of Berengaria floats before him, her cheek flushed with hope, and her eyes sparkling with love. He sees her leaning enchanted from the vessel's side, listening to the voice of her royal lover, while the wind with fairy fingers sweeps a wild symphony through the straining cordage of the gallant *Trenc-the-mere*. With the recollections come the long-forgotten emotions of that blissful season. Instinctively his hand grasps the harp; his spirit kindles with the inspiration; a melodious prelude rings out upon the still air, and he sings,

> *Your beauty, lady fair,*
> *None views without delight;*
> *But still so cold an air*
> *No passion can excite.*
> *Yet this I patient see,*
> *While all are shunn'd like me.*

215

Is it the voice of the warder mingling with his own in the concluding strain, or has his rapt fancy taught the echoes to mock his impatience with the loved tones of the royal troubadour? He pauses—'Tis
neither memory nor fancy. From the lonely turret and the closely
barred casements pours a liquid strain, and his fond ear drinks again
the clear tones that answered to his own, when in harmonious rivalry
each sought the rich reward of Berengaria's smile.

No nymph my heart can wound,
If favours she divide,
And smile on all around,
Unwilling to decide:
I'd rather hatred bear
Than love with other share.

It is the voice of Plantagenet!! The song, the tune are his! He lives!
He may yet be ransomed.

A rough hand is laid upon the shoulder of the minstrel, and a surly
voice bids him, Begone! He departs without question or reply. He
courts no danger; for on his safety depends the life of his friend. The
listless stroll of the harper is exchanged for the quick firm pace of one
who hastes to the accomplishment of a worthy purpose. He avoids
the populous cities, and tarries not in the smiling villages. He reaches
the sea-coast—he finds a vessel—he lands in England—he obtains
audience of the queen regent. She who subscribes herself "Eleanora,
by the *wrath* of God Queen of England," makes all Europe ring with
the infamy of those princes who have combined to keep her son in
chains. The power of the pope is implored, the mercy of the holy
mother is invoked. The Emperor Henry VI. requires the royal prisoner
at the hands of Leopold. Richard is brought before the diet at Worms,
to answer for his crimes.

He is accused of making an alliance with Tancred, of turning the
arms of the crusade against the Christian King of Cyprus, of affront-
ing the Duke of Austria before Acre, of obstructing the progress of
the *croises* by his quarrels with the King of France, of assassinating the
Marquis Conrad Prince of Tyre, and of concluding a truce with Saladin and leaving Jerusalem in the hands of the Saracen emperor.

The noble Plantagenet arises in the majesty of his innocence and,
"as the lion shakes the dewdrops from his mane," dispels the false ac-
cusations of his enemies. The eloquence of truth carries irresistible
conviction to the hearts of the congregated princes. They exclaim

216

loudly against the conduct of the emperor, the pope threatens him with excommunication, and the reluctant Henry is compelled from very shame to consent to the prisoner's release. But a heavy fine is required, and the monarch is remanded to his captivity till the sum shall be paid. Every vassal in England and Normandy is taxed for the ransom of his lord. The churches and monasteries melt down their plate, the bishops, abbots, and nobles, contribute a portion of their rent, the inferior clergy a tenth of their tithes, and Eleanor conveys the treasure to Germany, and brings back her long lost-son!

CHAPTER 12

Do you like letter-reading? If you do,
I have some twenty dozen very pretty ones:
Gay, sober, rapturous, solemn, very true,
And very lying, stupid ones, and witty ones.

LETTER FROM THE KNIGHTS OF ST. JOHN TO RICHARD.

To Richard Plantagenet, by the grace of God, King of England, your poor and unworthy servants of the Hospital of St. John, humbly set forth these things. We remember when it pleased the great Richard to depart from Palestine, leaving the Holy City still in the hands of the Moslems, that he pledged the honour of a knight, to return when the troubles of his own kingdom should be composed, and once more do battle in the cause of the saints.

According to our poor ability we preserved the conditions of the treaty, and the land had rest from war. The mighty sultan, Saladin, then kept his goods in peace. But God has called him to the judgment to answer for his crimes against the Christian nations. His brother Saphadin usurps the throne of Jerusalem, and his sons strive to rend the kingdom in pieces, that each may take his share.

Now the Scripture saith expressly, '*A house divided against itself shall not stand,*' and the fulfilment thereof is shown in that which they begin to do. A scarcity of food exhausts their forces, and it were easy for a Christian army, while they lie torn with faction and reduced by famine, to march through the length and breadth of the land, and make the strong places our own. But the forces of the military friars are insufficient for the pious work; therefore we turn our eyes towards Europe, we fix our regards upon the islands of the sea, and lift our hands to Heaven and pray that the lion-hearted monarch, with his valiant knights, would once more 'come up to the help of the Lord against the mighty.' May God and his saints incline your heart to the divine undertaking, and may the counsels of the Lord prevail. Amen.

Written from Palestine A.D. 1195.

Encyclical Letter of Celestin III.

To the most Potent Sovereigns of Europe, to the princes, nobles, and barons, who by the favour of God, hold authority over the dominions and vassals of our Lord and Saviour—to the cardinals, bishops, prelates, and other clergy that rule the Church of God, Pope Celestin III. called to be the vicar of Christ, and in virtue of his office heir to the Apostolic See, sendeth greeting.

My brethren, it hath been shown to us that Jerusalem, the city of the Saviour's life and passion, still lieth in the hands of the Moslems, that the *infidels* mock the rites of our holy religion even in the land where the sacred mysteries were first instituted, and that the Christians of Syria cry unto the brethren of the west for aid. Wherefore we command you all to spread again the crimson standard of the cross, and march against the persecutors of the faith.

By the authority of the blessed St. Peter, from whom we hold the keys of the kingdom of Heaven, whereby we open and no man can shut; we shut, and no man can open; we ordain that all those who in heart and truth obey this, our holy mandate, shall have claim to those indulgences needful for the flesh, in this toilsome warfare; absolution from those sins which they have heretofore committed, or shall hereafter fall into:—and we set before them an abundance of the honours of this life, and in the life to come life everlasting.

Given at Rome, under our hand and seal, this tenth day after Epiphany, in the Year of Grace 1196.

Letter From Elsiebede to Berengaria

Elsiebede to the most honoured Queen Berengaria. My noble mistress will pardon the wife of Saif Addin if she intrude upon her gracious attention the story of the changes that have befallen one whom Allah (blessed be his name) hath raised from the

218

low estate of a servant, to the dignity of sole wife of the monarch of the East. Though the voice of love charmed my ear, and made my heart tremble with sweet delight, yet tears overflowed my eyes when it was told me I should look no more upon the face of her whose fostering care had sustained my youth, and brought me to the land of my kindred.

My beloved lady and her valiant lord have departed for their own land, but still I hear their names echoed from the base of Carmel, to Damascus the garden of delights. The Arab horseman threatens his steed with the weight of King Richard's arm, the Saracen mother hushes her babe with the fear of the Melech Ric, and blesses her daughter with the benison, '*Allah* make thee fair as Berengaria.' But 'The strength of the mighty and the charm of the lovely availeth naught, since death, the terminator of delights, waiteth at the threshhold of every dwelling.' Scarce could the vessels that bore the *croises* have reached the shores of Frangistan, when Disease, more potent than even the sword of the lion-hearted Plantagenet, laid its hand upon Saladin the Powerful, the Illustrious, and his life was consumed beneath its burning touch.

Then the black banner that awoke thy terrors at the first sight of Palestine, and that so often like the wing of Azrael, waved over the fields of the slain, by his last command, was rolled in the dust, and the shroud that was to wrap his body in the grave, was borne aloft in the sight of his people, while the imams and muezzins cried aloud with an exceeding bitter cry, 'Behold all that remains to the mighty Saladin, the prince of the thousand tribes, the *vizier* of Egypt, the Conqueror of Syria, the Emperor of the East. Behold oh man, and prepare to die!'

Until his death the virtuous *soldan* had faithfully preserved the peace made with the Melech Ric, and it was the wish of his brother, my lord Saif Addin, upon whom the *emirs* and *atabeks* bestowed the kingdom of Syria, still to keep faith and truce with the Christians, but as your holy writing saith, '*A man's foes shall be they of his own household,*' even so hath it happened unto my lord. The undutiful sons of Saladin have seized Aleppo, Damascus, and Egypt. They have drawn the sword of battle, and our land again groaneth under the miseries of war. From these things it chanced that certain timid Christians, fearing again the renewal of all those sufferings, from which they had rested during the space of three years, called again on their brethren of Europe for aid. And there came a great company of crusading Germans, brutal and bloodthirsty, to wrest the territory of Palestine from the hands of the sovereign. When the Latins of Acre saw what manner of men they were, they represented to them the virtues and moderation of the noble Saif Addin, and entreated that the Christians of the Holy Land should have space for negotiation and treaty, before the commencement of hostilities. But they would not hear; and so the cruel war was again begun.

Then my lord girding himself for the conflict, showed that the spirit of Saladin survived in his brother. He advanced to the north to meet his foes, and a terrible slaughter took place in the vale of Sidon. The followers of the prophet were slain on every side, and the Latins also were greatly discomfited, and took refuge in Tyre. A portion of the Germans proceeded to Jaffa; thither Saif Addin pursued them, and after a continued siege, took the city and put them all to the sword. On the same night, Count Henry of Champagne, wearing the title, but not the crown of the King of Jerusalem, was killed by a fall, and the Christians being thus left without lord or ruler, concluded a peace with the emperor. Isabella, the widow of Count Henry, is again a wife, being taken in marriage by Almeric, brother of Guy de Lusignan.

The prophet saith truly, '*Though the storm rage without, there may be peace in the tent,*' and I dwell in safety within the sacred walls of Jerusalem. Cohr Eddin, my first-born, already assays to bend the bow of his father, and his infant brother nestling in my bosom, just lisps the name of his warlike sire. Farewell. The blessing of her who was ready to perish, rest upon thee and thine, and *Allah* make thee happy as Ayesha, the best beloved wife of the prophet, on whom be peace.

Written from Jerusalem in the year of the Hegyra 576, according to the era of the Franks, 1198.

******

The *Fourth Crusade*, which the French monarch regarded with indifference, and which the King of England despised as being the enterprise of his German enemies, ended thus without advantage or glory to Christendom. The hostilities which had been engendered in the Holy Land, continued to vex and agitate Europe long after the causes had ceased to operate. The Emperor Henry VI. died of poison administered by his wife Constance, and the pope prohibited his interment until the hundred and fifty thousand marks which he had received for Richard's ransom, should be paid over into the treasury of the Holy See.

Insignificant wars exciting the baser passions of human nature and developing few of its nobler qualities, occupied the remaining years of the two great rivals, Richard Plantagenet and Philip Augustus. The Princess Alice was at last surrendered to her brother, and at the mature age of thirty-five, with a tarnished reputation and a splendid dower, was given in marriage to the Count of Aumerle. Richard spent scarce four months of his reign in England, and Berengaria never visited the island. They resided upon his ducal estates in Normandy, or passed their time in Anjou and Aquitaine. It was at the siege of the castle of Chaluz, in the latter province, that Richard met his death. A peasant ploughing in the field, pretended that he had discovered a wondrous cave, in which were concealed golden statues, and vases of precious stones, of unrivalled beauty and value.

"The lively imagination of the king, heated by the splendid fictions of Arabian romance," led him at once to credit the report, and determined him upon securing the enchanted treasure. He immediately summoned the baron to give up to him as feudal lord, a share of the rich prize. The Castellan declared that nothing had been found but a pot of Roman coins which were at his service. The impetuous monarch could not be satisfied with this explanation of the affair, and immediately commenced a siege. He was pierced by an arrow from the walls, and the wound though not mortal was so inflamed by the unskilfulness of the physician, and the king's impatience under treatment, as to cause his death. Queen Eleanora was at this time in England; but Berengaria attended him in his last moments, and forgetting the years of neglect, and the ebullitions of ill temper that had poisoned her domestic happiness, watched and wept over him with the tenderest care.

Scarcely had he breathed his last, when Joanna, Countess of Toulouse, arrived in Aquitaine. She had come to entreat the assistance of the monarch against the haughty barons who had taken up arms against her husband. But when she looked upon the kingly form of her beloved brother stretched in the stillness of death; when she saw that the dull, cold eye kindled not as of yore at the recitative of her wrongs; and when she lifted the powerless hand ever ready for her defence, her long-tried courage gave way and she sank fainting by his side. The weight of this new grief, added to her former afflictions, pressed upon her enfeebled frame, and on the third day she expired, entreating Berengaria to bury her with her brother Richard. The sorrowing queen conveyed the royal remains of her husband and sister for interment to the stately abbey of Fontevraud, and laid them in the tomb of their father Henry II., and within a few short weeks after paid the last tribute of affection to her sweet sister Blanche, wife of Thibaut, Count of Champagne.

The world was now a desert to Berengaria. She retired to her dower estate of Orleans, where she founded the noble abbey of L'Espan, and passed the remainder of her life in acts of charity and beneficence.

ISABELLA OF ANGOULÊME.

Isabella

CHAPTER 1

The lady I love will soon be a bride,
With a diadem on her brow;
Oh why did she flatter my boyish pride,
She's going to leave me now.

It is a marvel to those unacquainted with the philosophy of navigation, that ships may sail with equal speed in opposite directions, under
the impelling force of the same breeze: and it is often an equal paradox
with casual observers of mental phenomena, that individuals may contribute as really to the success of an enterprise by the law of repulsion
as by the more obvious exercise of voluntary influence. Thus Isabella
of Angoulême, who was perhaps as little occupied with plans military
or religious, as any beauty that counted warriors among her conquests
could well be, as effectually impelled a noble knight and leader to undertake the Holy War, as did Adela, Countess of Blois, whose whole
heart was in the work.

Isabella was the only child and heiress of the Count of Angoulême.
Her mother was of the family of Courteney, the first lords of Edessa.
In very early youth Isabella had been betrothed to Hugh X. de Lusignan, the Marcher or guardian of the northern border of Aquitaine.
The little bride dwelt at the castle of her lord, flattered and caressed by
every vassal who hoped to win the favour of his master, while the gallant Hugh, surnamed le Brun, watched over her interests, and directed
her education with the care of a man anticipating full fruition in the
ripened charms and unrivalled attractions of one who looked upon
him as her future husband.

Count Hugh as a distinguished peer of France, had been summoned to form one of the splendid cortege which Philip Augustus

despatched into Spain, to bring home the fair Blanche of Castile, the bride of his son Prince Louis. During his absence the parents of Isabella sent messengers to the castle of Valence, to request their daughter's presence on the occasion of a high festival in Angoulême. The beautiful *fiancée* of Count Hugh was required to recognize King John of England, as the sovereign of Aquitaine, and feudal lord of the province of Angoumois.

Dressed in a simple robe of white, with her hair parted *à la vierge* upon the brow, and confined only by the golden coronet designating her rank, she advanced with a timid step through the assembly, and kneeling at the feet of the king, placed her tiny hands in his, while with a trembling voice she pronounced the oath of homage. The first peep which the fair child gained of the great world in this brilliant assembly, where she was made to act so conspicuous a part, intoxicated her youthful imagination; and the effect of her artless simplicity on the heart of the dissolute monarch, already sated with the adulation of court beauties, was such as one feels in turning from a crowded vase of gaudy exotics, to contemplate the sweetness of the native violet.

Hence was it that Isabella, though scarcely fifteen, entered into all the schemes of her parents, for preventing her return to the castle of her betrothed, and without opposition, gave her hand to a man who had been for ten years engaged in an ineffectual struggle against the canons of the church, for the possession of his beautiful cousin, Avisa, whom he had married on the day of Richard's coronation. Now smitten with the charms of Isabella, John submitted at once to his spiritual fathers, and the archbishop of Bordeaux having convoked a synod to consider the matter with the assent of the bishops of Poitou, declared that no impediment existed to their marriage. The nuptials were, therefore, celebrated at Bordeaux, in August, 1200.

Enraged at the loss of his bride, on his return from Castile, the valiant Count Hugh challenged the royal felon to mortal combat; but the worthless king despising the resentment of the outraged lover, sailed with Isabella in triumph to England, where they passed the winter in a continual round of feasting and voluptuousness. Thwarted in the usual method of redress, Count Hugh had recourse to the pope, the acknowledged lord of both potentate and peer. Innocent III. at once fulminated his thunders against the lawless prince; but as the lands, if not the person of the heiress of Aquitaine, were the property of King John as her lord paramount, not even the Church could unbind the mystic links of feudal tenure that barred the rights of Count Lusignan.

Disappointed in his hopes of vengeance in this quarter, the count became suddenly impressed with the right of young Arthur of Bretagne, to the throne of England, and being joined by the men of Anjou and Maine, he suddenly laid siege to the castle of Mirabel, where Queen Eleanor, then entering her eightieth year, had taken up her summer residence. The son of Geoffrey entered readily into the plot, for he had little cause to love the grandmother, who had advocated the setting aside his claims in favour of those of his uncle; and it was the intention of Count Hugh to capture the aged queen, and exchange her for his lost spouse.

In an age when decent people were expected to break their fast at the early hour of five, King John was surprised at his midday breakfast by a messenger, summoning him to his mother's rescue. Rising hastily in terrible wrath, and swearing a horrid oath, he overset the table with his foot, and leaving his bride to console herself as she could, set off immediately for Aquitaine. Arrived before the castle of Mirabel, he gave fierce battle to his enemies. The contest was very brief, and victory for once alighted upon the banners of John.

The unfortunate Count Hugh, and the still more unfortunate Arthur, with twenty-four barons of Poitou were taken prisoners, and chained hand and foot, were placed in tumbril carts and drawn after the Conqueror wherever he went. The barons, by the orders of King John, were starved to death in the dungeons of Corfe castle. The fate of the hapless Arthur was never clearly known. Many circumstances make it probable that he died by the hand of his uncle; and the twelve peers of France convened to inquire into his fate, branded John as a murderer, and declared the fief of Normandy a forfeit to the crown. Thus was this important province restored to the dominion of France, after having been in the possession of the descendants of Rollo nearly three centuries.

The only male heir now remaining to the House of Plantagenet, was the recreant John; and Queen Eleanor looking forward with fearful foreboding to the destruction of her race, sought an asylum in the convent of Fontevraud, where she died the following year.

The unhappy lover of Isabella dragged on a weary existence in the donjon of Bristol castle, and the heart of the queen, already wounded by the cruelty of John, and touched with pity for the sufferings of Lusignan, began to recount in the ear of her imagination the tender devotion of her first love, and to contrast her miserable, though splendid destiny with the peace and happiness she enjoyed in the castle of Valence.

★★★★★★

The controlling spirit of the thirteenth century was Innocent III. "Since Gregory the Seventh's time the pope had claimed the empire of the world, and taken upon himself the responsibility of its future state. Raised to a towering height, he but saw the more clearly the perils by which he was environed. He occupied the spire of the prodigious edifice of Christianity in the middle age, that cathedral of human kind, and sat soaring in the clouds on the apex of the cross, as when from the spire of Strasburg the view takes in forty towns and villages on the banks of the Rhine."

From this eminence Pope Innocent surveyed the politics of Europe, and put forth his mandates to bring the power and wealth of the nations into the treasury of the church. No measures had ever been adopted which combined so effectually to move the passions of an ardent age, in a direction indicated by papal authority, as the expeditions to the Holy Land. Louis and Philip of France and Henry of England had taxed their subjects for the benefit of the crusade. Pope Innocent went a step farther, and gave a new character to the sacred wars by imposing a similar tax upon the clergy. The eloquent *pontiff* described the ruin of Jerusalem, the triumphs of the Moslems, and the disgrace of Christendom; and, like his predecessors, promised redemption from sins and plenary indulgence to all who should serve in Palestine.

An ignorant priest, Fulk of Neuilly, took up the word of exhortation, and with less piety than Peter the Hermit and greater zeal than St. Bernard, itinerated through the cities and villages of France, publishing the command of the successor of St. Peter.

The situation of the principal monarchs was unfavourable to the pious undertaking. The sovereignty of Germany was disputed by the rival houses of Brunswick and Suabia, the memorable factions of the Guelphs and Ghibelines. Philip Augustus was engaged in projects to wrest from the King of England his transmarine dominions, and John was incapable of any project beyond the narrow circle of his personal pleasures and preferences.

Notwithstanding, therefore, the power of the pope and the fanaticism of Fulk, the whole matter might have fallen through but for the lofty enthusiasm of the descendants of Adela Countess of Blois. In every expedition to the Holy Land, there had not lacked a representative from the house of Champagne; and Thibaut, fourth Count of the name, was the first to unfurl the crimson standard in the *Fifth Crusade*. The young Thibaut held a grand tournament at Troyes, to which he invited all the neighbouring princes and knights for a trial in feats of derring-do. The festivities of the day were nearly over, and the victors were exchanging congratulations and commenting upon the well-won field, when the intrepid Fulk appeared in the lists and challenged the warriors to enforce an appeal to arms in the cause of Christendom. Geoffrey Villehardouin, the *marechal* of Champagne, who held the post of honour as judge of the combat, immediately gave place to the holy man, and the unbonneted chieftains drew around and with respectful regard listened while the subtle priest, from the temporary throne, descanted upon the sufferings of lost Palestina.

Encouraged by the example of his ancestors, animated by the distinction acquired by his elder brother as King of Jerusalem, fired with indignation against the Infidel that claimed that brother's crown, and stimulated by a holy ambition to inscribe his own name upon the rolls of honoured pilgrimage, the noble Thibaut came forward, and drawing his sword, laid it at the feet of the priest, who blessed and consecrated both it and him to the cause of God. His cousin Louis Count of Blois and Chartres, immediately advanced to his side and made a similar dedication.

Then followed his brother-in-law, Baldwin Count of Flanders, Matthew de Montmorenci, Simon de Montfort, Geoffrey Villehard-ouin, and a host of others, till the whole assembly becoming infected with the spirit of enthusiasm, sprang to their feet, and drawing their swords, held them up in the sight of heaven, and with unanimous voice vowed to engage in the Holy War. This vow was subsequently repeated in the churches, ratified in tournaments, and debated in public assemblies till, among the two thousand and two hundred knights that owed homage to the peerage of Champagne, scarce a man could be found willing to forfeit his share in the glorious enterprise by remaining at home.

As Sancho the Strong had died without children, Navarre acknowledged Thibaut, the husband of Blanche, as king; and bands of hardy Gascons from both sides of the Pyrenees flocked to his banners. The feudatories of the other pilgrim warriors, animated by this glorious example, joined the standards of their respective leaders, and crowds of prelates and barons waited but the final arrangements for departure. The perils of the land route to Jerusalem had been often tried. They were such as to intimidate the bravest, and check the impetuosity of the most ardent.

At the extremity of the Adriatic sea, the Venetians had found a shelter, during the dark and stormy interval that succeeded the downfall of the Roman Empire. There nestling in the sedgy banks of the islands that clustered around the Rialto, Commerce, through a long period of incubation, had nourished her venturesome brood, and now the white wings of her full-fledged progeny, like the albatross, skimmed the surface of the seas and found ready entrance to every harbour on the coast of the Mediterranean.

The Venetian republic had owed a nominal allegiance to the Greek empire, but entering the field as a rival to the Genoese and Pisans for the carrying-trade of Europe at the beginning of the crusades, she had displayed from her towering masts the banner of the cross, while she cultivated a friendly intercourse with the *infidels* of every clime. To this avaricious but neutral power the sacred militia determined to apply for a passage to the Holy Land, and six deputies, at the head of whom was Villehardouin,[1] were despatched to the island city to settle the terms of transportation.

The ambassadors were received with distinction, and a general assembly was convened to listen to their proposals. The stately chapel and place of St. Mark was crowded with citizens. The *doge* and the grand council of ten sat in solemn dignity while the *marechal* of Champagne unfolded thus the purposes of the embassy.

Illustrious Venetians: the most noble and powerful barons of France have sent us to you to entreat you in the name of God to have compassion on Jerusalem which groans under the tyranny of the Turks, and to aid us on this occasion in revenging the injury which has been done to your Lord and Saviour. The peers of France have turned their eyes to you as the greatest maritime power in Europe. They have commanded us to throw ourselves at your feet, and never to change that supplicatory posture till you have promised to aid them in recovering the Holy Land.

The eloquence of their words and tears touched the hearts of the people. Cries of "We grant your request," sounded through the hall. The honoured Doge Dandolo, though more than ninety years of age and nearly blind, consecrated what might remain to him of life to the pious work, and multitudes imitated his self-devotion. The treaty was

---

1. *Knights of the Cross: Chronicle of the Fourth Crusade and The Conquest of Constantinople & Chronicle of the Crusade of St. Louis* by Geoffrey de Villehardouin and Jean de Joinville is also published by Leonaur.

concluded, transcribed on parchment, attested with oaths and seals, and despatched to Rome for the approbation of the pope. Villehardouin repaired to France with the news of the success of his embassy. The gallant Thibaut sprang from his bed of sickness, called for his war-horse, summoned his vassals, and declared his intention to set off immediately upon the pilgrimage. The exertion was too great for his feeble frame; he sank fainting in the arms of his attendants, and expired in the act of distributing among his feudatories the money he had designed for the Holy War. A new leader was then to be chosen, and the lot finally fell upon Boniface of Montserrat, younger brother of the celebrated Conrad, Marquis of Tyre.

CHAPTER 2

I'll laugh and I'll sing though my heart may bleed,
And join in the festive train,
And if I survive it I'll mount my steed
And off to the wars again.

In the spring of the year 1202, the crusaders being joined by numbers from Italy and Germany, arrived at Venice.

On the Sunday before they were ready for embarkation, a great multitude assembled in the place of St. Mark. It was a high festival, and there were present the people of the land, and most of the barons and pilgrims. Before high mass began, the Doge of Venice, who was named Henry Dandolo, mounted the pulpit, and spoke to the people, and said to them, '*Signors*, there have joined themselves to you the best nation in the world, and for the greatest business that ever men undertook; and I am an old man and a feeble and should be thinking of rest, and am frail and suffering of body. But I see that no one can order and marshal you like I who am your lord. If you choose to grant to me to take the sign of the cross, that I may guard you and instruct you, and that my son may remain in my place to guard the land, I will go live or die with you and the pilgrims.'

And when they heard him they all cried out with one voice, 'We beg you in God's name to grant it, and to do it, and to come with us.' Then great pity took possession of the men of the land, and of the pilgrims, and they shed many tears to think that this valiant man had such great cause to remain, for he was an old man and had beautiful eyes in his head, but saw not with them, having lost his sight through a wound on the crown; exceeding great of heart was he. So he descended from the pulpit and walked straight to the altar, and threw himself upon his knees, pitifully weeping; and they sewed the cross on a large cape of cotton, because he wished the people to see it. And the Venetians began to take the cross in large numbers and in great plenty on that day, until which very few had taken the cross.

Our pilgrims were moved with exceeding joy even to over-flowing as regarded this new crusader, on account of the sense and the prowess that were his. Thus the *doge* took the cross as you have heard." But by a singular circumstance the expedition was diverted from its original design. Isaac Angelus, the vicious and tyrannical Emperor of Constantinople, had been deposed by his subjects, deprived of his eyesight, and cast into prison. His brother Alexius was invested with the purple, and rejecting the name of Angelus, assumed the royal appellation of the Comnenian race. Young Alexius, the son of Isaac, was at this time twelve years of age. Escaping from the guards of his uncle in the disguise of a common sailor, he found a refuge in the island of Sicily. Thence he set off for Germany, having accepted an invitation to reside with his sister Irene, wife of Philip of Suabia.

Passing through Italy, he found the flower of western chivalry assembled at Venice ready for the crusade, and it immediately occurred to his young and ardent mind that their invincible swords might be employed in his father's restoration. As he derived his birth in the female line both from the house of Aquitaine and the royal race of Hugh Capet, he easily interested the sympathy of the Franks, and as the Venetians had a long arrear of debt and injury to liquidate with the Byzantine court, they listened eagerly to the story of his wrongs, and decided to share the honour of restoring the exiled monarch. The place of their destination being thus changed, the crusaders with joyful haste embarked.

A similar armament, for ages, had not rode the Adriatic: it was composed of one hundred and twenty flat-bottomed vessels, or *palanders*, for the horses; two hundred and forty transports filled with men and arms; seventy store-ships laden with provisions; and fifty stout galleys, well prepared for the encounter of an enemy. While the wind was favourable, the sky serene, and the wa-

231

ter smooth, every eye was fixed with wonder and delight on the scene of military and naval pomp which overspread the sea.

The shields of the knights and squires, at once an ornament and a defence, were arranged on either side of the ships; the banners of the nations and families were displayed from the stern; our modern artillery was supplied by three hundred engines for casting stones and darts: the fatigues of the way were cheered with the sounds of music; and the spirits of the adventurers were raised by the mutual assurance, that forty thousand Christian heroes were equal to the conquest of the world.

As they penetrated through the Hellespont, the magnitude of their navy was compressed in a narrow channel, and the face of the waters was darkened with innumerable sails. They again expanded in the basin of the Propontis, and traversed that placid sea, till they approached the European shore, at the abbey of St. Stephen, three leagues to the west of Constantinople. As they passed along, they gazed with admiration on the capital of the East, or, as it should seem, of the earth; rising from her seven hills, and towering over the continents of Europe and Asia.

The swelling domes and lofty spires offive hundred palaces and churches were gilded by the sun, and reflected in the waters; the walls were crowded with soldiers and spectators, whose numbers they beheld, of whose temper they were ignorant; and each heart was chilled by the reflection, that, since the beginning of the world, such an enterprise had never been undertaken by such a handful of warriors. But the momentary apprehension was dispelled by hope and valour; and "Every man," says the Marechal of Champagne, "glanced his eye on the sword or lance which he must speedily use in the glorious conflict." The Latins cast anchor before Chalcedon; the mariners only were left in the vessels: the soldiers, horses, and arms were safely landed; and, in the luxury of an imperial palace, the barons tasted the first fruits of their success.

From his dream of power Alexius was awakened by the rapid advance of the Latins; and between vain presumption and absolute despondency no effectual measures for defence were instituted. At length the strangers were waited upon by a splendid embassy. The envoys were instructed to say that the sovereign of the Romans, as Alexius pompously styled himself, was much surprised at sight of this hostile armament:

If these pilgrims were sincere in their vow for the deliverance of Jerusalem, his voice must applaud, and his treasures should assist, their pious design; but should they dare to invade the sanctuary of empire, their numbers, were they ten times more considerable, should not protect them from his just resentment.

The answer of the *doge* and barons was simple and magnanimous. They said:

> In the cause of honour and justice we despise the usurper of Greece, his threats and his offers. *Our* friendship and *his* allegiance are due to the lawful heir, to the young prince, who is seated among us, and his father, the Emperor Isaac, who has been deprived of his sceptre, his freedom, and his eyes, by the crime of an ungrateful brother. Let that brother confess his guilt and implore forgiveness, and we ourselves will intercede, that he may be permitted to live in affluence and security. But let him not insult us by a second message; our reply will be made in arms in the palace of Constantinople.

Ten days after, the crusaders prepared themselves to attack the city. The navy of the Greek Empire consisted of only twenty ships. The vessels of the republic sailed without opposition, therefore, into the harbour, and the *croises*, with cheerful zeal commenced the siege of the largest city in the world. The Franks divided their army into six battalions: Baldwin of Flanders led the vanguard with his bowmen, the second, third, fourth and fifth divisions were commanded by his brother Henry, the Counts of St. Paul, Blois, and Montmorenci, and the rearguard of Tuscans, Lombards, and Genoese was headed by the Marquis of Montserrat. So far from being able to surround the town, they were scarcely sufficient to blockade one side; but before their squadrons could couch their lances, the seventy thousand Greeks that had prepared for the conflict vanished from sight. The Pisans and the Varangian guard, however, defended the walls with extraordinary valour, and victory was for a long time poised in the scales of doubt.

Meanwhile, on the side of the harbour the attack was successfully conducted by the Venetians, who employed every resource known and practised before the invention of gunpowder. The soldiers leapt from the vessels, planted their scaling-ladders, and ascended the walls, while the large ships slowly advancing, threw out grappling-irons and drawbridges, and thus opened an airy way from the masts to the ramparts. In the midst of the conflict, the venerable *doge*, clad in complete armour, stood aloft on the prow of his galley; the great standard of St. Mark waved above his head, while with threats, promises, and exhortations, he urged the rowers to force his vessel upon shore.

On a sudden, by an invisible hand, the banner of the republic was fixed upon the walls. Twenty-five towers were stormed and taken. The emperor made a vigorous effort to recover the lost bulwarks, but Dandolo, with remorseless resolution, set fire to the neighbouring buildings, and thus secured the conquest so dearly won. The discomfited Alexius, seeing all was lost, collected what treasure he could carry, and in the silence of the night, deserting his wife and people, sought refuge in Thrace. In the morning the Latin chiefs were surprised by a summons to attend the levee of Isaac, who, rescued from his dungeon, robed in the long-lost purple, and seated upon the throne in the palace of the Blaquernel, waited with impatience to embrace his son and reward his generous deliverers.

Four ambassadors, among whom was Villehardouin, the chronicler of these events, were chosen to wait upon the rescued emperor:

> The gates were thrown open on their approach, the streets on both sides were lined with the battle-axes of the Danish and English guard; the presence-chamber glittered with gold and jewels, the false substitutes of virtue and power; by the side of the blind Isaac, his wife was seated, the sister of the King of Hungary: and by her appearance, the noble matrons of Greece were drawn from their domestic retirement and mingled with the circle of senators and soldiers.

The ambassadors with courteous respect congratulated the monarch upon his restoration, and delicately presented the stipulations of the young Alexius. These were, "the submission of the Eastern empire to the pope, the succour of the Holy Land, and a present contribution of two hundred thousand marks of silver."

"These conditions are weighty," was the emperor's prudent reply: "they are hard to accept, and difficult to perform. But no conditions can exceed the measure of your services and deserts."

The ready submission of Isaac and the subjection of the Greek church to the Roman pontiff, deeply offended his subtle and revengeful subjects, and gave rise to so many plots and conspiracies, that the newly-restored emperor prayed the crusaders to delay their departure till order was re-established. To this they assented, but the odious taxes for rewarding their services were collected with difficulty, and Isaac resorted to the violent measure of robbing the churches of their gold and silver. Occasions of dissension ripened into causes of hatred. A devastating fire was attributed to the Latins, and in consequence desultory encounters took place, which resulted in open hostility. The feeble emperor died, it is said, of fear; his cousin, a bold, unscrupulous villain, assumed the imperial buskins, and seizing the young Alexius, put him to death.

The crusaders at once determined to make war upon the usurper. Constantinople, the empress of the East, the city that for nine centuries had been deemed impregnable to mortal arm, was taken by storm. The right of victory, untrammelled by promise or treaty, confiscated the public and private wealth of the Greeks, and the hand of every Frank, according to its size and strength, seized and appropriated the rich treasures of silks, velvets, furs, gems, spices and movables which were scattered like glittering baits through all the dwellings of that proud metropolis. When the appetite for plunder was satisfied, order was instituted in the distribution of spoils. Three churches were selected for depositories, and the magnitude of the prize exceeded all experience or expectation.

A sum seven times greater than the annual revenue of England, fell to the lot of the Franks. In the streets the French and Flemings clothed themselves and their horses in painted robes and flowing head-dresses of fine linen. They stripped the altars of their ornaments, converted the chalices into drinking cups, and laded their beasts with wrought silver and gilt carvings, which they tore down from the pulpits. In the cathedral of St. Sophia, the veil of the sanctuary was rent in twain for the sake of its golden fringe, and the altar, a monument of art and riches, was broken in pieces and distributed among the captors.

Having thus taken Constantinople and shared its treasures among themselves, the next step was the regulation of their future possessions and the election of an emperor. Twelve deputies were appointed, six to represent the interest of the Franks and six that of the Venetians; in the name of his colleagues, the Bishop of Soissons announced to the barons the result of their deliberations in these words: "Ye have sworn to obey the prince whom we should choose; by our unanimous suffrage, Baldwin Count of Flanders and Hainault, is now your sovereign and the Emperor of the East."

Agreeably to the Byzantine custom, the barons and knights immediately elevated their future lord upon a buckler and bore him into the church of St. Sophia. When the pomp of magnificence and dignity was prepared, the coronation took place. The papal legate threw the imperial purple over Baldwin; the soldiers joined with the clergy in crying aloud, 'He is worthy of reigning;' and the splendour of conquest was mocked by the Grecian ceremony, of presenting to the new sovereign a tuft of lighted wool and a small vase filled with bones and dust, as emblems of the perishableness of grandeur, and the brevity of life.

The splendid fiefs which the ambitious Adela had mapped out for the heroes of the first crusade, now fell to the lot of her descendants in the division of the Greek Empire. One was invested with the duchy of Nice; one obtained a fair establishment on the banks of the Hebrus; and one, served with the fastidious pomp and splendour of oriental luxury, shared the throne of Baldwin, the successor of Constantine the Great.

CHAPTER 3

But I'll hide in my breast every selfish care,
And flush my pale cheek with wine,
When smiles await the bridal pair,
I'll hasten to give them mine.

While the Eastern *Croises* were thus engaged in apportioning among themselves, the rich domains of the Greek Empire, Simon de Montfort, who had abandoned the expedition, when its destination was changed from Jerusalem to Constantinople, was not less actively employed in a domestic crusade, published by Innocent III., against the heretics of the south of France. In the province of Toulouse, certain sects had arisen variously known as Believers, Perfects, and Vaudois, but all rejecting some of the tenets of Rome, and from the city of Albi, designated by the general name Albigeois.

In his misguided zeal, Innocent III. despatched three legates to constrain these Albigeois to abjure their heresies and return to the bosom of the church. He empowered them to employ for this purpose, "the sword, water and fire, as these good monks should find it necessary to use one or the other, or all three together for the greater glory of God." Though the Albigenses, like other Christians, professed the doctrines of peace, they were somewhat infected with the warlike spirit of the age; consequently becoming exasperated at the executions deemed necessary to bring the lambs into the fold, they rose upon the missionaries, and stoned one of them to death. The pope retaliated by proclaiming the usual indulgence to those who should engage in the holy war, for exterminating the heretics. Count Raimond VI., the husband of Joanna, immediately took up arms in defence of his subjects, and against him Simon de Montfort headed the army of the church. With him came a monk of great austerity, afterwards St. Dominic, the founder of the Dominican order of friars, who encouraged the soldiers in their work of blood.

The city of Beziers long held out against them. It was finally taken, the inhabitants given up to slaughter, and when a difficulty arose about discriminating between the heretics and the Catholics, "Slay them all," said Dominic, "the Lord will know his own." It is estimated that the number that perished was sixty thousand. The war went on, characterized, as such wars always are, by the atrocity of private murder, and wholesale butchery, till de Montfort led his army to the siege of Toulouse. Count Raimond, beset on every side by foes, applied to his brother-in-law, the King of England, to the King of Arragon, whose sister he had married after the death of Joanna, and to Philip Augustus his liege lord. The first engaged in domestic broils, and the last involved in a contest with the pope, concerning the divorce of Ingeborge, could render him no assistance, but Don Pedro King of Arragon, entered warmly into the contest and fell bravely fighting in the Battle of Muret.

The count was at last compelled to conclude an ignominious peace with the pope; and thus the forces of the church were victorious in the south of France, as they were in the Greek Empire.

★★★★★★

To return to Isabella. The troubles with which King John had involved himself by the murder of the young Duke of Bretagne, seemed destined never to end. All Aquitaine had been in a state of revolt since the decease of his mother and the captivity of Count Hugh, and his queen finally persuaded him to trust to the magnanimity of her lover, for the peace of his dominions in France.

De Lusignan left England in 1206, and by his discretion and valour, soon restored the revolted provinces to the sway of the line of Plantagenet. The intolerance of the king next aroused the animosity of the English barons, and to prevent a popular outbreak, he demanded their sons as hostages, under the plausible pretext of requiring the services of the youthful lords as pages for his queen, and companions of his infant son, Henry.

The Lady de Braose, when her children were demanded, imprudently replied, "I will not surrender my boys to a king who murdered his own nephew." The unfortunate words were repeated to the malicious monarch, and measures for vengeance immediately instituted.

The Lord de Braose, with his wife and five innocent little ones, were confined in Windsor castle and starved to death.

While the husband of Isabella was thus alienating from himself the affections of his subjects, he had the temerity to dare the colossal power of Rome. A dispute arose as in the days of his father, concerning the incumbent of the see of Canterbury. The pope had commanded the monks to choose Cardinal Langton for their primate, without the ceremony of a writ from the king. They complied, and John sent one of his knights to expel them from the convent and take possession of their revenues.

The affair went on with admonitions from the spiritual father, and defiant retorts from the refractory king, till Innocent III. laid an interdict upon the realm. This terrible mandate at once covered the whole nation with the garb and the gloom of mourning. The priests with pious reverence stripped the altars of their ornaments, collected the crosses and relics, took down the images and statues of saints and apostles, and laying them upon the ground carefully covered them from the eyes of the profane.

No *matin* chime awoke the pious to their devotions, no vesper bell summoned the youths and maidens to unite in the evening hymn; no joyous peal invited the happy throng to the nuptial ceremony, no solemn toll gathered the sorrowing multitudes to the burial service. The bridegroom took the hand of his bride and whispered his vows with boding fear, standing in the churchyard, surrounded by the silent witnesses, whose very presence was a terror. The father relinquished the dead body of his child to unhallowed hands, that made for it an obscure and unconsecrated grave by the wayside; the tender infant was not presented at the font for baptism, but received the holy rite in the privacy of the monkish cell, and the dying man partook of the last sacrament under circumstances that rendered still more terrible the approach of death.

Men neglected their usual avocations, feeling that the curse of God rested upon them; children relinquished their amusements, subdued by the mysterious fear that pervaded all ranks of society.

But the tyrant John and his thoughtless queen felt no sympathy with the afflictions of their people, no reverence for the ordinances of religion. They made no concessions, they manifested no signs of repentance. Each was engaged in the pursuit of pleasure, without regard to the other's feelings, or the laws of God. If the fickle and wounded affections of Isabella wandered from her lord to some noble knight, who compassionated her wrongs, her crime was made known only by the terrible vengeance which her malignant husband inflicted upon her supposed lover; nor was she aware that the suspicions of the king had been awakened till retiring to her apartment at night, she beheld with horror the dead body of the nobleman, suspended above her couch, the bloodshot eyes fixed upon her with a ghastly stare, and the pale lips opened as if assaying to whisper in her ear the secret of the dark tragedy.

From this haunted chamber she was not suffered to depart for long weary years. But though John thus manifested his righteous horror of his wife's dereliction from the path of rectitude, he was himself unscrupulous in the perpetration of any species of iniquity. Parsimonious and cruel to his beautiful queen, he lavished upon his own person every extravagant indulgence; without honesty or honour. He was a bad son, a bad subject, a bad husband, a bad father, and a bad sovereign. The record of his thoughts is a disgrace to human nature, the record of his deeds, a recapitulation of crimes.

Finding his interdict of no avail, Innocent resorted to his most powerful weapon. He excommunicated John, pronounced utter destruction upon his body and soul, forbade all true Catholics to associate with him, absolved his subjects from their oath of allegiance to him, commanded all orders of religion to curse him, and exhorted all Christian princes to assist in dethroning him.

Philip Augustus found this crusade far more to his taste than the one he had before undertaken in the Holy Land, and Simon de Montfort having enjoyed a short repose from his work of blood in Languedoc, stood ready to enforce the authority of the church. To protect his transmarine dominions from these powerful foes, John found it necessary to solicit an alliance with his former rival Count Hugh de Lusignan, but the perverse bachelor was conciliated only on condition that the queen should be liberated from her irksome imprisonment, and that her eldest daughter, the Princess Joanna, should be affianced to him as a compensation for the loss of the mother. The necessity of the case did not admit of debate or delay, and the little princess was forthwith betrothed to her mature lover, and consigned to the castle of Valence; where she occupied the apartments and sported in the pleasance, that had formerly delighted the childhood of Isabella. With his heart thus reassured, Count Hugh repulsed the army of the French king, and kept the Poictevin border in peace.

Philip Augustus disappointed in this attempt, prepared for the invasion of England; but while his fleet waited in the ports of Normandy, the legate Pandulph sought an interview with John, and terrifying him with the prospect of certain ruin brought him to submit unconditionally to the pope. The pusillanimous monarch was thus induced to pass a charter in which he declared he had for his own sins and those of his family, resigned England and Ireland to God, to St. Peter, and St. Paul, and to Pope Innocent and his successors in the apostolic chair; agreeing to hold those dominions as feudatories of the church of Rome by the annual payment of a thousand marks.

He consented to receive Langton for the primate, laid his crown and sceptre at the feet of Pandulph, and kneeling down placed his hand in those of that prelate, and swore fealty in the same manner as a vassal did homage to his lord. The legate then revoked the sentence of excommunication, placed the crown upon the head of John, pocketed the first instalment of the tribute money, and returning to France informed Philip that England was a part of the patrimony of St. Peter, and it would be impious in any Christian prince to attack it.

★★★★★★

Isabella was residing with her children at Gloucester, when her inconstant husband, smitten with the charms of Matilda the fair daughter of Lord Fitz Walter, stormed the castle of her father, banished him from the kingdom, and bore away the trembling girl to the fortress of London. There confining her in one of the lofty turrets of the White tower he set himself to win her affections; but the noble maiden spurned all his overtures with virtuous indignation. When the hoary libertine found that flattery and coercion were alike vain, his adoration changed to hate, and the hapless lady fell a victim to poison. This crowning act of villainy completed the exasperation of the English nobles, and a confederacy was formed to resist farther aggressions upon their liberties. Cardinal Langton, in searching the records of the monasteries, had found a copy of the charter executed by Henry Beauclerk upon his marriage with Matilda the Good.

From this charter the primate drew up the bill of rights, which has become world-renowned as the Magna Charta. At Runnymede between Windsor and Staines the mail-clad barons met their guilty sovereign, and—

There in happy hour
Made the fell tyrant feel his people's power.

The signing of the great charter of English liberty was soon followed by the death of King John, and the diplomatic talents of Isabella were called into exercise to secure the vacant throne for her son Henry, then a boy of only nine years of age. The diadem of his father having been lost in Lincoln washes, and that of Edward the Confessor being in London, the little prince was crowned with a gold throat collar that she had worn in those happy days while the affianced bride of Count Hugh la Marche. Only a small part of England at first owned the sway of Prince Henry, but the nobles at length rallied around the young Plantagenet, and the valour and wisdom of the protector Pembroke soon drove the invading French from the island. No share in the government was committed into the hands of the dowager queen, and before the first year of her widowhood had expired she set out for her native city of Angoulême.

As she passed through the provinces of France her attention was attracted by groups of children, habited as pilgrims with scrip and staff, gathered about the doors of churches, repeating pious ascriptions of praise or tuning their infant voices to sacred hymns. Her curiosity was strongly excited, and she questioned them concerning the motives that influenced to so strange a proceeding. "Fair Solyma lies in ruins," replied the little fanatics, "and it may please God who out of the mouths of babes and sucklings hath ordained strength, to redeem it by our feeble hands."

These scenes occurred daily upon her route. In vain the queen employed argument and entreaty, threats and promises to induce them to return to their homes. They followed in the train of a company of monks who, with the diabolical design of profiting by a crime then too common, were working upon their superstitious hopes and fears to decoy them to the sea-coast, where they might be shipped to Egypt and sold as slaves. Thirty thousand misguided innocents were thus collected from Italy and Germany, and most of them fell a sacrifice to the mercenary motives of those who traded in the bodies and souls of men.

When Isabella arrived at Angoulême, the valiant Lusignan was absent from his territories, fighting under the banners of the cross, and her maternal heart was allowed the solace of frequent intercourse with Joanna, the little bride of her former lover.

I'll hang my harp on the willow-tree,
And off to the wars again;
My peaceful home has no charms for me,
The battlefield no pain"

Convinced by the crusade of the children that the spirit which had moved the former expeditions to the Holy Land was still active in Europe, Pope Innocent exclaiming, "While we sleep these children are awake," determined once more to arm the Christian world against the Moslem. The commands of the Vatican calling upon men to exterminate the Infidel were hurled upon every part of Europe. In a circular letter to sovereigns and clergy the pope declared that the time had at last arrived when the most happy results might be expected from a confederation of the Christian powers.

Count la Marche was among the first to hear and obey the mandate of the spiritual head. With the Duke of Nevers he commanded the French *croises* that in 1215 sailed for Egypt, where he was actively engaged in the Holy warfare when Isabella visited Valence. The siege of Damietta was carried on with the usual atrocities. Tidings of the death of Saphadin weakened the forces of the garrison, and Camel, younger son of Elsiebede, lord of the fertile country of the Nile, was compelled to seek refuge in Arabia. The first success of the crusaders was followed by disaster and discord; and when after a siege of seventeen months Damietta was taken, they found in pestilence and famine more terrible foes than in the sixty thousand Moslems that had perished beneath their swords.

Queen Isabella was seated in her former apartment in the castle of Valence describing to her daughter the person of the young King of England and his noble brother the Prince Richard, and painting to the imagination of the child the charms of the infant Princess Isabella, when the horn of the warder rang out shrill and clear on the evening air. The window of the turret commanded the view of the drawbridge. From that window where, eighteen years before, Isabella had watched with delight for the return of her gay knightly lover, she now beheld with palpitating heart the advance of a jaded, weary troop, at whose head rode one whose proud crest drooped as though the inspiration of hope had ceased to animate the warrior-frame, and the heart bereft of the blissful fervour of love no longer anticipated the sweet guerdon of his lady's smile.

A tide of recollections swept over her spirit; dizzy and faint she sank upon a seat in the embrasure of the window, and veiled her agitation in the curtaining drapery. She heard his tread upon the stair, no longer the elastic step that she had been wont to welcome with the sportive gaiety of a heart free from care; the door was thrown open, her daughter with bounding footstep so like her own in former days, flew to meet him as he entered. She saw the childish fingers unlace the helmet, unbind the gorget, unbelt the sword, and lay aside the armour. The form of the warrior was slightly bent, there were furrows upon the sunburnt cheek, deep lines upon the noble brow, and threads of silver among his dark locks. A heavy sigh was the first salutation of his little bride. He drew the fair girl to him and pressed his lip upon her cheek, but the anxious observer saw that the look and the smile were the expression rather of paternal regard than of lover like fondness; they were not such as had lighted up his countenance and kindled in his eyes when with gleesome alacrity she had rendered him the same gentle service.

Her agitation subsided, and when the little Joanna took the hand of the Count la Marche, and led him forward to present him to her mother, she received his embarrassed greeting with the stately courtesy of a queen and the dignity of a woman. The marvellous beauty that won for Isabella the appellation of the "Helen of the middle ages" soon eclipsed the infant graces of the princess, and reinstated her in the heart once all her own. We accordingly find in the records of the year 1220, that "Isabella, Queen Dowager of England, having before crossed the seas, took to her husband her former spouse, the Count of Marche, in France, without leave of the king, her son, or his council."

Notwithstanding this romantic change in their relations, Joanna continued to reside at the castle of Valence, under the care of the gallant count, who remained her steady friend and protector. She was of infinite service to her parents and her country. The English were greatly incensed at the marriage of Isabella, and the council of the regency withheld her jointure as the widow of John, and neither the representations nor threats of her valiant husband could induce them to repair the wrong.

A war soon after occurred between England and Scotland, and Alexander II., the chivalric descendant of Maude, declared that he could not trust the strength of a political treaty without the bond of a union with the royal family of England. King Henry therefore despatched a messenger with an affectionate letter to his mother, demanding the restoration of his sister. Count la Marche refused to resign the guardianship of his lovely step-daughter until the dower of his wife should be restored. The young king had then recourse to Pope Honorius III., traducing his mother and her husband in no measured terms, and praying him to lay upon them the ban of excommunication.

By a process almost as tedious as the present "law's delays," the pope investigated the affair, till Alexander becoming impatient, Henry was glad to accommodate the matter by paying up the arrears of his mother's dower. The little princess was then sent to England, and married to Alexander II., at York, 1221. She was a child of angelic beauty and sweetness, and though only eleven years of age, had thus twice stopped a cruel war. The English styled her Joan Makepeace.

The domestic bliss of Count Hugh and Isabella was less exquisite than might have been anticipated from the constancy of his love, and the romantic revival of her attachment: nor did the birth and education of eight beautiful children concentrate their affections or afford sufficient scope for their ambitious aspirations. Differences constantly arose between the King of France and her son Henry, and it was often the duty of her husband to fight in behalf of Louis, his liege lord, against her former subjects of Aquitaine. It was her sole study, therefore, to render French Poitou independent of the King of France. She "was a queen," she said, "and she disdained to be the wife of a man who had to kneel before another."

Causes of mortification on this point were constantly occurring. Count la Marche sought to obviate the difficulty by allying his family with the blood royal. He offered his eldest daughter in marriage to the brother of the French king, but the prince refused her, and gave his hand to Jane of Toulouse. On this occasion the king made his brother Count of Poictiers, and thus it became necessary for Count Hugh and his haughty wife to fill the *rôle* of honour, and do homage to the young couple as their suzerains. From this time forward the unfortunate count found that the only way to secure domestic peace was to make perpetual war upon the dominions of his sovereign. As a good soldier and a loyal knight who hangs his hopes upon a woman's smile, he perseveringly followed the dangerous path till he was utterly dispossessed of castle and patrimony, feudatory and vassal.

There remained then no resource but to cast themselves upon the charity of the good king. The repentant count first despatched his eldest son to the camp of Louis, and encouraged by the gracious reception of the youth, soon followed with the remainder of his family. The monarch compassionated their miserable situation, and granted to his rebellious subject three castles on the simple condition of his doing homage for them to Alphonso, Count of Poictiers. After this humiliating concession, Count Hugh was disposed to dwell in quietness: but the restless spirit of Isabella was untamed by disaster. The life of King Louis was twice attempted, and the assassins being seized and put to the torture, confessed that they had been bribed to the inhuman deed by the dowager Queen of England.

Alarmed for the consequences, she fled for safety to the abbey of Fontevraud, where, says a contemporary chronicler:

> She was hid in a secret chamber, and lived at her ease, though the Poictevins and French considering her as the cause of the disastrous war with their king, called her by no other name than Jezebel, instead of her rightful appellation of Isabel.

Notwithstanding the disgrace and defeat that Count Hugh had suffered, no sooner was the fair fame of his wife attacked than he once more girded on his sword and appealed to arms to prove the falsehood of the accusation upon the body of Prince Alphonso. Little inclined to the fray, Alphonso declared contemptuously, that the Count la Marche was so "treason-spotted" it would be disgrace to fight with him. Young Hugh, the son of Isabella, then threw down the gage in defence of his mother's reputation, but the cowardly prince again declined, alleging that the infamy of the family rendered the young knight unworthy so distinguished an honour.

The last interview between Hugh de Lusignan, Count la Marche, and Isabella of Angoulême, ex-Queen of England, took place in the general reception room in the convent of Fontevraud. The dishonoured noble sought his wife to acquaint her with the ruin of all their worldly prospects and the stain upon their knightly escutcheon. The last tones that he heard from those lips that once breathed tenderness and love were words of indignant upbraiding and heart-broken despair. All his attempts at consolation were repulsed with cruel scorn. She tore herself violently from his last fond embrace, sought again the secret chamber and assumed the veil, and for three years sister Felice, most inaptly so named, was distinguished among the nuns by her lengthened penances and multiplied prayers.

The land of his nativity no longer possessed any attractions for the bereaved and disappointed count. All the associations of his youth became sources of painful reflection, and anxious to escape from the scenes where every familiar object was but a monument of a buried hope, he determined to share the crusade which St. Louis was preparing against the *infidel*. He fell, covered with wounds and glory in one of the eastern battles, fighting beside his old antagonist Alphonso Count of Poictiers.

Violante

CHAPTER 1

'Twas but for a moment—and yet in that time
She crowded the impressions of many an hour:
Her eye had a glow, like the sun of her clime,
Which waked every feeling at once into flower!

The fall of Constantinople had not been without its effect upon eastern politics. The Christian Prince of Antioch acknowledged the feudal superiority of Baldwin, the new emperor, and Saphadin, the Sultan of Syria, justly apprehended that an easy and ready communication being thus opened with Europe through the Greek Empire, the splendid conquest might result in the carrying out of the original plan upon Palestine. To avert this danger, he repaired to Antioch to conclude, if possible, a treaty for six years' peace with the Christians. The sons of Elsiebede were permitted to accompany the army of their father on his most distant expeditions; and through the enlightened policy of Saphadin, or Saif Addin, during his absence, contrary to the usual Oriental observances, the Moorish European filled the office of regent of Jerusalem.

Under her benign administration the pilgrims had access to the holy places, and protection in the practice of all the rites of Christianity. Salaman, whose self-complacency and curiosity gave him a benevolent interest in all matters pertaining to politics, humanity, or religion, was the usual medium of communication between the empress and those who had occasion to solicit favours from her hand. He was the Mercury to convey safe conducts, the Apollo to usher petitioners into her presence.

The garb of the pilgrim had consequently become to her a familiar sight, and it was therefore without surprise that she saw her attendant

enter with a toil-worn man leaning upon a palmer's staff. Her beneficence to the Christians, and her affability towards all her dependents
had made her a frequent listener to the tales of pilgrims, and intent
upon her own thoughts she heard with an abstracted air the story of
the mendicant, till he uttered the name of Richard. Instantly she was
all attention.

The old man had been the confessor of Henry II., but won by the
cordial frankness and generous impulses of Cœur de Lion, he availed
himself of every opportunity afforded by his intimacy with Henry
to forward the interests of the young prince. The king had confided
to the priest, as his spiritual father, his attachment to the fair and frail
Alice of France; and the monk had betrayed the secret of the confes-
sional to Prince Richard. By a law of Henry I., all priests guilty of this
crime were condemned to perpetual wandering, and Richard, in his
first agony and remorse, at the death of his father, caused the penalty
to be strictly enforced.

The poor monk, therefore, had for nearly twenty years practised a
weary pilgrimage from one holy place to another, resting in monasteries, walking unshod before shrines of peculiar sanctity, and kneeling
or watching in every cave or hermitage where the hallowed remains
of a saint might be supposed to avail for his absolution. Pursued thus
by the furies of remorse, and the curses of the church, he had visited
the shrines of St. Wulstan, St. Dunstan, St. Thomas of Canterbury, St.
James of Compostella, the crucifix of Lucca, the congregated Saints at
Rome, the cave of St. Cyprian in Africa, and had now come to pray
God to release his soul at the church of the Holy Sepulchre.

At the mention of St. James of Compostella, Elsiebede seemed
agitated, and when the monk ceased his story, she anxiously inquired
whether in his travels through Spain, he had rested in Pampeluna.

"I tarried there some days," returned the pilgrim, "but it is several
years since, and but for a strange circumstance it might have faded
from my memory; for he who thinks ever upon his own sins has little
leisure to study that which pleases or benefits others."

"Relate to me this circumstance," cried Elsiebede, eagerly.

"As I knelt at high mass," resumed the priest, "a noble lady, closely
veiled, bowed at the altar by my side. When the solemn ceremony was
over, and she rose to depart, an attendant whispered me to follow. She
led the way to her oratory in the palace of the king, where she showed
me that she was the widow of my deceased lord, Richard Cœur de
Lion."

"My dear lady Berengaria," exclaimed Elsiebede, the tears falling from her eyes like rain.

"It was, indeed, that honoured queen," said the pilgrim; "who learning that I had loved and served the noblest prince in Christendom, sent for me to confess the follies of her past life, and to entreat me to perform for her in Palestine certain vows which she had made during the long and painful imprisonment of her royal husband. It was her purpose to expiate her own sins by a life of voluntary penitence and devotion in the convent of L'Espan: but before retiring from the world, she desired to make one more effort for the people of God in the Holy Land. She made me acquainted, therefore, most noble lady, with thy former estate in her household, and how God had exalted thee to be the spouse of a prince and ruler, as he did afore-time the royal Esther, who came to be Queen of Persia. She bade me remind thee of the kindness that had been shown thee, when thou wert a stranger in a strange land, and she commendeth her love to thee by this precious jewel, that thou mayest look upon it, and show mercy to those who are ready to perish for the faith of our holy church."

With a pious precision that mocked the impatience of Elsiebede, he drew from his scrip a small reliquary which he slowly unclasped, and taking thence the magic ring, around which clustered so many associations, presented it to the *sultana.* Salaman, who had lost not a motion nor a word of the pilgrim, at sight of the ring, forgot the respectful observance that had been enforced since his residence at the eastern court, pressed forward and gazed upon the precious talisman. The emotions of Elsiebede precluded utterance, and the monk waited her reply in silence, till Salaman comprehending her wishes in the matter, accompanied the pilgrim to the house of the patriarch, and made the necessary arrangements for the performance of his vows.

The gratitude of Elsiebede for the return of her long-loved, long-lost treasure, bringing before her as it did, the image of her widowed mistress, and the tender sympathy, which years of intimacy had engendered, warmed her heart still more to the Christians, and she studied to inculcate in the minds of her children, an amicable disposition towards the Latin inhabitants of Palestine.

The sister of Sybilla, Isabella, firstly, widow of Conrad, secondly, widow of Henry, Count of Champagne, and thirdly, widow of Almeric of Lusignan, the twelfth King of Jerusalem, at last died, leaving her proud pretensions and her disputed possessions to Mary, her daughter by Conrad. Alice, her daughter by Henry, was married to Hugh of Lusignan, the son of her last husband, and had been already proclaimed Queen of Cyprus. The claim of Mary, therefore, to the throne of Jerusalem was undisputed, and as Palestine was at that time without lord or ruler worthy to sway the ideal sceptre that cost so much blood and treasure, the Bishop of Acre, and the Lord of Cesarea were deputed by the Christian knights to wait upon Philip Augustus, King of France, and demand of him a husband for the young princess.

While the potentates of Palestine and Europe were thus occupied in the benevolent enterprise of procuring her a husband, the orphan, Mary, dwelt quietly at Acre; and it occurred to the politic Saif-Eddin, that a union between the young princess and his eldest son, Cohr-Eddin, might cement a peace between Syria and Palestine. The ambitious youth became very much interested in the affair, and readily entered into his parent's plan for his aggrandizement.

The magnificent embassy despatched by the Emperor of the East, to demand the hand of the fair heiress for his son, set out from Damascus loaded with most rare and costly gifts. Cohr-Eddin, with the enthusiasm of a lover, determined to exercise the liberty of the European princes and gain an interview with his intended bride. Before setting out he received from his mother a fragment of the true cross, and thus armed with what he thought would render him irresistible to the Christian maiden, he rode gaily along at the head of the splendid cavalcade, beguiling the way in converse with a celebrated *howadji*, learned in the precepts of the *Koran*, and in the gorgeous and metaphorical fictions of eastern poetry.

In the desert, as in the sea, the eye takes in a vast circle without obstruction from forest or dwelling: the scouts on the second day, therefore, easily discerned, far in the rear, a solitary horseman upon a fleet Arabian barb. He did not, however, join the troop, but passing it to the north, disappeared in the distance ere conjecture had settled upon his identity, or the cause of his sudden apparition.

When the hour for evening prayers arrived, on the last day of the journey, the *cortège* turned aside into a small grove of palms, and sought refreshment by a fountain, which threw up its clear waters, and with untiring voice, warbled its perpetual hymn. The breath of the evening was scented by the odour of the sorrowful *nyctanthes*, and as they entered, they observed that the place had been rendered sacred by the burial of one whose marble tomb, destitute of name or inscription, was shaded by the tender leaves of the sensitive mimosa.

The repast being over, the story-loving Saracens gathered around the *howadji*, who continued to unfold the stores of his learning, descanting upon the beauties of the place, and the influences of the stars, that, like the generations of the earth, follow each other in solemn procession, through the heavens; and drawing from his memory gems of poetry appropriate to the time and occasion. Thus said he:—

Open thine eyes to consider the Narcissus,
Thou wouldst say it is the circle of the Pleiades around the sun;
Yet since the Rose has removed the veil from before her cheek,
The Narcissus has become all eyes to gaze upon her."
The Violet has felt humbled and concealed her head under the purple
mantle that covers her;
One would say that the verdure has formed beneath her feet inviting
unto prayer."
"Yet as the sun among the stars, and the rose among the flowers of the
garden,
So is the Beloved to the partial eyes of the lover."

A voice singing or chanting in the Persian, seemed to reply from the precincts of the tomb:—

Child of Adam, heir of worldly glory, let not Hope deceive thee,
For I passed an undistinguished grave in the midst of a garden,
And the narcissus, and the rose, and the violet clustered round it,
And the star-like anemone shed its red light upon it.
And I said, whose tomb is this?
And the soil answered,
Be respectful, for this is the resting-place of a lover.
So I said, God keep thee, oh! victim of love,
For thou hast fallen beneath the simoom of passion,
Or perished with the mildew of disappointment.

The voice ceased—the company waited in silence for the renewal of the song: but the nightingale alone took up the strain, and the spreading of the tents and the sweet slumber that falls upon the weary, effaced the remembrance of the mysterious serenade from the minds of all but Cohr-Eddin. A superstitious fear weighed upon the spirit of the lover, and haunted his imagination. It was destiny warning him of disappointment, it was a rival triumphing in his chagrin; in either case it argued ill for the success of his suit, and robbed him of his rest.

When they set forward the following morning, they again caught a glimpse of the unknown cavalier, spurring on before them, and a messenger, mounted on the fleetest steed of the party, was despatched to overtake the stranger, and learn his purpose. The mission was unsuccessful, and the affair was passed over in silence.

The embassy was received with great distinction by the Christian lords in charge of Acre. The advantages of the proposed alliance were such as carried conviction to the most obtuse minds. The ardour of the lover, enforced by his presence, and by an animation unusual to the formal Orientals, gave to the Templars the strongest hopes of being able to make their own terms with the *sultan*, and they eagerly advocated the propriety of a betrothal between the parties, before the messengers could return from Europe with the husband provided by the French king.

But as the Princess Mary had been made fully aware of the importance of her hand to Christendom, and as her imagination might have been captivated by the glowing descriptions of the western knight who should lay his honours at her feet, the affair was considered of too delicate a character to admit of their interference: they concluded, therefore, to leave the lover to plead his own cause with the proud queen.

As Cohr-Eddin was conducted to the hall of audience, he encountered an individual, whose person seemed familiar, but whose face was studiously concealed, and who evidently sought to escape observation. When he entered the royal presence the lady appeared agitated, and despite her efforts at self-control tears forced themselves from her eyes, yet the unpropitious omen at the same time gave such a subdued and tender expression to her lustrous beauty, that the young Moslem acknowledged at once the power of her charms. But neither the stately courtesy, nor the florid flatteries of eastern compliment, nor the rich presents which he laid at her feet, nor the tempting offer of the crown matrimonial of Syria, nor even the piece of sacred wood which he brought to back his suit, had power to move the heart of the Christian maiden.

She steadfastly plead her engagement to abide by the arrangements of her ambassadors. The penetrating Saracen perceived, however, that it was the state of her affections, and not her principles that made his case utterly hopeless. He could not escape the suspicion that the mysterious horseman was in some way connected with his disappointment; but as he could not learn the name or rank of his rival, his wounded pride had not the usual alleviation of meditated revenge.

On his return to Damascus, he found that during his absence a

252

division of the Empire had been determined upon; that his younger brother had been made Sultan of Egypt, while to himself was committed the sovereignty of Syria and Palestine.

Affairs were in this posture when Jean de Brienne, the nobleman designated by Philip Augustus, with a train of three hundred knights arrived at Acre. The next day he received the hand of Mary in marriage, and shortly afterwards was crowned King of Jerusalem.

CHAPTER 2

—Death grinned horribly
A ghastly smile.—

A few years of unsuccessful conflict with the politic and warlike Saphadin, sufficed to acquaint the new king with the condition of affairs in Palestine. He displayed his valour in many a fierce encounter, and saved his states from utter annihilation, but he foresaw the approaching ruin of the holy cause, and wrote a letter to the pope, stating that the kingdom of Jerusalem consisted only of two or three towns, which by a vigorous action on the part of his foes, might be wrested from him at any moment.

Innocent III. answered by a circular letter, calling on all the sovereigns and clergy of Christendom, to seek a crown of glory in the sacred wars of Palestine; and by an epistle to Saphadin, in which he reminded the powerful *infidel*, that the Holy Land was in the possession of the Mussulmans, not on account of their virtues, but the sins of the Christians. The anger of Heaven, however, he said, was tempered with mercy, and the time was at hand when that mercy would be shown in an especial manner, and he finished by exhorting the *sultan* to resign peacefully, a country which was a source of more inconvenience than profit to the Moslems.

As the dignified Saracen made no overtures of capitulation, the pope found it necessary to put this boasted mercy to the proof, and the *Sixth Crusade* was accordingly preached in every church of Europe. A general council was held in the palace of the Lateran, *A.D.* 1215, for the important but dissimilar purposes of crowning Frederic II. grandson of Frederic Barbarossa, and for chastising vice in its various forms and condemning heresy in all its phases, and also for the sake of inducing princes and people to join the expedition to the Holy Land.

There were present the Patriarchs of Constantinople and Jerusalem, the ambassador of the Patriarch of Antioch, seventy-four metropolitan primates, and three hundred and forty bishops. The abbots and friars numbered eight hundred, but the representatives of the higher clergy could not be calculated. The Emperor of Constantinople, the Kings of France, England, Hungary, Jerusalem, Arragon, and the sovereigns of many other countries, were represented in the assembly.

After the general interests of the church had been considered and the heretics summarily given over to all the miseries of this life, and the pains of that to come, war against the Saracens, was declared to be the most sacred duty of the European world. The usual privileges and indulgences were accorded to the pilgrims, all tournaments during the three years appointed for the crusade, were prohibited, and universal peace was decreed, to all Christian kingdoms for the same period. Frederic II. was crowned on condition of joining the expedition.

The troubadours again took down their harps, and the voice of song echoing through castle and hall aroused the enthusiasm of youth, and awoke the slumbering energies of age. The *pontiff* himself declared his intention of visiting the Holy Land, and the warriors said one to another, "Let us spread our sacred banners and pass the seas; let us impress upon our bodies the sign of the cross; let us restore Christ to his inheritance, and by our deeds of arms merit the admiration of men, and the approbation of Heaven."

This crusade is divided into three parts. The expedition of Andrew II. King of Hungary; the war in Egypt, led by the Pope's legate and King Jean; and the campaign of the Emperor Frederic II., the first two divisions with their multiplied and sanguinary events, shaping the destiny and affecting the fortunes of Violante, the infant daughter of John de Brienne and Mary, King and Queen of Jerusalem.

Not long after Philip Augustus furnished from his dominions so wise and noble a knight to protect the rights of Mary and Jerusalem, he was called upon to exercise again his royal prerogative of matchmaker and king-maker by deputies from Constantinople.

The first Latin sovereign of the Greek Empire, Baldwin of Flanders, left his crown to his brother Henry. This prince dying without children, the next heir was his sister Yolande, widow of a French noble, and mother-in-law to Andrew II. King of Hungary. But the sceptre of empire in Constantinople, as well as in Jerusalem, could be swayed only by the firm hand of a warrior, and the deputies besought Philip

Augustus to provide at once a husband for Yolande, and an emperor for the throne of the Cæsars. The choice fell upon Peter Courtenay, cousin of the French king. The bridegroom—monarch elect, was conducted by a noble retinue to the Court of Hungary, where the marriage ceremony was performed by the successor of Innocent, Pope Honorius III. King Andrew then, in setting off for the crusade, accompanied the bridal party, dignified by the presence of the sovereign pontiff to the gates of Constantinople, where he witnessed the august ceremony of investing the monarch with the imperial purple, and saw the pope place the diadem of the East upon the head of his royal father-in-law. From Constantinople the Hungarian leader sailed for Cyprus, where he was admitted to an audience, with Hugh and Alice, king and queen of that island and thence with favourable winds passed over the Levant, and landed in safety at Acre.

This city was at that time the metropolis of the Holy Land, and in the palace formerly occupied by the queens Berengaria and Joanna, the stern western warriors knelt and did homage to Violante, the young princess of Palestine. Saphadin had retired from the constant toils of royalty, and blessed with the respect of his people, and the sweet affection of Elsiebede, resided in security at Damascus.

Cohr-Eddin, the reigning monarch, unprepared for the sudden invasion of his territories, was unable to call together his scattered tribes in sufficient force to hazard a general battle with the croises. The King of Hungary therefore led his army unmolested across "that ancient river, the river Kishon," over the plain of Jezreel, to the valley of the Jordan. They bathed in the sacred river; made the pilgrimage of the lake Gennesareth; visited the scenes made sacred by the miracles of the Saviour, and returned to Acre.

On the mount of Transfiguration the Saracens had built and fortified a tower of exceeding strength, and the soldiers, anxious to achieve something worthy the expedition, clamoured to be led to the siege of this fortress; but hordes of armed Mussulmans were every day crowding to the vicinity, and the restless Andrew, afraid to undertake anything further, resolved on a return to Europe.

Neither the entreaties nor threats of the Latin Christians, who had received him with hospitality, and exhausted their supplies in his entertainment, could persuade him to venture a blow for Palestine. Taking with him most of his soldiers, he returned through the Greek Empire, collecting relics from every holy place on his route, having so impoverished his kingdom by the expenses of the expedition, that it did not for years recover its pristine state. Thus ended the first division of the Sixth Crusade.

Still the Latins of Palestine were not left destitute. The Duke of Austria remained with a company of German crusaders, and the next year, when a reinforcement arrived, King Jean de Brienne with the Templars and Hospitallers, decided to transfer the seat of war to the dominions of Melech Camel, the youngest son of Saphadin and Elsiebede. Damietta was considered the key of Egypt, and thither the crusaders sailed in the month of May, A.D. 1216. A gallant band, selected from every nation in the army, led the assault against the citadel on St. Bartholomew's day. The garrison defended themselves with valour, but finally capitulated, and the rest of the city was looked upon as an easy conquest.

It was at this time that the Counts La Marche and Nevers arrived at the head of the French division of the crusade, but notwithstanding this new importation of knightly valour, the siege of Damietta went on but slowly. The legate of the pope advanced a claim to the office of commander-in-chief in right of his spiritual superiority; the Syrian Christians rallied around their King Jean de Brienne, and the French would yield obedience to none but their native leaders. Thus the captured castle of Damietta became a very Babel, from the confusion of tongues. Seventeen months were passed in furious attacks and idle skirmishes. The Saracens fought many well-contested battles with the Christians in their camp, but the issue of most of these conflicts was disastrous to the Moslems.

While the valiant Melech Camel was thus engaged in the gallant defence of his dominions, the death of Saif-Eddin deprived him of the counsels and assistance of the most successful chieftain that ever ruled the East.

When the news of the sad event reached Egypt, the subjects of the *sultan* withdrew from their allegiance and joined the standard of a young *emir* who attempted to make the sufferings of his country the means of his own aggrandizement. Melech Camel, obliged to escape for safety, fled over to Arabia, and thence directed his course toward Syria. Passing through El-akof, or territory of the winding sands, he came to the valley of Kadesh, where he descried a caravan encamped for the night. In doubt whether the convoy was guarded by the tributaries of his brother, or by a hostile tribe of Bedouins, he cautiously approached the well around which tethered horses and mules were browsing upon the scanty herbage, and multitudes of camels were lying in quiet repose. White tents like a setting of pearls around a central diamond encircled a silken pavilion of unrivalled magnificence, on the top of which gleamed a silver crescent, at once the symbol of the Moslem faith, and the reflection of its bright archetype in the sky. The watch-fires burned low, and no sounds of life broke the profound silence that reigned throughout the extended realm of night.

Dismounting and throwing the rein of his steed across his arm, to be prepared for any emergency, he advanced stealthily to the entrance of the circle. As he lifted the awning a small, dark, misshapen figure, like the fabled *genii* that guard the treasures of the East, rose up before him, and one glance at the ugly but welcome visage of Salaman assured him that he was among friends. The intelligence which he received from the faithful black, was even more gratifying than his appearance. The caravan was laden with provisions for the suffering soldiers in Egypt. Elsiebede herself occupied the royal pavilion, and Cohr Eddin was levying forces to come to the rescue of Damietta. Salaman led the way to a tent where, after listening to these satisfactory details, the fugitive monarch was left to the enjoyment of a repose to which he had long been stranger.

The meeting between Elsiebede and her favourite and unfortunate son, was of the most tender character. She acquainted him with the particulars of his father's death, and of the affairs that disturbed the peace of the empire. When Cohr-Eddin, returning from his unsuccessful suit to the heiress of Jerusalem, found that his brother had been sent to Egypt, he was confirmed in the suspicion that his rival was no other than Melech Camel. He recalled the figure of the solitary horseman, the voice at the tomb, and the disguised stranger, and, incensed at the thought that his brother had supplanted him in the affections of the princess, he determined to pursue him to his new dominions and take summary vengeance upon him.

To soothe the irritated and jealous feelings of Cohr-Eddin, Elsiebede had been under the necessity of revealing the secret which her younger son had confided to her on the eve of his departure for Egypt, namely, his early attachment for Mary formed during a residence at the Latin court, the hope he had cherished of uniting the kingdoms by a union with the object of his affections, and the struggle it had cost him to relinquish those pretensions. Cohr-Eddin, less noble than his brother, could scarcely be brought to credit the assertion that Camel's visit to Acre had originated in a desire to leave Mary free to accept his proposals, but as it was then the festival of the Ramadan,

257

in which it is not permitted for the faithful to make war upon each other, the execution of his revenge was necessarily delayed, and before the expiration of the sacred period, his presence was required upon the frontiers of his kingdom to repel the irruption of the Mongols.

★★★★★★

The timely relief afforded by the stores of the caravan, and the warlike fame and forces of his brother, soon reinstated Camel in his possessions; but their united efforts were insufficient to drive the Christians from Egypt. Before leaving Palestine, Cohr-Eddin apprehensive that his own territories might be garrisoned against him, destroyed the wall of Jerusalem, and broke down its defences with the exception of the tower of David, and the temple of the sepulchre; and after many gallant battles, deeming it impossible to raise the siege of Damietta, he proposed to the Crusaders peace. The Moslems, he said, would give up the piece of the true cross, release all the Christian prisoners in Syria and Egypt, rebuild the walls of Jerusalem, and relinquish the sacred city to its Latin king, John de Brienne.

The French and the Germans hailed with joy the prospect of a speedy termination of the war; but the fanatical devotees of the church, the Templars, legates, and bishops were deaf to the counsels of moderation, and it was decided to pursue the siege with vigour.

Damietta was taken; but with such determined valour had the Moslems defended their city, that of the population, which, at the commencement of the siege, consisted of seventy thousand souls, scarce three thousand upon the day of final attack appeared upon the ramparts. A gate was forced, and the warriors of the cross rushed forward to commence the work of plunder. They met neither a resistant nor a suppliant enemy. The awful silence struck a chill upon their souls. They passed along the deserted streets. The waysides were strewn with dead bodies in every state of putrescence.

They entered the dwellings. In every room ghastly corpses, with visages shrunken by famine or bloated by pestilence, glared upon them. Turk and Mameluke, Copt and Arab, master and servant, rich and poor, were heaped in undistinguished masses, the dying with the dead. Infants appealing in vain to the pulseless breasts of famished mothers, lifted their feeble cries for sustenance; dogs ran about the streets, and pestilential effluvia rose like an exhalation from the vast charnel-house, whose appalling stillness the Christians had invaded with songs of triumph and rejoicing. They had overcome the Moslems, but they found the Conqueror Death seated on the throne of dominion. Awestruck and abashed they fled from before the presence of the King of Terrors, gladly granting life and liberty to the surviving Moslems, on condition of their performing the horrid and melancholy task of cleansing the city from the remains of their relatives and friends.

The way into Palestine was now open, and King Jean proposed to the victorious Christians to march immediately thither; but the legate of the pope insisted that the complete conquest of Egypt should first be effected. His arrogance overruled wiser counsels, and it was resolved to pursue Melech Camel to Cairo. The *croises* accordingly advanced on the eastern bank of the Nile, till their progress was arrested by the canal of Ashmoun, on the south side of which the forces of Islam were stationed. Every *emir* of Syria had sent assistance to Melech, and the Latins were prevented from leaving their position, till the period of the annual influx of the Nile, when the Mussulmans opened their sluices, inundated their enemy's camp, cut off all communication with the sea-coast, and enclosed them like fish in a net.

The tents and baggage were swept away; the provisions spoiled, the terrible scourge that had destroyed the inhabitants of Damietta, appeared in the camp, and the humbled Christians made overtures of peace, promising to evacuate Egypt, on condition of being permitted to return in safety to Acre. The generous Melech Camel acceded to this proposal. Hostages were exchanged for the performance of the treaty, and the noble King of Jerusalem, together with his wife and their daughter, Violante, were among the number.

The Sultan of Egypt received his guests with distinguished honour, and provided for their princely entertainment in Cairo. As the sympathetic Latin chief took leave of his suffering followers, tears overflowed his manly cheeks.

"Why do you weep?" exclaimed the compassionate *sultan*.

"I have cause to weep," returned the king, "the people whom God has given to my charge, are perishing amidst the waters, dying with hunger, or falling a prey to the pestilence."

"Despair not," replied the noble Melech, "for what saith the proverb? '*To everything there is an end,*' therefore, mourn not, for misfortunes shall find a termination."

He turned to his soldiers, and gave orders that the granaries of Egypt should be opened for their suffering foes.

As the royal hostages approached the palace of the *sultan*, they were preceded by troops of vassals, called *apparitors*, who, sword in hand and with great clamour, led them through narrow and winding passages, where at every gate *cohorts* of armed Ethiopians, bowed with their faces in the dust before the *sultan*, and welcomed his triumphant return, with the harsh dissonance of the Saracen drum, and the shrill tones of the Syrian pipe. They entered next upon a broader space open to the clear light of day, where were galleries wainscoted with gold, and ornamented with marble pillars and sculptured images of the old Egyptian deities; and paved with mosaics of coloured stone.

There were basins filled with limpid waters, which glided in shining streams over rocks arranged to resemble the ravines and grottoes of the wilderness. The branches of the olive, pomegranate and fig were loaded with fruit, and the place resounded with the warbling of birds of varied and gorgeous plumage; while through *vistas* pleasantly opening to them as they passed, the eye caught glimpses of artificial forests in which bounded the silver-footed antelope, and the bright-eyed gazelle, with multitudes of graceful and beautiful animals, "Such as painters imagine in the wantonness of their art, such as poetic fancies describe, such as we see in dreams, and such as are found only in the lands of the Orient and the South."

The open court turned upon a corridor, and at the entrance beneath a crystal floor, there rolled a clear stream through which the glittering gold fish sported, and the mottled trout pursued the shining insects with restless avidity. The little Violante unpractised in the deceits of art, lifted her robe and stepped daintily upon the glassy surface, as if to lave her tiny feet in the translucent waters. Finding that the firm basis yielded not to the tread, she passed on with a puzzled look of surprise and pleasure, till her attention was attracted by the sound of a multitude of voices, and melodious harpings with which the satellites of the ante-chamber greeted their approach.

Bands of Mamelukes dressed in robes of the greatest magnificence, prostrated themselves thrice before their *sultan*, and then raised their feathery wands to bar the progress of the train to the inner court of the *harem*. The gates rolled back upon their golden hinges, and a troop of maidens fair as the *houries*, approached to receive the Christian females, while the *sultan* with the king and his knights turned away from the closing gates, like lost spirits banished from the bowers of Elysium.

Welcomed by the inmates of the *seraglio*, the royal ladies were conducted to baths, where all sense of fatigue was lost in the plastic embrace of the fragrant waters; after which reclining upon couches they enjoyed delicious repose, while their dark-eyed attendants plaited their hair according to the eastern fashion, and apparelled them with the flowing and graceful drapery of the Egyptian court. Thence they were ushered into a refectory, where seated upon divans, they regaled themselves with a simple collation of cakes and fruits, inhaling the balmy air redolent with accumulated sweets, gathered from the fragrant gardens that bordered the Nile.

From the banquet room they passed to an apartment magnificently adorned with all the appliances of Oriental luxury. Lofty windows admitted the light, which, shaded by curtains of varied colours, was tempered to a soft radiance that filled the apartment with an indefinable bloom. Suddenly the silken partitions inwoven with pearls and gold in the midst of the hall, were drawn aside, and Elsiebede, descending from a canopied throne, and resigning the stately dignity of the queen, greeted her European guests with the gracious familiarity that she had learned in the household of Richard Cœur de Lion.

Reclining upon cushions that offered rest and inspired a soft languor, they listened to her sweet assurances of favour uttered in the welcome language of Frangistan, or watched the airy motions of sportive girls, who keeping time to the tinkling ornaments that decorated their delicate limbs, sported before them in the joyous evolutions of the dance. The unaffected grace of the little Violante, who joined the performers, gave infinite delight to the *almé* or learned women, who accompanied by the Syrian lute, sang verses in compliment to the distinguished guests.

Upon the evacuation of Egypt by the Christians, the volunteers returned to Europe, and the Barons of Syria and the military orders retired to Acre. The hostages being now at liberty, the king set off for Palestine, leaving his wife and child to travel by the imperial caravan, under the safe conduct of the *sultana*. He found his kingdom in a distracted state. The Templars were in effect the lords of Palestine, and a cessation of hostilities with the *infidels*, was but a signal for the breaking out of animosities between the rival Christians.

Disheartened with the gloomy aspect of things, the disconsolate king sat in his palace at Acre, devising schemes to mend his broken fortunes, each one of which, upon mature consideration, he was forced to abandon as hopeless and impracticable, when the chamberlain entered and presented a letter. The epistle was from Elsiebede, and brought the melancholy intelligence of the death of his beloved Mary, whose remains, preserved in wax, and attended by her own Christian maidens, had been brought to Acre under the convoy of the fleet of

261

Melech Camel.

With the delicate tenderness of one who had tasted grief, the *sultana* dwelt upon the virtues of the deceased queen, and consoled the bereaved husband with assurances that her disease had been treated by the most learned leeches of the royal household, and her last hours been blest with the attendance of a Christian priest, and the performance of the rites enjoined by the Christian faith. Concerning the orphan, Violante, she continued, "Let the damsel, I pray thee, abide with me, that I may show kindness unto her for her mother's sake. She shall have the nurture of a princess in the house of the Egyptian, for God hath made her unto me as Moses to the daughter of Pharaoh. The angel of the storm rideth upon the sea, while the winter remaineth, but when the queen of the flowers shall ascend her throne of enamelled foliage, thou mayest require her, and she shall come to thee, by the blessing of *Allah* (whose name be exalted), and by the blessing also of thy prophet Jesus, in whom thou trustest."

The burial-ground of Acre was crowded with Christian graves. The best and noblest of the brave sons of the West, champions and martyrs of the cross, had there gained worthy sepulture; but it was meet that the Queen of *Jerusalem* should find her last resting-place among the ancient kings of that time-honoured metropolis. By the favour of Cohr-Eddin permission was gained to convey her body thither; mass was said for her soul in the church of the Holy Sepulchre; her grave was made in the valley of Jehoshaphat; and Christian and Saracen stood together in reverent silence, while the Patriarch of Jerusalem committed *"Earth to earth, and dust to dust,"* to wait the morning of the resurrection.

CHAPTER 3

The death of those distinguished by their station,
But by their virtue more, awakes the mind
To solemn dread, and strikes a saddening awe.

When the loss of Damietta and the evacuation of Egypt was known at Rome, Pope Honorius III. reproached the emperor, Frederic II. with being the cause of the signal failure of the Christian arms in the East, and threatened him with excommunication if he did not immediately fulfil his vow, by leading his armies against the *infidel.* This insolence roused the indignation of the prince, and excited him to hostility. He proceeded to claim the kingdom of the two Sicilies, in right of his mother, Constance, and marching thither, drove out the partisans of the Holy See, established bishops of his own choosing in the vacant benefices, and even threatened to plunder Rome. Honorius discovering that he had involved himself in strife with a powerful enemy, wrote a conciliatory letter to the emperor, saying, "I exhort you, my dear son, to recall to your recollection, that you are the protector of the Roman Church; do not forget what you owe to that good mother, and take pity on her daughter, the church of the East, which extends towards you her arms, like an unfortunate, who has no longer any hope but in you."

Frederic, too much occupied in his plans for adding Italy to the German Empire, to undertake a distant expedition that afforded so little prospect of an increase of patrimony or glory, was, notwithstanding, willing to avail himself of the popular enthusiasm. He professed his intention to obey the mandate of the holy father, and prepared for the pious work, by causing his son Henry to be crowned King of the Romans, and by adding the imperial to the kingly diadem upon his own head, 1220. It is even probable that the subjugation of Italy, and the assertion of the rights of the temporal against the spiritual power, might have prevented Frederic from ever attempting anything for Palestine, had not the sagacious *pontiff* found an irresistible ally in the beautiful Violante, Queen of Jerusalem.

Wearied of endeavouring to convert his marital rights to the sovereignty of Jerusalem, into actual and firm dominion, Jean de Brienne listened to the suggestions of the Roman legate, that his claims to the nominal crown might be transferred with the hand of his daughter to some powerful prince of Europe.

Accompanied by the patriarch of Jerusalem, Jean de Brienne sailed for Egypt on his route to Italy. Melech Camel received his guests with a pompous distinction calculated to impress them with the security and prosperity of his government; and Violante, whose sojourn with Elsiebede had been protracted to several years, welcomed her father with the timid reserve consequent upon the harem-like seclusion in which she had been nurtured. Her dress was Oriental, both in richness of material and peculiarity of costume. She returned the king's embrace gracefully and affectionately, but when the patriarch fixed his admiring eyes upon her, she instantly concealed her blushing countenance behind the folds of her veil, and the prelate observed that though the prayers she repeated in her agitation, were such as the church prescribed, she held in her hand an "Implement of praise," or Moslem rosary, of thrice three and thirty precious stones, and that she involuntarily mingled with her more orthodox devotions, "*Ya Alla khalick, ya Alla kareem.*" He would fain have relieved her of the Infidel charm, but the spoiled princess resisted his pious endeavour, and sought refuge from his remonstrances in the female apartments of the palace.

The stay of Jean de Brienne in Egypt was marked by an event of great consequence, both to the Christians and Mussulmans. The health of Elsiebede had long been declining; and in the maturity of years, passed in benevolent efforts to harmonize the discordant interests of those among whom she dwelt a stranger and a sovereign, she sank to her rest. Violante wept bitterly at the loss of her patron and friend, but the Moorish maidens, to whom she had rendered herself inexpressibly dear, were not permitted by their law to indulge in expressions of sorrow, though an involuntary tear accompanied the consolatory words with which they addressed Melech Camel: "*Alla* wills it. May the blessing of the All-merciful rest upon thee."

Violante had so long dwelt in the house of Elsiebede, that the distinctions of faith were forgotten, and she was allowed to mingle with the mourning-train that carried the body to the burial: but King Jean de Brienne and the patriarch of Jerusalem were prohibited from profaning the sacred ceremony by their presence.

The serene dawn of an Eastern morning was gilding the domes and minarets of Cairo, as the body of Elsiebede was carried forth to the mosque, to be prepared, according to the faith of her fathers, for its final home. As the bearers entered the door, the congregation repeated in solemn cadence, "Praise be to God, the Lord of the worlds, the most merciful, the king of the day of judgment. Thee do we worship, and of thee do we beg assistance. Direct us in the right way, in the way of those to whom thou hast been gracious; not of those against whom thou art incensed, nor of those who go astray."

The *imam* then stood up and called upon one and another to testify concerning the life of the illustrious dead; and each vied with the other in recounting her acts of beneficence and piety, till the priest concluded with, "She was more glorious than the four perfect women who dwell in the bowers of the blest. She was more bountiful than Fatima; she had the virtue of Kadijah; she was more constant than Asia; she had the purity of Mary."

Wrapped in fine linen impregnated with spices and perfumes, and laid in a coffin of cypress, the remains were then carried to the place of interment, where a crowd of females who were not permitted to enter the mosque, sat closely veiled upon the ground in the utmost abandonment of silent sorrow. Others embraced the pillars that ornamented the graves, and cried out, "A leaf hath withered on the tree of life, a new guest cometh to the City of the Silent."

The body was preceded by a noble Moor, who bore upon his head a box of cendal wood inlaid with mother-of-pearl. Arrived at the grave, the bearers set down the bier, and the imam called upon all to join him in prayer. Scarcely had the air ceased to vibrate with their voices, when the *muezzins*, placing frankincense in golden censers, touched it with burning coals, and a fragrant cloud laden with the breath of their petitions, seemed to float away towards heaven. The *imam* standing at the head of the grave, opened the cendal box, and taking thence the leaves of the *Koran*, distributed them among the people, and all began to read in a low recitative chant, the words of the holy book:

> By the brightness of the morning; and by the night, when it groweth dark; thy Lord hath not forsaken thee, neither doth he hate thee. Verily the life to come shall be better for thee than the present life; and thy Lord shall give thee a reward wherewith thou shalt be well pleased. Did not he find thee an orphan, and hath he not taken care of thee? And did he not find thee wandering in error, and hath he not guided thee into the truth? And did he not find thee needy, and hath he not enriched thee? Wherefore declare the goodness of thy Lord.

The coffin was deposited in the ground, and every friend and every bystander cast a portion of dust upon it, until the grave was filled. The *imam* then called out to the loved one, "Oh Elsiebede! daughter of Eve, say that God is thy God, say that Mohammed is the prophet of God." He paused a moment as if listening for her response, and then continued, "Certainly thou hast acknowledged God for thy God, Islamism for thy religion, Mohammed for thy prophet, the *Koran* for thy priest, the sanctuary of Mecca for thy *Kibla*, and the faithful for thy brethren." He turned to the congregation, and spreading forth his hands repeated the benediction, "Oh Lord pour patience on us, and cause us all to die Moslems."

Melech Camel, as chief of the household, then approached, and planted a sprig of cypress on the right and on the left of the grave, and each friend and relative performed the same sad duty, and then all standing together with their hands stretched out above the resting-place of the beloved *sultana*, repeated the portion of the sacred writings appointed for the closing service: "By the sun and its rising brightness—by the moon when she followeth him—by the day when he showeth his splendour—by the night when it covereth him with darkness—by the heaven and him who built it—by the earth and him who spread it forth—by the witness and the witnessed—by the soul and him who completely formed it, and inspired into the same its faculty of distinguishing and power of choosing wickedness and piety—now is he who hath possessed the same happy—"

The procession then slowly and sadly departed from the hallowed precincts, and none marked the bowed and wasted figure of Salaman leaning upon the broken turf that hid from his dimmed and aged eyes the face of his only friend. His attachment for Elsiebede had been such as is common to animals remarkable for sagacity and fidelity, and the range of his intellect introducing him to no personal aspirings, all his thoughts had been concentrated in the one idea of serving his mistress. He had shared her confidence and favour in weal and in woe, and followed her fortunes with a zeal and industry that engrossed all his powers. Now that she was no more, there remained for him neither aim nor purpose, neither hope nor desire.

Without a country, without a religion, he had worshipped Mass with the Christians, and repeated the Creed with the Moslems; but since Elsiebede had entered upon an untried state, his desire to insure to her every possible good, led him, at great personal inconvenience, to procure an ebony cross, that if she failed of the Mohammedan paradise, she might, through its influence, gain an entrance into the Christian's heaven. With a feeble hand that scarce obeyed the promptings of his generous affection, the faithful black hollowed a place for the venerated symbol, and with great difficulty planted it firmly at the head of the grave. The pious task accomplished, he knelt to repeat a Christian prayer which they had learned together in the household of Berengaria. The familiar words overwhelmed him in a tide of long-forgotten reminiscences, and he fell prostrate upon the mound.

The following morning Violante obtained permission to accompany the maidens to the burial ground, and assist in garlanding the grave of the *sultana*. At the sight of the silent worshipper they hushed their voices, but he heeded not their approach. The princess ventured to lift the hand that rested upon the cross. It was stiff and cold. She drew aside her veil and gazed upon his face. The faithful Salaman had expired upon the grave of Elsiebede.

Her lot is on you—silent tears to weep,
And patient smiles to wear through suffering's hour
And sumless riches from Affection's deep,
To pour on broken reeds—a wasted shower!
And to make idols, and to find them clay,
And to bewail that worship—therefore pray!

Violante, the eastern beauty, whose hand held the keys of all the seaports of the Levant—the sceptre of the Latin kingdom of Palestine, and the diadem of Jerusalem—and whose voice alone could pronounce the magic "*Sesame*" that should open the gates of commerce, and pour the treasures of Sheba, and Dedan, and Ophir into the coffers of the church, created a great sensation in Europe.

The titular king, John de Brienne, was ready to resign all the real or fancied good that might appertain to his daughter's dominions, in favour of any candidate whom the pope should select as her future husband; and the presumptive queen, whose eastern preferences led her still to retain the timid reserve in which she had been educated, was not supposed to have any choice in the matter. The wily *pontiff* desirous to bind the Ghibelline faction like a victim to the horns of the altar, proposed a union between the son of the Emperor Frederic, and the daughter of John de Brienne. The young prince was delighted with his brilliant prospects, and readily assured the legate of the pope, that his sword should be ready at all times and in all places to execute the decrees of the church.

Since her arrival at Rome, Violante had lived in almost utter solitude, mourning for the girlish sports that had given wings to the flying hours in the palace of Cairo, and weeping at the remembrance of the constant beneficence and tender counsels of the good Queen Elsiebede. She received the advances of the royal heir of Hohenstaufen with an embarrassment that might portend either success or failure to his suit. He repeated his visits, and at each interview made desperate efforts to impress her with a sense of his devotion and to win in return some token of her regard; but his self-felicitations reached no farther than a general conviction, that she was very beautiful and very bashful. John de Brienne represented to his daughter the necessity of fixing the affections of the young king. She listened with respectful silence, and interposed no objections to the arrangements making for her future happiness.

The nuptials were to be celebrated on the occasion of a high festival, at Ferentino, and the emperor with the chief dignitaries of his court was to grace the splendid ceremony. The week before the appointed day, Frederic arrived in Italy, and prompted by curiosity, sought an interview with his prospective daughter. Violante received the majestic emperor with the same maiden coyness that had characterized her interviews with her lover; but Frederic, whose ardent fancy was captivated by the fascinating Oriental, was not to be baffled by her shyness. After attempting an indifferent conversation, in the French language, he changed his tactics, and modulating his voice to the low, deep tones of the Arabic, spoke to her of her former life, of her mother, of her future home.

Suddenly the countenance of the delighted girl became radiant with animation, the eloquent blood mounted to her cheek, her eyes dilated with joy, and the admiring monarch listened in mute surprise, while in the graceful and poetical language of the East she narrated the particulars of her sojourn at Cairo, and described the games and sports she had enjoyed in the company of the Moorish maidens. She showed him her jewel rosary, with its pendant charm, the talisman of the Gyptianos, the last gift of Elsiebede; but when she essayed to speak of the virtues of the sultana, tender recollections crowded so fast upon her, that her lips refused their office, and gushing tears alone finished her tale of gratitude and love.

Her royal auditor soothed her agitation with assurances of sympathy and kindness, and on leaving the apartment, was flattered by her urgent request, that he would visit her again. Engagements of this sort, the amatory monarch seldom failed to fulfil. Each interview increased the charm, and deepened her affection; and before the expiration of the week, he waited upon the pope to apprize his holiness, that Violante had rejected the son, in favour of the father. The *pontiff*, well pleased with the turn affairs had taken, interposed but one condition, and Frederic having solemnly promised to undertake the crusade within two years, took the place of Henry at the altar, and espoused the heiress of Jerusalem.

Pleased with his lovely acquisition, and occupied with the affairs of his realm, Frederic delayed under various pretexts the fulfilment of his vow, and neither the expostulations of pope nor peer had any influence upon his purposes, till he learned that Honorius had entered into a league with his son Henry, the disappointed bridegroom, and instigated the cities of Lombardy to revolt. Alarmed at the disaffection of his subjects, Frederic renewed his promise, and went so far as to consign his kingdom to the protection of the church, during his absence. The death of the pope, in 1227, afforded him another temporary respite.

He had, however, in this change of *pontiffs*, as little matter of congratulation, as the fox in the fable: Gregory IX. proving a more voracious and intolerant scourge, than his predecessor. After making arrangements to prosecute the designs of Honorius upon the Albigenses, the new pope published the eastern crusade, and called upon Frederic to set out without loss of time.

The lovely Violante was drooping in her European home. The harsh and guttural language of the Germans, offended her ear, their rude and unpolished manners presented an effectual barrier to the light and graceful amusements, which she sought to introduce in her court, and her delicate frame chilled by the severity of a climate to which she was unaccustomed, shrank from every exposure. She pined to revel once more, in the bland and balmy airs that sweep the fragrance from Hermon, and to be served with the courteous reserve, and graceful observances which she had enjoyed in the harem of Cairo. Her only hope of returning to her native land, was in the fulfilment of her husband's vow; but finding that her mild entreaties served only to irritate his imperious temper, she refrained to press the subject, and confined her anxieties to her own breast.

While the lovely exotic was thus withering under the blighting influence of the uncongenial atmosphere of the north, Jean de Brienne visited the German court. Alarmed at his daughter's pale and wasted appearance, he regarded her with a tender sympathy, such as he had never before manifested towards her; and the heart-broken queen poured out her sorrows before him, and entreated him to take her back to Palestine. The sweet pensiveness so like the expression of her mother's countenance, and which had already become habitual to her youthful features touched a secret chord in his heart, and the thought that Frederic had squandered the wealth of her affection, and repulsed her winning caresses with coldness and contempt, roused his indignation.

He expostulated with the monarch in no measured terms. The emperor admitted, that he had won the affections of Violante, by his apparent interest in the Holy Land, and gained her hand by a promise to restore to her, her rightful inheritance; but he sneeringly insinuated, that these courteous condescensions, were the fanciful gages staked by all lovers, which as husbands they were not bound to redeem. He laid down the proposition that oaths in religion, politics, and love were but means to an end, only binding, in so far as they accorded with the convenience of those who made them. He cited examples of the clergy, with the pope at their head, who wedding the church, and professing to live alone for her interests, made her the means of their own aggrandizement, the pander of their base passions; the policy of kings, who, receiving the sceptre of dominion for the ostensible purpose, of securing peace and happiness to their subjects, pursued their own pleasure, without regard to civil commotion or discord; and he illustrated his theory by multiplied instances in the domestic life of the sovereigns of Europe, who, for the gratification of personal pique, put away those whom they had promised to love and cherish to the end of life.

Violante listened to this discourse like one who for the first time comprehends the solution of a problem, that has long taxed the ingenuity and embarrassed the reason. His sentiments explained the mystery in his manner, the discrepancy between his professions and performances, and like the spear of Ithuriel, dispelled at once the illusion of her fancy, and made him assume before her his own proper character. She fixed her large dark eyes upon his countenance, as though striving to recall the image she had worshipped there. She saw only the arrogant sneer of scepticism, and the smile of selfish exultation. Her sensitive heart recoiled with horror at the prospect of the cheerless future, which in one fearful moment passed like a vision before her, and with a piercing cry she fell fainting to the floor.

The husband calmly summoned the maids as he left the apartment, while the father, with a heart distracted between pity and anger, tenderly lifted her lifeless form and conveyed her to a couch.

Robert, the second son of Peter Courtenay and Yoland, succeeded his father upon the throne of Constantinople. An inglorious reign of seven years left the empire in a distracted state, and an early death transferred the crown to his infant son Baldwin. The barons of the Greek Empire felt the necessity of placing the sceptre in the hands of a man and a hero; and messengers were despatched to the veteran King of Jerusalem, to beg him to accept the imperial purple, and become the father of the young prince, by bestowing upon him the hand of his second daughter in marriage. The position and authority of Jean de Brienne as the Emperor of Constantinople, gave him power to punish Frederic's baseness, and he speedily signified to the emperor, that the might of his sword, backed by the strength of the Greek forces, was now ready to enforce the decrees of the pope.

Frederic, finding that he could no longer with any safety defer his pilgrimage, ordered a general rendezvous of his troops at Brundusium preparatory for departure. Before however the appointed time for sailing had arrived, a pestilence broke out in the camp, numbers died and greater numbers deserted, and the emperor himself, after having embarked and remained at sea three days, returned, declaring that his health would not admit of his taking the voyage. Exulting in the fortunate circumstance that had released him from the dreaded expedition, he hastened his march to Germany.

As he entered his palace, he was struck by the grave and serious manner with which his retainers, usually so enthusiastic, received him. An ominous gloom reigned in the court, and as with lordly tread he passed through the long corridors, he felt that his step was breaking the silence of death. In the anteroom of the queen's apartment, he found her maidens indulging in the utmost expressions of grief. The feeble wail of an infant smote upon his ear, and striding through the hushed and darkened chamber, he sought the couch of the neglected Violante. That couch was a bier. Those lips, upon whose sportive accents he had hung with exquisite though momentary rapture, were forever dumb. Those features, that had kindled with a glow of love at his every word of tenderness, were now settled in their last calm repose.

Poor Violante! Thy pilgrimage was brief. The first sweet stage of childhood scarcely passed, Fancy led thy willing footsteps through the Elysian fields of Love, and robed the object of thy young affections with a halo of purity and truth.—The life-long experience of woman—the indefinable slight and wrong that press home upon her, the bitter sense of utter helplessness and dependence, the inexplicable woe of the primeval curse,—crowded into the little span of a few short months, brought thee early to the sepulchre,—seventeen summers, and a winter whose rigor congealed the very fountain of thy life,—to hope, to love, to give thy life to another, and die.—Such is thy history, beautiful Violante, Queen of Jerusalem, Empress of Germany, Heroine of the Sixth Crusade.

271

Eleanora

Chapter 1: The Parents of Edward I

Of all the royal suitors that ever stooped to woo the love of woman, Henry III. son of John Lackland and Isabella of Angoulême, appears to have been the most luckless and unfortunate. He first fixed his affections upon the Princess of Scotland, who was dissuaded from listening to his suit, by her brother's assurance that the king was a squint-eyed fool, deceitful, perjured, more faint-hearted than a woman, and utterly unfit for the company of any fair and noble lady.

Disappointed in Scotland, the monarch next offered his hand to the heiress of Brittany, but the rugged Bretons, too well remembering the cruelty of his father, to their beloved Prince Arthur, returned a haughty refusal.

He then proposed to confer the honour of his alliance upon a daughter of Austria, but the fair descendant of Leopold inherited all her grandfather's enmity to the princely house of Plantagenet, and rejected his addresses with disdain.

The Duke of Bohemia, to whom he next applied, civilly answered that his child was already plighted to another, and it was not until Henry reached the mature age of thirty that he received a favourable response to his matrimonial proposal; and when at last the marriage contract was signed between himself and Joanna, daughter of Alice of France, the roving affections of this royal Cœlebs were beguiled from their allegiance by the sweet strains of the youthful poetess of Provence.

Eleanor la Belle, second daughter of Count Berenger, perhaps the youngest female writer on record, attracted the attention of the fickle King of England, by a poem which she composed on the conquest of Ireland.

Dazzled by her genius and personal charms, Henry's vows to Joanna were forgotten, and his ambassadors received orders to break off the negotiations, while his obliging counsellors recommended a union with the very lady he so ardently admired.

His habitual covetousness intruded however into the courtship, and had well-nigh subjected him to a sixth disappointment. He intrusted his *seneschal* to demand twenty thousand *marks* as the dower of Eleanor, but privately empowering him to lessen the sum if necessary to fifteen, ten, seven, five or three thousand. He quite disgusted the haughty count her father, by his sordid bargaining, and at last wrote in great terror, to conclude the marriage forthwith, either with money or without, but at all events to secure the lady for him and conduct her safely to England without delay.

In the splendid festivities with which Henry welcomed his young bride to London, and in the preparation of her coronation robes, he displayed a taste for lavish expenditure altogether inconsistent with the state of his finances, and in ridiculous contrast to his former penuriousness.

Like his father the greatest fop in Europe, but not like him content with the adornment of his own person, he issued the most liberal orders for apparelling the royal household in satin, velvet, cloth of gold and ermine, expending in the queen's jewellery alone a sum not less than one hundred and fifty thousand dollars.

About the same time he bestowed his sister Isabella upon the Imperial widower Frederic II., and personally designated every article of her sumptuous wardrobe.

It was on this occasion that he first learned how imperative a check a sturdy British Parliament may be on the lawless extravagance of a king; for when he petitioned the Lords for a relief from his pecuniary difficulties, they told him they had amply supplied funds both for his marriage and that of the empress, and as he had wasted the money he might defray the expenses of his wedding as best he could.

It would be difficult to say whether the king, the queen, or the royal relations, proved the greatest scourges to Britain during the long and impotent reign of Henry III.

One of Eleanor's uncles became prime minister; to another was given the rich Earldom of Warrenne, and a third was made Archbishop of Canterbury, and numerous young lady friends of the romantic queen were imported from Provence and married to the king's wealthy wards.

Henry's mother, not content with sending over all her younger children to be provided for by the impoverished monarch, involved him in a war with Louis IX., which ended disastrously for the English arms, in the loss of a great part of the rich southern fiefs and the military chests and costly ornaments of the king's chapel.

Henry's ambition for his children brought still greater difficulties upon the realm. His eldest son, Edward, was appointed viceroy of the disputed possessions in Aquitaine, and being too young to discharge his important trusts with discretion, so mismanaged affairs as greatly to increase the discontent of his father's French subjects.

His eldest daughter Margaret, married to her cousin Alexander III., the young King of Scotland, was taken prisoner by Sir John Baliol, and subjected to the most rigorous confinement, thus making it necessary for Henry to undertake a Northern campaign for the rescue of his child.

But his second son, Edmund, proved more expensive to the British nation, and innocently did more to project the civil war than any other member of the royal family; for the pope, having conferred the crown of Sicily upon the young prince, the delighted father eagerly engaged in a prospective war, and promised to defray the whole expense of substantiating the claim.

Again the barons resisted the onerous tax which this new attempt at family aggrandizement would impose upon them, and the first subsidy was raised from the benefices of the church only by the exercise of spiritual authority. When the ambitious king had exhausted all his resources, the *pontiff* coolly transferred the coveted crown to Charles d'Anjou, brother to the King of France, leaving poor Henry to cancel his debt with the lords of exchequer as best he might, getting to himself in the eyes of his subjects little glory and great loss.

Such was the character, the political and the social position of the parents of Edward I., who commenced about the middle of the thirteenth century to take an active part in the affairs of Europe.

A splendid concourse were gathered in the spacious palace of the old temple at Paris, *A.D.* 1254. The royal families of England and France were convened on terms of cordiality and kindness, such as they had never enjoyed since the day when Normandy was wrested from the descendants of Charlemagne. The banquet was given in honour of Edward, the heir-apparent of England, and his sweet young bride, Eleanora of Castile. In the place of honour sat the good St. Louis King of France, on his right, Henry III. of England, and on his left, the King of Navarre, the royal descendant of Thibaut of Cham-

pagne, and Blanche the sister of Berengaria. At this magnificent enter-
tainment, Beatrice the Countess of Provence enjoyed a reunion with
her beautiful daughters, their noble husbands and blooming offspring.
The eldest, Margaret, was the wife of Louis IX., Eleanor, of Henry
III., Beatrice, of Charles d'Anjou, and Sancha, of Richard of Cornwall,
King of the Romans.

But the queen of this Feast of kings, the fair young *infanta*, around
whom were gathered the nobility of a Continent, though but a child
of scarce ten years, concentrated in herself more romantic associations
and excited higher hopes than any of the crowned heads present. Her
brother Alphonso X., the astronomer, was the most learned prince
in Europe, and neither priest or peer could boast that devotion to
the arts, or that success in scientific discoveries that characterized the
King of Castile, surnamed *Il Sabio*, the wise. Her mother Joanna, had
been the affianced bride of her royal father-in-law Henry III., had
been rejected for the more poetic daughter of the Count of Provence;
and her grandmother, Alice of France, had been refused by the gallant King Richard, in favour of Berengaria of Navarre. Her brother
Alphonso, and her husband's uncle, Richard of Cornwall, were candi-
dates for the crown of the German Empire, in opposition to the rights
of Conrad, son of Frederic and Violante, and her husband, a graceful
youth of fifteen, who had received the honours of knighthood at his
wedding tournament, was heir to the goodly realm of England and
the beautiful provinces of Southern France.

The tourney, the banquet, and the procession, had marked their
progress from Burgos, in Spain, to the Parisian court. At Bordeaux,
King Henry expended 300,000 *marks* on their marriage feast, a sum,
at that time so extravagant, that when reproached for it, he exclaimed
in a dolorous tone, "Oh! *pour la tête de Dieu*, say no more of it, lest men
should stand amazed at the relation thereof." At Chartres, the palace
once occupied by Count Stephen and Adela, was ornamented with
the most brilliant decorations to honour their presence. St. Louis advanced to meet, and escort them to Paris. The cavalcade consisted of
one thousand mounted knights in full armour, each with some lady
by his side, upon a steed whose broidered housings rivalled the richness of the flowing habiliments of the fair rider, while a splendid train
of carriages, sumpter mules, and grooms, and vassals completed the
magnificent retinue.

The nuptial festival with its usual accompaniments of hunting,
hawking, and holiday sports, continued through eight days, and a bril-

liant *cortége* attended the bridal party to the coast of France, on their departure for England. The passage was rough and gloomy, and the fleet that conveyed Eleanora to her new home encountered a storm upon the Channel, and approached the harbour under the cover of a fog so dense, that the white cliffs of Dover were entirely veiled from sight.

The child queen, terrified at the profound darkness, strove to silence her own agonizing apprehensions, by repeating those words of sacred writ, which she supposed exercised some mysterious influence upon the elements. Suddenly a terrible crash made the ship groan through all its timbers. Piercing shrieks from without told a tale of horrors, and the echoing screams within rendered it impossible to ascertain the nature or extent of the danger. At length it was found, that the royal vessel had in the darkness encountered and sunk a small bark, supposed to be a fishing smack, that had been driven out to sea by the wind.

Prince Edward immediately ordered the small boat to be lowered, and despite the entreaties of his parents and little bride, sprang into it, in hope of rescuing the perishing crew.

Alarmed for his safety, Eleanora added to the anxieties of her parents, by hastening to the deck, where leaning from the vessel's side, she scanned with intensest gaze the narrow circle of waters illuminated by the lights of the ship. A brave sailor, buffeting the waves with powerful arm, escaped the eddies made by the sinking craft, and grasping the rope which was flung to his assistance, sprang up to the vessel's side. Another object soon after appeared rising and sinking upon the crest of the billow. Now it seemed but the sparkling foam, and now it lay white and motionless in the dark trough of the sea.

At length it floated beyond the line of light, and seemed lost in the impenetrable gloom, but not till the prince had fixed his eye upon it, and ordered his rowers to pull in the direction of its disappearance. One moment of agonizing suspense, and the heir of England again appeared nearing the vessel, carefully folding a motionless form in his arms; the sailors plied the windlass, and the boat with its crew was safely received on board.

Scarcely heeding the curious inquiries of those who gathered around him, the prince made his way to the cabin and deposited the precious burden upon a couch. The dripping coverings were speedily removed, and delight, admiration, and pity, were instantly excited in the hearts of the spectators, at the sight of a lovely child, apparently less than two years of age. Eleanora watched the resuscitation of the little stranger, with anxious tenderness. She chafed its dimpled hands in her own, and strove to recall animation by soft kisses and gentle caresses. As vital warmth gradually returned, and the faint hue of life glowed on the pallid cheek, the suffering one opened her blue eyes, and whispering some indistinct words, among which they could distinguish only "Eva," sank again into unconsciousness.

The clothing of the little foundling was such as indicated rank and wealth, and a bracelet of Eastern manufacture, clasped upon her tiny arm, excited much wonder and curiosity among the queens and their attendants. The prince had found the infant lashed to an oar with a scarf of exquisite embroidery. There seemed to be also an armorial design upon it, but the green shamrock, with a rose of Sharon, was a device which none present could decipher. The rescued sailor stated that the lost ship was a coasting vessel, and that, in an Irish harbour, they had taken on board a lady and child; but, as he had only seen them at the time of their embarkation, he could give no farther account of them.

The partiality which Eleanora manifested to the orphan, thus suddenly bereft of every friend, gained for it a home in the bosom of the royal family, and at the castle of Guilford, where her father-in-law established her with much state, she passed many pleasant hours in the care of her tender charge. The little Eva added to her infantile charms a disposition of invincible sweetness, relieved by a sportive wilfulness that elicited a constant interest, not unmixed with anxiety, lest a heart so warm might become a prey to influences against which no caution or admonition could shield her. She could give no account of her parentage or home; but sometimes spoke of her mamma, and birds and flowers, as though her childish memory retained associations that linked her thoughts with pleasant walks and tender care.

Her perceptions were exceedingly quick, but her best resolutions were often evanescent, and she lacked a steadiness of purpose in the pursuit of the studies to which Eleanora invited her attention. An appeal to her heart never failed to induce immediate repentance for any fault, and she was altogether the most winning, but vexatious pupil, that ever engaged the affections of a queen. But the accomplishments of Eleanora herself were not complete, and in 1256 she was again conveyed to Bordeaux, for the purpose of receiving instruction from masters better qualified to conduct her education. At her earnest request, Eva was permitted to accompany her.

Her young husband was meanwhile engaged perfecting himself in every knightly accomplishment, "haunting tournaments," and carrying off the prizes from all competitors, with a skill and grace that gave him a renown, not inferior to that of his great uncle Richard Cœur de Lion. At Paris, he formed an intimacy with the Sire de Joinville, companion of St. Louis in the seventh crusade, and he listened to the account of affairs in the East with an interest that inflamed his young and ardent imagination. The Lord de Joinville, high seneschal of Champagne, was one of the most erudite and affable nobles of the thirteenth century, and it was an agreeable occupation for the experienced soldier, to enlighten the mind of the young prince with an account of the customs and manners of the East, and the state of the Latin kingdom in Jerusalem, which had so much influenced the politics of Europe.

After the return of Frederic, Gregory IX. excommunicated him for declining to combat the enemy of God; but so long had been the contest between the emperor and the pontiff, and so divided were the minds of men upon the rights of the cause, that the clergy published the sentence with many explanatory clauses, that greatly modified its effect. A *curé* at Paris, instead of reading the bull from the pulpit in the usual form, said to his parishioners, "You know, my brethren, that I am ordered to fulminate an excommunication against Frederic. I know not the motive. All that I know is, that there has been a quarrel between that prince and the pope. God alone knows who is right. I excommunicate him who has injured the other; and I absolve the sufferer."

Frederic, in revenge, employed his Saracen troops, of which he commanded not a few, in southern Italy, to ravage the dominions of the church, and convinced all his subjects of the wisdom of his former refusals, by taxing them heavily for the expenses of the expedition on which he determined to embark. Finding that Frederic was thus placing himself in a posture to enlist the sympathies of Christendom, the pope prohibited his undertaking the Holy War till he should be relieved from ecclesiastical censure. The emperor notwithstanding sailed directly for Acre, and was received with great joy by the Christians. The next ships from Europe brought letters from the *pontiff* to the patriarch, repeating the sentence of excommunication, forbidding the Templars and Hospitallers to fight under the banner of the son of perdition.

In this state of embarrassment, Frederic found his military operations limited to the suburbs of Acre; and dwelling in the palace, and gazing on the scenes which Violante had so often and so eloquently portrayed, his mind reverted, with a touch of remorseful tenderness, to the enthusiasm with which she had anticipated a return to her eastern home. The rapture with which she had dwelt upon the virtues of the Empress Elsiebede, and her noble son Melech Camel, inspired him with the thought that he might avail himself of the generous friendship entertained for his much injured wife, to further his own plans in Palestine. Acting upon this selfish policy, he opened negotiations with the Sultan of Egypt, now heir to all Saphadin's dominions by the death of Cohr-Eddin. The Saracen emperor lent a gracious ear to the overtures of the successor of Jean de Brienne, and a truce of ten years was concluded between the belligerent powers.

Jerusalem, Joppa, Bethlehem and Nazareth, with their appendages, were restored to the Latins. The Holy Sepulchre was also ceded, and both Christians and Mussulmans, were guaranteed the right to worship in the sacred edifice, known to the former as the temple of Solomon, and to the latter as the mosque of Omar. The emperor repaired to Jerusalem, but no hosannas welcomed his approach. The patriarch forbade the celebration of all religious ceremonies during his stay, and no prelate could be induced to place upon his brow accursed, the crown of Godfrey of Boulogne. Frederic, notwithstanding, advanced to the church of the Sepulchre, took the crown from the altar, placed it upon his own head, and then listened with great apparent satisfaction, to a laudatory oration, pronounced by one of his German followers. Thus the memory of the gentle and loving Violante, more powerful than the heroic frenzy of King Richard, or the misguided devotion of the military orders, established the kingdom of Palestine, once more upon a firm basis, and gave the sceptre into the hands of one able to defend its rights.

CHAPTER 2: DE JOINVILLE'S STORY OF THE SEVENTH CRUSADE

These particulars de Joinville faithfully narrated, at various times, to Prince Edward, who was an indefatigable listener to whatever pertained to feats of chivalry and arms.—But he dwelt with far greater circumlocution and precision upon the events of the Seventh Crusade, in which he was personally engaged with Louis IX.

"You must know, gracious prince," said the good knight, in the quaint language of the times, "that though the Christians in Asia had possession of the holy places, by the treaty with Melech Camel, the mildew of discord continually blighted all their plans for the improvement of the state, and as soon as the truce had expired, the Saracens again fell upon them in their weakened condition, and slaughtered great multitudes of pilgrims. For this cause it was, that Gregory IX. called again upon the devout children of the church, to take arms against the *infidels.*"

"I remember," replied Edward, "the departure of my uncle Richard of Cornwall, and the valiant Longsword, with their knights, and retainers for Palestine, and I have heard that his very name was a terror to the Saracens, inasmuch as they mistook him for the great Richard Cœur de Lion. God willing, Sire de Joinville, the name of Edward shall one day, frighten his enemies as well."

To this De Joinville gravely replied, "Thou wouldst do well to remember that which the good King Louis said, when, to secure the tranquillity of his subjects, he relinquished so great a portion of his territory to thy royal sire: I would rather be like our Lord, who giveth freely to all, than like the Conquerors of the earth who have made to themselves enemies in grasping the rights of others!"

"In sooth," replied Edward, "the sentiment savoureth more of the saint than of the king," a little piqued that his ambitious tendencies elicited no warmer approbation.

"And yet," returned de Joinville, "King Louis is the greatest monarch in Europe, and often by his wise counsel accommodates those differences which involve other countries in bloodshed. He has, thou knowest well, already composed the dissensions between thy father and his haughty brother-in-law, Earl Leicester."

"Aye, verily," returned Edward, his eyes flashing with the presentiment of vengeance, "this good sword shall one day teach the misproud earl better manners.—Had my father, less of those meek virtues which thou prizest so highly, he would never have ratified the statutes of Oxford, and made England the prey of Simon de Montfort's rapacity."

"The poor inhabitants of Albi and Carcassonne, albeit many of them, I fear me, were miserable heretics, teach their children to curse the name even more bitterly," answered de Joinville, "than thou dost."

"He who slaughters women and children," answered Edward, with proud disdain, "even though it be by the commands of the church, stains his fair fame more deeply than his sword. To my poor wit it seems good sire, that this crusade against our own vassals in happy France, bears a hue far different from the wars in Palestine."

So thought my good lord," returned de Joinville, "for though his soul loveth peace, his conscience was often unquiet with the thought of the sufferings of the Christians, who, pressed by the Turks, cried out for aid, and yet he knew not how he might leave his people for a foreign war. At length his doubts were resolved on this wise.—Being grievously ill at Paris, his soul as it were departed from his body. He saw standing before him Count Raimond of Toulouse, who, being in the torment of purgatory, cried out, 'Oh! that I had employed my people in chasing the children of Satan from the Holy Land, then would they not have had leisure to have devised those heresies by which they have destroyed both their souls and bodies in hell.'

"When the soul of the king returned, he heard those who had nursed him speaking together, and one would have covered his face with a cloth, thinking that all was over, but another (so God willed it) declared continually that he was alive. Then he opened his eyes and looked upon them, and he desired one of them to bring him the crucifix, and he swore upon it that if God should please restore him to health, he would, in person, undertake the Holy War. In like manner as the king put on the cross, so did his three brothers, Robert, Count d'Artois, Alphonzo, Count de Poitiers, and Charles, Count d'Anjou, the venerable Hugh le Brun, Count le Marche and his sons, with many others of rank and dignity, and many lords whom Simon de Montfort had deprived of their patrimony in Languedoc, and many others who had fought against the heretics.

"Thus did the pious king make the Holy War the means of expiation and of universal reconcilement. But so wise was he withal, and so careful of his people, that he thought also to make the expedition the foundation of a great colony in Egypt. Thus many of the transports were laden with spades, pitch-forks, ploughs, and other implements for the tilling of the ground, together with seeds of various kinds, for the better prospering of the new state. You must know, before the king left the realm, he summoned all the barons to Paris, and there made them renew their homage and swear loyalty to his children, should any unfortunate event happen to himself during this expedition.

"Magnificent dresses were on this occasion bestowed upon all the courtiers, and the next day the cavaliers were surprised to find, that to every cloak a splendid gold cross had been affixed by the art of the goldsmith, thereby intimating the king's desire that they should join him in the Crusade.

"It was in the month of August that we embarked at the rock Marseilles, and the priest and clerks standing round the king, sang the beautiful hymn, 'Veni Creator,' from the beginning to the end. While they were singing, the mariners set their sails in the name of God, and soon, with a favourable wind, the coast disappeared from our view, and we saw nothing but the sea and sky. We landed first at Cyprus, where we made a long stay, waiting for Count Alphonzo, who headed the reserve. Here ambassadors from all nations came to pay their court to the French monarch. The great *Chan* of Tartary paid him many fine compliments, and bade his servants say that their master was ready to assist him in delivering Jerusalem from the hands of the Saracens. The King of France sent likewise to the *Chan* a tent, in the form of a chapel, of fine scarlet cloth, embroidered on the inside with the mysteries of our faith. Two black monks had charge of it, and were also instructed to exhort the Tartars, and show them how they ought to put their belief in God."

"Are not the Tartars of the same race as the Turks?" inquired Edward, with great curiosity.

"I understand not well the genealogy of the people of the East," replied de Joinville, "but I consider Tartary as a general name for a vast country, whence have issued, at various times, certain tribes called Scythians, Hungarians, Turks, and Mongols, which have overrun the fertile provinces that skirt the Mediterranean."

The prince, feeling greatly enlightened at this comprehensive answer, listened respectfully while de Joinville resumed. "There came also ambassadors from the Christians of Constantinople, Armenia and Syria. Envoys likewise from the 'Old Man of the Mountain,' of whom there runs so many strange stories. King Louis also formed a league with the leader of the Mongols against the two great popes of Islamism, the Sultans of Cairo and Bagdad. From Cyprus we sailed to Damietta, which King Louis attacked sword in hand. The *infidels*, by the favour of God, were put to the worse, and the city fell into our hands. We found great spoil in Damietta, and were comfortably lodged there. But the king's officers, instead of well-treating the merchants, who would have supplied the army with provisions, hired out to them stalls and workmen, at so dear a rate, that they departed from us, which was a great evil and loss.

"Barons and knights began to give sumptuous banquets, one to the other; the commonalty also gave themselves up to all kinds of dissipation, which lasted until the day we set forward toward Cairo, on the route formerly travelled by Jean de Brienne. We were stopped at Mansourah many days by a branch of the Nile, where it was necessary to construct a dyke, and there they assailed us with the Greek fire, by which we were in great danger of perishing. This fire was in appearance like a great tun, and its tail was of the length of a long spear, and the noise which it made was like thunder, and it seemed a great dragon of fire flying through the air, giving such light by its flame, that we saw in our camp as clearly as in broad day; and when it fell upon a knight in armour, it penetrated through the scales thereof, and burned to the very bone. Thus our army suffered greatly, and were prevented from making farther progress.

"The king called his barons to council, and it was concluded to return to Damietta. But so many of our army had fallen sick, that it was necessary to make preparations to embark upon the Nile. The king himself suffered greatly with the pestilence, and our march was stopped by the Saracens, who lay in wait for us upon the banks of the river, and as the prince would not desert his people, we were all made prisoners together. After we had suffered many things, both in body and spirit, the *sultan*, who had been recently elected by the Mamelukes, agreed to accept as ransom for the captives, the city of Damietta and the sum of 500,000 *livres*. When the *sultan* found that King Louis complied with the first demand without striving to drive a bargain, 'Go and tell him from me,' he said, 'that I retract one-fifth of the sum, because I have found him both generous and liberal.'

"After the affair was concluded, my royal master empowered me to accompany the envoys to Damietta, and to receive from Queen Margaret the money for the ransom. When I came to the palace where the queen was lodged, I found her apartment guarded by an aged knight, whom, when she heard of her royal husband's captivity, she had caused to take oath that, should the Saracens enter the town, he would himself put an end to her life before they could seize her person. My royal mistress received me graciously, and gave me the money which the king had commanded, and she also bade me look upon the son she had borne to Louis during his absence, that I might assure him of their health and comfort. The misfortunes that had attended our arms caused us to quit Egypt; and, sailing at once for Acre, we were received with great joy by the Christians of the East. We employed ourselves in restoring the fortifications of the principal towns, but the monarch, through dejection at the failure of his enterprise, returned to France without making a pilgrimage to the holy places."

"By my faith," replied the young prince, "it were a matter of surprise that such well-appointed expeditions should suffer such total loss. Methinks a good soldier should never sheathe his sword till the hour of victory."

De Joinville regarded the inexperienced youth with a benevolent smile, remarking only, that caution and prudence are virtues as essential to a ruler, as courage and prowess.

Chapter 3: The Relics Brought From Constantinople

The young bride Eleanora, in her residence at Bordeaux, had formed the acquaintance of Guy de Lusignan, second son of the ex-queen Isabella and Count Hugh le Marche, and through his kindly attentions she had been apprized of the events that agitated England. She learned that her royal parents had been under the necessity of taking up their residence in the Tower of London, almost in the condition of state prisoners, and that her gallant husband had exchanged the sports of a knight for "the game of kings." Anxious for his safety, and desirous to assist in the release of the royal family, or share their captivity, she besought Count Guy to conduct her thither. He represented the danger of such a proceeding, and strove by every argument to induce her to remain in France, but in vain. The traits of character, that subsequently made her the heroine, already developed in unchanging affection, and invincible firmness, overbore all opposition, and with a retinue scarcely suitable for her rank, and insufficient for her protection in case of attack, she set off for England.

They reached the island without accident, and had approached in sight of London, when the great bell of St. Paul's startled them with its hurried peal, and they almost instantly found themselves surrounded by an infuriated mob. The simplicity of their attire shielded them from observation, and they passed some time unmolested among the crowd, but the vindictive shouts of the multitude, crying, "Down with the Jews! down with the followers of the virago of Provence!" so alarmed the little Eva, that she was unable to keep her seat upon the pillion of the knight who had her in charge, and Sir Guy at length obtained for them a shelter in an humble tenement upon the banks of the Thames.

From the window of the cottage, they beheld the terrible massacre that characterized the first popular outbreak against the government of Henry III. The harmless Jews were dragged from their houses and mercilessly slaughtered, amidst protestations of innocence, and heart-rending cries for pity, while the furniture of their dwellings, and valuables of every kind, were hurled into the streets, and distributed among the crowd. A venerable man, Ben Abraham, of majestic demeanour, was pursued to the door of the house in which the royal fugitives had taken refuge.

Count Guy in his agitation sprang to bar the entrance, but the young queen with readier tact removed the bolt, and throwing open an opposite door, motioned all the armed retainers to retire. Scarcely had the helpless old man crossed the threshold, when the mob with demoniac cries, rushed in after him, and the leader seizing him by his long white beard, severed his head from his body, and held it up a grim and ghastly spectacle for the plaudits of his followers. The terrified Eva, clinging close to Eleanora, shrunk behind the open door, and the queen controlling her own agitation, placed her hand over the child's mouth to repress her screams, while the murderers dragging the bleeding corpse upon the pavement, began to search the body for gold. Down the street rolled the tide of blood. Mad yells of vengeance and frantic cries of terror mingled on the air, and swept away toward the river.

Now the roar seemed advancing and now retreating, when a barge loosing from the tower stairs, drew the concourse in that direction. It was the Queen of Henry III. with her children, seeking to escape to Windsor castle, where Prince Edward was quartered with his troops. Cries of "Drown the Witch! Down with the Witch! No favour to foreigners! Death to the Italians!" rent the air. The mob tore up the paving stones, stripped the tiles from the houses, plundered butchers' shambles, and hucksters' shops, and a shower of deadly missiles rained upon the river. The boat approached the bridge, at the west end of which thousands of fierce eyes glared for its appearance, and thousands of bloody hands were raised for its destruction.

At this moment the figure of an armed knight, of lofty stature, appeared upon the bridge. Forcing his way through the mob, he shouted to the sailors as the boat was about to shoot the arch, "Back! Bear back!! upon your lives!!! Return to the tower!!!!" The frightened boatmen turned at the critical moment, and the knight, by the prowess of his single arm, diverted the attack to himself, till the queen was again sheltered by the walls of the fortress.

Roar upon roar again swelled through the streets. The crowd hurried on in search of prey, swaying to and fro, like trees in a tempest. Again the feeble walls that sheltered the fair Castilian, felt the terrible presence of demons in human form. The sight of a French attendant again raised the cry of "Death to foreigners," and madly they rushed to the onslaught. But the strange knight was already at the door, and backed by Guy de Lusignan and the retainers, for some hours kept the infuriated multitude at bay, but at every moment the crowd became denser, the cries more terrific, and Eleanora drawing the little Eva to her bosom, and surrounded by her own maidens, and the females of the household, was striving to recall the prayers for the dying, when a distant shout of rescue swelled upon the breeze. The shrill blast of a trumpet confirmed the uncertain hope, and the defiant threats of the multitude began to give place to the howlings of baffled rage.

On came the tramp of horsemen, the clangor of armour; louder roared the din of the fight; not now the sounds of falling dwellings, flying missiles, and female shrieks, but the ringing clash of Damascus steel, and the regular tramp of mounted horsemen. The warlike shout of "Edward to the rescue," "Give way to the prince," drove on the motley mass like sands before the desert wind, and scattered them through all the lanes and alleys of the vast metropolis.

At the sound of her husband's name, Eleanora sprang from her knees and rushed to the door-way, where she beheld, advancing at the head of the troops, taller than all his compeers, more firmly seated upon his noble *destriar*, and more gracefully managing the rein and wielding the sword, her long-absent lord. He raised his visor, as he paused to return the salutation of his uncle, De Lusignan, and his fine, manly features, radiant with pleasure, and flushed with triumph, his fair hair curling round his helmet, made him appear to Eleanora, more brave and beautiful than a hero of romance. But the eye that "kindled in war, now melted in love" at the unexpected apparition of his bride, who with tearful eyes gazed upon him, uncertain whether her presence would more embarrass or pleasure him.

It was not, however, in the heart of a chivalric prince to frown upon any distressed damsel, much less upon the beautiful young being, whose fair face, the sensitive index of every emotion, now paled with fear, now flushed with joy, seemed each moment changing to a lovelier hue, while she awaited his approach in doubt as to the greeting she should receive from her lord. The generous prince hastily dismounting, and clasping her in his arms, tenderly reassured her with words of affectionate welcome, not however, without a gentle upbraiding, that she had not tarried at Dover till he had been able, with a retinue befitting her rank, himself to escort her to Windsor.

The little Eva, meanwhile, had found a safe asylum in the arms of the stranger knight, and, through the bars of his visor, obtained a glimpse of eyes, whose colour and expression she never forgot, and listened to words that made a lasting impression upon her mind.

Prince Edward found it necessary to establish his mother and queen, with the ladies and attendants, under a strong guard, at Bristol castle, where they remained during a part of that stormy period, consequent upon Leicester's rebellion. Restricted to the narrow enjoyments which the castle walls afforded, and to the society of the few knights who had them in charge, the royal ladies found their chief entertainment in the volatile spirits, and restless gaiety of the orphan Eva.

No caution nor command could prevent her mingling with the dependents, and listening to and relating to her mistress every flying report that reached the castle. But so gentle was her temper, and so ready her submission, that it was impossible to be seriously offended with her, and her light footsteps and joyous laugh were equally welcome in the royal apartments, and in the servants' kitchen. The maids of honour, who were the most frequent victims of her pranks, surnamed her, "Dame Madcap," while her cordial interest in inferiors caused the retainers to dub her with the equally appropriate soubriquet of "Little Sunbeam."

One day, the Princess Eleanora, passing the hall of audience, was surprised by hearing shouts of irrepressible laughter. Suspecting that her *protegée* was engaged in some frolic, she cautiously opened the door and stood an unobserved spectator. Every piece of furniture capable of being moved, had been torn from its mooring, and placed in some fantastic position. The arras had been stripped from the walls, and hung in grotesque festoons at the farther extremity of the room, above and around a throne, ornamented with every article of embroidered velvet and silk brocade, that the royal wardrobe afforded, on which was seated her Madcap majesty, bedecked and bedizened with all sorts of holiday finery, while every maid and retainer, not on duty, was passing before her, and repeating the oath of fealty in giggling succession.

The fair queen, meanwhile, diversified her state duties by lecturing her new subjects upon the indecorum of such ill-timed levity. The princess, in doubt what notice to take of the affair, prudently withdrew, but not till Eva had caught sight of her retreating figure, whereon, she assured her vassals, that they had all been guilty of high treason, and that, no doubt, the Don Jon, or some other Spanish cavalier would soon have them in close keeping.

When Eva again appeared in the presence of the princess, she fell on her knees and begged pardon with an air of mock humility that changed Eleanora's frowns to smiles in spite of herself, though she felt it necessary to remonstrate with her upon the oft-reiterated subject of her undignified familiarity with dependents. "I was but acting the queen, your majesty, and would be glad of more exalted subjects," said she, archly, in extenuation of her fault. "Royalty is but a pageant, and I shall doubtless exercise the prerogative of a sovereign, when it is proved that the wicked little Eva de la Mer is heiress of the gallant Strongbow."

"Thou, Queen of Ireland!" exclaimed Eleanora. "Who has put this foolish conceit into thy young head? Thou must beware, sweet one, of these odd fancies. Rememberest thou not the words of the confessor, that the pomps and vanities of the world lead the soul astray?"

Tears filled the blue eyes of Eva, but instantly dashing them away with spirit, she exclaimed, "And why not I a queen! 'Tis sure I would be a better sovereign than most. They should not say as they do of our liege, King Henry, that I robbed my subjects to make presents to my favourites."

"Eva, Eva," gravely rejoined the princess, "the Scripture saith we should not speak evil of dignities." But Eva was in the vein, and her volubility was not to be silenced.

"I would not be a queen," exclaimed she, "for then I should have none to love me or to tell me the truth."

"None to love thee!" replied Eleanora. "Do not the people love her gracious majesty, my royal mother?"

"Thou shouldst hear what all men say of her," exclaimed the child, almost frightened at her own audacity.

"And what do men say?" inquired Eleanora, her curiosity getting the better of her judgment.

"They say," continued Eva, "that all the troubles in England are owing to the queen and her relations. That King Henry took the marriage portion of his sister Isabella to furnish the decorations for the coronation; and thou knowest well, my lady, that she hath nine garlands for her hair, besides a great gold crown most glorious with gems."

"In sooth," returned the princess, "thou knowest more than I of the queen's wardrobe. But how learnedst thou these things?"

"Her maidens, who love her none too well, tell me everything."

"And dost thou encourage them in evil speaking of their mistress, by listening to their idle tales?"

"Nay, I told them they were sinners, and that the father of evil would surely get them; but they only laughed, and said, in that case, I should certainly bear them company."

Eleanora, looking gravely, said, "I fear my darling is learning sad ways, and I must henceforth keep her always by my side."

Eva threw her arms around the princess, and pillowing her fair cheek upon her bosom, whispered, "Let not my noble mistress omit this punishment, for in her presence 'tis easy to be good." There was a pause of some minutes, when the child gently resumed, "My lady will one day be a queen, shall Eva then speak only the words of adulation, such as the false *dames d'honneur* employ in the presence of her majesty? I heard them whispering low concerning the queen's gold, and the extortions and exactions she had brought upon the people, and when she inquired what they whispered, they turned it with some fine compliment.

"I sought to tell her of the falsehood, but the ladies would not give me entrance to her apartment. I will tell thee, for thou art wise and mayest perchance warn her of her false friends. What first caught my ear was the name of my lord, Prince Edward. They said that when he was a lad of eight years, his royal father brought him forth with his brother Edmund and his sisters Margaret and Beatrice, and had them all weighed up like the calves at the butchers, and then scattered their weight in coin among the ragged beggar children that stood in the court below, laughing at the screams of the royal babies."

"Eva! Eva! How couldst thou listen to such vain parlance?"

"Oh! my lady, this is not the half of the vile things they told. They said that when the king had oppressed the people till he could wring no more money from them, he broke up his court, and then, to avoid the expense of keeping his family, he invited himself with his retinue to the castles of the nobles, and after being feasted right royally, he begged gifts at his departure, telling them it was a greater charity to bestow alms upon him than upon any beggar in the realm."

"Eva! darling! no more of this," said Eleanora, in a decided tone. "I will give thee for thy penance three paternosters and a creed. Repair to my oriel, and let me hear thee prate no more."

Eva received so much spiritual benefit from her devotions in the oratory, that the next day she was permitted to go where she pleased, and her first works of supererogation were distributed among those who had participated in her offence. Accordingly, the princess found her robed in the chaplain's gown, and receiving the confessions of those who had assisted at her coronation the previous day, in which capacity she exhibited a wonderful facility in prompting treacherous memories and callous consciences. In the midst of the scene, a sharp blast from the warder's horn startled the merry group. In times of public calamity, every unexpected event seems fraught with a fearful interest. Each vassal hurried to his post, and the females hastened away, while Eva, dropping her sacred character, ran with all speed to reconnoitre from the arrow-slit of the turret.

The portcullis was raised, the sound of hoofs was heard upon the drawbridge, and the next moment a messenger, toil worn and travel-stained, dashed into the court. The tidings which he brought were of the most important character. King Henry, apparently on the most friendly terms with Leicester, was, in reality, a prisoner in his castle, and subject to the will of the earl. Prince Edward was rapidly preparing for war with the rebel barons, and, deeming the royal ladies unsafe in England, had sent to bid them haste with all speed to the court of the good King of France. Straining her eyes to command a view beyond the castle walls, Eva discerned a band of huntsmen lingering in the skirts of an adjoining wood, but in the bustle of departure, she could not find opportunity to communicate the suspicious circumstance to any in authority.

Apparelled in the utmost haste, the parties set forth, and slacked not their riding till they reached the port. There seemed to be a great crowd in the vicinity, of sailors, boatmen, clowns, in cartmen's frocks, and occasionally a man in armour. Eva fancied that she discerned among them the huntsmen of the wood, and her fears were confirmed when a moment after the royal train were completely environed by the band. But so adroitly was the manœuvre effected, that the fugitives had scarcely time to feel themselves prisoners, when a troop of Leicester's men appeared in the distance, and they comprehended that, but for the timely interposition of these unknown friends, their retreat would have been cut off. As the vessel receded from shore, swords were drawn, and a fierce contest ensued between the huntsmen and the soldiers, and Eva recognized in the leader of their defenders the figure of the tall knight who had rescued them at London bridge.

At the court of Queen Margaret, the exiled princesses received a cordial welcome, and the piety of Eleanora was strengthened by intercourse with the good St. Louis: while Eva's vivacity soon made her a favourite with the ladies of the French court. The unaffected piety of the saintly monarch was scarcely a fit subject for the humour which Eva exercised without discrimination, upon the grave and gay. But many of the superstitious observances of the church, ridiculous in themselves, excited her native merriment; nor could all the penances of the confessor restrict the playful license of her tongue.

The Latin dynasty of Constantinople was now tottering to its fall. The young Greek emperor Baldwin, deprived of the counsels of his father-in-law, Jean de Brienne (who had taken the habit of St. Francis, and died on a pilgrimage to Jerusalem), was exposed to the attacks of every disaffected noble that chose to rebel against him. He had made every possible concession to avoid open warfare with his enemies, and had suffered every conceivable inconvenience from utter poverty. He had given his niece in marriage to a Turkish *emir*, and ratified a treaty with a haughty pagan by tasting his blood. He demolished vacant houses in Constantinople for winter fuel, stripped the lead from the churches for the daily expense of his family; mortgaged his father's estates in France to increase the public revenue; and pawned the heir of the purple at Venice, as security for a debt.

One only treasure yet remained, the Holy Crown of Thorns; but piety forbade him to make merchandise of that which all Christendom regarded with such superstitious veneration. It was therefore determined to present the precious bauble to the most honourable prince in Europe, and rely upon his pious gratitude to make suitable return. A wooden box conveyed the inestimable relic to France. It was opened in the presence of the nobility, discovering within a silver shrine in which was preserved the monument of the Passion, enclosed in a golden vase. St. Louis, with all his court, made a pilgrimage to Troyes, to receive the precious deposit.

And the devout monarch, barefoot, and without other clothing than a simple tunic, carried it in triumph through the streets of Paris, and placed it in La Sainte Chapelle, which he prepared for the purpose. This solemn ceremony roused all the mirthfulness of Eva, nor could the habitual reverence of Eleanora so far prevail over her good sense, as to prevent some slight misgivings concerning the authenticity of the various and multiplied relics that then formed so lucrative a branch of commerce.

"I warrant me," said the madcap, Eva, to the maidens, "we shall all of us be compelled to kneel upon the cold pavement before that prickly emblem, as a punishment for our many transgressions." Shocked at her impiety, yet inwardly amused, the merry party mingled their reproaches with encouraging peals of laughter.

"No doubt," continued she, "it will cure all diseases, at least it has humbled the holy king like St. Paul's thorn in the flesh. For me, though I strove to wear a devout face, I could not help laughing at the sight of his royal shins." The volatile French ladies, who had experienced very much the same sensation, joined in the merriment. "I hear," said Eva, "we are to have another procession of the same kind ere long, and mayhaps they will require us to transport the holy relic in the same flimsy guise. Thou, Felice, who art so jealous of Sir Francis d'Essai's attentions to me, shall carry the cross. And the sharp-witted Beatrice shall bear the lance. Thou, Caliste, who hearest all and sayest naught, shall wear the sponge, and as for me, I shall take the rod of Moses and smite your rocky hearts, till the waters of repentance flow forth."

"Hush! hush!" exclaimed the damsels, "her majesty approaches."

Scarcely were their countenances composed to the approved pattern of court propriety, and their eyes fixed upon their embroidery, when Queen Margaret entered, and, in her serenely gracious manner, informed them that his highness, the Emperor Baldwin, had presented another invaluable gift to her royal husband, and she counselled them, by fasting and prayer, to put themselves in readiness to join the court in a procession to deposit the sacred relic in St. Chapelle. While each maiden dropped her head with apparent assent, but in reality to conceal her smiles brought up by the prospective realization of Eva's panorama, the facile girl devoutly crossed herself, and with a demure look replied, "We have heard of the noble Courtenay's munificence, and have endeavoured, according to our poor ability, to prepare our minds for the solemn duty."

No sooner had the queen departed, than in a tone of mock gravity, she exhorted them to be diligent in their worship, for now she thought of it, she resolved to smile upon the young Squire Courtenay, who had besought her to embroider a shamrock upon his pennon. Winning him, she should doubtless one day share the imperial purple, in which case she should reclaim those sacred treasures, and they would then be under the necessity of making a pilgrimage to Constantinople, for as Baldwin's last heir was in pawn, the crown would doubtless descend to the younger branches of his house.

CHAPTER 4: THE ESCAPE

In the court of France, the royal princesses received constant intelligence of the progress of the struggle between the English barons and the king, or rather, between Simon de Montfort and Prince Edward, who headed the opposite factions. Their hopes were raised by accounts of the gallant conduct of the young prince, and by the disaffection that arose between the confederate barons, but sudden misery overwhelmed them, when, after several years of torturing suspense, Wm. de Valence arrived at Paris, bringing news of the death of Guy de Lusignan, in the disastrous action at Lewes, and the captivity of King Henry and his gallant son.

Queen Eleanor immediately determined to proceed to England, and her daughter-in-law Eleanora insisted upon accompanying her. Young de Courtenay, who had recently received the honours of knighthood, from his royal master, and Sir Francis, who had enlisted as his rival for the smiles of Eva, now a beautiful girl of fifteen, begged permission to join the escort, with a band of armed retainers. They landed at Plymouth, and lay concealed for some time in the wilds of Devonshire, while the gallant knights, Sir Henry and Sir Francis, scoured the country in all directions, for information concerning the captive princes. They learned that the royal army had retreated to Bristol castle, under the command of seven knights, who had reared seven banners on the walls, and with determined valour held out against Leicester, and that the princes were confined in Kenilworth castle. The difficulty of communicating with the prisoners exercised the ingenuity of the little council for many days, but every plan involved danger, both to themselves and to the royal cause.

Eleanora, whose clear sense and unwavering reliance on a higher power, led her to a practical demonstration of the sentiment, "To hope the best is pious, brave, and wise," was the life and soul of every arrangement, and the soother of those fainter spirits, who were ready to yield, to despair at every sign of failure. Their residence was in a little hamlet of the better class of peasants, faithful to the interests of the king. A deep forest extended on the west to a great distance, and in those wilds, spite of all caution, Eva delighted to ramble. One day she had been so long absent that even Eleanora, becoming alarmed, despatched her attendant in quest of her, and herself joined the search.

As she passed along through the glades of the deep wood, her attention was arrested by the sight of a pretty boy, lying asleep beneath the shade of a spreading oak, whose dress from his embroidered shoes, to the ruby that fastened the plume in his velvet cap, was of the most exquisite beauty, and taste. The page was clad in a hunting suit of "Lincoln green," slashed with cloth of gold, that gleamed from the mossy bank upon which he rested, as though the sunshine had fallen and lingered there. A crimson baldric curiously wrought with strange devices, lay across his breast, a sword with burnished sheath, was suspended from his belt. As Eleanora approached, and gazed upon the sleeping boy, she thought she had never beheld so lovely a youth, and an instinctive desire rose up in her heart, to enrol him in her service.

"Wake, pretty one," said she, softly touching his cheek, "wake, and go with me." The youth started and gazed upon her, and a flush of surprise and pleasure suffused his countenance. "Whose page art thou?" said Eleanora, "and how hast thou wandered into this wild?"

"Noble lady," returned the boy, casting down his eyes with modest hesitation, "my hawk hath gone astray, and I sought him till aweary, I fell asleep."

"Thy friends have left thee in the greenwood," returned the princess, "and thou may'st not find them. Wilt go with me, and I will give thee gold and benison, and if thou art loyal, an errand worthy thy knightly ambition."

"Nay, treason may be loyal, or loyalty treason, in these troublous times," said the boy. "One says follow my lord of Leicester, another, draw thy sword for the good Prince Edward."

"And if I say, draw thy sword for the good Prince Edward, wilt follow me?"

The youth replied evasively, "I love my lady, and I may not engage in other service, till I bring her proud bird back to the perch."

Something in his earnest tone arrested the attention of the princess, and scanning the countenance of the youth with more curious scrutiny, she marked the rosy hue in his cheek, and the tear trembling in his blue eye, and exclaimed,

"Eva! Eva!! How is this?"

"Nay, an thou knowest me, I will e'en venture on thy knightly errand," said the blushing girl, falling on her knees, and repeating the oath of fealty, rapidly as possible to hide her emotions.

"Rise," said the princess, with all the sternness she could command, "and tell me whence this disguise."

"I know not, lady, more than thou, save this. Scarce a week since, I met in this wood the tall knight who hath so nobly defended us, and yesternight I braved the fear of thy frown, and came to this trysting-place. He hath concerted a plan for the liberation of my royal master, and brought me this disguise, which must be sufficient, since it so long baffled thy quick discernment. Accident has betrayed me, else it had not rested with my lady, whether Eva should trust the stranger, and aid in restoring the proud bird of England to his royal perch." Eleanora paused one moment, while her mind, ever clearest and most active in emergency, poised between the possibility of danger to her favourite, and rescue to her lord.

"The knight has twice preserved our lives, he must be bold and true, and heaven hath raised him up for our deliverance, since God conceals us from our enemies, and reveals our lurking-place to him. It were treason to doubt this divine Providence, since it would imply neither trust in man, nor faith in God. Go, Eva," said the princess, her eyes filling with tears, as she pressed her to her bosom, and imprinted a warm kiss upon her cheek. "Heaven will protect and prosper thee, and my noble Edward know how to reward thy devotion." She stood gazing fondly on her in silence, while Eva's colour went and came as though she essayed, what yet she feared, to utter. At length she stammered forth, "My lady will send Sir Francis with his band to guard the fords of the Exe till my return."

"Sir Francis," reiterated the queen, in a tone of surprise; "methought Sir Henry were more agreeable escort."

Eva tried to hide her crimson blushes beneath her delicate fingers, as she whispered, "If my mistress please, I would that Sir Henry should be ignorant of this unmaidenly disguise."

"Thou lovest Sir Henry, then?" said Eleanora.

"Nay, lady, I know not that," replied Eva; "but there is something in him that commands my regard despite my will, and I would not needlessly forfeit his esteem."

"I will answer for thee, sweet," replied the princess. "Sir Francis shall go according to thy wish. But must I leave thee here alone and unprotected?"

"The monarch of the forest spreads his broad arm for my protection, and thou shalt envy my repose, in my sylvan eyrie," replied Eva, lightly springing into a fantastic seat, formed by the twisted branches of a gnarled oak, and completely concealed by the foliage. Firmly ensconced in her rustic lodge, she leaned forward and whispered a gentle farewell, as the princess, bearing in her mind a vision of a bright face, peeping out from among the green leaves, turned and rapidly retraced her steps to the hamlet.

That night Sir Francis set out with his train, and as two maidens accompanied the band, one wearing the dress of Eva, her absence excited no suspicion.

Meanwhile the sprite remained in her place of concealment, till the gathering shadows of the trees stretched stealthily across the glade the appointed signal for the gathering of the outlawed bands. The tall knight soon appeared, and, lifting her gently from the tree, placed her on a beautiful Spanish jennet, and smilingly handing her an ivory whistle, terminating in a silver cross, bade her summon her satyrs. She placed it to her lips, and blew a shrill call, and forthwith from the leafy bosom of every bush and shrub there issued a huntsman, clad in forest green, and carrying only such weapons as were used in the chase.

The knight gave them hasty directions for the different points of rendezvous, at which they were to watch the safety of the young squire, warned them against those places where they would be most likely to encounter the malcontents, and then mounting the noble steed that stood pawing the turf in impatience by his side, and laying his hand upon the rein, recalled Eva to herself, by saying, with emphasis, "Sir Launfal, we must away, or morning will dawn ere we cross the fords of Exe."

They rode at a brisk pace for some time in silence, the mind of each being too much occupied for words.

The knight at length spoke abruptly. "Thou hast a turn for adventure, pretty page, and I'll warrant me, ready tongue, but how dost thou think to gain speech with Prince Edward?"

"Nay, that I leave with thee," returned Eva, "since I know neither the place to which I am bound, nor the duty I am to perform."

"And that I scarce know myself," replied the knight. "The lady Maud Mortimer has the swiftest courser in all England, a coal-black Arabian, brought by Richard of Cornwall as a gift to her ladyship, on his return from the Holy Land. My Lord Mortimer is a partisan of Leicester, but is somewhat cooled in his devotion to the proud earl, from an affront received since the battle of Lewes. The lady, therefore, to be revenged, has volunteered her steed for the escape of Edward. There riseth, however, another difficulty. The prince is constantly surrounded with guards, so that no stranger may accost him. My merry men have beset the castle in every kind of disguise, but to no purpose. Of late, the prince rides forth of a morning, closely attended, and I have brought thee, hoping that thy woman's wit may effect more than all our dull brains have yet accomplished."

As the captive prince, sick with hope deferred, languidly mounted his horse and rode forth upon his monotonous round, he was surprised by the appearance of a saucy-looking page, who mingled carelessly among the attendants, and challenged the younger squires to test the speed of their horses.

"And who art thou, pert boy?" inquired the captain of the guard.

"Who but the squire to my Lord de Mortimer? Thou must be learned in heraldry an thou knowest not the device of the noble earl," replied the page, with an air of nonchalance that easily satisfied his interrogator, and eager of sport the whole party joined in the race. They were thus led far beyond their usual limits. But the prince, whose heart was sad, evinced little interest in the animated scene till the page, loudly entreating him to put his steed to the mettle, found opportunity at intervals to whisper, "Tomorrow when the horses of the guards are blown, seek the copse by the Hazel Glen." As if disgusted with the familiarity of the page, the prince slowly turned away, but not till he had exchanged a glance of intelligence with his new friend.

The following morning the gallant Sir Launfal stood in the copse holding the reins of his own palfrey, and the steed of Lady Mortimer, till he was faint and weary. The expected hour for Edward's arrival had long passed, and notwithstanding his effort to appear the brave squire he personated, it must be confessed he felt very like a timid girl, whose active imagination peopled the wood with a thousand unknown dangers. He turned the whistle nervously in his fingers, and almost essayed to try its magic powers in summoning around him the brave outlaws who waited his bidding, when the welcome sound of advancing hoofs reassured him, and a moment after the prince dashed into the thicket.

"Keep to the highway till we meet at the cross-roads," said the page, resigning the rein into his hand.

The shouts of the pursuers were already on the air, as the prince vaulted into the saddle and took the direction indicated. Striking into a bridle path, Sir Launfal reached the cross-roads just as the prince appeared, and together they rode gaily on towards Bristol. The pursuers soon after gained the same point, where they encountered a woodman, jogging on slowly after two loaded mules, of whom they inquired concerning the fugitive.

"He be's gone yonder," replied the boor, pointing in the direction opposite to the one which the prince had taken, where upon an eminence appeared an armed force. The baffled guards, fearing that the conspiracy might have been more extensive than they had anticipated, made the best of their way back to Kenilworth.

"And who art thou, my pretty page?" inquired Edward, "that hast so dexterously redeemed thy prince, and whither dost thou conduct me?"

"I wear the badge of Mortimer," replied Sir Launfal. "The Lady Maude is the constant friend of thy royal mother."

"Canst tell me aught of the movements of the rebel barons, or the fate of my brave knights?"

"Nay, my giddy brain recks little of politics or war," returned the boy, "but there are can give thee tidings."

A moment after they turned an angle in the road, and the boy putting the whistle to his mouth sounded a sharp note, and a party of huntsmen, apparently in quest of game, darted across the path, while one shouted, as if to his companions, "To the right, the game lies by the Hermit's Cross." The page immediately turned his palfrey, motioning to silence, and led off into the path through the wood, and after several hours' hard riding arrived at the appointed place of rendezvous.

At the foot of a large wooden cross, weather-stained and somewhat decayed, sat a monk, closely robed in gown and cowl, who rose at their approach, saying in a low voice, "The benison of our Lady of Walsingham rest upon you;" and with great strides conducted them deeper and deeper into the wood, till they came to a hunter's lodge, which, though much in ruins, gave signs of having been recently repaired, with some view to the rank and comfort of those who were to occupy it.

The prince made light of the trifling inconveniences to which they were subjected, remarking, "A soldier has little choice of resting-place." But poor Eva, wearied almost to death from the unaccustomed fatigues of the day, now that the stimulus of excitement was over, had leisure to think of her own situation; and scarcely able to restrain her tears, crept silently to her couch of fern, and beneath the russet covering, soon slept from very exhaustion. The prince and the monk meanwhile conferred apart in low tones, concerting measures for present and future security.

"Gloucester is with us," said the priest, "and Sir Roger de Mortimer has a party of picked men on the road to Evesham. My band have charge of every ford and pass between this and Hereford. The scouts report that Leicester's men are much wasted by their long residence on the Welsh frontier, and my jolly fellows are this night engaged in breaking down the bridges across the Severn. For we churchmen have a fancy, that baptism is necessary to wash away the sins of rebels."

"I fear not all the rites of the Church can absolve the black-hearted traitor," returned Edward, with great asperity. "But proceed with thy news."

"The country is beset with Leicester's spies," continued the monk, "else had I been less guarded in my communications with thee. Bands of men are daily mustering in every direction, making the high-roads unsafe for honest travellers like myself."

"Thou wilt join our forces with the brethren of thy chapter," suggested the prince.

"Our chapter are somewhat too much tinctured with heresy to hail the ascendency of the odious De Montforts," replied the monk; "thou mayst, therefore, depend upon their most earnest intercessions in thy behalf. But for me, I must restore pretty one," nodding his head significantly towards the spot where Eva lay asleep, "to his mistress. It is a matter, not of selfish interest alone, that the loyal page be restored unharmed."

"Thou art right," returned Edward. "I would not that the charming boy should lose one raven curl for me, though he hath risked his freedom and, perhaps, his life to save me."

CHAPTER 5: THE DETERMINATION

After the Battle of Evesham, in which Edward entirely overthrew the party of the rebel barons, and re-established Henry's throne, Eleanora resided alternately in the palace of Savoy and at Windsor castle. The care of her three beautiful children occupied much of her attention, and in their nurture the streams of her affection deepened and widened, until they embraced all who came within the sphere of her influence. The now charming, but still volatile, Eva occasioned her infinite anxiety.

Since the day when Sir Francis had received her from the tall knight, at the ford of the Exe, he had held her by the two-fold cord of obligation and the possession of a secret; and from the first moment he discovered that she was sensitive upon the subject, he had not ceased to use his power to his own advantage. She was thus obliged to treat him with a favour which he ill deserved; yet such was the natural transparency of her character, that her real sentiments so often betrayed themselves, as to keep him in a constant state of irritation.

Sir Henry de Courtenay, whose sincere and ardent nature gave him little taste for mysteries, could not brook the inconsistencies that constantly presented themselves in her manner, and determining that his hand should never be bestowed where there was not the basis of confidence, withdrew himself from the sphere of her attractions. Eva grieved at his departure, but it was in vain that the princess represented, that the readiest escape from her difficulties was a courageous and candid confession of the truth.

Eva "did not care if he could be piqued by such trifles, as her smiling upon Sir Francis, when she heartily wished him among the Turks, he might e'en seek his fortune elsewhere. And for the matter of that, who could tell that it was desirable for the heiress of Strongbow to marry a simple knight." But these heroics usually ended in violent fits of weeping, and profound regrets that she had ever forfeited the confidence of De Courtenay.

Meanwhile, Edward began to feel the languor of inglorious ease, and as his dreams of ambition returned upon him, his thoughts reverted again and again to the unsolved problem that had exercised the political mathematicians of Europe for nearly two centuries. Could a permanent Christian kingdom be founded in Palestine? All the blood which the French had shed, and all the wise counsel that Louis lavished in the Seventh Crusade, had failed to erect the necessary defence, or compose the disorders that oppressed the Syrian Christians. Nor were the Mussulman lords of Syria in much better condition. The noble dynasty of Saphadin had fallen a prey to the ruthless Mamelukes, and a blood-stained revolution in Egypt had placed the fierce Almalek Bibers on the throne. An excuse was not wanting for the invasion of Palestine, and the holy places were again bathed in the blood of their gallant defenders. The military orders were nearly annihilated, and the country was ravaged with fire and sword, almost to the very walls of Acre.

About this time an event, no ways connected with the East, turned Edward's attention to the adoption of the cross. He had challenged Sir Francis to a game of chess. In the midst of the play, from an impulse unaccountable to himself, he rose and sauntered towards the embroidery frame, to relate to Eva his adventure with the page whose ingenuity had once saved his life. Sir Francis, curious to enjoy her artful evasions, followed him; and a moment after, the centre stone of the groined ceiling fell with a terrible crash on the very spot where they had been sitting.

This almost miraculous preservation induced the prince to believe that he was destined to perform some great service for God. It recalled to his mind the benison of our Lady at Walsingham, and, accompanied by Eleanora and a goodly train, he set off the following day to offer on her shrine at Norfolk an altar-cloth of gold brocade, and to crave her protection upon the expedition that he now seriously meditated.

"Eva," said the princess, very gravely, when they sat one day alone, "thou knowest my lord contemplates a pilgrimage."

"The saints preserve us!" said Eva. "Are there not holy places enough in England, but my lord must risk his life upon the sea, and encounter the black *infidels* whose very presence is a terror?"

"'Tis not alone to visit the holy places," replied Eleanora, "though that were a work well worthy knightly daring; but to redeem our Christian brethren from the power of their foes, and to establish the kingdom of Christ, in the land where He died for his people."

"And have not the holiest men and the bravest warriors in Europe, from Peter the Hermit to Fulk of Neuilly, and from Godfrey of Boulogne to the good St. Louis, all attempted it and failed? My lord, I warrant me, has been reading the tales of the romancers, or been deceived by the cunning manifestos of the pope," returned Eva.

"Eva, dear one, when shall I teach thee to treat with respect those in authority."

"I know that I am wrong," said Eva, "but why does not his Holiness take the cross himself, if he considers it such a pious work?"

"And if the Sovereign Pontiff be one of those who say and do not, the Scriptures still require us to obey those who sit in Moses' seat," replied the queen.

"Thy goodness reproveth me beyond thy words. I would that I could be always truthful and pure as thou," said Eva.

"Nay," returned the queen, "I do but repeat that which the confessor this morning told me."

"Forgive my irreverent prating," replied the maiden, "but it seemeth strange to me that one, who lacks the grace of Christian charity himself, should dictate the devotions of my lady who is love itself."

"Ah! partial one," returned the princess, "hadst thou lived in Beziers, St. Dominick would have had thy head for thy heresy. But seriously, my Eva, thy praises humble me, for methinks had my life really exhibited those graces for which thy partial fondness gives me credit, I might ere this have taught thy restless spirit the composure which trust in God always gives."

Alarmed by the grave tone of her mistress, and anxious to conceal the emotions that welled up in her heart, Eva replied, with assumed gaiety, "Nay, what canst thou expect from a sea-sprite? Surely I must

301

rise and fall like my native element."

"Ah! darling, this is that which hath so often forced home upon me the thought I would not willingly apply to thee, 'Unstable as water, thou shalt not excel.' And this it is makes me solicitous to gain thy candid ear while I unfold my husband's plans." Tears rolled over the fair girl's cheeks, but she remained perfectly silent. "Sir Warrenne Bassingbourn, whose noble heart thou knowest well, hath demanded thee of Edward, being pleased to say that thy fair hand would be sufficient guerdon for his gallant conduct in the wars. My royal father will give thee fitting dowry, and I would see my sweet friend well bestowed with some worthy protector before I embark upon that voyage from which I may never return."

"Thou embark for Palestine!" exclaimed Eva, forgetting her own brilliant prospects in the contemplation of her lady's purpose. "Bethink thee, my most honoured mistress, of all the perils that beset thy course."

"I have counted them over, one by one," replied the princess, calmly.

"Thou hast thought of the dangers of the sea, perhaps, but rememberest thou the dreadful pestilence?—the horrors that Queen Margaret told?—how the leeches cut away the gums and cheeks of the sufferers, that they might swallow a drop of water to ease their torments?"

"I remember all—I have considered well," returned the princess. "And this also do I know, that nothing ought to part those whom God hath joined; and the way to heaven is as near, if not nearer, from Syria as from England, or my native Spain."

"Then I go with thee," said Eva, throwing herself at the feet of Eleanora, and pressing her lips upon her hand, "for if God hath not joined me to thee, he hath left me alone in the world. Thou hast been to me more than Naomi, and I shall not fail to thee in the duty of Ruth. Where thou goest I will go, where thou diest I will die, and there will I be buried. Thy people shall be my people, and thy God my God. The poor, lone Eva, whose mother lieth in the deep, deep sea, and whose father is perchance a wanderer or an outlaw, shall no more strive to veil the sadness of her orphan heart by the false smiles and assumed gaiety that grieve her truest, only friend. Henceforth I will learn the lesson thou hast, with such gentle patience and sweet example, ever strove to teach me."

Eleanora mingled her tears with those of the impassioned maiden, and, anxious to end the painful scene, said, "Thou shalt go with me, love, to danger, and perhaps to death, since such is thine election; but what answer shall Edward return to Sir Warrenne Bassingbourn?"

"Let my lord assure Sir Warrenne," said she, rising proudly, "that Eva de la Mer is not insensible of the honour he intends, but that she will never add the shamrock to a knight's escutcheon, till she knows by what title she claims the emblem."

Chapter 6: The Old Man of the Mountain

The benevolent Louis could not rest in the palace of Vincennes while the Mamelukes were slaughtering the Christians, or destroying their souls by forcing them to renounce their faith. In his protracted devotions in the Sainte Chapelle, he fancied he heard the groans of the dying in Palestine, and his soul was stirred for their relief. He convened the barons in the great hall of the Louvre, and entered bearing the holy crown of thorns. He took the cross in their presence, and made his sons and brothers take it, and after those no one dared refuse. Especially did he exert himself to gain the concurrence of the English. Edward joyfully assented to the proposal, and Eleanora, with her female train, departed in the spring of 1270 for Bordeaux, where she superintended the preparations for the crusade campaign.

Thither Edward followed her when his own arrangements were complete. From Bordeaux they sailed for Sicily, where they remained the winter, and where they heard the melancholy intelligence of the death of King Louis, who had advanced as far as Tunis on his way to Egypt. With his last breath, the sainted king whispered the name that was set as a seal upon his heart. "Oh! Jerusalem! Jerusalem!" His brother, Charles d'Anjou, King of Sicily, attempted to dissuade Edward from prosecuting the expedition. But the noble prince, striking his hand upon his breast, exclaimed, with energy, "*Sangue de Dieu!* if all should desert me, I would redeem Acre if only attended by my groom."

When Edward turned the prow of his vessel up the Mediterranean, Acre was in a state of closer siege than it had formerly been, at the advent of Richard Cœur de Lion. But now it was the Mussulmans who lay encamped around its walls, and the Christians who feebly defended it from their fierce attack. The fate of the principality of Antioch was closely connected with that of the Latin kingdom of Jerusalem.

The family of Bohemond, the first sovereign, who married Constantia, daughter of Phillip I., King of France, had reigned there in unbroken succession nearly to the period of the last Crusade—though the State was tributary to Frederic II. and to his son Conrad. The last king was made a knight by St. Louis. When the Egyptians commenced their conquests in Syria, Antioch surrendered without even the formality of a siege, and thus the link between the Greek Empire and Palestine was sundered, and all prospect of aid from that quarter entirely cut off.

In Acre were assembled the last remains of all the Christian principalities of the East; the descendants of the heroes who, under Godfrey of Boulogne, took up their residence there; the remnants of the military friars who had so long and so strenuously battled for the ascendency of the "Hospital" and the "Temple" no less than for the redemption of the Holy Sepulchre; and all the proselytes who, through years of missionary efforts, had been gathered from the Pagan world. But the defenceless were more numerous than the defenders, and the factions which divided their councils would have ripened into treachery and ended in ruin, had it not been for the presence of Sir Henry Courtenay. From the day of his estrangement from Eva, he had bestowed his devotion upon those objects which he thought best calculated to fill the void in his heart

At the first news of the disasters in Palestine, he had assembled all the partisans and vassals of the noble house of Courtenay, and, furnishing them from his own purse, rallied them around the standard *or torteaux*, and led them to the rescue of their eastern brethren. He reached the city at the critical moment when, wearied with the strife, the Templars had begun to negotiate with Melech Bendocar upon the terms of a capitulation. His courteous and noble bearing harmonized the jarring spirits, and his ardent valour inspired them with new hopes, and enabled them to maintain the last stronghold in Palestine, till the arrival of Edward.

The knowledge that a Plantagenet had come to lift the dishonoured banner of the cross from the dust, spread terror and dismay among the ranks of the Moslem, the Sultan of Egypt fled from the city of Acre, all the Latins in Palestine crowded round the standard of the English prince, and Edward found himself at the head of seven thousand veteran soldiers. With this force he made an expedition to Nazareth, which he besieged with the most determined valour. In the fight, Edward was unhorsed, and might have perished in the *mêlée*, had not Henry Courtenay relinquished his own steed for his master's use.

The gallant youth then took his station by the side of a tall knight, whose falchion gleamed in the front of the battle like the sword of Azrael. They were the first to mount the scaling-ladders and drive the Moslem from the walls. Nazareth was thus, by one decisive blow, added to the dominions of Christendom. But the wing of victory was paralyzed by the scorching sun of Syria. Edward was prostrated by the acclimating fever that wasted the energies of Richard Cœur de Lion, and in the palace of Acre he longed, in vain, for the cooling draughts of iced sherbet, that the courteous Saladin had bestowed upon his royal predecessor. Sir Francis d'Essai had followed the fortunes of Edward, or rather of Eva, to Palestine, hoping to win the favour of his lady's smiles. The sight of de Courtenay roused all his former jealousy, and the cordial manner of Eva towards his rival almost drove him to desperation. Various circumstances had excited an apprehension in Edward's mind, that the count was seeking to make common cause with the Arabs, but as no tangible proof of treasonable practices appeared, the suspicion passed away.

The illness of the monarch continuing, Eleanora determined to make a pilgrimage to the Jordan, to pray at the shrine of St. John for her husband's recovery, and, at his own earnest solicitations, Sir Francis was permitted to conduct the party. Eleanora afterwards remembered that he rode most of the way in close attendance upon Eva, and seemed engaged in earnest conversation, though several muttered oaths gave her the impression that the colloquy was not so satisfactory as he could have wished. They accomplished their pilgrimage safely, and commenced their return, when, stopping to refresh themselves in a small grove near Mount Tabor, a band of mounted Saracens fell upon them.

There was a fierce struggle, and, for a few moments, the gleaming of swords and the flash of scimitars seemed to menace instant destruction. Both the assailants and defenders were scattered through the wood, and a few of the frantic females attempted flight. The Moslems at length retreated, but when the princess summoned her retainers to set forward, neither Sir Francis nor Eva could be found.

Alarmed for the safety of her lovely companion, Eleanora caused the vicinity to be searched in every direction. Her palfrey was discovered idly cropping the grass, but all trace of its fair rider was lost. With a bursting heart the princess gave orders to proceed with all haste to Acre, that scouts in greater numbers might be sent in quest of the lost jewel.

The state of Edward's health was such, that it was not deemed advisable to acquaint him with the melancholy result of their pious enterprise. But de Courtenay at once comprehended the plot. Such a *mêlée*, without bloodshed, proved no hostile intention on the part of the Arabs, and there could be no doubt that Sir Francis was the instigator of the attack, and the possession of Eva, its object. His impatience to set off for her rescue did not prevent him from taking every precaution, both for the safety of Acre, and the success of his expedition. Eleanora, whose characteristic self-possession had left her at liberty to observe, described with the most scrupulous exactness the circumstances of the fray, and each trifling peculiarity in the appearance of the robbers.

Fortified with this intelligence, he set off at once, with a select party, and a few hours after leaving Acre, was unexpectedly joined by the tall knight, and a reinforcement of converted *Pullani*. From him he learned that the Arabs had taken the direction of Mt. Lebanon, and from his knowledge of the Assassin band, his heart sunk within him, at the thought of what might have been the fate of his lovely Eva. In his anxiety for her rescue, all her faults were forgotten, and he only remembered the gentle kindness that characterized every action, and the nameless charm, that made her friends as numerous as her acquaintances. Prompted by these considerations, they spurred forward, stopping only to refresh their wearied steeds, till they began to wind among the rocky passes of Mt. Lebanon.

The tall knight seemed perfectly familiar with the locality, and guided the pursuers directly to the tower, called The Vulture's Nest, which was the chief residence of the Old Man of the Mountain. There seemed to be an intelligence between the tall knight and all the *marabouts* who guarded the entrance to this "Castle Dangerous." Leaving their followers, the two leaders advanced, and the knight presenting a piece of shrivelled parchment to an Arab, who filled the office of porter, they were ushered into a long hall, at the door of which stood a swarthy Turk, partly leaning upon an immense battle-axe, the handle of which was stuck full of daggers.

The *sheik* received them with an obsequiousness scarcely to be expected from one of his bloody trade, and in answer to the knight's eager inquiries, motioned his attendant, and instantly that which had appeared a solid masonry, rolled silently back, as if by magic, revealing an apartment fitted up with every appliance of eastern magnificence. Before they recovered from their surprise, voices were heard from the farther extremity of the room, soft female pleading, and then the loud menacing tones of passion.

"Eva, thou shalt be mine! I swear it by all the fiends of hell. Nay, anger me not by thy cold repulse. Thou art now beyond the protection of the smooth-tongued de Courtenay." He seized her arm as he spoke, and a piercing shriek rang through the hall.

"Traitor! viper! release thy hold," exclaimed de Courtenay, springing forward and receiving the fainting girl in his arms.

"And who art thou, that darest to cross the purpose of D'Essai? By what right dost thou interfere between me and my bride?"

"By the right of a father," said a deep, stern voice at his side, and the tall knight advancing, tenderly clasped his unresisting daughter to his heart, and stood by like one lost in a tide of long-repressed emotions, while the two nobles fiercely drew their swords, and with deadly hatred, each sought the life of his foe. But the *sheik* interposed, reminding them, that his castle walls were sacred, and that if his tributaries chose to slay one another, they must seek the open field for the pastime. Reluctantly, and with eyes that glared with baffled vengeance, the lords sheathed their swords, and the tall knight, laying his daughter gently upon a couch, spake a few words apart to the *sheik*.

The Old Man made a sign of assent, and instantly two Arabs sprang forward, seized D'Essai, bound him with thongs, and conveyed him from the apartment. Relieved of her fears, and reassured by the presence of a father, for whose affection she had always pined, and a lover, on whom she now contrived to smile in a way that completely satisfied his heart, Eva declared herself impatient to set off immediately for Acre. The *sheik* pressed them to partake of some refreshments, and while Eva enjoyed a few moments' delicious conversation with her sire, a troop of slaves prepared and set before them an entertainment that would have done honour to the palace of a king. As the cavalcade set out, the tender heart of Eva was pained to see Sir Francis placed upon the back of a mule, blindfolded, with his face to the crupper, and his arms firmly pinioned to the body of the Arab who had him in charge.

"Thou seemest on excellent terms with the *sheik* of the mountain, noble Clare," said de Courtenay, as they rode along. "Had I not a guarantee in thy kindred," said he glancing at Eva, "I should somewhat challenge the familiarity that has given such success to our expedition."

"Nay, and that thou well mightst," returned the Clare, "for the history of mankind does not furnish the idea of so daring and desperate a band as these assassins of Mt. Lebanon."

"Heaven save us!" exclaimed Eva, her lips white with fear. "From what terrible fate have I been delivered! That vile Sir Francis declared that he had snatched me from the hostile Arabs, and would bring me safe to Acre, and that it was in pity for my fatigue he turned aside to a castle of Christian natives. It makes me shudder, even now, to think that I have been in the presence of the man whose very name hath made me tremble, when beyond the sea, in merrie England."

"Nay, love," said her father, tenderly, "the *sheik* owed thee no malice, and might have rescued thee, had not Sir Francis been his tributary."

"They exact, then, toll and custom?" said Courtenay, inquiringly.

"Thou sayest well *exact*," replied the knight. "Didst not mark the battle-axe of the rude *seneschal*? 'Tis said the Danish weapon once belonged to the founder of the band, and each dagger stuck in the oaken helve, inscribed with a sentence in a different dialect, is significantly pointed against the prince or ruler who shall dare withhold tribute from their chief. One of my ancestors, I reck not whom, once resided in the vicinity of Croyland, and received from the venerable abbot the parchment which thou sawest me use with such marvellous effect. My ancestor fought in the first crusade under the Atheling, and, unlike most of his companions, returned in safety, whence a tradition arose in the family that the scroll was a charm.

"On my setting out for the holy wars, I placed the heirloom in my *aumonière*, and had nearly forgotten its existence, when a startling circumstance recalled it to memory. My plan for the redemption of Palestine (for I have not been without ambition) was the organization of troops collected from the mixed races which are now an important part of the population. I was warned at the outset that tribute would be demanded by the chief of the assassins, but I steadily resisted every tax-gatherer who presented his claims, till I awoke one morning in my tent, surrounded by my faithful guard, and found a dagger stuck in the ground not two fingers' breadth from my head.

"I examined the inscription upon the weapon and found it the same with that upon the scroll, and forthwith determined to form the acquaintance of this rival chief. He respected my passport and showed me the wonders of his habitation, which heaven grant I may never see again. So perfect is the discipline of his followers, so invincible their faith, that every word of their chief is a law. He led me up a lofty tower, at each battlement of which stood two Fedavis. At a sign from him, two of these devotees flung themselves from the tower, breaking their bones, and scattering their brains upon the rock below. 'If you wish it,' said the chief, 'all these men shall do the same.' But I had seen enough, and I resolved from that hour never to tempt the enmity of the Old Man of the Mountain.

"I have ransomed yon traitor, at heavy cost, for I would that Edward should know and punish his baseness. You are now beyond the reach of danger. I may not enter Acre—the reasons shall be told ere long. Farewell, my daughter, sweet image of thy sainted mother; guard my secret safely till we meet again. *Adieu.*"

He dashed the rowels into his steed, and was soon lost among the hills.

CHAPTER 7

Meantime the palace of Acre had been witness of a fearful scene. Since the fall of Nazareth the Emir of Joppa had opened negotiations with Edward, professing a desire to become a Christian convert. So eager was the king for this happy consummation that he cherished the deceitful hope, held out by the Infidel, and granted him every opportunity for gaining information concerning the tenets and practices of the church.

Letters and messages frequently passed between them, and so accustomed had the English guards become to the brown *haick* and green turban of the swarthy Mohammedan, who carried the despatches, that they gave him free ingress to the city and admitted him to the palace, and even ushered him into the king's ante-chamber almost without question or suspicion.

The day had been unusually sultry, even for the Syrian climate. The heat of the atmosphere somewhat aggravated the symptoms of the disease from which Edward was slowly recovering, and Eleanora had passed many weary hours in vain endeavours to soothe his restlessness and induce repose.

As the sun declined a cooling breeze sprang up from the sea, seeming to the patient wife to bear healing on its wings, and the invalid, stretched on his couch before the casement, began at length to yield to the soothing influence of slumber, when the chamberlain entered to say that the emissary from Joppa waited an audience.

"Now have I no faith in the conversion of this *infidel*," said Eleanora, with an impatience unusual to her gentle spirit, "since his messenger disturbs my lord's repose."

"Verily thou lackest thine accustomed charity," replied Edward. "I had thought to hear thee declare the conversion of this Saracen my crowning glory in Palestine. But thou art weary, my love. Go to thy rest, thy long vigils by my side have already gathered the carnation from thy cheek."

"Yet, my lord—" interposed Eleanora.

"Nay, nay," said Edward, "disturb not thy sweet soul; perchance more than my life depends upon the interview. I will straight dismiss the envoy, and then thou canst entrust my slumbers to the care of the faithful Eva."

At the mention of Eva a new and not less painful train of associations was awakened in the mind of Eleanora, and with a heavy sigh she withdrew as the messenger entered.

A moment after there were sounds as of a violent struggle and of the fall of a heavy body, and Eleanora, who had lingered in the ante-chamber, scarcely knowing why, rushed back into the apartment, followed by the chamberlain and guards.

The assassin lay upon the floor in the agonies of death, his head broken by the oaken tressel from which she had just risen. Prostrate by his side lay the prince, in a state of insensibility, the blood faintly oozing from a wound in his arm. The princess comprehended at once the risk her husband had incurred, and shuddered with apprehension at the thought of the danger that yet might menace him; and while the attendants lifted him from the floor, she tenderly raised his arm to her lips, and began to draw the venom from the wound. But no sooner did Edward revive from his swoon, than, forcibly thrusting her aside, he exclaimed, "Eleanora my life, knowest thou not the dagger was poisoned?"

"Even so, my lord," said she, with steadfast composure, still firmly persisting in her purpose, notwithstanding his constant remonstrance.

The fearful intelligence of their leader's peril spread with lightning speed through the city, and self-sent messengers hurried in every direction, and summoned leeches and priests to cure or shrive the dying monarch. The Grand Master of the Temple, who was somewhat practised in the habits of the assassins, appeared in the midst of the exciting scene, and commending the timely application of Eleanora's loving lips, bound up the wound with a soft emollient, and prescribed for the princess an antidote of sovereign efficacy.

Scarcely had silence resumed her dominion in the palace, when the porter was again aroused to admit de Courtenay and his rescued

Eva. The traitor D'Essai had been lodged in the tower of Maledictum, to wait Edward's pleasure concerning him; and Eva, her heart overflowing with rapture in the assurance of Sir Henry's restored confidence, and the security of a father's love, passed the livelong night with Eleanora, in that free communion of soul which generous natures experience when the gushings of a common emotion overleap the barriers of conventionalism and formality.

★★★★★★

Edward was himself again. The steady ray of reason had subdued the fevered gleam of his eye, and the ruddy hue of health replaced the pallor of wasting sickness upon his cheek. His athletic frame had wrestled with disease, and come off Conqueror over weakness and pain; and as he assumed his seat of judgment, clad in his warlike panoply, the royal Plantagenet "looked every inch a king." The great church of Acre was thrown open, and knights in brilliant armour, and Templars and Hospitallers in the habiliments of their orders, bishops and priests in their sacred robes, and vassals in their holiday array, crowded up the long aisles, and filled the spacious choir, as though eager to witness some splendid ceremonial. But instead of gorgeous decorations, wainscot and window draped with black diffused a funereal gloom, and the solemn reverberation of the tolling bell seemed to sound a requiem over the grave of Hope.

Sir Francis d'Essai had been tried in a council of his peers, and found guilty of treason to religion and knightly devoir; and this day, the anniversary of his admission to the rank of knighthood, his companions in arms, the vassals whom he despised, and all those actuated by curiosity or enmity, were assembled to witness his *degradation*. Eva shuddered at the terrible doom of her former lover, and de Courtenay, with instinctive delicacy, had obtained permission to absent himself from the scene on a visit to the Holy Sepulchre. As king-of-arms, and first in rank, it was the duty of Edward to preside over this fearful ceremony, which, by the true and loyal, was regarded as more terrible than death itself.

At the first stroke of the great bell, the *pursuivants*, having robed Sir Francis for the last time in his knightly habiliments, conducted him from the *Cursed Tower* toward the church. As they entered the door, the doleful peal sank in silence, and, after one awful moment, his fellow-knights, with broken voices, began to chant the burial service.

An elevated stage, hung with black, had been erected in the centre of the nave, and upon this the *pursuivants*, whose business it was to divest him of every outward insignia of courage and truth, placed the culprit, in full view of all the vast concourse.

When the chanting ceased, Prince Edward spoke in a voice that thrilled to every heart, "Sir Francis d'Essai! thou who didst receive the sword of knighthood from the hand of the good St. Louis, dost stand before us this day attaint of treason to thy God, thy truth, and the lady of thy love. Wherefore thy peers have willed that the order of knighthood, by the which thou hast received all the honour and worship upon thy body, *be brought to nought*, and thy state be undone, and thou be driven forth outcast and dishonoured according to thy base deserts." Instantly the brazen tongue from the belfry ratified the fiat, and announced the hour of doom.

At the word, the squire with trembling hand removed the helmet, the defence of disloyal eyes, revealing the pale and haggard countenance of the recreant knight, and the choir resumed the mournful dirge. Then each pursuivant advanced in his order to the performance of his unwelcome duty. One by one the knightly trappings of D'Essai were torn from his body, and as *cuirass*, greaves, brassarts, and gauntlets rang upon the pavements, the heralds exclaimed, "Behold the harness of a miscreant!"

Trembling and bent beneath the weight of shame, the craven stood, while they smote the golden spurs from his heels, and brake his dishonoured sword above his head, and the terrible requiem wailed over the perished emblems of his former innocence.

The Grand Master of the Templars then entered upon the stage, bearing a silver basin filled with tepid water, and the herald, holding it up, exclaimed, "By what name call men the knight before us?"

The *pursuivants* answered, "The name which was given him in baptism,—the name by which his father was known,—the name confirmed to him in chivalry is Sir Francis d'Essai."

The heralds again replied, "Falsehood sits upon his tongue and rules in his heart; he is miscreant, traitor, and *infidel*."

Immediately the Grand Master, in imitation of baptism, dashed the water in his face, saying, "Henceforth be thou called by thy right name, Traitor!"

Then the heralds rang out a shrill note upon the trumpets, expressive of the demand, "What shall be done with the false-hearted knave?"

Prince Edward in his majesty arose, and in a voice agitated with a sense of the awful penalty, replied, "Let him with dishonour and shame be banished from the kingdom of Christ—Let his brethren curse him, and let not the angels of God intercede for him."

Immediately each knight drew his sword, and presenting its gleaming point against the now defenceless D'Essai, crowded him down the steps to the altar, where the *pursuivants* seized him, and forced him into his coffin, and placed him on the bier, and the attendant priests completed the burial-service over his polluted name and perjured soul. At a sign from the king, the bearers took up the bier, and all the vast congregation followed in sad procession, to the city-gates, where they thrust him out, a thing accursed, while the great bell from the lofty tower of the cathedral told the tale of his infamy in tones of terrible significance, "Gone—gone—gone—virtue, faith, and truth;lost—lost—lost—honour, fame, and love." From Carmel's hoary height to Tabor's sacred top, each hallowed hill and vale reverberated the awful knell, "Gone and lost—lost and gone"—and the breeze that swept the plain of Esdraelon caught up the dismal echo, and seemed hurrying across the Mediterranean to whisper to the chivalry of Europe the dreadful story of his *degradation*.

Stung by the weight of woe that had fallen upon him, the miserable D'Essai rose and gazed across the plain. An arid waste spread out before him like the prospect of his own dreary future, blackened and desolate by the reign of evil passions.

Life, what had it been to him? A feverish dream, a burning thirst, a restless, unsatisfied desire! Virtue—honour—truth—idle words, their solemn mockery yet rang in his ears. He ran—he flew—anywhere, anywhere to flee the haunting thoughts that trooped like fiends upon his track.

He neared the banks of the river, its cooling waters rolling on in their eternal channel, promised to allay his fever and bury his dishonoured name in oblivion. He plunged in—that ancient river swept him away, the river Kishon, and as he sank to rise no more, a deep voice exclaimed, "So perish thine enemies, O Lord!" It was the voice of Dermot de la Clare, who, passing southward at the head of his troop, from the opposite bank became an involuntary witness of the frantic suicide.

The week following the ceremony last described, Eva entered the apartment of Eleanora, each fair feature radiant with pleasure, bearing in her hand a carrier-pigeon, whose fluttering heart betokened the weary length of way that had tried the strength of its glossy pinions.

"Whence hast thou the dove, and what is his errand?" exclaimed the princess, equally eager for any intelligence that might affect the fate of the East.

"A Pullani brought it to the palace," she replied, and hastily cutting the silken thread, she detached a letter from beneath the wing of the bird. It contained but these words: "The Sultan of Egypt is hard pressed by the Moslems. It is a favourable moment to commence negotiations."

The seal of the Shamrock was the only signature, but Eva well understood that the Clare had been engaged in devising an honourable scheme to release Edward from an expedition which could not result in glory to the Christian arms.

The prince had now been fourteen months in the Holy Land. His army, never sufficient to allow of his undertaking any military enterprise of importance, was reduced by sickness, want and desertion, and he therefore gladly accepted the hint of his unknown friend, and despatched de Courtenay to Egypt with proposals of peace.

It was a glad errand to the knight, though the timid and (she could not conceal it) loving Eva warned him most strenuously against the artifices of the Sultan, Al Malek al Dhaker Rokneddin Abulfeth Bibers al Alai al Bendokdari al Saheli, whose name, at least, she said, was *legion*.

"And were he the prince of darkness himself, the love of my guardian Eva would protect me against his wiles," gallantly returned the count.

"Alas!" said Eva, humbly, "thou little knowest the broken reed on which thou leanest. My weak will mocks my bravest resolutions, and makes me feel the need of a firmer spirit for my guide."

"Heaven grant that I may one day receive the grateful office," returned her lover.

"Heaven help me become worthy of thy noble devotion," said Eva, remembering with regret the cruel test to which she had subjected his generous affection.

De Courtenay found little difficulty in settling the terms of a ten years' truce with the formidable Mameluke; for the *sultan* had far greater reason to fear his Moslem than his Christian foes.

There was no occasion for the farther sojourn of the English in Palestine; and Edward, having accomplished nothing more than his great-uncle, and leaving a reputation scarcely inferior to Cœur de Lion, departed with his retinue for Europe.

Notwithstanding the peaceful termination of the expedition, this crusade, the last of the chivalrous offspring of Feudalism and Enthusiasm, like its elder brethren, found a premature grave in darkness and gloom.

The son of St. Louis, Philip the Hardy, returning from Tunis, deposited five coffins in the crypts of St. Denis. They contained the remains of his sainted father, Louis IX., of his brother Tristan, of his brother-in-law, Thibaut, descendant of Adela, of his beloved queen and their infant son. Weak and dying himself, he was almost the only heir of his royal family. The ambitious Charles d'Anjou, the rival and the murderer of Corradino, grandson of Frederic and Violante, plundered the stranded vessels of the returning crusaders, and thus enriched his kingdom of Sicily, by the great shipwreck of the empire and the church.

Death, too, had been busy in the palace of Windsor. The two beautiful children of Edward and Eleanora had been laid in the tomb, and their grandfather, Henry III., with their Aunt Margaret,[1] Queen of Scotland, soon followed them to the great charnel-house of England, Westminster Abbey. The melancholy tidings of these repeated bereavements met the royal pair in Sicily, and cast a pall over the land to which they had anticipated a triumphant return.

The great problem of the conquest of Palestine was not yet solved to the mind of Edward, but the progress of the age trammelled his powers and limited his ambitious aspirations. The orders of knighthood, exhausted by the repeated drafts made upon their forces, by these eastern expeditions, began to decline in the scale of power; and the lower ranks, finding new avenues to wealth in productive labour and commerce, began the great battle with military organizations and hereditary aristocracy, which has been going on with increased advantage to the working classes from the middle ages to the present glorious era.

Gregory X. made some feeble attempts to rouse Europe once more for the redemption of the Holy Sepulchre, but his earnest appeal received no response from the sovereigns of Christendom, and within three years the last strain of the great anthem "*Hierosolyma liberati*" that began with the swelling tones of mustering warriors and sounded on through two centuries in the soul-stirring harmonies of jubilante *peans*, alternating with the mournful measures of funeral dirges, ended in a last sad refrain over the diminished remnants of the military orders, who, in a vain defence of Acre, dyed the sands of Syria with their blood.

---

1. *Margaret Queen of Scotland* by Henry Grey Graham also published by Leonaur.

From Sicily the royal crusaders proceeded to Rome, where they were cordially welcomed and splendidly entertained by Pope Gregory X., who, having long filled the office of confessor in their household, had been recalled from the Holy Land, to occupy the chair of St. Peter.

In the train of the King of England was his cousin, Henry, son of Richard of Cornwall, a gallant young noble who had led the detachment that opposed the band of Leicester, and, by his warlike prowess, greatly contributed to the successful issue of the sanguinary conflict at Evesham. His zeal and loyalty during this doubtful period, commended him to the confidence of Edward, and he had still more endeared himself to his royal patron, by his ardour in battling against the *infidels*, and his brilliant achievements at the siege of Nazareth.

The young Henry was the affianced husband of the Princess Mary, in consequence of which, Eleanora had admitted him to an intimacy, and evinced for him an affection almost equal to that enjoyed by the royal children themselves.

During the stay of the king at Rome, the devoted Henry obtained permission to make a pilgrimage to a celebrated shrine near Naples, for the consecration of sundry relics which he had collected in Palestine. As he knelt at the foot of the altar and closed his eyes in prayer, he was not aware of the entrance of his mortal enemy, Guy de Montfort, son of the Earl of Leicester. With stealthy tread the assassin approached, bent over the suppliant youth, and exclaiming, "Die! murderer of my father!" thrust his sword into the heart, beating warm with life and hope, and sprinkled the holy relics with the blood of another martyr. With a vengeful frown of satisfied hate, he wiped the sword, returned it to its scabbard, and strode from the church. One of his knights, fit follower of such a master, inquired as he rejoined his troop,

"What has my lord Guy de Montfort done?"

"Taken vengeance," was the fiendish reply.

"How so?" rejoined the knight. "Was not your father, the great Leicester, dragged a public spectacle, by the hair of the head through the streets of Evesham?"

Without a word the demon turned to his yet more malignant triumph, and seizing the victim, whose pale lips yet moved with the instinct of prayer, dragged him from the attendants, who were vainly striving to staunch the life-blood welling from the wound, to the public place, and left him a ghastly spectacle to the horror-stricken crowd.

316

It was now necessary for the murderers to think of self-defence. The English retainers of Earl Henry had raised the cry of revenge, and the Italian populace excited by the fearful tragedy that had been enacted in the very presence of the virgin and child, began to run together and join the parties of attack or defence. The train of de Montfort immediately raised the shout of, "d'Anjou! Down with the Ghibelines!" and when the armed forces of the Duke Charles rode into the midst of the throng to investigate the cause of the tumult, Sir Guy joined their ranks, and departed for Naples under their escort.

Tidings of this melancholy event were soon carried to Rome, and Edward immediately appealed to the pope for justice upon the murderer. Gregory, who feared to offend Edward, and who was almost equally alarmed at the prospect of a rupture with the tyrant of Sicily, had recourse to various ingenious methods of delay. Finding however that the King of England had determined to postpone the obsequies of his noble relative, until a curse was pronounced upon the assassin, he was forced to the exercise of ecclesiastical measures.

Clothed in his *pontifical* robes, Gregory X. entered the church at Orvietto, and proceeding to the high altar, took the bible in his hand, and, after setting before the awestruck assembly the guilt of the culprit, proceeded thus to fulminate his anathema against the assassin.

"For the murder of Henry of Germany, slain before the shrine of St. Mary, in the face of day, we lay upon Guy de Montfort the curse of our Holy Church. In virtue of the authority bestowed upon us as the successor of St. Peter, we do pronounce him excommunicate, and alien to all the privileges and consolations which our blessed religion affords. We permit everyone to seize him—we order the governors of provinces to arrest him—we place under interdict all who shall render him an asylum—we prohibit all Christians from lending him aid, and we dispense his vassals from all oaths of fidelity they have made to him; may none of the blessings of this holy book descend upon him, and may all the curses contained therein, cleave unto him;" and he dashed the bible to the ground.

Lifting the waxen taper, he continued, "Let the light of life be withdrawn from him, and let his soul sink in *eternal night*." With the word he threw the candle upon the pavement, and instantly every light in the church was extinguished, and amid the gloom, the trembling congregation heard the voice of the *pontiff*, ringing out full and clear, "I curse him by book, by candle, and by bell." A solemn toll proclaimed the malediction, and amid the darkness and the silence,

317

the multitude crept one by one from the church, as though fearful of being implicated in the terrible denunciation.

Edward, having thus placed his cousin under the ban of the church, disdained to persecute him with farther vengeance, and taking an amicable leave of the pontiff continued his route to France. Learning that England was quiet under the regency of the queen-mother, he improved the opportunity to make the tour of his southern dominions, and, in gallant sports and knightly adventures passed several months upon the continent.

Edward and Eleanora arrived in England, August 2nd, 1273. The English welcomed their return with the greatest exultation. Both houses of parliament assembled to do honour to their entrance into London, and the streets were hung with garlands of flowers and festoons of silk; while the wealthy inhabitants, showered gold and silver on the royal retinue as they passed.

Preparations were made for their coronation on a scale of magnificence hitherto unrivalled. Fourteen days were spent in erecting booths for the accommodation of the populace, and temporary kitchens for the purpose of roasting oxen, sheep, and fowls, and preparing cakes and pastry, for the expected banquet. Hogsheads of Bordeaux wine, and pipes of good stout English ale, were ranged at convenient intervals, and flagon-masters appointed to deal them out to the thirsty crowds.

The night before the expected ceremony, the presumptive king and queen were indulging in reminiscences of the early days of their married life, and comparing those troublous times, with the splendid future that seemed to stretch in bright perspective before them.

"Methinks, sweet life," said Edward, tenderly taking her hand, "those days when thou dwelt a fugitive in the wilds of Devonshire, and I languished within the walls of Kenilworth, gave little promise of our present peaceful state."

"True, my lord, yet had I not dwelt in the humble hamlet, I might never have known the pure loyalty of English hearts."

"By our Lady, thou hast a better alchemy than thy clerkly brother, the Castilian monarch, for his science finds only *gold* in everything, while thy diviner art finds *good* in all, and loyalty in outlaws."

"I remember me," replied Eleanora, with an arch smile, "there was a gallant outlaw, in whom my woman's heart discerned every noble and knightly quality. But small credit can I claim for my science, since it was the alchemy of love that revealed his virtues."

318

"No other alchemy hath e'er found good in man, and, sinner as I am, I might fear the judgment of thy purity, did not the same sweet charity that discovers undeveloped virtues transmute even errors into promises of good. Tomorrow, God willing, it will be in Edward's power to constitute Eleanora the dispenser of bounty. Whom would she first delight to honour?"

"Since the prince of outlaws puts it in my power," said Eleanora, with a look of grateful affection, "I would e'en reward those bold foresters who delivered my Edward from the enemies that sought his life."

"Thou sayest well, dearest," replied Edward, "and now that thou remindest me of my escape from thraldom, I pray our Lady of Walsingham aid me to discharge an obligation that hath long laid heavy on my conscience. Yesternight, methought I saw, among the yeomen busy in the preparations for the approaching pageant, the tall outlaw, who, in his gown and cowl, one moment gave me priestly benison, and the next, advised me of Leicester's movements, with the sagacity of a practised warrior. Such length of limb and strength of arm, once seen, does not escape my memory; and, if my eye deceive me not, 'twas he, with Courtenay, who led the assault at Nazareth; and furthermore, it runneth in my mind, that I have seen him elsewhere and in other guise."

"Mayhap it was the tall knight who defended Eleanora at the Jews' massacre, till thy arrival dispersed the rabble mob," returned the queen.

"By the soul of St. Bartholomew thou divinest well," said the king; "and, since thou knowest the monk, perhaps thou canst give me tidings concerning the shrewd-witted boy, who managed to gain speech with me, when all my partisans had failed. So fair a squire must, ere this, have earned the spurs of knighthood; and much would it pleasure me, to lay the accolade upon his shoulder, in return for his dextrous plotting. That the lad pertained not to the household of Mortimer, I knew right well; but whether he were a retainer of the bold outlaw who organized the royal forces, or some young noble whose love of adventure set him upon the work, I could never yet decide."

"And if he were retainer of the outlaw?" said Eleanora, inquiringly.

"My gratitude should none the less reward the service of one who risked his life for mine," replied the king.

A smile of satisfaction beamed on the countenance of Eleanora, and opening her gypsire, and taking thence the small ivory whistle, she despatched an attendant with the token to Eva.

Shortly after, the conversation was interrupted by the entrance of an attendant, who announced that a page from Lady Mortimer craved an audience of his majesty.

"Let him be at once admitted," said Edward, casting a significant glance at Eleanora.

The door was thrown open, and the beautiful boy, whose image at that moment filled the mind of the king, entered with trembling step, and proceeding straight to the monarch, knelt at his feet, and with clasped hands began to plead earnestly for the pardon of the banished Earl Dermot de la Clare.

"How is this?" exclaimed Edward, gazing with astonishment, first upon the kneeling page, and then upon his wife. "How is this? by the Holy Rood, my heart misgives me, thou art witch as well as alchemist. Here is the identical page I have vainly sought for nine long years, conjured up by the magic of an ivory whistle."

"Earl Dermot de la Clare!" said he to Eva, lifting the boy tenderly from his knees, "why has the banished outlaw sought thy fair lips to plead his cause? Let himself present his claims to our clemency, and we will promise justice for ourself, and perchance a better guerdon from our loving spouse, who would ever have mercy rejoice above judgment.

"And thou, sweet dove," said he, gazing admiringly upon the doubting Eva, "'who wearest the badge of Mortimer,' and whose 'giddy brain recks not of politics,' demandest manor and lordship for an outlawed man! Didst crave it for thyself, not twice the boon could make me say thee nay."

"'Tis for myself I crave the boon, royal liege," said Eva, falling again upon her knees. "Dermot de la Clare is the sire of thy poor orphan charge."

"Thy sire!" exclaimed the prince, greatly moved. "How knowest thou this?"

"First, by the story of the rescued sailor, who was one of the band with which my father thought to regain possession of his fief, when the act of attainder had branded him an outlaw. He it was with the cartman's frock, who waited our coming at the cross-road on the memorable day of my lord's escape. Next, by the shamrock, the ancient cognizance of the house of Strongbow, and by the rose of Sharon, which my mother wrought upon the scarf in memory of her husband's pilgrimage. But Eva finds the strongest proof in the promptings of her heart; for from the day since she rested in his arms at London bridge, to the time when he drew her from the Vulture's Nest at Mount Lebanon, she hath trusted in his love, and obeyed his bidding, with such confidence as none but a father could inspire."

"Thy eloquence hath proved thy cause," said the king, raising her and seating her by his side; "and were I a needy knight, requiring royal favour, I'd bribe thy pleading eyes to back my suit, and never fear denial."

Eva essayed to stammer forth her thanks, but tears choked her utterance, and Eleanora, pitying her confusion, reassured her with playful allusions to her childish aspirations for the sovereignty of Ireland.

"I fear me," said Edward, gazing upon her varying colour with admiration, "that to reward all my subjects and vassals, according to their merit, will exhaust my exchequer. The audacity of these benefactors exceeds all belief! It was but this morning that one more bold than his fellows demanded the fairest flower of our court as a recompense for his knightly service in the eastern campaign."

The conscious Eva looked imploringly at her mistress, who graciously accorded her permission to depart, while Edward continued his raillery.

"I referred the gallant unto thee, love," said he, "for he must be a brave man who dares transfer the possessions of his wife."

"To the marriage of de Courtenay with our beautiful ward," returned the queen, "there riseth but one objection. From the similarity of her name, she ever fancied herself the heiress of the former King of Leinster, and hath cultivated a taste for decorations befitting royalty. I fear me that Sir Henry, being but the younger branch of his house, will scarce be able to maintain a state suited to her desires."

"God grant she have not the ambition of Earl Strigul, else might we find it necessary to do battle for our fief of Ireland," said Edward.

"Nay, from the ambition of Eva, thou hast nought to fear; her heart would incline her rather to bestow benefices upon her friends, than to hoard treasures for herself. Therefore it is that I desire for her worthy alliance and princely dower," returned the queen.

"Thou hast it in thy power, best one, to obviate thine own objections and to bless the loyal hamlet that protected thy seclusion, by giving them so gracious a mistress."

Tears of gratitude filled the eyes of the queen, as looking affectionately upon her husband she replied, "How lost were Eleanora to the love of God did she not daily thank Him for making her the wife of one who finds his own happiness in promoting the welfare of his subjects."

"Not all his subjects regard him with thy partial fondness," said the king. "Our brother, Alexander of Scotland, has refused to renew the oath of homage, which his ancestor made to Henry II. for his crown, and will attend our coronation only as kingly guest; while the bold Llewellyn refuses to set foot in London."

"The troublous period through which the realm so lately passed, pleads their best excuse for these unjust suspicions," suggested the queen. "When the wisdom and magnanimity of my Edward shall become known, they will learn to trust their interest in his hands with the confidence of vassals."

"Thou would'st fain persuade me," said Edward, laughing, "that I may love my enemies."

"I would persuade thee," said Eleanora, with a smile of confident affection, "to make thine enemies thy friends. Suspicion ever breeds hatred. There be many warm, true hearts in England, at this hour, who, having followed the fortunes of Leicester, for what they deemed the public good, are withheld by fear, from uttering the shout of loyalty."

"And how would'st thou purpose that I should bind them to their allegiance?" said Edward, curiously.

"By the same rule that our blessed Lord restored this fallen world," returned the queen, timidly. "He declareth his love toward us, even while we are sinners, and thus we learn to confide in Him."

"Verily, there seems truth in what thou sayest," said the king, thoughtfully; "but it were a thing unheard of—for a ruler to illustrate the principles of forgiveness, and place his kingdom at the mercy of traitors."

"The good St. Louis," urged Eleanora, almost fearful of pressing the matter too far, "leaned ever to the side of mercy; and no king of France hath enjoyed a more peaceful or glorious reign."

"It shall be as thou sayest," said Edward, after a pause, during which he gazed upon her pleading countenance, whose every feature mirrored the intense interest of her heart in the welfare of their subjects, and the honour of her lord. "It shall be as thou sayest. Heaven cannot suffer me to err in this matter, since it hath sent an angel for my counsellor." Then resuming his accustomed tone of affectionate pleasantry, he added, "Thou think'st it well, dearest, for a warrior like myself to perform some work of supererogation, to cancel the sins into which my love of power may yet lead me. But small merit may I claim for my clemency, since it were not in the nature of man to withstand the sweet earnestness with which thou dost enforce thy gentle counsels."

CHAPTER 8: THE CORONATION

Nearly a century had elapsed since an occasion like the present had called together the different ranks and orders of the English population. Native Britons, Saxons, Danes and Normans, hereditary enemies, had, by years of unavoidable intercourse, and by a community of interests, been fused into one mass, and now vied with each other in manifesting their loyalty to a king in whose veins mingled the several streams of the great Scandinavian race. The independent Franklin, the stout yeoman from the country, and the rich citizen and industrious artisan, the curious vassal, the stately knight, and lordly baron, alike instinct with love for feasting and holiday show, hastened to witness the ceremony.

The coronation of John had been unpopular, both from the well known malevolence of his disposition and the rival claims of his injured nephew. That of Henry III. took place in a remote part of the kingdom, when a portion of the island was in the possession of the French, and the minds of the people were distracted between a fear of foreigners and a detestation of the reigning family. Not a man in the realm, therefore, could remember so grand a spectacle as the coronation of Edward and the beautiful Eleanora of Castile.

When the crown was placed upon their heads by the Archbishop of Canterbury, a murmur of joy arose from the assembled throngs; but when the herald stood forth and proclaimed an *indemnity* to all those who had been engaged in the civil commotions of the former reign, and the repeal of the cruel statutes, that had made so many worthy citizens outlaws and aliens in the sight of their English homes, the enraptured multitude made the welkin ring with shouts of—Long live King Edward!—Long live our gracious Queen Eleanora!

Tears dimmed the beautiful eyes of the gratified queen, for she read in the enthusiastic acclamations with which the act of Indemnity was received, an incontrovertible testimony to the wisdom of the course she had so warmly advocated, and an earnest of the peace which this display of her husband's magnanimity would secure to his realm.

Foremost among those who hailed his accession, Edward discerned the commanding figure of the outlaw, who had so long and so successfully eluded his search. No sooner was he seated upon his throne, than he commissioned the lord-high *seneschal* to cause the mysterious personage to approach. As he came forward, and knelt at the monarch's feet, Eleanora recognized the tall knight to whom she owed her own life and her husband's liberty, and heard him with more pleasure than surprise announced as Dermot de la Clare.

"Rise, noble Clare!" exclaimed Edward, "to thee thy monarch owes his life and the security of his realm, and the honours and titles of thy house are henceforth restored, to which we add the forfeited manors of Leicester, not more a recompense for thy knightly service than a guerdon for the sweet affection of thy lovely daughter." Scarcely had Earl Dermot retired among the nobles, who crowded around him with words of congratulation, when the monarch summoned Henry de Courtenay, and, in consideration of his services in the holy wars, created him Earl of Devon—whispering aside to the conscious noble, "Our gracious queen, who excelleth in charity, will give thee pity and dole of that which she hath in royal keeping, and for which thou wilt doubtless be more grateful than for all the lands of which we have this day made thee lord."

Other faithful vassals of the crown were rewarded, and then the joyous multitude adjourned to the feasting and games, with which the day was closed; and the marriage of Eva and Sir Henry, which took place the following day, added another fête to the coronation festivities.

Among the various disorders to which the kingdom had fallen a prey during the weak and uncertain rule of Henry III., none excited more universal dissatisfaction, than the adulteration of the coin. As the Jews were the principal money-lenders in the kingdom all embarrassments of this kind, were by common consent attributed to their characteristic avarice.

Edward's crusade to the Holy Land, had not softened his prejudices towards this people, who, more than the *infidels* poured contempt upon the rites of Christianity. In his zeal for the public welfare he proscribed the obnoxious race and confiscated their estates to the crown, and banished no less than fifteen thousand valuable inhabitants from the kingdom. Notwithstanding these rigorous measures he still retained in his employ certain of the hated sect to assist in the correction of the currency.

The trivial circumstance of a change in the form of the penny gave rise to some of the most important occurrences that transpired during his eventful reign.

The Welsh, deriving their ancestry from the early Britons, placed the most implicit confidence in the prophecies of Merlin, which in an oracular manner set forth the destiny of the nation. One of these half-forgotten traditions, asserted that when the English penny should become round, a prince, born in Wales, should be the acknowledged king of the whole British island. No sooner, therefore, had the new coin begun to circulate west of the Menai, than the bards commenced to ring their changes upon the mysterious circumstance, and to inflate the minds of their countrymen with the hopes of conquest. The successes of Llewellyn, their prince, in reconquering all the territory that had been wrested from them by the Normans, gave great encouragement to their ambition.

Not availing himself of the act of indemnity the Welsh prince still maintained his allegiance to the party of the Montforts, and was plotting with the remaining adherents of that powerful faction for assistance from France. To intercept these hostile communications, Edward ordered his fleet into the channel under the command of Earl Dermot de la Clare, both to testify a regard for the Irish noble, and a confidence in his abilities. De Courtenay was residing with his bride at Exeter, when he received intelligence that the Earl of Clare was on his way to pay them a visit, and the following day Eva welcomed her father to her new home. The earl was accompanied by a lady whom he intrusted to his daughter's care, desiring that she might be kept in safety till Edward's pleasure concerning her should be known.

At first the fair captive was inconsolable, but she at length found some alleviation of her grief in recounting her eventful history in the sympathizing ear of Eva, now Marchioness of Devon. The Lady Eleanora was the only daughter of Simon de Montfort, and inherited the firm and relentless characteristics of her house, which the sedulous instructions of her mother Eleanor Plantagenet had somewhat softened and subdued. Her brother Guy, having gained absolution from the terrible malediction of the church, had sought to carry out his plans of vengeance by making an alliance with the Welsh, and to cement the treaty, he had consented to bestow his sister upon Llewellyn, and the young lady was on her way to meet her bridegroom when her vessel was intercepted, and herself made prisoner by Earl Clare.

Her position as the prospective Queen of Wales more than the enmity of her brother, made her fear the severity of her cousin, the King of England, but Eva assured her that the sentiments of Edward were characterized by the most generous chivalry, and that no feelings of malice or revenge could actuate him to any ungallant procedure against her. Notwithstanding the confidence with which Eva made this asseveration, the fair bride of Llewellyn listened with a faint smile of incredulity, and answered with a sigh, "Ah! lady, the poor daughter of de Montfort covets thine ignorance of the dark passions that rankle in the human breast!" "Thy fair young face gives little evidence of experience in worldly ills," returned Eva, with some surprise.

"Events, not years, confer experience," replied Elin, "and young as I am, I have marked cherished resentment ripen into deadly enmity. The unjust aspersion of Henry III. wrought upon the mind of my father, till it well nigh ruined the broad realm of England. Thou canst never know the bitter sorrow that weighed upon my mother's heart during all the cruel strife between her husband and her brother. I well remember," said the agitated girl, proceeding impetuously with her sad reminiscences, "the fatal day of Evesham—how, chilled with fear at my mother's agony, I laid aside my childish sports and crept cowering to a corner of her apartment in Kenilworth castle, while she paced the floor beseeching heaven alternately to spare her husband and save her brother. O! it was terrible," added she, pressing her hands upon her eyes, while the tears gushed between her fingers, "when my brother Guy rushed in with the tidings of our father's defeat and death, and took his awful oath of vengeance."

"Speak not of it," exclaimed Eva, shuddering in her turn at the recollection of the murder of young Henry, and the subsequent anathema pronounced upon Sir Guy.

"It is little pleasure to recall these dreadful scenes," said Elin, gloomily, "but thou mayst learn from my brief history how little hope I have in one who aspires to power or has aught to revenge."

"But her gracious majesty Queen Eleanora," said Eva, "will delight to soothe thy sorrows, and the sweet companionship of her daughters will win thee to happier thoughts."

"Nay, sweet lady, think me not ungrateful that I cannot trust thy kind presages. Whether it be a retribution, I know not, but since my grandsire's crusade against the Albigeois, evil has been the lot of our house. Hope, that seems ever to light the pathway of the young, hath never smiled on me."

This despondency continued to depress the mind of the captive during all the period of her residence at Exeter, nor could Eva's ingenuity in devising schemes for her diversion, nor hopeful predictions concerning her future happiness with Llewellyn lure her to happier thoughts. But the courteous manner of Edward, when he came to receive his cousin and conduct her to Windsor, confirmed these promises; and the unaffected kindness of Eleanora, while it soothed her afflictions, had the effect to awaken some degree of confidence in the mind of the despairing maiden. The capture of his bride infuriated Llewellyn beyond all bounds, and led him to invade England with the fiercest valour. His efforts were repulsed by the gallant conduct of the troops under the command of the Earl of Devon, and after four years of fruitless endeavour he consented to the required homage, and came to Worcester to claim his bride.

The cherishing sympathy of Eleanora had not been lost upon the heart of her stricken ward, and these years of tranquillity, the first the orphan Elin had enjoyed, so enhanced to her mind the blessings of peaceful security that she steadfastly refused to fulfil her engagement with Llewellyn, without his solemn pledge of continued amity to the English nation. When the bridegroom finding all other expedients in vain consented to the required homage, the King of England gave away his fair kinswoman with his own hand, and Eleanora supported the bride at the altar and presided at the nuptial feast with the affability and grace so peculiarly her own.

The Prince and Princess of Wales then accompanied their suzerains to London and performed the stipulated ceremony, the Snowdon barons looking on fiercely the while, with the air of warriors who were resigning their ancient rights. This discontent gave rise to various murmurings. They disdained the English bread, they were disgusted with the milk of stall-fed kine, they detested the acridity of the London porter, and they pined for the sparkling mead concocted from the honeyed sweets gathered from their own breezy hills. They saw that their national costume and dialect conferred an uncomfortable notoriety upon them, and they more than suspected that they were the objects of jeering contempt.

They therefore endured with great impatience the protracted entertainments with which Edward honoured his guests, and finally left their uncomfortable quarters murmuring with stifled imprecations, "We will never more visit Islington except as Conquerors." The unremitting influence of Elin, notwithstanding, counteracted the complaints of the malcontents, and Llewellyn religiously maintained friendly relations with England during her brief life. This interval of uninterrupted peace was employed by Eleanora in prompting her husband to measures for the public good, and England long enjoyed through the wise administration of her beneficent sovereign a respite from those evils under which the nation had groaned since the Norman conquest.

By a royal patent Edward erected boroughs within the demesne lands and conferred upon them liberty of trade, and profiting by the example of Leicester, permitted them to send representatives to parliament, which was the true epoch of the House of Commons—the first dawn of popular government in England. The lower or more industrious orders of the state were thus encouraged and protected, and an interest in the commonwealth diffused through all the ranks of society.

CHAPTER 9: CONQUEST OF WALES

The death of Joanna, mother of Eleanora, leaving the domains of Ponthieu and Aumerle, made it necessary for the king and queen to visit France, to do homage to Philip the Bold for their new possessions. They passed several months on the continent ordering the affairs of their feudaltories, but their return was hastened by tidings of fresh disturbances in Wales.

On her arrival at Windsor her daughter, Joanna of Acre, presented the queen with a letter which she said had been brought to the castle by a strange-looking priest who refused for some time to give it into any hand save that of Eleanora, but who was finally persuaded to intrust the precious document to herself on her promise to deliver in person to her mother. The letter was from Elin the Princess of Wales. It read as follows:—

To my gracious sovereign Lady Eleanora of England the wife of Llewellyn sendeth love and greeting.

I had hoped once more to see the face of my noble mistress, and to visit the scenes hallowed by the first happy hours of my sad life. I had thought to crave thy blessing on my lovely infant, for my lord had promised that on the return of spring we should be conveyed to England, and this hath cheered me through the weary hours of sickness and languishing when my heart hath pined for the sweet communion which I sometimes enjoyed in the castle at Windsor.

But the hills are already changing under the softening airs of spring, and my step is more feeble and my breath more faint, and I no longer indulge the anticipation of thanking thy goodness for the pleasant thoughts with which thy holy counsels hath blessed my memory. But I am resigned to die! and I know that before the flowers come forth my sad heart will find rest in the grave. One anxiety alone disturbs the serenity of my few remaining days.

Already my little Guendoline returns her mother's smile. Who will cherish her infant years and guide her youthful footsteps to those fountains of peace which the light of thine example hath so lately revealed to my erring sight?

Struggling with weakness and pain, thy dying Elin pens this last earnest prayer. Let the damsel abide with thee. Let her be nurtured in the practice of those gentle virtues which her obdurate race have abjured.

Commend me to Edward, our sovereign, and those fair daughters that cluster round thy board and gladden thy life with their smiles. Again let me beg a place in thy heart for my orphan child, and oh! remember in thy prayer the soul of the exile, who from thy lips first learned to hope in the mercy of Heaven.

The letter bore the date of March, and it was now early June, and to Eleanora's anxious inquiries for further tidings concerning the lady Elin and her child no answer could be given. The king however had better sources of information. Scarcely was he recovered from the fatigue of travel when the lords were summoned in council to deliberate upon the petition of David and Rodric, brothers of Llewellyn, who had applied to the English court for assistance.

From these barons Edward learned that the Welsh prince had violated the promise made to his princess on her death-bed, of conveying their daughter to the care of Eleanora, and that stimulated by the songs of the bards and the long-smothered anger of the malcontent barons, he had resolved to break his oath of allegiance to the King of England, and had dispossessed his brothers of their inheritance as a punishment for their loyalty.

The council decided to assist David and Rodric in the recovery of their possessions, and Edward not displeased with the occasion of making an absolute conquest of the country, advanced with his army into Wales.

The English at first suffered some reverses, but in the great battle of Builth, Llewellyn was slain, his forces put to flight, and the gold coronet taken from his head was offered by Prince Alphonso at the shrine of Edward the Confessor. But the war was not yet ended. Prince David now claiming the title of king, as the heir of his brother, assumed the command of the Welsh, and it needed the constant presence of Edward to keep down the rebellious spirit of the people. The same steadfast affection which had supported Eleanora during the tedious hours of her anxious sojourn in the wilds of Devon, and that had prompted her to brave the varied dangers of the Syrian campaign, led her now to follow her lord's fortunes through the rugged defiles and rocky fastnesses of the Welsh mountains.

For her security, Edward built and fortified the strong castle of Caernarvon, which now, after the lapse of nearly six centuries, presents the same external appearance as on the day when Queen Eleanora first entered its stupendous gateway in company with her royal lord.

The battlements with which the walls were defended, stand unchanged in their hoary strength and grandeur, and the statue of Edward I., carved to the life, still protects the entrance of the castle, and with its drawn dagger, menaces the intruder who would venture within its guarded precincts. The eagle tower yet nestles in the defences of the rocks, though the royal fledglings have deserted the comfortless eyrie of Snowdon for the softer luxuries of Windsor Castle and Hampton Court, and the oaken cradle of the second Edward, suspended by ring and staples from carved supporters, yet occupies its little nook in the secluded chamber where his infant eyes first opened on the light.

Eleanora's experience of the conquering power of love, made her solicitous to employ a Welsh attendant for her son, but such was the fear which her husband's name had inspired among the families of the fierce mountaineers that she was forced to abandon the project till accident procured for the amiable queen the domestic she needed not only, but threw into her hands the fate of Wales.

From the irregular surface of their territory the Welsh were necessarily a pastoral people, and their simple manner of life exposed them to certain defeat when the conquest of their country was steadily and prudently pursued by the well-trained warriors of England. But like the hardy sons of all mountainous districts, the Welsh seemed to inhale the spirit of liberty from the free breath of their native hills, and hunted as they were from one retreat to another, they still rallied around their ancient standard, and listened with rapture to predictions of their future greatness. Edward followed them with untiring patience through rugged defiles and rocky fastnesses till his heavy armed troops were ready to sink with fatigue.

Everywhere they found evidences of the straits to which the miserable inhabitants were reduced. Deserted hamlets, abandoned fields, and famishing animals, betokened the last extremity of suffering. It was just at nightfall when they came suddenly upon a strong body posted within the narrow precincts of a valley.

The lowing of the herds that began to suffer from the want of forage, was the first sound that attracted the attention of the English scouts, and by a circuitous path the whole detachment were conducted to a position commanding a full view of the enemy. The bivouac consisted of rude huts or booths, constructed for shelter rather than defence, in and around which sat barbarians in various attitudes of attention or repose.

The watch-fires gleamed luridly upon the wild figures that circled around them, with dark and frowning brows, while from the centre of the encampment echoed the sounds of hoarse voices, accompanied by the martial strains of music. The barbarous language made the song of the bards incomprehensible to the English, but they divined its spirit from the effect upon the rude auditors, who, at every pause in the agitating refrain, sprang to their feet, struck their spears upon their shields, and mingled their shrill voices in a responsive chorus of muttered vengeance.

In the enthusiasm which the patriotic songs awakened, Edward read the secret of the protracted resistance, and saw that the destruction of these bards would insure his conquest. The trumpets were immediately ordered to sound, and his army, wearied as they were, summoned their fainting energies and rushed to the conflict.

The Welsh, surprised in the midst of their fancied security, stood to their arms, and fought with the courage of desperation, the exhilarating strains of the bards rose to a shrill wail of agony, then sank in the voiceless silence of death.

This final strain of the national poetry, was the requiem of Welsh liberty. King David made his escape through the defile of a mountain followed by a few of his nobles, and the Earl of Devon, in attempting to cut off his retreat, surprised and captured a company of frightened females who had been lodged in the rocky fastness for greater security. With knightly courtesy he extended to his helpless captives every delicate attention that would soften the rigor of their fate.

His sympathies were especially excited by the distress of a woman of an appearance somewhat superior to her companions, who exhibited the greatest solicitude for the safety of a child that, all unconscious of the tumult, lay quietly sleeping in its cradle of twisted reeds.

331

De Courtenay approached, anxious to relieve her fears, when the nurse, expecting to be torn from her tender charge, exclaimed, in barbarous English, "Take not the princess from me! I promised the Lady Elin never to resign her save to the hands of the good Queen of England."

"Comfort thee, good woman," said the earl, kindly. "I will myself convey thee, with the babe, to Caernarvon, where thou mayest discharge thy trust by bestowing the little orphan with the royal friend of her mother." Consigning the other captives to the care of his knights, he gave the nurse in charge to his groom, and himself carefully lifting the wicker cradle with its lovely occupant to the horse before him, led the way towards the castle.

Eleanora received the daughter of Elin de Montfort with tears of tender welcome, and lavished upon the child the same affection that she bestowed upon her own infant Edward. The little cousins were nurtured together, and the nurse soon became tenderly attached to both children, and conceived an almost reverential devotion to the pious queen; and as Eleanora gave her frequent opportunities for communion with the natives of the vicinity, she lost no occasion of publishing the virtues of her mistress.

She represented that Eleanora and little Edward were scarce inferior in beauty to the Madonna and child, and that they were as good as they were beautiful; and, she added, on her own responsibility, that since the queen treated Guendoline with as much affection as though she were her own daughter, there could be no doubt that she looked upon her as the future bride of the young prince.

Meantime, Edward had prospered in his military plans. David could never collect an army sufficient to face the English in the field, being chased from hill to hill, and hunted from one retreat to another, and was finally betrayed to his enemy and sent to England.

The Snowdon barons, deprived of their leader, and aware that their princess Guendoline was in possession of the English king, and somewhat mollified by the prognostication of her future greatness, at length obeyed the summons of Edward to a conference at Caernarvon. The hardy mountaineers agreed to tender their final submission to him as lord paramount, if he would appoint them a native Welshman for their prince, who could speak neither Saxon nor French, for those barbarous languages they declared they could never understand.

Edward graciously acceded to the request, and the preliminaries being arranged he brought from the eagle tower the little Edward, assuring them that he was a native of Wales, could speak neither of the reprobated tongues, and, under the tutelage of his lovely instructress Guendoline, would doubtless soon become a proficient in Welsh. "The fierce mountaineers little expected such a ruler. They had, however, no alternative but submission, and with as good grace as they might, kissed the tiny hand which was to sway their sceptre, and vowed fealty to the babe of the faithful Eleanora."

CHAPTER 10: THE ASTRONOMER AND THE JEW.

Peace being thus happily established, King Edward transferred the residence of his queen from the rugged strength of Caernarvon to the magnificent refinements of Conway castle; where, surrounded by her ladies and children, she enjoyed, for a brief period, a repose from anxiety and care.

Here seated in a chamber of state, whose windows of stained glass opened upon a terrace, commanding a beautiful view of the varied landscape, Eleanora passed her mornings, receiving those who were honoured by being present at her *levée*, while her tire-women combed and braided the long silken tresses which shaded and adorned her serene and lovely features.

This condescension of the queen, had a most gracious and softening effect upon the rude customs of the Welsh, and the first aspirations of this semi-barbarous nation for Christian refinement, date from the period in which they felt the winning influence of her gentle manners.

But though Eleanora was thus happy in her domestic relations, blessed in the love of her subjects, and thrice blessed in the consciousness of exercising her power for the happiness of others, she did not forget the kindred ties that bound her to her native Spain.

Indeed there seems to be this peculiarity, observable in the influence of the gospel on the character, a paradox in philosophy, but a fact in Christian experience, that while it increases the intensity of the social affections, it expands the heart to the remoter relations of life, awakening a cordial response to the command, "*Thou shalt love thy neighbour as thyself.*"

For Eleanora to know that she could render assistance to another, was sufficient motive to arouse her activity; and constant habit made that an inspiring impulse, which had commenced in a rigid adherence to the requisitions of duty. When she learned, therefore, that her beloved brother Alphonso X. had been deposed by his undutiful son,

Sancho, she besought her heroic husband to undertake the difficult task of his restoration.

Edward, whose principles of government were of a very different character from those of the royal philosopher, listened somewhat reluctantly to her anxious pleadings, but at last consented to accompany her into Castile.

The royal progress was one of the utmost pomp and splendour. Their cousin Philip received them in Paris with the greatest distinction. They reposed some months among the elegancies of Bordeaux, and thence journeyed across the Pyrenees to Burgos.

The brave Sancho welcomed them to his palace with unaffected pleasure, and listened with easy good-humour to the questions and remonstrances of the queen.

"My father," said he, "is happier in the retirement of his prison, than he was ever in the administration of public affairs. In truth, he has for these last years been so occupied with the motions of Mars and Jupiter, that he has had little leisure to attend to the movements of his subjects, and, but for what seemeth my undutiful interposition, our fair Castile would have been one scene of anarchy and confusion."

"But if my brother desired the repose of private life, he had surely the right to appoint his successor," suggested Eleanora.

"Nay, concerning that, men differ in opinion," replied Sancho. "Our ancestors, the Goths, confer the crown upon the second son, in preference to the heirs of the elder brother, and by this right I reign."

"But by this right, thou takest from the prince all power," returned the queen.

"And wherefore," said Sancho, "should the word of a prince prevail against the will of the people, whose interest no king has a right to sacrifice to his ambition?"

"Certes, there is great semblance of truth in what thou sayest," added Eleanora, thoughtfully; "and much I wonder me that, while some are born to such high estate, others in heart possessed of noble feelings are doomed to perpetual servitude. My poor brain has been ofttimes sadly puzzled in this matter; but when I bethink me of the miseries fair England suffered during the rebellion of Leicester, I content myself to believe the holy writ, 'The powers that be, are ordained of God.'"

"Thy scripture well establishes my claim," cried Sancho, laughing heartily.

Eleanora sighed. "Forgettest thou, brave Sancho," said she, "that the

God who gave to thee the estate and rule of king, (since thou dost so wrest my words to prove thy usurpation,) forgettest thou that *He* hath also ordained, 'Thou shalt honour thy father?'"

"Nay, nay, my most gracious aunt, now thou accusest me beyond my desert. The wise Alphonso is not restrained from his clerkly studies, but—"

"He is in prison," interrupted Eleanora.

"It is my care," continued Sancho, "to grant him everything, but freedom to disturb my kingdom. Jews and Arabs, his chosen friends, doctors of Salerno and Salamanca, friars and priests, (though, sooth to say for them, he careth little save as they bring him mouldy manuscripts from the monasteries,) jugglers and mummers, a worthy retinue, have free access to his presence. Tomorrow thou mayest see the philosopher, surrounded by his motley courtiers, and methinks thou wilt then pronounce him as do others, either fool or madman."

King Edward, who from conversation with the nobles of Castile, no less than with Sancho, had arrived at the same conclusion with his royal nephew, made no efforts to release Alphonso from his confinement, but gladly accepted an invitation to accompany the King of Castile on an expedition against the Moors in southern Spain.

During their absence Eleanora remained in Burgos, and devoted herself to the care of her brother, for whose sanity she began to entertain serious fears. Alphonso's affection for his lovely sister so far prevailed over his excitable temperament, that he permitted her to enter his apartments at all hours without exhibiting any annoyance, and often turned aside from his abstruse studies to indulge in reminiscences of their youthful sports, and to satisfy her inquiries concerning his present pursuits.

Eleanora possessed that genial spirit which discovers something of interest in every occupation, and that exquisite tact which enabled her to insinuate a truth, even while seeming not to contradict an error; and it was soon apparent that, though the philosopher still uttered his absurdities with great complacency,—his temper became more tranquil, and his manners far more affable to all who approached him. The queen listened patiently to his tedious explanations of the motions of the planets, and exerted her utmost powers of perception to comprehend the diagrams which he contended were illustrative of the whole theory of Nature, and the great end and purpose of her solemn mysteries inscribed on the scroll of the heavens, forming an elder Scripture more authoritative than the divine oracles themselves.

"Thou seest, my sister," said the enthusiast, "that our maturity like our childhood is amused by fables: hence do the ignorant believe that this great array of worlds was formed for the contemptible purpose of revolving around our insignificant planet, and all the glittering circle of the stars made to serve no better end than to enliven a winter night."

"In truth the doctrine savours much of the arrogance of man," gently returned the queen, "and reminds one of the false systems of a monarch who considers his subjects but tributaries to his pleasure."

"False systems," returned the astronomer, apparently unheeding the point of her remark, "have disgraced the world in every age. Pythagoras approached nearest the true idea, and yet was lost in the wilderness of error."

"Heaven save us from a fate so evil," solemnly ejaculated the queen.

"The philosopher, who rejecting the dogmas of the church, listens to the voice of Nature speaking to the ear of reason, is in no danger of error," said Alphonso pompously. "Thy Mosaic Testament asserts that God created the heavens and the earth in six days; but they bear no marks of such creation. Their course is eternal. And as for appointing the glorious sun with no higher mission than to enlighten the earth, had the Almighty called me to his counsel, I would have taught Him a wiser plan of compassing day and night."

Shocked at his impiety, Eleanora calmly replied, "The Holy Word which thou despisest, directs us to 'prove all things.' How canst thou sustain such assertions?"

Alphonso, pleased with what he considered her docility, lifted a small globe, and placing it at a convenient distance from the lamp, caused it to revolve upon its axis, making her observe that the regular vicissitudes of light and darkness were produced without any change in the position of the luminary.

"At what infinite expense," said he, "would the lamp revolve around the globe to produce only the same effect, and to furnish only one world with light; while any number of globes might gyrate about the lamp without loss, save an occasional eclipse."

Struck with the simplicity and evident truth of the illustration, Eleanora gazed admiringly upon her brother, but scarcely had she essayed to frame an answer, when the conversation was interrupted by the entrance of an individual—the expression of whose countenance awoke a painful association in her mind, although in vain she tasked her memory to decide where or when she had before beheld him. His figure, though concealed by a Spanish doublet, and slightly bent with age, had evidently been once tall and commanding, and his swarthy countenance was illuminated by keen black eyes, whose quick penetrating glance, seemed at once to fathom the purposes, and divine the thoughts of those about him; and a long flowing beard, somewhat inclining to gray, imparted an air of dignity to his whole appearance. With a profound, though silent salutation to the royal pair, he crossed the apartment, and carefully laying aside his cloak, quietly seated himself at a side table covered with manuscripts, and commenced his labours; while Alphonso answered the inquiring gaze of Eleanora, by remarking, "'Tis our excellent Procida, my trusty Hebrew scribe."

"Hebrew or Arab," said Eleanora, in a low tone, "I have seen that face before."

At the sound of her voice the stranger looked up, while Eleanora placed her hands before her eyes, as if to shut out some dreadful vision.

"It cannot, cannot be," she exclaimed, "but so looked the Jew, slain at my feet on that dreadful day when I first entered London."

"My good Procida," said Alphonso, misinterpreting her emotion, "I fear me we must dispense with thy presence, since my sister is too good a Christian to look upon a Jew, save with feelings of abhorrence."

The Jew arose. "Nay, my good brother," said the queen, "forgive this weakness. I would fain speak with thy friend."

Procida came forward and stood in respectful silence waiting her commands.

"Hast ever been in London?" inquired she, earnestly regarding him.

"My noble queen recalls not then the face of Raymond Lullius, who coined *rose nobles* for her royal lord. She may, perhaps, remember the curiosity of the young Prince Alphonso, whose little hand no doubt still bears the scar of the melted metal he snatched from the crucible."

At the mention of her son, the mother's tears began to flow. "My sweet Alphonso sleeps in the tomb of his ancestors," replied she, when she had somewhat recovered her composure; "but I mind me of the accident, though surely 'tis another scene that hath impressed thy features on my memory."

"Your majesty refers to the slaughter of the Jews," returned Proc-

337

ida, in a sorrowful tone, "and the victim slain at your feet was my aged father Ben-Abraham. Of all my family I alone escaped, through the timely interposition of the gallant Prince Edward."

"Ah! now I comprehend thy haste to serve my brother," interrupted Alphonso. "Thou must know, sweet sister mine," said he, turning to the queen, "that the secrets of our art are for the learned alone, but king as I am, I found it impossible to prevent my worthy Procida from leaving my court to aid the English sovereign in increasing his revenue by transmuting mercury into gold."

"It is then true that metals can be thus transmuted," said Eleanora, with an incredulous smile.

The alchemists exchanged glances of intelligence, but Alphonso, remembering her ready appreciation of his astronomical theory, answered Procida's hesitating look, with "Nay, 'tis but for once—our sister is an earnest seeker of truth, and if she comprehend will not betray our secret." Thus saying, Alphonso threw open a door and conducted the queen, followed by Procida, into a small laboratory filled with all the mysterious appurtenances of his art. The learned doctor busied himself in clearing a space in the centre of the apartment and arranging in a circle sundry jars and a brazier, while the philosopher king, opening a cabinet, took thence some dried and withered sea-weed, which he threw into the brazier and kindled into a flame. The blazing kelp was soon reduced to ashes, which Procida carefully gathered into an old empty crucible, and set before the queen. Alphonso advancing took up the crucible, saying, "What seest thou, my sister?"

"A dull, gray powder," she replied.

He then placed a tube from one of the jars within the crucible, and bidding her regard it attentively, submitted it to a chemical process which she did not understand, repeating his question.

"I now see," replied Eleanora, with astonishment, "the dull powder transformed into little shining globules like silver."

"Thou mayst take them in thine hand," said the philosopher, after a pause; "they will not harm thee."

With some timidity the wondering queen received the metallic drops, almost fearing that her brother was a necromancer as the priests affirmed.

"Canst judge if it be a metal?" said Alphonso, enjoying her confusion.

"My sight and touch assure me of the fact. Yet whence—"

"Is it not a miracle," interrupted the philosopher, laughing, "more real than thy fancied transubstantiation?"

A frown gathered on the serene brow of the lovely queen—but commiserating his impiety as sincerely as he pitied her ignorance, with forced gayety she replied, "Nay, heaven works not miracles by the hands of such unbelievers as thou. I fear me lest evil spirits have aided thee, as they did the Egyptians with their enchantments;" and she handed the globules to the philosopher.

"Keep them safely until the morrow," said he, "they may form the basis of another experiment."

As the Queen of England left the prison, Procida followed her and craved an audience.

CHAPTER 11: THE JEWESS

The conference between the queen and Procida was not limited to one audience. Day after day he sought her presence, under various pretexts—some unimportant business, some message from Alphonso—and each time he lingered as if anxious to prolong the interview; till at length his strange manner convinced Eleanora that something more momentous than philosophical researches detained him in Castile.

When the mind is agitated upon any particular subject, fancy connects every mysterious appearance with the prevailing thought; and the lovely queen became impressed with the idea that some impending danger threatened her royal brother.

She therefore strove to win the confidence of Procida, and encouraged him to confide his secret to her keeping.

"Is there aught," said she, "of interest to thyself or others in which I can aid thee?" finding that his anxiety and hesitation seemed rather to increase than diminish.

"Most gracious sovereign," returned Procida, apologetically, "the despised outcasts of Israel have little hope to enlist the sympathies of Christians in their behalf."

"Nay," replied the queen, "thou forgettest that our gospel saith, God hath made of one blood all the nations of the earth."

"And if I have forgotten it," said Procida bitterly, "it is because the practice of the church agreeth not with the precept."

"It is true," returned Eleanora, with a sigh, "that our lives exhibit too little the holy influence of the faith we profess: but tell me, how can the wife of Edward serve the alchemist?"

"Noble queen," said Procida, speaking earnestly and with great agitation, "thou knowest not the peril in which thy generosity may involve thee."

"Speak, and fear not," reiterated she, "Eleanora fears no evil in the practice of kindness."

Fixing his keen eyes upon her face, as if to detect every emotion which his words might awaken, the Jew replied bitterly, "Procida for his attachment to the noble house of Swabia, is proscribed and hunted from Sicily, his daughter, a Jewess, can scarce claim the protection of law; and concealed as she is in the suburbs of Burgos, her beauty has already attracted the curiosity of those from whom her father cannot defend her. Did I dare claim so great a boon I would beg a place for her among thy maidens."

Eleanora paused. The prejudice against the Jews was so intense as to affect even her upright mind; and the scandal it might bring upon the royal household to enrol an unbeliever among its inmates, startled her apprehensions: but the father stood before her with the air of one who had intrusted his last treasure to her keeping, and she could not find it in her heart to crush his confidence in her generosity.

"Bring thy daughter hither," added she, thoughtfully, "with me she shall be safe."

"The blessing of him that is ready to perish, rest upon thee," said the scholar, fervently, as he left her presence.

When the Queen of England next visited the apartments of her brother, she was accompanied by a young girl of such surpassing loveliness as to attract the attention of the philosopher himself. Her features were of that perfect form generally described as Grecian, while her dark hair and soft black eyes, suggested the idea of a brunette; but the fairness of her complexion and the brilliant colour of her cheek, that varied with every emotion, gave a character of exquisite delicacy and sensibility to her countenance.

"Does thy realm of England abound in such comely damsels?" inquired Alphonso, while Agnes blushed at the king's encomium.

"England may rival Spain in the beauty of her daughters," answered Eleanora, evasively. "My gentle Agnes is curious like her mistress to learn the wonders of thy art: hence do we crave thine indulgence to pass some weary hours of my lord's absence among thy folios."

"Thou art ever welcome," returned Alphonso, benignantly, "and this young disciple shall receive the benefit of serving so good a mistress."

"I have pondered much," said the queen, who had been for some

340

time attentively regarding the care-worn lineaments of his face, "upon thy theory of the planets. The globe moved around the lamp because thou didst bear it in thine hand. By what power is our earth carried around the sun?"

"There is some invisible influence which retains it with its sister-orbs in the eternal round, but the subtle essence has thus far eluded my investigations," replied Alphonso.

"Thou believest then, my brother," said Eleanora, in her gentlest tone, "in a power whose existence thou canst not demonstrate by thy 'Tables' or diograms?"

"Verily, such a power is a matter of *necessity*," returned the monarch.

"And thy unlearned sister," replied the queen, hesitating, "finds the same *necessity* to believe in a God, whose existence she can demonstrate only by the contemplation of his glorious works."

"It is well for the ignorant to repose in this idea," replied Alphonso, "and it may perchance restrain the wicked from his misdeeds, to believe that an ever-present Intelligence regards his actions."

"And it may comfort the sorrowing," said Eleanora, "to feel that this Infinite Power can satisfy the needs of the human soul."

"Hast thou brought the metal I gave thee?" said Alphonso, abruptly changing the conversation.

"I have it in my gypsire," said she, unclasping the bag and unfolding the paper—"Lo! my brother, what a transformation is here," exclaimed the queen, in amazement. "Thy silver has again become ashes."

"Grieve not," said the alchemist, with an air of superior wisdom, "Science will achieve new wonders with these dull atoms."

He now placed the powder in the crucible as before, and taking from a shelf what seemed a fragment of rock, pulverized it to a like powder, and mingled both in the crucible, which he placed upon the brazier and subjected it to a most intense heat.

"What dost thou now observe?" said the alchemist.

"A melted glowing mass of a ruby colour," said Eleanora, with great interest.

Taking a small rod in his hand he lifted the adhering particles, and drew them into thin, fine hair, like threads of a shining whiteness, which he presented to Agnes, saying, with a smile, "I will bestow these frail crystals upon thee, fair one; perchance thou mayst preserve them in memory of the mad philosopher."

Every day the Queen of England became more interested in the society of her lovely ward, whose sprightliness was tempered by a sweetness, and a delicate discrimination, that never gave offence. It was gratifying to observe, in a fancy cultivated by the poetic legends of the South, and stored with the splendid fictions of Arabian romance, an ardent love of *truth*, and a strict adherence to its dictates; and Eleanora saw with pleasure that her most playful and entertaining sallies, though sometimes pointed at the peculiarities of those around her, never betrayed ill-humour, nor degenerated into sarcasm. Her beauty and gayety forcibly recalled the image of Eva; but the reliance which the obedient Jewess inspired, was in strong contrast to the anxiety ever awakened by the lovely, but volatile daughter of Clare.

The charming Agnes not only amused the queen with her vivacity, but afforded her a sense of repose, by her amiable observance of every admonition, and her evident desire to regard the wishes no less than the positive commands of her royal benefactress, and especially did she win the love of the mother by her graceful attentions to the infant Princess Beatrice.

While Agnes was actuated by the most dutiful affection to her father, she seemed by a happy trustfulness to escape participation in that gloom and care which daily deepened upon the clouded brow of the Sicilian.

Desirous to relieve what she deemed his apprehensions for the future welfare of his daughter, the queen took occasion, upon one of his visits, to assure him of her increasing attachment to her lovely charge.

"Thy generous interest in the despised exile softens my bitter fate," said he, "but could the unhappy Procida enlist the influence of England's gracious sovereign in the great project that preys upon his being, he would feel that he had not lived in vain."

"My lord the king is ever ready to assist the unfortunate," said Eleanora, encouragingly, "and is free from those prejudices which embarrass weaker minds. If thou deemest it proper to reveal thy secret, his queen will herself endeavour to redress thy wrongs."

"Procida seeks not the redress of a personal affront, nor restoration to his island home; my project is," said the Sicilian, drawing near the queen, and speaking in a low tone of terrible emphasis, "*revenge!*— death to the infamous Charles d'Anjou!"

The startled Eleanora essayed no reply, but gazed in mute terror at the dark and malignant face of the conspirator.

"Yes," continued he, his tall figure dilating with long repressed and cherished passion, "I will rouse all Europe with the wrongs of the

342

noble house of Suabia."

"I know," said the queen, the words faintly struggling through her white lips, "the woes inflicted upon our cousins of Suabia by the relentless fury of the Guelphs, but I dare not assume the office of their judge. It is written, '*Vengeance is mine, I will repay it, saith the Lord.*'"

"Aye, verily," replied the Jew, fiercely, "but how does the Lord repay vengeance? Is it not by the hand of man he brings retribution upon the guilty? Did he not commission the sword to cut off the Canaanites, the Midianites, the Assyrians, and those who vexed his people in every age? Who can say he hath not inspired the heart, and nerved the arm of the proscribed and outcast Jew to execute his wrath upon the proud tyrant of Sicily?"

"*Thou*," inquired the queen. "By what title claimest *thou* allegiance to that fallen house?"

"I know," said Procida, stung by her remark, "full well I know, that your Holy Church denies to the son of Abraham all the tender ties that bind the lord to his vassal, or the vassal to his lord. He may have neither house nor land, he may not dwell in Jerusalem the city of his fathers, or be buried in consecrated ground. His possessions become the spoil of the tyrant, his innocent offspring the victims of brutal passion; and yet your priests say,—Be meek—Be patient—Obey the precepts of that gospel which we trample under foot."

He paused, struck by the compassionate gaze of Eleanora, who, for the first time, comprehended the hopeless misery of the hapless race.

"Thy pardon, noble queen," said Procida, softened by her tender pity." Were there more like thee, 'twere easier for the Jew to embrace the faith of the Nazarene. Thou didst inquire by what tie I followed the changing fortunes of Hohenstaufen." In a gentler tone he continued—

"The Jew loves gold. Loves he aught else? Yea, to the death his friend. The Emperor Frederic was free from the chains of superstition. Christian, Saracen, or Jew, found equal favour in his eye, and learning and genius not less than military prowess were rewarded with titles and lands.

"Know me, then, royal lady, miserable and destitute as I appear, as favourite physician of the emperor, created by him Count de Procida, lord of the fairest island in the Bay of Naples."

Chapter 12: The Fate of the House of Suabia

The soft climate of the south, and the rich and varied scenery upon the banks of the Arlanzon, invited Eleanora to long walks in the suburbs of Burgos: and she found the greatest delight in watching the changing foliage, which announced the approach of the mellow autumn.

Her recent interviews with the philosopher had given a new direction to her thoughts. She experienced a pleasure before unknown in studying the various aspects of nature, and contemplating the subtle arrangement by which all these beautiful phenomena were produced. New proofs of an All-creative Intelligence were daily forced upon her with peculiar distinctness, and her mind was thus fortified against the cold, insinuating doubts, with which her brother continually assailed her faith. Often she became so lost in reflection as to be insensible to all external circumstances, and her ladies, loosed from the restraints of court etiquette, revelled in the unwonted freedom of these rural strolls. Eleanora was often lured from her speculative abstraction by the sportive gayety of their amusements, and she saw with benevolent pleasure the ready tact with which the young Jewess avoided every inquiry that might lead to a discovery of her nation or position, without in the least compromising her truthfulness or transgressing the rules of courtesy.

During one of these rambles, a mendicant of the order of St. Francis approached the queen, and asked an alms. The smoothly-shaven chin of the monk, closely clipped hair, and unsandalled feet, at first completely imposed upon her credulity, but his voice at once betrayed Procida.

With a troubled look she gave him a few *denier*, as if desirous to escape all parley. But the monk lingered; and after a pause, hesitatingly remarked in a low tone, "I am about to leave Burgos, and I would fain confer with the queen before my departure."

"But wherefore the monkish habit? Has the Jew resolved to do penance for his sins?" inquired Eleanora.

"Nay," replied Procida, evasively, "if my gracious mistress will grant me an audience, I will unfold to her the purpose that hath moved me to this disguise."

"I cannot tell," replied the queen, with a tone of unwonted reproach, "if it be desirable to entrust thy plans to my keeping, since I may not encourage deceit, and I would not that thy Agnes, so innocent of guile, should learn that her father, for some dark purpose, has assumed the garb he abhors."

Tears glistened in the eyes of Procida, as he replied, "Thou sayest well and wisely. The sweet child knoweth not more of the secret

344

schemes of her father, than do the angels of the dark deeds of fiends. But—"

"I hear the voice of my maidens," exclaimed the queen impatiently, "expose not thyself to their observation."

"*Benedicite*," murmured the counterfeit priest, turning away to avoid the scrutiny of the approaching group.

But Procida was so determined to secure the approbation of the queen, that the following day he craved an audience at the palace.

"My royal mistress," said he, "must permit me once more, to plead the rights of the illustrious house of Suabia, before I depart on my pilgrimage, that if I never return, she may justify my acts in the eyes of my daughter."

"Speak," said Eleanora, moved by the sorrowful earnestness of his manner.

"My royal master Frederic," began the Jew, "had little cause to love the church. Hated by the pope, for that with a strong arm he claimed his hereditary possessions in Italy, he was excommunicated for refusing the pilgrimage, and again cursed for fulfilling his vow; and had not the honest pagan, Melech Camel, been more his friend than the Christian troops by whom he was surrounded, he would have perished by treason in the Holy City itself.

"Freed from superstition, he looked upon all religions as formed to impose upon the vulgar; and it was through his instructions, that I learned the policy of conforming to the prejudices of mankind, and now avail myself of the privileges of an order, who wander everywhere, and are everywhere well received.

"The emperor, like thy brother Alphonso, was a man of science. He opened schools in Sicily, and maintained poor scholars from his own purse, and by every means promoted the welfare of his subjects; but he could not escape the toils spread around him by his great enemy the church."

As he said these words the queen beheld in his eyes the same vengeful fire that once had before so startled and shocked her.

"Thy pardon, sovereign lady," said he, recollecting himself, "but the wrongs of the master have well-nigh maddened the brain of the servant.

"His own son Henry, wrought upon by the malicious representations of the pope, revolted, and his beautiful boy Enzio, pined away his young life in the prison of Bologna. The great Frederic died; and his wretched Procida vowed to avenge him upon his murderers." He paused a moment overcome by his emotions, and then continued, "There yet remained Conrad and Manfred: the former, only son of the Queen of Jerusalem, and the latter, illegitimate offspring of a Saracen woman. Conrad passed into Italy to claim his inheritance, only to be poisoned by the pope; while Manfred, calling around him the friends of his mother, battled for his father's strongholds and treasures. He was brave, generous and noble. He would have made peace even with his enemy, but the tyrant d'Anjou spurned his overtures, and insultingly replied to the messenger, 'Go tell the Sultan of Nocera, that I desire war only, and this very day I will send him to hell, or he shall send me to Paradise.'

"He prepared for the conflict. As he fastened on his helmet it twice slipped from his grasp. 'It is the hand of God,' was his exclamation, and with a presentiment of his fall, he hurried to the fight. I stood by his side in the bloody battle of Benevento, and we made a holocaust of our enemies; but a fatal spear pierced his brain! The implacable d'Anjou would have the poor excommunicated corpse remain unburied, but the French soldiers, less barbarous than their master, brought each a stone, and so reared him a tomb."

"Tell me no more horrors," exclaimed the queen, with a look of painful emotion.

"Ah! lady," said the artful Procida, sadly, satisfied that his recital had so moved his royal auditor, "thou art grieved at the very *hearing* of these atrocities, but bethink thee of the misery of the poor daughter of Frederic, wife of the Duke of Saxony. When the family fell, the duke repented of his alliance with the house of Suabia. From cold neglect and scorn, he proceeded to violence—he brutally struck her. She, unhappy woman, thinking he sought her life, endeavoured to escape. The castle rose upon a rock overhanging the Elbe. A faithful servant kept a boat upon the river, and by a rope, she could let herself down the precipitous descent.

"An agonizing thought stayed her footsteps. Her only son lay asleep in the cradle. She would once more fold him to her breast. She would imprint her last kiss upon his cheek. With a maddening pang she closed her teeth in the tender flesh, and fled, pursued by the screams of her wounded child. The treacherous rope eluded her grasp, and the frantic mother fell, another victim from the doomed race of Hohenstaufen.

"The little Corradino, who should have been King of Jerusalem, had also a mother, tender and fond, who would fain have detained him from funereal Italy, where all his family had found a sepulchre; but ere he attained the age of manhood the Ghibelline cities called to him for aid, and no entreaties could withhold the valiant youth. Accompanied by his dearest friend, Frederic of Austria, and a band of knights, he passed the Alps to claim his inheritance. There was a battle—there was a defeat—there was a prisoner—The Vicar of Christ, showed he mercy? He wrote to d'Anjou, 'Corradino's life is Charles's death.' Judges were named, a strange and unheard-of proceeding; but of these some defended Corradino, and the rest remained silent.

"One alone, found him guilty, and began to read his sentence upon the scaffold. But outraged nature asserted her rights, d'Anjou's own son-in-law leaped upon the scaffold and slew the inhuman judge with one stroke of his sword, exclaiming, ''Tis not for a wretch like thee to condemn to death so noble and gentle a lord.' But the execution proceeded. I stood among the spectators a shaven priest, *honouring the decrees of the church*! I heard the piteous exclamation of the hapless youth, 'Oh my mother, what sad news will bring thee of thy son.'

"His eye caught mine, he slipped a ring from his finger, and threw it into the crowd. I seized the precious jewel, and renewed my vow of vengeance. The faithful Frederic of Austria stood by his side, and was the first to receive the fatal stroke. Corradino caught the bleeding head, as it fell, pressed his own upon the quivering lips, and perished like his friend. 'Lovely and pleasant in their lives, in death they were not divided.'"

Tears for a moment quenched the fire in the old man's eyes, and Eleanora wept in sympathy. "And Enzio—?" she said, mournfully.

"Enzio yet languished in prison, the delicate boy, the idol of his imperial father. I found my way to Bologna, gold bribed his guard. An empty wine-cask was at hand, I enclosed him therein, and brought him safely to the gates. A single lock of hair betrayed my secret. 'Ha!' exclaimed the sentinel, ''tis only King Enzio has such beautiful fair hair.' I escaped with difficulty, but the boy was slain."

"Lives there not one of all the princely house?" inquired the queen.

"Frederic the Bitten lives, the deadly enemy of his father, and the daughter of Manfred is the wife of the Prince of Arragon. To her I carry the ring. A Saracen servant of the emperor ascribes to it magic virtues. It shall be the talisman to bind Europe in a league against the infamous d'Anjou."

"My brother! knows he of thy purpose?" inquired Eleanora, apprehensively.

"I entered Castile to secure his assistance, and devoted myself to the practice of alchemy, to gain his confidence; but the philosopher is too intent upon the science of dull atoms to mingle in political strife."

"Thank heaven! that his studies keep him innocent of human blood," ejaculated the queen. "Wouldst ought with me?" inquired she, after a pause, observing that the Jew remained silent with his eyes fixed upon her.

"Let my gracious queen pardon her servant, that he hath so long detained her with his tale of horror. Something I would add concerning my sweet Agnes. Call her not a Jewess. Her father hath long since abjured the burdensome rites of Judaism, and her mother—'tis enough to say that she resembled the Queen of England. Though I trust not in the pious fables of the priests, they seemed to charm her gentle spirit into peace. Let Agnes, therefore, I pray thee, be instructed in her mother's faith."

"Thy wishes shall be strictly regarded," replied Eleanora, "and may the same peace thou covetest for thy daughter, yet find its way to thy own unquiet breast."

CHAPTER 13: TRANSLATION OF THE BIBLE

Each time the queen visited the laboratory of Alphonso, he made her acquainted with some new fact in philosophy, or some new device of alchemy, which awakened curiosity and gave rise to inquiry. The Spanish king, having made some discoveries in advance of the age, had fallen into the popular error of philosophers, that of repudiating all pre-established doctrines and maxims. Having laid down the theory that matter was eternal, and all external appearances the result of natural change, he was at infinite pains to account for all phenomena so as not to conflict with this proposition. The unbiased mind of Eleanora often detected in his assertions a vagueness of expression which passed for argument, but which evidently imposed less upon his auditors than upon himself.

"Nature," said he, "arranges her work in circles: hence is the sky a dome, the earth a convex ball, and each minute atom of a globular form. The seasons roll their perpetual round, and as a ring hath neither beginning nor end, so must the material universe be eternal. The acorn groweth into the oak, and the oak again produceth the acorn; all outward manifestations are but parts in the great universal machine."

348

Eleanora, who had been attentively regarding an ingenious invention of the king's, interrupted this tirade, by remarking, "A few months before I left England, I visited the cell of Friar Bacon, in Oxford. But I saw nothing in his laboratory so curious and wonderful as this work of my brother's."

The philosopher, flattered with the encomium, turned at once to exhibit the design of the machine. She followed his explanation with the greatest apparent interest; and when he had finished, replied, "In all these curious arrangements, I trace the wisdom of my brother; and it is that which gives me the greatest pleasure; and when I see the beneficent purposes for which it is designed, I feel a deeper veneration for the mind that could plan so skilfully."

She took a bunch of flowers from the hand of Agnes and approached the king. "I have been observing," said she, "the curious arrangement of these frail leaves, five green supporters, five yellow petals, five slender threads, and one central spire. I have gathered thousands of them in my rambles, and the same perfect number is found in every one. It has led me to inquire if Nature be not like my brother, a mathematician."

The workings of Alphonso's face showed how closely the simple truth of this proposition had driven home. "Nature," said he, "is an active principle, whose changes neither add to, nor detract from, the original matter of the universe. The metals," continued he, seeing she was about to respond, "the metals, my philosophical sister, form the basis of everything. I have detected iron in human blood, and a lustrous substance like that thou sawest in common ashes; hence do the alchemists believe that gold, the most precious of all, is scattered through nature, as the seeds of vegetation are scattered in earth, requiring only the proper gases to develop it and make it abundant as the pebbles on the shore."

"And have these gases been able to effect the desirable changes?" inquired the queen.

"There are innumerable obstacles in the way of these momentous inquiries," said the enthusiast. "Nature resists intrusion into her arcana, and I grieve to say, that we have not yet been able to bring about a definite result. Science has achieved only the procuring of the gases, while there remains still the nicer problem—to mix them in their right proportions, at their proper temperatures; for the nascent metal is more delicate than the embryo plant, and an excess of heat or cold destroys like frost or blight."

"Ah, me!" said Eleanora, with a sigh; "before this great end be accomplished I fear me my brother will have passed away, and then all this toil and research will be lost."

"My sister," said Alphonso, abandoning his labours and seating himself, "thou hast unconsciously touched the thorn that rankles deepest in my breast. In nature, nothing seems made in vain; even decay produces new life, and man alone, the crowning work of all, seems made to no purpose."

"I have sometimes thought," said Eleanora, as if answering her own reflections, rather than replying to her brother's remarks, "that man might perhaps be made for the pleasure of a higher order of intelligence, as the lower orders of creation seem formed for our gratification, and that all our miseries spring from an attempt to thwart this plan."

"If thy thought be not the true solution of man's destiny, I know not what end he serves in the great scheme of existence," returned Alphonso, sadly; "I have passed through various vicissitudes of life, from the greatness of earthly state to the poverty of a prison, and I have derived more pleasure from the achievements of science than from all my hereditary honours. And yet even these do not satisfy the longings of my nature."

"The scripture teaches us, that the superior intelligences find delight in benefitting mortals; and acting upon this hint the good have taught us, that to be blest ourselves we must seek to bless others," said Eleanora.

"True," replied the philosopher, breaking out once more into his old enthusiasm, "I have sometimes found alleviation from the weariness of my thoughts in the reflection, that the sciences in which I am engaged will one day exercise a wider and more perfect control over the destiny of the human race, than all the military orders backed by the sanction of ecclesiastical decrees. Science will open the door to Art; and her triumphant offspring, in a train of skilful inventions, shall pass on through long ages, breaking down the stern barriers of kingdoms, and uniting mankind in a common interest; war shall give place to useful Labour, and Science abrogating labour in its turn, shall satisfy the wants of the human race, accomplishing by a touch that which requires the might of thousands. Men shall then have leisure to perform the rites that lift the veil of Isis, and perhaps find means to *question* Nature even in the innermost recesses of her temple."

"Oh! life! life!" said the philosopher, in an accent of despair, "why art thou so brief? Why must I die without discovering the sublime agencies?"

Eleanora waited in compassionate silence till her brother resumed in a calmer tone, "Think me not mad, my sister. If the feeble attempts of an imprisoned king, and a cloistered friar, can produce the wondrous results of which thou hast been witness, what shall the end be, when men free to pursue these investigations shall win the rich guerdon of fame and pecuniary reward? Thou hast heard, perchance, of the magician Albertus Magnus, who constructed a human figure, which performed the office of a servant; and of the stupid priest Thomas Aquinas, who, alarmed by the appearance of the automaton which opened the door and ushered him in with ceremonious obeisance, destroyed with one blow the work of years."

"I can forgive his terror," said Eleanora, "for I well remember my own affright, when the brazen head contrived by Friar Bacon, rolled along on the table towards me, and uttered '*pax vobiscum*' with startling distinctness."

"Albertus Magnus performed a still more astonishing work," continued Alphonso. "At a banquet which he gave in the garden of his cloister, in the depth of winter, trees appeared covered with leaves and flowers, which vanished as if by enchantment, when the guests rose to depart."

"By what means were these wonderful works produced?" said Eleanora, with astonishment.

"With the mode of this operation I am not familiar," returned the philosopher. "Doubtless by some of the powerful agents alchemy reveals to its votaries."

"And what dost thou consider the chief agent in the universe?" said Eleanora, with the air of one inquiring after truth.

"Nature," returned the philosopher, emphatically.

"And will it pain my brother, if his unlearned sister call that great agent, who brings the flowers and leaves upon the trees in their season, by the name of God?"

"Certainly, the name can affect nothing," replied Alphonso; "and if thy priest require it of thee, sin not against him, by a more liberal view."

"And if the ignorant mass, who cannot be enlightened by thy theories, are restrained from vice by the thought that an Omniscient Being takes note of their actions, would it be well to free them from the necessary monitor?" inquired his sister.

351

"It is doubtless well for man to be deterred from evil by salutary fear, till he rises to more exalted capabilities," replied Alphonso.

"And art willing," suggested Eleanora, cautiously, "to administer to this wholesome necessity until thy divine philosophy become sufficiently perfected to renovate their character."

"What priestly scheme hast thou in hand?" said her brother, regarding her with a look of mirthful curiosity.

"Thou knowest how dearly I love the Castilian language," returned the queen, "and I would that my brother should perpetuate his fame by that which will benefit his subjects. The sight of thy Jewish scribes, suggested the thought that it would be easy for thee to procure the translation of the Scriptures into our mother tongue."

The philosopher remained silent for a moment, and then answered, "knowest thou the effect of the measures thou proposest?"

"I conceive," replied Eleanora, "that it will make thy people more virtuous and happy, and," added she, mindful of his foible, "prepare them to receive all the additional light to which thy investigations may lead."

"There will be another effect, which, perhaps thou dost not anticipate," replied Alphonso. "It will overthrow the power of the priesthood; for as now each man inquires of his confessor concerning his duty, he will, if enabled to read the boasted oracles, claim the right to interpret for himself. But thy experiment shall be tried, and now I bethink me, those learned scribes which *our benevolent son Sancho* hath permitted us to employ in transcribing the laws of Spain into the language of Castile, shall be placed under thy direction for this important work."

Thus the object for which Eleanora had so long and so patiently prayed and planned, progressed under the auspices of a man who affected to despise the truths he yet condescended to propagate; and while the philosopher gave critical attention to the correctness of the work, he found leisure to complete his Astronomical tables, and to commence the first general history of Spain.

Chapter 14: An Accident

To the monotony of a winter which the absence of the gallant cavaliers had rendered doubly tedious to the ladies of the royal household, succeeded a balmy spring. The favourite haunt of Eleanora, by the side of a noisy stream, which escaping from its icy chain among the hills, hurried away through the ravine, leaping up to clasp the overhanging rock in its wild embrace, and showering its silver spray upon the weeping boughs that fringed its bank, was again carpeted with mossy green, and draped with the bright garniture of May.

The view from this romantic spot commanded upon the right the city of Burgos, built upon the declivity of a hill, and on the left, a flowery path leading along the bank of the stream, which it crossed by a foot-bridge, wound up the cliff till it entered upon extensive plains that stretched out to the west, and afforded rich pasturage for numerous flocks which fed upon the luxuriant herbage.

One sunny afternoon, Eleanora, becoming deeply absorbed in her brother's history of the reign of their father, Ferdinand the Holy, allowed the maidens, protected by the squires and pages, to climb the prohibited cliff, which, ever since it had begun to assume its summer garb, had been a strong temptation to their footsteps. Occupied with her manuscript, she was unconscious of the lapse of time, but an occasional sound of merry voices, mingling harmoniously with the pleasant reflections that filled her mind, inspired her with a feeling of security and peace. It was nearly sunset when she finished her task, and the chill dews admonished her of the lateness of the hour; but when she raised her eyes, not a human being was within call.

The sentinel page, presuming upon his mistress' abstraction, had strolled across the bridge and ascended the hill after his companions, and the queen began to be alarmed lest the giddy party should defer their return till darkness had increased the danger of the mountain path. She gazed in every direction, and listened intently to every sound. The breeze rustled the branches, and the river gurgled on its way, but all else was still. Suddenly she perceived on the extremity of the cliff, the rocks of which sank sheer down to the water's edge, her maidens hurrying to the rescue of a lamb, that, having strayed from the care of the shepherd, startled the echoes with its piteous cries.

Agnes was foremost, and as she tripped along unconscious of the abyss which the pendant foliage concealed from her sight, and clasped the snowy foundling to her lovely breast, her slight figure bathed in the bright gold of the western sky seemed the impersonation of the angel of mercy. With a glad shout of exultation she turned to exhibit her prize, when the treacherous earth gave way beneath her feet, and with her fleecy burden she was precipitated into the stream, nearly opposite the spot which the queen, breathless with alarm, had just reached. Screams of helpless terror rent the air.

The squires ran each in a different direction, hoping to find some point from which they could descend the cliff, while the poor girl floated rapidly down the stream, rising and sinking with the swelling waves. Quick as thought, Eleanora caught up a fallen branch that lay upon the bank, and extended it for her rescue. The drowning Agnes seized it with one hand, and the queen, with great exertion, had drawn her almost to the shore, when the frail support gave way, and the mad waters again enveloped her form. As she sank, the animal struggled from her grasp and gained the bank.

"Save her! Oh God in mercy save her!" exclaimed Eleanora, clasping her hands in agony. At this moment a solitary pedestrian turning an angle in the path, approached, and attracted by the cry of distress quickened his pace. "There! there!" exclaimed the queen, pointing with a frantic gesture to the spot where Agnes had disappeared. Without a word, the stranger threw his staff and cloak upon the ground, and plunged into the stream. But the rapacious tide had borne her beyond his reach. On he swam, buffeting the waves with a strong arm, now searching the depths, and now scanning the ruffled surface, till finding every effort unavailing, he paused amid the whirling eddies, as if irresolute to seek the shore or continue the fruitless search.

At this moment a small fair hand gleamed in the water before him, vainly clasping the idle waves, as if reaching for the broken reed that had so deceived its hope. He grasped the tiny hand in his own, raised the sinking form, and, renerved by the joy of success, and the shouts of those who approached in tumultuous haste, by a few strokes of his powerful arm gained the shore. Every hand was extended for his assistance; but the stranger heeded not the proffered aid, and kneeling upon the velvet turf he pressed the senseless form in his arms, and regarded the face that lay so fixed and still upon his breast, with a mute anxiety that held his features almost as rigid as those on which he gazed.

While the balance thus trembles between life and death, every voice is dumb and every breath suppressed. The queen hangs motionless over her unconscious favourite, and the attendants stand chilled and paralyzed with doubt and dread, till a sudden gleam of satisfaction irradiates the stranger's face, and a faint sigh heaves the bosom of Agnes. "My God, I thank thee!" exclaims Eleanora, fervently, while every frame dilates with a full deep inspiration of returning hope. But the stranger, with an authoritative wave of his hand, repels all attempts to relieve him of his lovely charge.

Gently he disengages the long silken locks that cling dripping to his arm, tenderly he raises her head to catch the breeze that fans her pallid cheek, and 'tis not till returning life quivers in the languid eye-lids, that pressing his lips upon her snowy hand, he resigns her to her royal mistress. At once the maidens crowded around, some weeping and some laughing under the excess of the same emotion, eager to as-sist in the resuscitation of their lovely friend; and the squires and pag-es busied themselves in constructing a litter of boughs, upon which Agnes was conveyed to the palace.

Meanwhile, the innocent cause of the catastrophe crept shivering to the feet of the queen, who compassionately ordered one of the attendants to carry it forward; and thus while the shades of evening stretched over the landscape, the saddened party re-entered the streets of Burgos. In the general confusion the strange deliverer had disap-peared, and no one knew the direction he had taken; but the ladies had not been so much occupied with their anxiety, that they had failed to mark his noble figure and princely bearing; and Eleanora remembered that his face was one of peculiar beauty, though marked by a scar, conspicuous upon the right cheek.

CHAPTER 15: FREDERIC THE BITTEN

The slight illness that followed the accident which had so nearly proved fatal to the young Jewess, was attended by no dangerous symp-toms, and the maidens amused her convalescence with conjectures concerning her mysterious deliverer. Their pleasantries acquired new zest, when they discovered that a rosy blush, no less than an evasive reply, answered their reiterated prediction that the stranger would one day return, no longer a simple knight, but a noble lord, or powerful prince, and claim the fair hand on which he imprinted his parting kiss. Thus the weeks wore away, and the affair at length ceased to be the engrossing topic of conversation: the inhabitants of the palace resumed their accustomed employments, and indulged in their usual rambles.

Eleanora received frequent despatches of the most satisfactory character from her husband. The Christian arms had been everywhere successful against the Moors, and the King of Arragon had added to his former conquests, Majorca and Valencia, together with numerous castles and churches taken from the *infidels*. Edward proposed to re-turn by sea to Bordeaux, where he appointed his queen to meet him within the following month.

But the tidings she received from Procida, through an ambassa-dor that craved a private audience, created a more agitating interest than even the affairs of their own realm could awaken. At sight of the stranger, she recognized the saviour of Agnes, and her first impulse was to thank him for his generous exertions in behalf of her fair ward. But the grave formality of his manner checked the graceful condescension. He seemed but the bearer of a letter, and received her greeting merely as the messenger of Procida, and presuming upon his avowed character, she proceeded to peruse the despatch in his presence.

The epistle from the Jew commenced abruptly without date. It acquainted the queen with the rank and title of the bearer, "Frederic the Bitten," Duke of Saxony, grandson of the illustrious Emperor of Germany, and commended him to her courtesy as the suitor of the young Agnes. Procida alluded darkly to negotiations and plots, which he trusted would accomplish the deliverance of his country, but towards the close of the epistle, the *father* triumphed over the *conspirator*, and the expressions of paternal love subdued the tone of vengeance to the accents of tenderness and apprehension.

"I was anxious my royal friend," said he, "now that rugged winter has been smoothed by a softer breath, I was anxious to write and to address thee some grateful strain, as the first-fruits of the spring. But the mournful news presages to me new storms; my songs sink into tears. In vain do the heavens smile; in vain do the gardens and groves inspire me with unseasonable joy, and the returning concert of the birds tempt me to resume my own. I cannot behold with dry eyes the approaching desolation of my kind nurse Sicily. Which shall I choose for her, the yoke, or honour? I see that in the confusion of insurrection numbers of her innocent children must perish. Shall I then leave her under the power of the tyrant?

"Shall our beautiful Palermo be defiled by strangers? Shall the powerful and noble Messina rest in quiet with the foot of her oppressor on her neck; or shall I, while feigning peace, organize a war, rousing Sicily and the world to revenge? Revenge! at the word all thoughts of pity and tenderness leave me. The concentrated rage of Etna seems warring in my bosom; it heaves at sight of the miseries of my unhappy people. The island is full of preparations against the Greeks: but, when the sword is drawn, shall it not be buried in the breast of him who drains the life blood from his helpless subjects?

"But in that hour Procida may perish, and the King of Arragon fail to restore the sister of Manfred to her ancient rights. There will then remain of the house of Suabia only 'Frederic the Bitten.' If the daughter of Procida favour his suit, detain him till the '*Ides of March*' be

356

passed, for with Frederic, dies the last hope of the Hohenstaufen."

Eleanora closed the letter and pondered a moment upon its contents. In the plan of Procida to detain Frederic from the approaching conflict in Sicily, she most readily acquiesced, but the difficulty of managing so delicate an affair became instantly apparent to her ready perception. When, however, she adroitly endeavoured to draw from the young duke his knowledge of the purposes of Procida, her apprehension was relieved by discovering that the affair had been planned in such a manner as to require from her, neither entreaty nor subterfuge, since the wily Jew had exacted a promise from the young noble, that he would spend a twelvemonth, at the court of his cousin Edward, before he demanded the hand of Agnes in marriage.

Procida had not indeed, left the duke ignorant of his ultimate purpose, but he had led him to look for its accomplishment at a much more distant date than that designated in the letter, and Frederic consequently feeling no anxiety for an immediate return to Sicily, readily accepted the queen's invitation to form part of the royal escort to Bordeaux.

Eleanora in taking leave of her brother, was comforted with the thought, that he was occupied with a more healthful and profitable pursuit than were the abstruse researches into the mysteries of nature, in which she had found him engaged. She had also the satisfaction of knowing that the deposed monarch had laid aside all his ambitious projects for empire, and now busied his thoughts in calculating the immense advantage and glory that would accrue to mankind from the Castilian literature he had in preparation. The affectionate farewells were exchanged, and, accompanied by her two beautiful children, Beatrice and Berengaria, her maidens and the attendant squires, and a small band of Spanish cavaliers, among whom rode the Duke of Saxony, she set off to meet her lord in Aquitaine.

In the genial society of the queen and her maidens, whose spirits were exhilarated by the exercise and incidents of the journey, Frederic seemed to breathe an atmosphere to which he had been unaccustomed, and which served to enliven his habitual gravity, and develop the gentler qualities of his naturally generous character. The maidens amused themselves with constant allusions to the happy accomplishment of their prediction, and the wit of the fair Agnes was sorely tested, in meeting and parrying their playful attacks. The courteous attentions of the duke, were so impartially distributed among the ladies, that not even jealousy itself could find cause for complaint; yet it was only the voice of Agnes that had power to rouse him from his frequent reveries, and when he spoke, his eye instinctively turned to read in her countenance approbation or dissent.

Disciplined in the school of adversity, he manifested a strength and severity of character, tempered by a pensive tenderness, which showed that his mother's wrongs had wrought in his heart a sentiment of sympathy for the suffering which made him hesitate to involve his country in the exterminating wars, that he foresaw would follow a renewal of the strife between the Guelphs and Ghibellines; and though he felt an enthusiastic admiration for the ardour and zeal of Procida, yet the unscrupulous Jew, who studied the character of all he met with reference to their availability in the approaching crisis, too accurately estimated the probity and truth of the young noble, to attempt to engage him in the dark plot for the overthrow of d'Anjou.

Still he loved the duke, as the descendant of his great patron, and honoured him for those qualities, of which he felt himself destitute; and thus it was with a feeling of joyful security, rather than of pride at the princely alliance, that he consented to bestow his only treasure upon the man, who least of all sympathised in the one purpose of his life.

The royal party arrived at Bordeaux a few days in advance of the King of England, and during these hours of leisure, Frederic unfolded to the queen the mystery of his first appearance in Burgos.

Procida had entrusted him with despatches for the King of Arragon; and to execute his commission with the more secrecy, and at the same time to enjoy the freedom of the mountain solitudes, he travelled without retinue or insignia of rank. Thus he was leisurely pursuing his way along the bank of the stream, communing pleasantly with his own thoughts, when the cries of Eleanora attracted him, just in time to save Agnes from a watery grave. Time had so developed her loveliness that at first he failed to recognize in the fair being before him, the beautiful child he had been accustomed to admire in her father's castle of Prochyta; but when the first flush of returning life glowed upon her countenance, his admiration became lost in a deeper emotion, and from that hour he determined to lay the ducal coronet of Saxony at the feet of the beautiful daughter of Sicily.

The return of the royal family was an era in the annals of English prosperity, from the number of valuables imported from Spain. In the catalogue of the queen's plate, mention is made of a crystal fork, the parting gift of her brother Alphonso, from which the first idea of these articles of table luxury was derived: but the lamb, which had so nearly cost the life of Agnes, proved a benefit to the nation, whose value can never be estimated; and the shepherd of Cotswold to this day, has reason to bless the queen, who bestowed the cherished pet in an English fold.

During his southern campaign, King Edward had contracted an alliance between his eldest daughter Eleanora, and Alphonso, the young Prince of Arragon. The next sister, Joanna of Acre, who most of all resembled her mother in beauty and strength of character, was about the same time, married to the first peer of the realm, Gilbert the red Earl of Gloucester, and the third daughter wedded to John, the Duke of Brabant. At these nuptials the queen presented a golden cup of benison to each of the brides, inscribed with appropriate passages of Holy Writ; and though, in consequence of Frederic's promise to her father, the betrothment between himself and Agnes could not then take place, Eleanora bestowed upon her lovely ward a similar gift, bearing these words, "Thou hast been unto me as a daughter."

CHAPTER 16:
LETTER FROM PROCIDA TO DON PEDRO, KING OF ARRAGON

Thou didst tell me in Arragon, that to restore Sicily to the house of Suabia, was the chimera of a maddened brain; that the strong arm of the church would be lifted to crush the Ghibellines in their final struggle; that gold was wanting to bribe the soldier to draw his sword in behalf of the doomed race, and that the enemies of Charles of Anjou could not be brought to act together against their common foe. Recall now the cruel words that drove Procida from thy court, a Mendicant, '*Conquer these impossibilities, and the fleet of Arragon is ready to substantiate the claim of the daughter of Manfred to the throne of Sicily.*' Goaded by the mocking promise, the mendicant wanders in Sicily.

Now, companion of the tax-gatherer, he wrings the last *drachmè* from the hard hand of toil, and now with the agents of tyranny, he hides the skins of stags or deer in the huts of the peasant, and then robs the goatherd as a penalty for the offence. Thus, he listens and observes. Thus, he tugs at the chain that festers in their shrinking flesh, to show his countrymen their thraldom. *Anon*, a *shepherd* or a *herdsman*, he traverses the valley, or scales the rock, joins the youthful throng that stealthily sport beneath the mountain chesnut, or mingles with the vexed vassals who wait their sovereigns' will, and whispers in the ear of each repining soul, 'The avenger of Manfred holds the vigils of Freedom in the cave of the forest of Palermo.' At sunset, a *traveller*, he seeks the rendezvous: the husbandman is returning to his cottage, his reaping-hook hanging idly from his arm, the Frenchman has gathered the grain from his fields. The herdsman drives his lowing flocks across the lea—the kine and the goat have been robbed of their young, and their fleecy robes been stripped from the bleating tenants of the fold.

The peasant of Hibla returns mourning the swarm which the wind bore beyond his reclaim, but still more the honied stores which during his absence the hand of the spoiler ravished from his unprotected apiary. There comes no voice from the vineyard—the vintagers have trodden the wine-press, but the ruby current flows in the goblets that enliven the banquets of their foreign masters. Oh my people, Sicilians! Listen to him who whispers in the ear of each, 'Carry thy wrongs to the cave of the forest of Palermo.' They come—barbarians, Arabs, Jews, Normans and Germans—those who rejoiced in the tolerant reign of the Suabians, those who have suffered from the tyrant French—Etna groans with the prescience of coming vengeance, and with her thousand tongues of flame, summons the guilty oppressor to abide the 'judgment of God' before the altar.

★★★★★★

A vessel sails from Brundusium, the mariners, hardy Calabrians, spread their sails and bend to their oars with patient purpose; but there is *one* among them who never leaves his post, in calm or in storm—one thought gives strength and vigour to his iron arm; and though a scorner of puerile beadsmen, he almost prays the God of the wind to speed him on his course. Should the Greek Emperor refuse his aid—*he* will tell him that, which will make him tremble for his throne and force the gold from the reluctant coffers. The crafty Paleologus hesitates, but he stands aghast, when Procida acquaints him that Venice hath lent her ships to D'Anjou, and another Dandolo is already embarked to repeat the *Fifth Crusade*!

The Greek exclaims in despair, 'I know not what to do.' 'Give me money,' replies the *mariner*, 'and I will find you a defender, who has no money, but who has arms.' Michael Paleologus opens his treasures and satisfies even a Jew's thirst for gold.

360

Most of all, Paleologus desires a complete reconciliation with the pope; most of all Procida desires an interview with the sovereign *pontiff*.

More swiftly returns the galley; and the ambassador of the Greek stands upon the prow, wrapped in courtly vestments; but not the less anxiously does he watch the winds and waves that return him to Rome. The feeble Nicholas trembles at thought of the vast undertaking, but Procida has fathomed the old man's ambition for his house. He reminds him of the reply of D'Anjou, when the pope proposed a marriage between his niece and Charles' son, 'Does Nicholas fancy because he wears red stockings that the blood of Orsini can mingle with the blood of France?' The stinging remembrance of the taunt determines the pontiff, and the treaty with Paleologus is delivered into the hands of the ambassador. Behold now, King of Arragon, *'The impossibilities are conquered,'* and thou art bound by the very vow of thine unbelief to *'substantiate the claim of the daughter of Manfred to the throne of Sicily.'*

Before the letter of Procida reached Don Pedro, Pope Nicholas died, and Charles had sufficient interest with the college of cardinals to procure the election of one of his own creatures to the Holy See.

These events darkened the horizon above the Sicilians: but the dauntless spirit of Procida rose superior to this alarming turn of affairs. Though aware that Charles had been made acquainted with his designs, he remained upon the island, stealthily riveting the links of the conspiracy, and binding the discordant interests of the various ranks in an indissoluble confederacy, for the overthrow of foreign oppression. The cave of the forest of Palermo was piled with bundles of faggots, in which were concealed the weapons that the inhabitants had forged in secrecy and in darkness, for by the prohibition of the French no Sicilian was permitted to wear arms.

The grand conspirator knew well the Sicilian character, ardent, gay, voluptuous,—he chose his time with his wonted sagacity, when the beautiful island rejoicing in the fullness of bloom, invites her children to banquet upon her charms; when the long abstinence of Lent being over, the senses, reanimated by flesh and wine, start from languor to revel in the enjoyment of luxury and the exhilaration of passion. Easter-Monday, March 30th, 1282, dawns upon Sicily with fair promise for the festal day. The citizens of Palermo look one upon another with furtive glances of restrained impatience, and prepared for the annual *fête* with busy alacrity, while the foreigners, made apprehensive by the gathering multitudes, come armed to assist in garlanding the very church of God.

At sunset a bride and bridegroom go forth, attended by all the inhabitants of the city, both men and women, up the beautiful hill Monréale, to present their vows at the altar of the blessed Virgin:—a traitor whispers the warning, "The Sicilians have arms beneath their robes." The leader of the French hurries forward and seizes the weapon of the bridegroom—he lays his licentious hand upon the bride. Procida draws his sword, and with a cry of "Death to the French!" buries it in the heart of the brutal enemy. At the moment the sound of the Vesper bell floats from the temple of our lady, on the mount of Monréale. It is the appointed signal for vengeance, and "Death to the French!" echoes from lip to lip, through all the ranks of the Sicilians. Everywhere the tyrants are cut down—the houses of the foreigners bear each a fatal mark, and the Destroying Angel spares not even women and children, and the night spreads her solemn pall over the bodies of slaughtered thousands.

Intelligence of the accomplishment of Procida's purpose soon reached Eleanora; but the horrors of the massacre were suppressed, nor did Agnes ever know the cruel part her father had played in the grand tragedy of the *Sicilian Vespers*. She learned, indeed, that the Queen of Arragon had rescued the only son of D'Anjou from his pursuers, and conveyed him away in safety from the island; but the insurrection had not reached its final triumph, when she left the court of England as the Duchess of Saxony; and it was from that time the care of her husband that her gentle spirit should not be pained by a knowledge of the sanguinary scenes that resulted in the death of D'Anjou, and in the re-establishment of the house of Suabia upon the throne of Sicily.

It would have been natural for Edward, in this struggle, to throw the weight of his influence on the side of his uncle D'Anjou; but the circumstance of his daughter's betrothment to Alphonso of Arragon, held him neutral. He, however, negotiated a peace between the pope and Alphonso, by which D'Anjou's son, Charles the Lame, was released from his captivity in Arragon, and permitted to assume his authority in Naples.

Eleanora's love for her husband, not less than her delicate appreciation of excellence, had led her to weigh with wise discrimination the effect of political events upon his character; and the truth was reluctantly forced upon her, that ambition, nurtured by the uniform success of his enterprises, was gradually absorbing the nobler qualities of his nature, and steeling his heart against the claims of justice and humanity.

King Alexander III. of Scotland, the last direct heir in the male line from Maude, died 1285, and this circumstance was the precursor of that period, fatal to Edward's honour, and to the long-established amity between the two kingdoms.

To avert the consequences which she foresaw would follow Alexander's demise, she had influenced Edward to propose a matrimonial alliance between the Prince of Wales and the Maid of Norway, heiress of the Scottish crown. The states of Scotland readily assented to the proposition of the English, and even consented that their young sovereign should be educated at the court of her royal father-in-law. But, while Eleanora was anticipating the pleasant task of rearing the future Queen of England, she was overwhelmed with sorrow by the intelligence, that the tender frame of the priceless child, unable to sustain the rigors of the voyage, had fallen a victim to death at the Orkneys, on her way to England. Her loss was the greatest calamity that ever befell the Scottish nation, fully justifying the touching couplet,

The North wind sobs where Margaret sleeps,
And still in tears of blood her memory Scotland steeps.

The succession of the Scottish crown became at once a matter of dispute, and all the evils which Eleanora had foreseen began to darken the political horizon.

The line of Alexander being extinct, the crown devolved on the issue of David, Earl of Huntington, who figures as Sir Kenneth, in the *Talisman.* The earl had three daughters, from one of whom descended John Baliol, from another Robert Bruce; and the rival claims of these two competitors having for some time agitated the kingdom, it was agreed to submit the arbitration of the affair to Edward, in the same manner as Henry III. had made Louis IX. umpire of his difficulties upon the continent. But the noble virtues of the saintly monarch were poorly represented in the English king. Edward at once claimed the crown for himself as lord paramount of the country, appointed Baliol as his deputy, and sent six regents to take possession of Scotland. The brave men of the north resisted this aggression with a spirit that fully proved their Scandinavian origin, and Edward hastened to the Scottish border to enforce his claims.

Queen Eleanora was absent in Ambresbury, to witness the profession of her daughter Mary, who there, with the Welsh Princess Guendoline, was veiled a nun under the care of her royal mother-in-law, Eleanora of Provence. But no sooner was the ceremony concluded, than she complied with her husband's earnest request, that she should follow him to Scotland.

Regardless of fatigue, she hurried forward, though sensible that an incipient fever preyed upon her strength. As the dangerous symptoms increased, she redoubled her speed, hoping at least to reach Alnwick castle, and die in her husband's arms. But at Grantham, in Lincolnshire, her strength utterly failed, and in the residence of a private gentleman, who had belonged to their household in Palestine, she awaited the coming of the King of Terrors. A courier was immediately despatched to Edward, with news of her alarming illness. At the gentle call of conjugal love, all other considerations gave way in the heart of Edward. He turned southward instantly, and by forced stages, hurried towards Grantham.

The dying Eleanora watched for his coming with an anxiety born of an intense devotion to the welfare of her husband and his subjects. She longed to repeat with her last breath the tender counsels that had ever influenced him to clemency and mercy, and which she had enforced by the strongest of all arguments, the daily example of a holy life. But the last sad duty to the cold remains of his beloved consort, was the only consolation left to the bereaved monarch, when he arrived at Lincolnshire. With a sorrow that found relief in every outward testimonial of woe, he followed her corpse in person during thirteen days in progress of the funeral to Westminster.

In every town where the royal bier rested the ecclesiastics assembled, and in solemn procession conducted it to the high altar of the principal church, and at each resting-place, Edward set up a crucifix in memory of "*La chere reine,*" as he passionately called his lost Eleanora. Charing Cross, erected upon the site now occupied by the statue of Charles I., was the London monument of this saintly queen.

An English writer, in a tribute to her memory, thus enumerates her virtues, "To our nation she was a loving mother, the column and pillar of the whole realm; therefore, to her glory, the king her husband caused all those famous trophies to be erected, wherever her noble corpse did rest; for he loved her above all earthly creatures. She was a godly, modest and merciful princess; the English nation in her time was not harassed by foreigners, nor the country people by the purveyors of the crown. The sorrow-stricken she consoled, as became her dignity, and she made them friends that were at discord."

Her sorrowing lord endowed the Abbey of Winchester with rich donations for the perpetual celebration of dirges and masses for her soul, and waxen tapers were burned about her tomb, till the light of the Reformation outshone the lights of superstition; but her imperishable virtues survive every monumental device, illume the annals of history, and illustrate the true philosophy of female *Heroism*.

Notes

Note A.—Page 15.

"*The Lady Matilda.*"—Hlafdigé, or lady, means the giver of bread. Few of the Queens of England can claim a more illustrious descent than this princess. Her father, Baldwin V., was surnamed the gentle Earl of Flanders: her mother Adelais, was daughter of Robert, King of France, and sister to Henry, reigning sovereign of that country, and she was nearly related to the Emperor of Germany, and most of the royal houses in Europe.—*Queens of England*, p. 24.

Note B.—Page 15.

"*Woden and Thor.*"—Two of the most powerful deities in northern mythology. The ancient Saxons honoured Woden as the God of War, and the Germans represented Thor as the God of Thunder.

Note C.—Page 16.

"*The Royal Children.*"—The sons of Matilda and William the Conqueror, were Robert, afterwards Duke of Normandy, Richard, who died young, William and Henry, afterwards kings of England, Cicely, Agatha, Adela, Constance, Adeliza and Gundred. No two writers agree as to the order of their ages, except that Robert was the eldest and Henry the youngest son, Cicely the eldest and Gundred the youngest daughter.—*Vide Queens of England*, p. 33-82.

Note D.—Page 16.

"*The Mora.*"—While the fleet destined to invade the island waited in the port for a favourable wind, William was agreeably surprised by the arrival of his duchess at the port, in a splendid vessel of war called the Mora, which she had caused to be built, unknown to him, and adorned in the most royal style of magnificence for his acceptance. The effigy of their youngest son, William, in gilded bronze, most writers say of gold, was placed at the prow of this vessel, with his face turned towards England, holding a trumpet to his lips with one hand, and bearing in the other a bow with the arrow aimed towards

England.—*Queens of England*, p. 40.

Note E.—Page 16.

"*William the Conqueror*" was of low origin on the mother's side. He was not ashamed of his birth, and drew around him his mother's other sons. At first he had much difficulty in bringing his barons, who despised him, to their allegiance. He was a large, bald-headed man, very brave, very greedy, and very sage, according to the notions of the times, that is very treacherous.—*Michelet's History of France*, p. 193.

Note F.—Page 17.

"*Edgar Atheling.*"—Edward, the son of Edmund Ironside, being sent to Hungary to escape the cruelty of Canute, was there married to Agatha, daughter of the Emperor Henry II. She bore him Edgar Atheling, Margaret, afterwards Queen of Scotland, and Christina, who afterwards retired to a convent.—*Hume*, p. 115.

Note G.—Page 18.

"*The one keeping strict lenten fast.*"—By a mixture of vigour and lenity, he had so soothed the mind of the English, that he thought he might safely revisit his native country, and enjoy the triumph and congratulation of his ancient subjects. He left the administration in the hands of his uterine brother, Odo, Bishop of Bayeux, and of William Fitz Osberne. That their authority might be exposed to less danger, he carried over with him all the most considerable nobility of England, who, while they served to grace his court by their presence and magnificent retinues, were in reality hostages for the fidelity of the nation. Among these, were Edgar Atheling, Stigand the primate, the Earls Edwin and Morcar, Waltheof the son of the brave Earl Siward, with others eminent for the greatness of their fortunes and families, or for their ecclesiastical and civil dignities.

He was visited at the Abbey of Fescamp, where he resided during some time, by Rodulph, uncle to the King of France, and by many powerful princes and nobles, who having contributed to his enterprise, were desirous of participating in the joy and advantages of its success. His English courtiers, willing to ingratiate themselves with their new sovereign, outvied each other in equipages and entertainments; and made a display of riches which struck the foreigners with astonishment.

William of Poictiers, a Norman historian, who was present, speaks with admiration of the beauty of their persons, the size and workmanship of their silver plate, the costliness of their embroideries, an art in which the English then excelled, and he expresses himself in such terms as tend much to exalt our idea of the opulence and cultivation of the people. But though everything bore the face of joy and festivity, and William himself treated his new courtiers with great appearance of kindness, it was impossible altogether to prevent the insolence of the Normans; and the English nobles derived little satisfaction from those entertainments, where they considered themselves as led in triumph by their ostentatious Conqueror.—*Hume*, vol. 1, p. 184.

Note H.—Page 18.

The celebrated Bayeaux tapestry, distinguished by the name of the *Duke of Normandy's toilette*, is a piece of canvass about nineteen inches in breadth, but upwards of sixty-seven yards in length, on which is embroidered the history of the conquest of England by William of Normandy, commencing with the visit of Harold to the Norman court, and ending with his death at the battle of Hastings, 1066. The leading transactions of these eventful years, the death of Edward the Confessor, and the coronation of Harold in the chamber of the royal dead, are represented in the clearest and most regular order in this piece of needle-work, which contains many hundred figures of men, horses, birds, beasts, trees, houses, castles, and churches, all executed their proper colours, with names and inscriptions over them to elucidate the story. It appears to have been designed by Turold, a dwarf artist, who illuminated the canvas with the proper outlines and colours.— *Queens of England*, vol. 1, p. 54.

Note I.—Page 18.

"*Cicely, the betrothed of Harold.*"—William also complained of the affront that had been offered to his daughter by the faithless Saxon, who, regardless of his contract to the little Norman princess, just before King Edward's death, strengthened his interest with the English nobles by marrying Algitha, sister to the powerful Earls Morcar and Edwin, and widow to Griffith, Prince of Wales. This circumstance is mentioned with great bitterness in all William's proclamations and reproachful messages to Harold, and appears to have been considered by the incensed duke to the full as great a villainy as the assumption of the crown of England.—*Queens of England*, vol. 1, p. 35.

Note J.—Page 19.

"*Condemned her former lover.*"—Brithric, the son of Algar, a Saxon Thane, is stated in Domesday, to have held this manor in the reign of Edward the Confessor; but having given offence to Maud, the daughter of Baldwin, Count of Flanders, previous to her marriage with William, Duke of Normandy, by refusing to marry her himself, his property was seized by that monarch on the conquest, and bestowed seemingly in revenge upon the queen.—*Ellis's History of Thornbury Castle.*

Note K.—Page 20.

"The terrible Vikings."—Sea kings among the Danes or Normans; leaders of piratical squadrons who passed their lives in roving the seas in search of spoil and adventures. The younger sons of the Scandinavian kings and jarls, having no inheritance but the ocean, naturally collected around their standards the youth of inferior order, who were equally destitute with themselves. These were the same who, in England and Scotland, under the name of Danes, and on the continent under the name of Normans, at first desolated the maritime coasts, and afterwards penetrated into the interior of countries, and formed permanent settlements in their conquests.—*See Encyclopaedia.*

Note L.—Page 22.

"The Danes confided much in the Fylga or Guardian Spirit."—They have certain Priestesses named Morthwyrtha, or worshippers of the dead.

Note M.—Page 23.

Edgar Atheling, dreading the insidious caresses of William, escaped into Scotland, and carried thither his two sisters, Margaret and Christina. They were well received by Malcolm, who soon after espoused Margaret, the elder.—*Hume's History of England,* vol. 1.

Note N.—Page 23.

"The laying waste of Hampshire."—There was one pleasure to which William, as well as all the Normans and ancient Saxons, were extremely addicted, and that was hunting; but this pleasure he indulged more at the expense of his unhappy subjects, whose interests he always disregarded, than to the loss or diminution of his own revenue. Not content with those large forests which former kings possessed in all parts of England, he resolved to make a new forest near Winchester, the usual place of his residence; and for that purpose he laid waste the country in Hampshire for an extent of thirty miles, expelled the inhabitants from their houses, seized their property even, demolished churches and convents, and made the sufferers no compensation for the injury.

At the same time he enacted new laws, by which he prohibited all his subjects from hunting in any of his forests, and rendered the penalties more severe than ever had been inflicted for such offences. The killing of a deer or bear, or even a hare, was punished with the loss of a delinquent's eyes; and that, at a time, when the killing of a man could be atoned for by paying a moderate fine.—*History of England*, vol. 1, p. 214.

Note O.—Page 23.

"*Odious Danegelt, and still more odious Couvrefeu.*"—William, to prevent the people of the land from confederating together in nocturnal assemblies, for the purpose of discussing their grievances, and stimulating each other to revolt, compelled them to *couvrefeu*, or extinguish the lights and fires in their dwellings at eight o'clock every evening, at the tolling of a bell, called from that circumstance, the curfew or couvrefeu.—*Queens of England*, vol. 1, p. 57.

Note P.—Page 24.

"*Lanfranc will absolve thee from thy oath.*"—Lanfranc exchanged his priory for the Abbey of St. Stephen, at Caen, in Normandy, and when William, the sovereign of that duchy, acquired the English throne by conquest, the interest of that prince procured his election, in 1070, to the Archbishopric of Canterbury, then become vacant by the deposition of Stigand.—*See Encyclopaedia.*

Note Q.—Page 29.

"*A maiden's needle wounds less deeply than a warrior's sword.*"—It was on the field of Archembraye, where Robert, unconscious who the doughty champion was, against whom he tilted, ran his father through the arm with his lance, and unhorsed him.—*Queens of England*, vol. 1, p. 71.

Note R.—Page 30.

"*Accolade.*"—The more distinguished the rank of the aspirant, the more distinguished were those who put themselves forward to arm him. The romances often state that the shield was given to a knight by the King of Spain, the sword by a King of England, the helmet from a French sovereign. The word dub is of pure Saxon origin. The French word *adouber* is similar to the Latin *adoptare*, for knights were not made by adapting the habiliments of chivalry to them, but by receiving them, or being adopted into the order. Many writers have imagined that the accolade was the last blow which the soldier might receive with impunity.—*Mill's History of Chivalry*, p. 28.

Note S.—Page 33.

"*Adela stood again in the old Abbey of Fescamp.*"—In the year 1075, William and Matilda, with their family, kept the festival of Easter with great pomp at Fescamp, and attended in person the profession of their eldest daughter Cicely, who was there veiled a nun, by the Archbishop

John.—*Queens of England*, vol. 1, p. 63.

Note T.—Page 38.

"*I craved a portion of the Holy dust.*"—Even the dust of Palestine was adored: it was carefully conveyed to Europe, and the fortunate possessor, whether by original acquisition or by purchase, was considered to be safe from the malevolence of demons. As a proof that miracles had not ceased in his time, St. Augustine relates a story of the cure of a young man who had some of the dust of the Holy City suspended in a bag over his bed.—*Mill's Crusades*, p. 14.

Note U.—Page 38.

"*Pilgrim, and Palmer.*"—On his return, he placed the branch of the sacred palm tree, which he had brought from Jerusalem, over the altar of his church, in proof of the accomplishment of his vow; religious thanksgivings were offered up; rustic festivity saluted and honoured him, and he was revered for his piety and successful labours.—*Mill's Crusades*, p. 14.

Note V.—Page 38.

"*The Saxon Secretary Ingulphus.*"—In the year 1051, William, Duke of Normandy, then a visitor at the court of Edward the Confessor, made Ingulphus, then of the age of twenty-one, his secretary. He accompanied the duke to Normandy—went on a pilgrimage to the Holy Land, and upon his return was created abbot of the rich monastery of Croyland—*See Encyclopaedia*.

Note W.—Page 39

"*Joined the Archbishop.*"—The clergy of Germany had proclaimed their intention of visiting Jerusalem; and Ingulphus, a native and historian of England, was one of a Norman troop which joined them at Mayence. The total number of pilgrims was seven thousand, and among the leaders are the names respectable for rank of the Archbishop of Mayence and the Bishops of Bamberg, Ratisbon, and Utrecht. Their march down Europe, and through the Greek Empire, was peaceable and unmolested; but when they entered the territory of the infidels, they fell into the hands of the Arab robbers, and it was not without great losses of money and lives that the band reached Jerusalem.—*History of Crusades*, p. 17.

Note X.—Page 39.

"*The Gog and Magog of sacred writ.*"—Magyar is the national and oriental denomination of the Hungarians; but, among the tribes of Scythia, they are distinguished by the Greeks under the proper and peculiar name of Turks, as the descendants of that mighty people who had conquered and reigned from China to the Volga.—*Gibbon's Rome,* vol. 5, p. 411.

Note Y.—Page 40.

"Battle Abbey."—William laid the foundation of the Abbey of St. Martin, now called Battle Abbey, where perpetual prayers were directed to be offered up for the repose of the souls of all who had fallen in that sanguinary conflict. The high altar of this magnificent monument of the Norman victory was set upon the very spot where Harold's body was found, or, according to others, where he first pitched his gonfanon.—*Queens of England,* vol. 1, p. 50.

Note Z.—Page 41.

"Did not that for his own sins."—It is a maxim of the civil law, that whosoever cannot pay with his purse must pay with his body; and the practice of flagellation was adopted by the monks, a cheap, though painful equivalent. By a fantastic arithmetic, a year of penance was taxed at three thousand lashes, and such was the skill and patience of a famous hermit, St. Dominic, of the iron *cuirass,* that in six days he could discharge an entire century by a whipping of three hundred thousand stripes. His example was followed by many penitents of both sexes; and as a vicarious sacrifice was accepted, a sturdy disciplinarian might expiate on his own back the sins of his benefactors.—*Gibbon's Rome,* vol. 5, p. 58.

Note AA.—Page 42.

The story of the noble Magyar is taken from early travels in Palestine.

Note BB.—Page 48.

"The assassin band of Mount Lebanon."—Hassan, with his seven successors, is known in the East, under the name of the Old Man of the Mountain, because his residence was in the mountain fastness in Syria. These Ismaelians, therefore, acquired in the West the name of Assassins, which thence became in the western languages of Europe a common name for murderer.—*See Encyclopaedia.*

Note CC.—Page 54.

"Thou shouldst have been King."—His eldest son, Robert, was absent in Germany, at the time of his death. William was on his voyage to England; Henry, who had taken charge of his obsequies, suddenly departed on some self-interested business, and all the great officers of the court having dispersed themselves,—some to offer their homage to Robert, and others to William, the inferior servants of the household plundered the house, stripped the person of the royal dead, and

left his body naked upon the floor.—*Queens of England*, vol. 1, p. 85.

Note DD.—Page 55.

"*Our uncle Odo hates Lanfranc.*"—The Duke William was brave, open, sincere, generous; even his predominate fault, his extreme indolence and facility, were not disagreeable to those haughty barons, who affected independence, and submitted with reluctance to a vigorous administration in their sovereign. Odo, Bishop of Bayeux, and Robert, Earl of Montaigne, maternal brothers of the Conqueror, envying the great credit of Lanfranc, which was increased by his late services, enforced all these motives with these partisans, and engaged them in a formal conspiracy to dethrone William Rufus.—*Hume's History of England*, vol. 1, p. 221.

Note EE.—Page 57.

"*Siege of St. Michael's Mount.*"—Prince Henry, disgusted that so little care had been taken of his interests in this accommodation, retired to St. Michael's Mount, a strong fortress on the coast of Normandy, and infested the neighbourhood with his incursions. Robert and William, with their joint forces, besieged him in this place, and had nearly reduced him by the scarcity of water, when the eldest, hearing of his distress, granted him permission to supply himself, and also sent him some pipes of wine for his own table. Being reproved by William for his ill-timed generosity, he replied, "What, shall I suffer my brother to die of thirst—where shall we find another when he is gone?"— *Hume's England*, vol. 1.

Note FF.—Page 59.

"*Crowds followed the steps of the monk.*"—The lower order of people attached themselves to one Peter the Hermit, a monk of the city of Amiens. He had at first led a solitary life under the habit of a monk; but afterwards, men saw him traversing the streets, and preaching everywhere. The people surrounded him in crowds,—overwhelmed him with presents, and proclaimed his sanctity with such great praises, that I do not remember like honours having been rendered to anyone. In whatever he did or said, there seemed to be something divine in him, so that they would even pluck the hairs out of his mule, to keep them as relics; which I relate here, not as laudable, but for the vulgar, who love all extraordinary things. He wore only a woollen tunic, and above it a cloak of coarse dark cloth, which hung to his heels. His arms and feet were naked; he ate little or no bread; and supported himself on wine and fish.—*Michelet*, p. 209.

Note GG.—Page 62.

"Deus Vult."—Urban was about to continue, when he was interrupted by a general uproar; the assistants shed tears, struck their breasts, raised their eyes and hands to heaven, all exclaiming together, "Let us march, God wills it! God wills it!"—*History of the Popes*, p. 384.

Note HH.—Page 64.

"Stitch the red cross."—All mounted the red cross on their shoulders. Red stuffs and vestments of every kind were torn in pieces; yet were insufficient for the purpose. There were those who imprinted the cross upon themselves with a red-hot iron.—*Michelet*, p. 210.

Note II.—Page 66.

"Walter the Penniless."—Sixty thousand were conducted by the Hermit. Walter the Penniless led fifteen thousand footmen, followed by a fanatic named Godeschal, whose sermons had swept away twenty thousand peasants from the villages of Germany. Their rear was again pressed by a herd of two hundred thousand, the most stupid and savage refuse of the people, who mingled with their devotion a brutal license of rapine, prostitution, and drunkenness. Some counts and gentlemen, at the head of three thousand horse, attended the motions of the multitude to partake in the spoil; but their genuine leaders (may we credit such folly) were a goose and a goat, who were carried in the front, and to whom these worthy Christians ascribed an infusion of the divine spirit.—*Gibbon's Rome*, vol. 5, p. 553.

Note JJ.—Page 67.

"Inquire if that be Jerusalem."—In some instances the poor rustic shod his oxen like horses, and placed his whole family in a cart, where it was amusing to hear the children, on the approach to any large town or castle, inquiring if the object before them were Jerusalem.—*Mill's Crusades*, p. 31.

Note KK.—Page70.

"Adela's Letter from Stephen."—Alexius expressed a wish that one of the sons of Stephen might be educated at the Byzantine court, and said a thousand other fine things, which Stephen reported to his wife as holy truths.—*Mill's Crusades*, p. 49.

Note LL.—Page 85.

"Of English laws and an English Queen."—Matilda is the only princess of Scotland who ever shared the throne of a king of England. It is, however, from her maternal ancestry that she derives her great interest as connected with the annals of this country. Her mother, Margaret Atheling, was the granddaughter of Edmund Ironside, and the daugh-

ter of Edward Atheling, surnamed the Outlaw, by Agatha, daughter of the Emperor Henry II. of Germany.—*Queens of England*, p. 91.

Note MM.—Page 89.

"*We fought in the Plains of Ramula.*"—The small phalanx was overwhelmed by the Egyptians! Stephen, Earl of Chartres, was taken prisoner and murdered by his enemy; he was the hero who ran away in the Crusade. His wife was Adela, a daughter of King William I. of England, and this spirited lady vowed she would give her husband no rest till he recovered his fame in Palestine. He went thither, and died in the manner above related.—*Mill's Crusades*, p. 95.

Note NN.—Page 90.

"*The daughter of Earl Waltheoff, Matilda,*" was the wife of David, afterwards King of Scotland, and the mother of the first Earl of Huntingdon.—*Dr. Lingard.*

Note OO.—Page 91.

"*Lucy lies in the sea.*"—Besides the heir of England, Prince William, there were lost in the White ship, Richard, Earl of Chester, with his bride, the young Lady Lucy, of Blois, daughter of Henry's sister Adela, and the flower of the juvenile nobility, who are mentioned by the Saxon chronicle as a multitude of "incomparable folk."—*Queens of England*, p. 131.

Note PP.—Page 96.

"*Courts of Love.*"—Eleanora was by hereditary right, chief reviewer and critic of the poets of Provence. At certain festivals held by her after the custom of her ancestors, called Courts of Love, all new *sirventes* and *chansons* were sung or recited before her by the troubadours. She then, assisted by a conclave of her ladies, sat in judgment and pronounced sentence on their literary merits.—*Queens of England*, p. 188.

Note QQ.—Page 97.

"*Romance Walloon.*"—The appellation of Walloon was derived from the word Waalchland, the name by which the Germans to this day designate Italy. William the Conqueror was so much attached to the Romance Walloon, that he encouraged its literature among his subjects, and forced it on the English by means of rigorous enactments, in place of the ancient Saxon, which closely resembled the Norse of his own ancestors.

Throughout the whole tract of country from Navarre to the dominions of the Dauphin of Auvergne, and from sea to sea, the Provençal language was spoken—a language which combined the best points of French and Italian, and presented peculiar facilities for poetical composition. It was called the langue *d'oc*, the tongue of "yes" and "no;" because, instead of "*oui*" and "*non*" of the rest of France, the affirmative and negative were "*oc*" and "*no*." The ancestors of Eleanora were called *par excellence*—the Lords of "*oc*" and "*no*."—*Queens of England*, pp. 60-186.

Note RR.—Page 98.

"*In a Province fair.*"—This ballad is from the early English Metrical Romances.

Note SS.—Page 104.

"*The Lady Petronilla.*"—The sister of the queen, the young Petronilla, whose beauty equalled that of her sister, and whose levity far surpassed it, could find no single man in all France to bewitch with the spell of her fascinations, but chose to seduce Rodolph, Count of Vermandois, from his wife.—*Queens of England*, p. 189.

Note TT.—Page 106.

"*Abelard.*"—Abelard, Peter, originally Abailard, a monk of the order of St. Benedict, equally famous for his learning and for his unfortunate love for Héloise, was born in 1079, near Nantes, in the little village of Palais, which was the property of his father, Berenger.—*Encyclopaedia*.

Note UU.—Page 108.

"*St. Bernard.*"—St. Bernard, born at Fontaines, in Burgundy, 1091, was of noble family, and one of the most influential ecclesiastics of the middle ages. He was named the *honeyed teacher*, and his writings were styled *a stream from Paradise*.

He principally promoted the crusade in 1146, and quieted the fermentation caused at that time by a party of monks, against the Jews in Germany.—*Encyclopaedia*.

Note VV.—Page 110.

"*Valley of Laodicea.*"—The freaks of Queen Eleanora and her female warriors were the cause of all the misfortunes that befell King Louis and his army, especially in the defeat at Laodicea. The king had sent forward the queen and her ladies, escorted by his choicest troops, under the guard of Count Maurienne. He charged them to choose for their camp the arid, but commanding ground which gave them a view over the defiles of the valley of Laodicea. Queen Eleanora insisted upon halting in a lovely romantic valley, full of verdant grass and gushing fountains.—*Queens of England*, p. 190.

Note WW.—Page 114.

"*Series of Coquetries.*"—Some say that she was smitten with Raymond, of Antioch; others with a handsome Saracen slave; and it was, moreover, rumoured that she received presents from the *sultan.*—*Michelet,* p. 233.

Note XX.—Page 115.

"Twenty days."—The "Queens of France" record that he learned the Provençal tongue in twenty days.

Note YY.—Page 1163.

"Knights of the Temple."—A celebrated order of knights, which, like the order of St. John and the Teutonic order, had its origin in the crusades. It was established in 1119, for the protection of the pilgrims on the roads in Palestine. Subsequently, its object became the defence of the Christian faith, and of the Holy Sepulchre against the Saracens.

Uniting the privileges of a religious order with great military power, and always prepared for service by sea and land, it could use its possessions to more advantage than other corporations, and also make conquests on its own account; in addition to which it received rich donations and bequests from the superstition of the age.

The principal part of the possessions of the order were in France: most of the knights were also French, and the grand-master was usually of that nation. In 1244, the order possessed nine thousand considerable bailiwicks, commanderies, priories and preceptories, independent of the jurisdiction of the countries in which they were situated.

The order was destroyed in France by Philip the Fair, about the beginning of the fourteenth century.—*Encyclopaedia.*

Note ZZ.—Page 117.

"Hospitallers."—The Knights of St. John, or Hospitallers of St. John, afterwards called Knights of Rhodes, and finally Knights of Malta, were a celebrated order of military religious, established at the commencement of the crusades to the Holy Land. It was the duty of the monks, who were called brothers of St. John or hospitallers, to take care of the poor and sick, and in general, to assist pilgrims. This order obtained important possessions, and maintained itself against the arms of the Turks and Saracens by union and courage.

In 1309 the knights established themselves on the island of Rhodes, where they remained upwards of two hundred years. In 1530, Charles Fifth granted them the island of Malta, on conditions of perpetual war against the infidels and pirates. From this period, they were commonly called *Knights of Malta.*—*Encyclopaedia.*

Note AAA.—Page 119

"On her way Southward."—Eleanora stayed some time at Blois, the

count of which province was Thibaut, elder brother to King Stephen, one of the handsomest and bravest men of his time. Thibaut offered his hand to his fair guest. He met with a refusal, which by no means turned him from his purpose, as he resolved to detain the lady prisoner in his fortress till she complied with his proposal. Eleanora suspected his design, and departed by night for Tours. Young Geoffrey Plantagenet, the next brother to the man she intended to marry, had likewise a great inclination to be sovereign of the south. He placed himself in ambush at a part of the Loire called the Port of Piles, with the intention of seizing the duchess and carrying her off and marrying her. But she, pre-warned by her good angel, turned down a branch of the stream toward her own country.—*Queens of England*, p. 114.

Note BBB.—Page 123.

"*Becket.*"—Thomas Becket, the most celebrated Roman Catholic prelate in the English annals, was born in London, 1119. He was the son of Gilbert, a London merchant. His mother was a Saracen lady, to whose father Gilbert was prisoner, being taken in the first crusade. The lady fell in love with the prisoner, and guided by the only English words she knew—"Gilbert—London"—followed him to London, where he married her.

He was recommended by Archbishop Theobald, to King Henry II., and in 1158 he was appointed high chancellor and preceptor to Prince Henry, and at this time was a complete courtier, conforming in every respect to the humour of the king.

He died in the fifty second year of his age, and was canonized two years after. Of the popularity of the pilgrimages to his tomb, the *Canterbury Tales* of Chaucer will prove an enduring testimony.—*Encyclopaedia.*

Note CCC.—Page 126.

"*Regular Drama.*"—Besides the mysteries and miracles played by the parish clerks and students of divinity, the classic taste of the accomplished Eleanor patronized representations nearly allied to the regular drama, since we find that Peter of Blois, in his epistles, congratulates his brother William, on his tragedy of Flaura and Marcus, played before the queen.—*Queens of England*, p. 199.

Note DDD.—Page 134.

"*Adrian IV.*"—Adrian IV., an Englishman, originally named *Nicholas* Breakspear, rose, by his great talents, from the situation of a poor monk, to the rank of cardinal, and legate in the north. He was elected pope in 1154, and waged an unsuccessful war against William, King of Sicily.

The permission which he gave to Henry II., King of England, to invade Ireland, on the condition that every family of that island should pay annually a penny to the papal chair, because all islands belong to the pope, is worthy of remark. On this grant the subsequent popes founded their claims on Ireland.—*Encyclopaedia.*

Note EEE.—Page 150.

"The wasted form of Rosamond."—It is not a very easy task to reduce to anything like perspicuity the various traditions which float through the chronicles, regarding Queen Eleanor's unfortunate rival, the celebrated Rosamond Clifford. No one who studies history ought to despise tradition, for we shall find that tradition is generally founded on fact, even when defective or regardless of chronology. It appears that the acquaintance between Rosamond and Henry commenced in early youth, about the time of his knighthood by his uncle, the King of Scotland; that it was renewed at the time of his successful invasion of England, when he promised marriage to the unsuspecting girl. As Rosamond was retained by him as a prisoner, though not an unwilling one, it was easy to conceal from her the facts that he had wedded a queen and brought her to England; but his chief difficulty was to conceal Rosamond's existence from Eleanor, and yet indulge himself with frequent visits to the real object of his love.

Brompton says, "That one day, Queen Eleanor saw the king walking in the pleasance of Woodstock, with the end of a ball of floss silk attached to his spur, and that, coming near him unperceived, she took up the ball, and the king walked on, the silk unwound, and thus the queen traced him to a thicket in the labyrinth or maze of the park, where he disappeared. She kept the matter secret, often revolving in her own mind in what company he could meet with balls of silk.

"Soon after, the king left Woodstock for a distant journey; then Queen Eleanor, bearing this discovery in mind, searched the thicket in the park, and found a low door cunningly concealed; this door she had forced, and found it was the entrance to a winding subterranean path, which led out at a distance to a sylvan lodge, in the most retired part of the adjacent forest." Here the queen found in a bower a young lady of incomparable beauty, busily engaged in embroidery. Queen Eleanor then easily guessed how balls of silk attached themselves to King Henry's spurs.

Whatever was the result of the interview between Eleanor and Rosamond, it is certain that the queen neither destroyed her rival by sword nor poison, though in her rage it is possible that she might threaten both.

The body of Rosamond was buried at Godstow, near Oxford, a little nunnery among the rich meadows of Evenlod. King John thought proper to raise a tomb to the memory of Rosamond; it was embossed with fair brass, having an inscription about its edges, in Latin, to this effect,

This tomb doth here enclose
The world's most beauteous rose
Rose passing sweet erewhile,
Now nought but odour vile.

Queens of England.

Note FFF.—Page 151.

"*Imprisonment of Queen Eleanor.*"—Queen Eleanor, whose own frailties had not made her indulgent to those of others, offended by the repeated infidelities of the king, stirred up her sons, Richard and Geoffrey, to make demands similar to that of their brother, and persuaded them, when denied, to fly also to the court of France. Eleanor herself absconded; but she fell soon after into the hands of her husband, by whom she was kept confined for the remainder of his reign.—*Pictorial History of England.*

Note GGG.—Page 153.

"*Turning proudly to the rebel lords.*"—Hoveden, and some other English writers, have recorded a story, that the Count of Tripoli and his friends proffered their allegiance to the queen, upon the reasonable condition that she should be divorced from Lusignan, and should choose such a person for the partner of her throne as would be able to defend the kingdom. She complied, and after she had been crowned, she put the diadem on the head of Lusignan.—*Mills' Crusades*, p. 137.

Note HHH.—Page 156.

"*Thy brother William and his beautiful bride.*"—The Earl of Salisbury was the son of King Henry II., by fair Rosamond. His Christian name was William, and his wearing a longer sword than was usual gave him his surname. His half brother, King Richard I., gave him in marriage Ela, eldest daughter and coheiress of William de Eureux, Earl of Salisbury and Rosemer; and also raised him to the title of earl. Ela was granddaughter of Patric Earl of Salisbury, murdered by Guy de Lusignan.—*Mills' Crusades*, p. 198.

Note III.—Page 158.

"*The well Zemzem.*"—Zemzem is believed by the followers of

380

Mohammed, to be the identical spring which gushed forth in the wilderness for the relief of Hagar and Ishmael; and marvellous efficacy is ascribed to its waters, in giving health to the sick, imparting strength of memory, and purifying from the effects of sin.—*Encyclopaedia.*

Note JJJ.—Page 162.

"*Pampeluna*"—a city of Spain, and capital of Navarre, situated on the Arga, in a plain near the Pyrenees, founded by Pompey.—*Encyclopaedia.*

Note KKK.—Page 178.

"*Blood oozed.*"—When Richard entered the abbey he shuddered, and prayed some moments before the altar, when the nose and mouth of his father began to bleed so profusely, that the monk in attendance kept incessantly wiping the blood from his face.—*Queens of England—Eleanora of Aquitaine,* p. 220.

Note LLL.—Page 184.

"*Driven from the harbour.*"—Queen Joanna's galley sheltered in the harbour of Limoussa, when Isaac, the Lord of Cyprus, sent two boats, and demanded if the queen would land. She declined the offer, saying, "all she wanted was to know whether the King of England had passed." They replied: "they did not know." At that juncture Isaac approached with great power, upon which the cavaliers who guarded the royal ladies, got the galley in order to be rowed out of the harbour at the first indication of hostilities.—*Bernard le Tresorier.*

Note MMM.—Page 195.

"*Battle of Tiberias.*"—In the plain near Tiberias the two armies met in conflict. For a whole day the engagement was in suspense, and at night the Latins retired to some rocks, whose desolation and want of water had compelled them to try the fortune of a battle. The heat of a Syrian summer's night was rendered doubly horrid, because the Saracens set fire to some woods which surrounded the Christian camp. In the morning, the two armies were for awhile stationary, in seeming consciousness that the fate of the Moslem and the Christian worlds was in their hands.

But when the sun arose, the Latins uttered their shout of war, the Turks answered by the clangour of their trumpets and atabals, and the sanguinary conflict began.

The piece of the true cross was placed on a hillock, and the broken squadrons continually rallied round it. But the crescent had more numerous supporters than the cross, and for that reason triumphed.—*Mills' History of the Crusades,* p. 139.

Note NNN.—Page 202.

"*Courtesies of life.*"—Through the whole of the war Saladin and Richard emulated each other as much in the reciprocation of courtesy, as in military exploits. If ever the King of England chanced to be ill, Saladin sent him presents of Damascene pears, peaches, and other fruits. The same liberal hand gave the luxury of snow, in the hot season.—*Hoveden*, p. 693.

Note OOO.—Page 205.

"*Union between his brother.*"—Political disturbances in England demanded the presence of Richard, and he was compelled to yield to his necessities, and solicit his generous foe to terminate the war. He proposed a consolidation of the Christian and Mohammedan interests, the establishment of a government at Jerusalem, partly European and partly Asiatic; and these schemes of policy were to be carried into effect by the marriage of Saphadin with the widow of William, King of Sicily. The Mussulman princes would have acceded to these terms: but the marriage was thought to be so scandalous to religion, that the imams and the priests raised a storm of clamour, and Richard and Saladin, powerful as they were, submitted to popular opinion.—*Mills' Crusades.*

Note PPP.—Page 207

"*This way sire.*"—A friend led him to a hill which commanded a view of Jerusalem: but, covering his face with a shield, he declared he was not worthy to behold a city which he could not conquer.—*Mills' History of the Crusades*, p. 164.

Note QQQ.—Page 214.

"*Count Raimond.*"—The young count so well acquitted himself of his charge, that he won the affection of the fair widow, Queen Joanna, on the journey. The attachment of these lovers healed the enmity that had long subsisted between the houses of Aquitaine and that of the Counts of Toulouse, on account of the superior claims of Queen Eleanora on that great fief.

When Eleanora found the love that subsisted between her youngest child and the heir of Toulouse, she conciliated his father by giving up her rights to her daughter, and Berengaria had the satisfaction of seeing her two friends united after she arrived at Poitou.—*Berengaria of Navarre*, p. 16.

Note RRR.—Page 2215.

The song of Richard and Blondell is found in *Burney's History of Music*, vol. 2, p. 236.

Note SSS.—Page 219.

"*The black banner.*"—Finding his end approaching, Saladin commanded the black standard, which had so often led the way to victory, to be taken down, and replaced by the shroud which was to wrap his body in the grave. This was then borne through the streets, while the cries called all men to behold what Saladin, the mighty Conqueror, carried away with him of all his vast dominion. Saladin died, a monarch in whose character, though the good was not unmixed with evil, the great qualities so far preponderated, that they overbalanced the effects of a barbarous epoch and a barbarous religion, and left in him a splendid exception to most of the vices of his age, his country and his creed.—*James' History of Chivalry*, p. 264.

Note TTT.—Page 220.

"*The Fourth Crusade.*"—Saphadin marched against them, and the Germans did not decline the combat. Victory was on the side of the Christians; but it was bought by the death of many brave warriors, particularly of the Duke of Saxony, and of the son of the Duke of Austria. But the Germans did not profit by this success, for news arrived from Europe, that the great support of the crusade, Henry VI., was dead. The Archbishop of Mayence, and all those princes who had an interest in the election of a German sovereign, deserted the Holy Land.—*Mills' History of the Crusades*, p. 172.

Note UUU.—Page 225.

"*Blanche of Castile.*"—This queen, so justly celebrated for her talents in the administration of government, as well as her lofty character and the excellent education her son received under her direction, was granddaughter of Eleonor of Guyenne. She was born at Burgos, in Spain, in 1185, and was the daughter of Alphonso IX., King of Castile, and of Eleonor, daughter of Henry II. of England.—*Queens of England*, p. 164.

Note VVV.—Page 231.

"*Suabia.*"—In 1030, Frederic of Staufen, Lord of Hohenstaufen, displayed so much courage in battle, that the Emperor, Henry IV., bestowed upon him the Duchy of Suabia, and his daughter Agnes in marriage. Thus was laid the foundation of the future greatness of a house, whose elevation and fall are among the most important epochs in the history of the German empire. The inextinguishable hatred of the Guelphs, against the house of Hohenstaufen (Ghibelines) resulted in a contest which involved Germany and Italy in accumulated sufferings for more than three hundred years.—*See Encyclopaedia.*

Note WWW.—Page 234.

"*Submission of the eastern Empire to the Pope.*"—If the French would place Alexius on the throne, religious schism should be healed; the eastern church should be brought into subjection to the church of Rome; and Greece should pour forth her population and her treasures for the recovery of the Holy Land.—*See Encyclopaedia.*

Note XXX.—Page 237.

"*St. Dominic.*"—The Dominicans originated in 1215, at Toulouse. The principal objects of their institution was to preach against heretics. This passion for heresy-hunting established the order of the Inquisition. The Dominicans were called Jacobins in France, because their first convent at Paris, was in the *rue* St. Jaques. Their order is now flourishing only in Spain, Portugal, Sicily and America.—*See Encyclopaedia.*

Note YYY.—Page 240.

"*Magna Charta.*"—The Great Charter of Liberties, extorted from King John, in 1215. The barons who composed the army of God and the Holy Church, were the whole nobility of England; their followers comprehended all the yeomanry and free peasantry with the citizens and burgesses of London. John had been obliged to yield to this general union, and, June 15th, both encamped on the plain called Runneymede, on the banks of the Thames, and conferences were opened, which were concluded on the 19th. The thirty-ninth article contains the writ of *habeas corpus*, and the trial by jury, the most effectual securities against oppression which the wisdom of man has ever devised.—*See Encyclopaedia.*

Note ZZZ.—Page 247.

"*Filled the office of Regent of Jerusalem.*"—In the 13th century we find woman seated, at least as mother and regent, on many of the western thrones. Blanche, of Castile, governed in the name of her infant son, as did the Countess of Champagne for the young Thibaut, and the Countess of Flanders for her captive husband. Isabella, of Manche, also exercised the greatest influence over her son, Henry III., King of England. Jane, of Flanders, did not content herself with the power, but desired manly honours and ensigns, and claimed at the consecration of St. Louis, the right of her husband to bear the naked sword, the sword of France. By a singular coincidence, a woman, in the year 1250, succeeded, for the first time, a sultan. Before this, a woman's name had never been seen on the coin, or mentioned in the public prayers. The Caliph of Bagdad protested against the scandal of this innovation.—

Michelet's History of France.

Note AAAA.—Page 248.

"*St. Dunstan.*"—Dunstan, Abbot of Glastonbury, in the year 948, possessed complete ascendancy over King Edred and the councils of state. He lived for some time in a cell so small that he could neither stand nor sit in it, and was honoured with remarkable dreams, visions, and temptations. He it was who introduced the order of Benedictine monks into England.—*Parley's History.*

Note BBBB.—Page 249.

"*Convent of L'Espan.*"—Queen Berengaria fixed her residence at Mans, in the Orleannois, where she held a great part of her foreign dower. Here she founded the noble Abbey of *L'Espan.*—*Queens of England.*

Note CCCC.—Page 253.

"*Sultan of Egypt.*"—Saphadin's son, Coradinus, the Prince of Syria and Palestine, did not proclaim the death of his father till he had secured himself in the possession of the royal coffers. Discord and rebellion were universal throughout Egypt when the news arrived of the death of Saphadin, and his son Carnel, lord of that country, was compelled to fly into Arabia for protection from his mutinous people.—*Mills' Crusades.*

Note DDDD.—Page 258.

"*Mongols.*"—Genghis Khan, the chief of a mongrel horde, in 1260, conceived the bold plan of conquering the whole earth. After the death of Genghis Khan, in 1227, his sons pursued his conquests, subjugated all China, subverted the Caliphate of Bagdad, and made the Seljook Sultans of Iconium tributary.

Note EEEE.—Page 260.

"*Wainscoted with gold.*"—This description of the *sultan's* palace is taken from William of Tyre's glowing account of the "House of Wisdom," found in a note of *Michelet's France*, vol. 1, p. 206.

Note FFFF.—Page 263.

"*Moslem Rosary.*"—A rosary of ninety-nine beads, called Tusbah, or implement of praise. In dropping the beads through the fingers, they repeat the attributes of God, as, O Creator, O merciful, &c., &c. This act of devotion is called Taleel. The name *Allah* is always joined to the epithet, as "*Ya Allah Kalick, Ya Allah Kerreem,*" found in note to the Bahar Danush.

Note GGGG.—Page 264.

"*Congregation repeated 'Praise be to God.'*"—See *Griffith's description of Mahomedan funeral.*

Note HHHH.—Page 265

Kibla, or Cabbala, signifies oral tradition. The term is used by the Jews and Mahomedans to denote the traditions of their ancestors, or, most commonly, their mystical philosophy.—*Encyclopaedia.*

Note IIII.—Page 268.

"Tones of the Arabic."—Frederic II., the grandson of Barbarossa, was successively the pupil, the enemy, and the victim of the church. At the age of twenty one years, in obedience to his guardian, Innocent III., he assumed the cross; the same promise was repeated at his royal and imperial coronations, and his marriage with the heiress of Jerusalem forever bound him to defend the kingdom of his son Conrad. For suspending his vow, Frederic was excommunicated by Gregory IX.; for presuming the next year, to accomplish his vow, he was again excommunicated by the same pope.

He was well formed, of a fair and fine complexion, and a gentle and kind expression of the eye and mouth. He was brave, bold, and generous, and possessed great talents, highly cultivated. He understood all the languages of his subjects—Greek, Latin, Italian, German, French and *Arabic*. He was severe and passionate, mild or liberal, as circumstances required; gay, cheerful, and lively, as his feelings dictated. He was a noted Freethinker, and regarded men of all religions with equal favour.

Note JJJJ.—Page 279.

"Opened Negotiations with the Sultan of Egypt."—Frederic signed a treaty with Camel, which more effectually promoted the object of the Holy Wars than the efforts of any former sovereign. For ten years the Christians and Mussulmans were to live upon terms of brotherhood. Jerusalem, Jaffa, Bethlehem, Nazareth, and their appendages, and the Holy Sepulchre, were restored to the Christians.

Note KKKK.—Page 280.

"Simon de Montfort."—The family of Montforts seems to have been fiercely ambitious. They trace their origin to "Charlemagne."

Simon de Montfort, the true leader of the war against the Albigeois was a veteran of the crusades, hardened in the unsparing battles of the Templars and the Assassins. On his return from the Holy Land he engaged in this bloody crusade, in the South of France.

His second son seeking in England the fortune which he had missed in France, fought on the side of the English commons, and threw open to them the doors of Parliament. After having had both king and kingdom in his power, he was overcome and slain. His son (grandson of the celebrated Montfort, who was the chief in the crusade against the Albigeois) avenged him by murdering in Italy, at the foot of the altar, the nephew of the king of England, who was returning from the Holy Land.

This deed ruined the Montforts. Ever after they were looked upon with *horror and detestation.*—*Michelet.*

Note LLLL.—Page 280.

"*Richard of Cornwall,*" in the spring of the year 1240, embarked for the crusade. The Christian name of the Earl of Cornwall alarmed the Saracens. The very word Richard was dreaded in Syria; so great was the terror which Cœur de Lion had spread.

Note MMMM.—Page 280.

"*King Louis.*"—The superstition of a French king, and the successes of the savage Korasmians, gave birth to the seventh crusade. One night during the Christmas festival (*A.D.* 1245), Louis caused magnificent crosses, fabricated by goldsmiths, to be sown on the new dresses, which, as usual upon such occasions, had been bestowed upon the courtiers. The next day the cavaliers were surprised at the religious ornaments which had been affixed to their cloaks; but piety and loyalty combined to prevent them from renouncing the honours which had been thrust upon them.

Note NNNN.—Page 280.

"*Statutes of Oxford.*"—The English barons assembled at Oxford, on the 11th of June, 1258, and obliged the king and his eldest son, then eighteen years of age, to agree to a treaty by which twenty-four of their own body, at the head of whom was De Montfort, had authority given them to reform all abuses.—*History of England.*

Note OOOO.—Page 283.

"*Greek Fire.*"—This was invented in the 7th century. When the Arabs besieged Constantinople, a Greek architect deserted from the Caliph to the Greeks, and took with him a composition, which by its wonderful effects, struck terror into the enemy, and forced them to take flight. Sometimes it was wrapped in flax attached to arrows and javelins, and so thrown into the fortifications and other buildings of the enemy to set them on fire.

At other times it was used in throwing stone balls from iron or metallic tubes against the enemy. The use of this fire continued at least until the end of the 13th century, but no contemporary writer has handed down to us any accurate account of its composition.

Note PPPP.—Page 283

"Mamelukes."—Slaves from the Caucasian countries, who, from menial offices, were advanced to the dignities of state. They did not, however, form a separate body; but when Genghis Khan made himself master of the greatest part of Asia, in the thirteenth century, and carried vast numbers of the inhabitants into slavery, the Sultan of Egypt bought twelve thousand of them, and had them instructed in military exercises, and formed a regular corps of them. They soon exhibited a spirit of insubordination and rebellion, and in 1254 appointed one of their own number Sultan of Egypt. Their dominion continued two hundred and sixty-three years.—*Encyclopaedia.*

Note QQQQ.—Page 286.

"Damascus Steel."—Damascus was celebrated in the middle ages for the manufacture of sabres, of such peculiar quality as to be perfectly elastic and very hard.

Note RRRR.—Page 288.

"Eva Strongbow."—Dermot, King of Leinster, formed a treaty with Pritchard, surnamed Strongbow, earl of Strigul. This nobleman who was of the illustrious house of Clare, had impaired his fortune by expensive pleasures, and being ready for any desperate undertaking, he promised assistance to Dermot on condition that he should espouse Eva, daughter of that prince, and be declared heir to all his dominions.—*Hume's History of England.*

Note SSSS.—Page 289.

"Queen Gold."—One great cause of the queen's unpopularity in London originated from the unprincipled manner in which she exercised her influence to compel all vessels freighted with corn, wool, or any peculiarly valuable cargo, to unlade at her hithe, or quay, called Queen-hithe, because at that port the dues which formed a part of the revenues of the queens-consort of England, and the tolls, were paid according to the value of the lading.

In order to annoy the citizens of London, Henry, during the disputes regarding the queen's gold, revived the old Saxon custom of convening folkmotes which was in reality the founding the House of Commons.—*Queens of England.*

Note TTTT.—Page 291.

"Holy crown of Thorns."—This inestimable relic was borne in triumph through Paris by Louis himself—barefoot and in his shirt, and a free gift of ten thousand marks reconciled the emperor, Baldwin de Courtenay, to his loss. The success of this transaction tempted him to

send to the king a large and authentic portion of the true cross, the baby linen of the Son of God, the lance, the sponge, and the chain of his Passion.—*Gibbon*, vol. vi. p. 122.

Note UUUU.—Page 293.

"*Lay concealed.*"—During the captivity of her husband and son, it is asserted that Eleanor, of Provence, made more than one private visit to England, but she ostensibly resided in France with her younger children, under the kind protection of her sister, Queen Marguerite. Robert, of Gloucester said that she was *espy* in the land for the purpose of liberating her brave son.—*Queens of England.*

Note VVVV.—Page 297.

"*Shouts of pursuers.*"—Lady Maud Mortimer having sent her instructions to Prince Edward, he made his escape by riding races with his attendants till he had tired their horses, when he rode up to a thicket where dame Maud had ambushed a swift steed. Mounting his gallant courser, Edward turned to his guard, and bade them "commend him to his sire the king, and tell him he would soon be at liberty," and then galloped off; while an armed party appeared on the opposite hill, a mile distant, and displayed the banner of Mortimer.—*Queens of England.*

Note WWWW.—Page 308.

When the Old Man rode forth, he was preceded by a crier who bore a Danish axe with a long handle, all covered with silver, and stuck full of daggers, who proclaimed, "Turn from before him who bears the death of kings in his hands."—*Joinville*, p. 97.

Note XXXX.—Page 309.

"*Fedavis.*"—Henri, Count of Champagne, visiting the grand-prior of the Assassins, the latter led him up a lofty tower, at each battlement of which stood two fedavis (devotees). On a sign from him, two of these sentinels flung themselves from the top of the tower. "If you wish it," he said to the count, "all these men shall do the same."—*Michelet.*

Note YYYY.—Page 310.

"*Loving lips.*"—"It is storied," says Fuller, "how Eleanor, his lady, sucked all the poison out of his wounds without doing any harm to herself. So sovereign a remedy is a woman's tongue, anointed with the virtue of a loving affection. Pity it is that so pretty a story should not be true (with all the miracles in love's legends); and sure he shall get himself no credit, who undertaketh to confute a passage so sounding to the honour of the sex."

Note ZZZZ.—Page 324.

"Earl of Devon."—The Courtenays derive their ancestry from "Louis the Fat." Beside the branch that was established upon the throne of Constantinople, a part of the family settled in England, and twelve Earls of Devonshire of the name of Courtenay were ranked among the chief barons of the realm, for a period of more than two hundred years.

By sea and land they fought under the standard of the Edwards and Henrys. Their names are conspicuous in battles, in tournaments, and in the original list of the Order of the Garter; three brothers shared the Spanish victory of the Black Prince. One, the favourite of Henry the Eighth, in the Camp of the Cloth of Gold broke a lance against the French monarch. Another lived a prisoner in the Tower, and the secret love of Queen Mary, whom he slighted perhaps for the princess Elizabeth, and his exile at Padua, has shed a romantic interest on the annals of the race.—*Gibbon's Rome.*

Note AAAAA.—Page 325.

"Merlin."—Merlin Ambrose, a British writer who flourished about the latter end of the fifth century. The accounts we have of him are so mixed up with fiction, that to disentangle his real life from the mass would be impossible. He was the greatest sage and mathematician of his time, the counsellor and friend of five English kings, Voltigern, Ambrosius, Uther, Pendragon, and Arthur. He uttered many prophecies respecting the future state of England.—*Encyclopaedia.*

Note BBBBB.—Page 326.

"Unjust Aspersion."—When Leicester brought his newly-wedded wife, the king's sister, to pay his devoir to Eleanor of Provence, he was received with a burst of fury by Henry, who called him the seducer of his sister, and an excommunicated man, and ordered his attendants to turn him out of the palace.

Leicester endeavoured to remonstrate, but Henry would not hear him, and he was expelled, weeping with rage, and vowing vengeance against the young queen, to whose influence he attributed this reverse.—*Queens of England.*

Note CCCCC.—Page 332.

"Daughter of Elin de Montfort."—The first mischance that befell the Welsh was the capture of the bride of Llewellyn, coming from France.

The young damsel, though the daughter of Simon de Montfort, Edward's mortal foe whom he had slain in battle, was at the same time, the child of his aunt, Eleanor Plantagenet. He received her with the courtesy of a kinsman, and consigned her to the gentle keeping of his queen, with whom she resided at Windsor Castle.

The fair bride of Llewellyn died after bringing him a living daughter. This daughter whose name was Guendolin, was brought to Edward a captive in her cradle; she was reared and professed a nun in the convent with her cousin Glades, only daughter of Prince David.—*Queens of England.*

Note DDDDD.—Page 335.

"*Motley courtiers.*"—Alphonso was not in good repute with his people, either as a Spaniard or a Christian. A great clerk, devoted to the evil sciences of Alchemy and Astrology, he was ever closeted with his Jews, to make spurious money or spurious laws—adulterating the Gothic laws by a mixture of the Roman.—*Michelet's France.*

Note EEEEE.—Page 336.

"*I would have taught him.*"—Alphonso, tenth King of Castile who flourished in the 18th century. When contemplating the doctrine of the epicycles, exclaimed, "Were the universe thus constructed, if the deity had called me to his councils at the creation of the world, I would have given him good advice." He did not however mean any impiety or irreverence, except what was directed against the system of Ptolemy.

Note FFFFF.—Page 337.

"*Raymond Lullius.*"—A story is told of this famous alchemist, that during his stay in London, he changed for King Edward I., a mass of 50,000 pounds of quicksilver into gold, of which the first *rose nobles* were coined.

Note GGGGG.—Page 345.

"*Everywhere well received.*"—The Mendicants strayed everywhere—begged, lived on little, and were everywhere well received. Subtle, eloquent, and able men, they discharged a multiplicity of worldly commissions with discretion. Europe was filled with their activity. Messengers, preachers, and at times diplomatists, they were then what the post and press now are.—*Michelet's France.*

Note HHHHH.—Page 347.

"*Slipped a ring.*"—Procida offered the ambitious Peter of Arragon, the crown of Sicily, which that monarch might justly claim by his marriage with the daughter of Mainfroy, and by the dying voice of Conradin, who from the scaffold had cast a ring to his heir and avenger.—*Gibbon.*

Note IIIII.—Page 349.

"*Friar Bacon.*"—Though an extraordinary man, could not entirely free himself from the prejudices of his times. He believed in the philosopher's stone, and in astrology. There are to be found in his writings new and ingenious views on optics, on the refraction of light on the apparent magnitudes of objects, on the magnified appearance of the sun and moon when in the horizon. He also states that thunder and lightning could be imitated by means of saltpetre, sulphur, and charcoal. Hence he had already an idea of gunpowder.

Note JJJJJ.—Page 351.

"*Albertus Magnus.*"—During the year 1280, died the celebrated Albert the Great, of the Order of Preaching Friars, less known as a monk than a magician. The prodigious diversity of his learning, and the taste which he had for experiments in alchemy, which he himself called magical operations, caused a superhuman power to be attributed to him. Besides the automaton which St. Thomas de Aquinas, his disciple, broke with a club, it is affirmed that Albert entertained William, Count of Holland, at a miraculous banquet in the garden of his cloister and that though it was in the *depth of winter*, the trees appeared as in spring, covered with flowers and leaves, which vanished as if by enchantment, after the repast.—*History of the Popes.*

Note KKKKK.—Page 356.

"*I was anxious.*"—This passage is quoted from Falcando, an Italian historian of the twelfth century.

Note LLLLL.—Page 359.

"*Shepherd of Cotswold.*"—To Eleanora, is due the credit of introducing the Spanish breed of sheep into England.

Note MMMMM.—Page 361.

"*Red stockings.*"—According to Michelet, Procida influenced the pope to sign the treaty with the Greek Emperor, by repeating the insulting allusion of Charles to the purple buskins worn by the pontiff.

Note NNNNN.—Page 361.

"*Easter Monday, 1282.*"—The intelligent readers of history will observe an anachronism in placing the Sicilian vespers after the Welsh war. They will also discover a mistake in representing Alphonse as the rival of Conrad, rather than of Rodolph, of Hapsburg, for the crown of the German empire.

Note OOOOO.—Page 362.

"*Rescued.*"—Constance of Arragon, fortunately arrived in time to prevent the Sicilians, from putting Charles the Lame to death. She carried him off from Messina in the night and sent him to Spain. When Charles of Arragon was informed of the defeat of his troops, and the captivity of his son, he fell as though struck down by a thunderbolt, and succeeding attacks of epilepsy carried him to the tomb in a few months. Through the mediation of Edward, Charles the Lame, surrendered to Alphonse of Arragon, all claims to the crown of Sicily, and thus gained his liberty. He reigned over Provence in right of his mother, and was the progenitor of Margaret of Anjou.

LEONAUR

ALSO FROM LEONAUR

AVAILABLE IN SOFTCOVER OR HARDCOVER WITH DUST JACKET

THE WOMAN IN BATTLE *by Loreta Janeta Velazquez*—Soldier, Spy and Secret Service Agent for the Confederacy During the American Civil War.

BOOTS AND SADDLES *by Elizabeth B. Custer*—The experiences of General Custer's Wife on the Western Plains.

FANNIE BEERS' CIVIL WAR *by Fannie A. Beers*—A Confederate Lady's Experiences of Nursing During the Campaigns & Battles of the American Civil War.

LADY SALE'S AFGHANISTAN *by Florentia Sale*—An Indomitable Victorian Lady's Account of the Retreat from Kabul During the First Afghan War.

THE TWO WARS OF MRS DUBERLY *by Frances Isabella Duberly*—An Intrepid Victorian Lady's Experience of the Crimea and Indian Mutiny.

THE REBELLIOUS DUCHESS *by Paul F. S. Dermoncourt*—The Adventures of the Duchess of Berri and Her Attempt to Overthrow French Monarchy.

LADIES OF WATERLOO *by Charlotte A. Eaton, Magdalene de Lancey & Juana Smith*—The Experiences of Three Women During the Campaign of 1815: Waterloo Days by Charlotte A. Eaton, A Week at Waterloo by Magdalene de Lancey & Juana's Story by Juana Smith.

NURSE AND SPY IN THE UNION ARMY *by Sarah Emma Evelyn Edmonds*—During the American Civil War

WIFE NO. 19 *by Ann Eliza Young*—The Life & Ordeals of a Mormon Woman During the 19th Century

DIARY OF A NURSE IN SOUTH AFRICA *by Alice Bron*—With the Dutch-Belgian Red Cross During the Boer War

MARIE ANTOINETTE AND THE DOWNFALL OF ROYALTY *by Imbert de Saint-Amand*—The Queen of France and the French Revolution

THE MEMSAHIB & THE MUTINY *by R. M. Coopland*—An English lady's ordeals in Gwalior and Agra duringthe Indian Mutiny 1857

MY CAPTIVITY AMONG THE SIOUX INDIANS *by Fanny Kelly*—The ordeal of a pioneer woman crossing the Western Plains in 1864

WITH MAXIMILIAN IN MEXICO *by Sara Yorke Stevenson*—A Lady's experience of the French Adventure